Roman Law and Language

STUDIES IN COMPARATIVE LEGAL HISTORY

Roman Law and Language

Collected Works of David Daube
Volume 6

Edited by
Calum Carmichael and Laurent Mayali

Foreword by David Johnston

The Robbins Collection
Berkeley

The Robbins Collection in Religious and Civil Law
The University of California, Berkeley
School of Law
Berkeley, California 94720
(510) 642–5094
law.berkeley.edu/research/the-robbins-collection/

ISBN: 978-1-882239-25-2   *Roman Law and Language*

ISBN: 978-1-882239-01-6   Collected Works of David Daube

Library of Congress Catalog Card number: 92-61641

Earlier versions of parts 1 through 3 were published as *Roman Law* (Edinburg: Edinburg University Press, 1969). Reproduced with the persmission of Edinburgh University Press Limited through PLSclear.

Chapter 7 was published as "'Suffrage' and 'Precedent,' 'Mercy' and "Grace'" in *Tijdschrift voor Rechtsgeschiedenis* 47, no. 3, (1979).

Chapter 8 was published as "Withdrawal: Five Verbs" in *California Studies in Classical Antiquity*, 7, (1975). Reproduced with the permission of University of California Press.

Part 5 was published as "Greek and Roman Reflections on Impossible Law" in *Natural Law Forum*, 125, (1967).

Contents

ROMAN LAW: LINGUISTIC, SOCIAL, AND PHILOSOPHICAL ASPECTS

Part I. Linguistic Aspects

An agent noun is narrower in meaning than the verb from which it derives (e.g., scriptor, professional writer, from scribere, "to write") and is usually confined to the extraordinary. Failure to recognize the difference in meaning between verb and noun commonly results in mistaken conclusions in every field of research.

In the history of a language, the appearance of a noun to signify the action of a verb represents conceptualization of the activity and is of fundamental importance in studying the history of ideas. The emergence of an action noun is one of the most revealing developments in any branch of a culture. Conceptualization of many matters in Roman law often does not occur until the late classical period, or even the Middle Ages.

LEGAL CONCEPTS AND SOCIAL
CONVENTIONS

Part IV. Linguistic Variations

Part V. Greek and Roman Reflections on Impossible Laws

Foreword

Roman law and language: the theme of this latest volume of the collected works of David Daube is one that Daube made peculiarly his own. Think, for example, of Daube's fundamental analysis of the language of Roman statutes in *Forms of Roman Legislation* (1956); or of his equally foundational contribution to understanding the *lex Aquilia* in "On the use of the term *damnum*" (1948). The theme of law and language is so bound up with Daube's entire oeuvre that we have to have a degree of sympathy for the editors of this volume who, from a remarkable number of candidates for possible inclusion, had to make a selection in order to keep it within manageable bounds.

Daube was much influenced by form criticism and by historical criticism, both disciplines originally developed in criticism of the Bible. The papers reproduced here, and indeed Daube's work beyond the confines of Roman law, such as on the Talmud and the Bible, are deeply impregnated by these disciplines. What they have in common is an insistence on paying the closest possible attention to texts. In the study of Roman law, this is a matter of trying to understand the meaning and significance in context of a legal proposition or opinion attributed to a classical jurist. The Roman texts which we scrutinize or criticize are mediated largely through Justinian's *Digest*, a compilation composed several centuries after the classical jurists lived. The fact that almost none of the works of the classical jurists are preserved in anything resembling their original form necessarily adds to the difficulty for the interpreter. Nonetheless, the task of form criticism remains that of seeking to comprehend why the jurist's text uses the language that it does in the form that it does. Historical criticism, on the other hand, insists on placing the text within its historical,

XDAVID JOHNSTON

social or economic context, so that the ideas or reasoning a jurist expresses can be interpreted and understood not as abstract propositions of law (the approach favoured by the Pandectists in the nineteenth century) but as expressions shaped by, and to be understood in the context of, a specific historical reality.

The papers included here were first published in the 1960s and 1970s. Forty (or more) years later, it is evident that they have stood the test of time.

The volume opens with the three lectures Daube gave to the Faculty of Classics at Cambridge University as the Gray lectures for 1966: *Roman Law: Linguistic, Social and Philosophical Aspects.* For those who have yet to discover Daube, this is a good place to start. The pages give a flavour of what Daube the man was actually like: they show not just an astonishing breadth and depth of learning but an extraordinary engagement with all aspects of Roman law and an unquenchable curiosity about how it developed as it did, when, why, and by what means.

Only the first lecture is avowedly concerned with language. Here, in exploring the formation of legal rules, Daube insists on a close focus on language and how it develops. Two classic examples are the agent noun and the action noun. Daube points out that the agent noun (for instance, "baker") emerges later than the cognate verb ("bake"). Why? Because many people bake without being bakers: the description of a person as a "baker" identifies that there is an especially close relationship (perhaps a professional one) between that person and baking. The verb simply describes an activity, while the noun indicates a process of abstraction, that the activity is being conceptualized as such.

A similar approach can be taken to the action noun: for example, acquisition is formed from acquire. Again, the noun is formed once the action described by the verb has become an abstract concept. Here too there is explanatory force in attempting to identify when the noun first appeared: Daube notes that the noun acquisition (*acquisitio*) appeared much later than the noun alienation (*alienatio*) and asks why. His explanation is that the notion of alienation, and especially restrictions on the power of alienation, were recognized in the abstract in early Roman law, in order to describe generically those who were unable to dispose of property. In relation to acquisition on the other hand, the tendency was to use a specific word (usually in fact the verb) referring to a specific mode of acquisition (such as deliver or occupy): acquisition as an abstract concept encompassing numerous such modes came only later.

Daube employs these insights in order to arrive at conclusions about the evolution of institutions in legal history. This sensitivity to the forms of language used in law can assist us when we try to identify when particular developments in the law occurred. And it can enable us to avoid ahistorical or anachronistic conclusions, if for example we take note of the fact that (as is often the case) the agent or action noun appeared only in post-classical or even medieval times.

The lecture on the social aspects of Roman law shows the questioning Daube at his best, wondering how the traditional explanation of damages under chapter 3 of the *lex Aquilia* can possibly be correct, given its remarkable punitive consequences; trying to make sense of the Romans' supposed "horror of intestacy" (Henry Maine's expression); attempting to understand how lifelong paternal power could actually function in practice, if for instance a son subject to paternal power was elected to high office. On some of these issues the linguistic argument plays an important part in the overall exploration: for example, close analysis of key texts leads Daube to the conclusion that *intestatus* in those texts does not mean "intestate". His wider theme, however, is that it is a mistake to make assertions about the Romans and testation or intestacy without recognizing that in doing so we are referring only to the upper strata of Roman society. Thus, the supposed horror of intestacy is an ahistorical fiction. On other issues Daube discusses in this lecture sensitivity to language is never absent (for instance, in his discussion of the meaning of *filiusfamilias*, or of tips and gratuities), although the emphasis is on how the law (can have) worked in Roman society.

The third lecture, on philosophical aspects, includes an extended treatment of the standards of liability in Roman contract law: *dolus*, *culpa, casus.* The context of Daube's analysis is indeed philosophical: it is a rebuttal of the notion that this categorization of standards of liability derives from Greek thought, in particular Aristotle's *Nicomachaean Ethics*. Once again, however, language plays a key part in Daube's examination. He shows that there is no such categorization in Aristotle: the notion of negligent commission of a wrong is absent there. The supposition that the Roman analysis derives from Aristotle rested in the first place on a mistranslation of *amartema* as importing negligence; and in the second on a failure to take proper account of the context, in particular the fact that Aristotle's discussion is directed at criminal liability, whereas the texts of the Roman jurists are directed at civil liability for damages, in which the notion of negligence inevitably plays a more central role.

The next two papers are fine examples of Daube's sensitive exploration of language. In "Suffrage and precedent, mercy and grace" Daube investigates the shifting meaning in Latin of each of these terms. To take but one example, *suffragium* has a particularly interesting history: initially it means "vote"; under the Roman emperors, as the meaningfulness of votes declined, it took on the sense of influence or patronage; later still it came to refer to honours or privileges; and later still to intercession (including in the context of religion). Now it has essentially reverted to its original meaning, "vote." Of the following paper, "Withdrawal: five verbs" here it is enough to say that the title conveys the content perfectly: the paper is made up of five studies of the evolution in meaning of verbs with a common theme of withdrawal.

The remainder of this volume reproduces Daube's 1967 paper "Greek and Roman reflections on impossible laws." Some of the issues considered involve a good deal of legal technicality. One is the discussion of texts on succession in relation to various kinds of legal familial relationship (cognatic and agnatic). The broad context of Daube's examination is an attempt to understand and then to refine the jurist Pomponius's observation, in relation to succession to an inheritance on death, that the civil law cannot destroy the rights of blood (*iura sanguinis*). Daube rightly points out that Pomponius is quite wrong: while it is true that the civil law cannot turn a relative into a non-relative as a matter of fact, what it certainly can do is remove from a relative the rights that relatives enjoy.

The Romans certainly knew of laws which rewrote the past. In the public sphere, the obvious example is *abolitio memoriae* (although Daube is careful to note that the abstract noun appears late): a law to that effect would have the effect that a hated ruler had in fact never ruled. The *fasti* would be amended to remove all references to the "abolished" person. In this context Daube aptly quotes from George Orwell's *1984*: "Who controls the past, controls the future, who controls the present, controls the past."

There is an absorbing discussion of *ingenuitas*, the status of being freeborn. That is straightforward enough when it is a simple matter of fact. It starts to become more complicated legally with the development of procedures to allow a person who was not freeborn to obtain a declaration that he was in fact freeborn. Declarations that rewrite history cause conceptual difficulties. The late jurist Marcian attempted to address these by construing the effect of the declaration not simply as a (factually incorrect) *ex post facto* statement about the individual freedman but instead as a restoration to that freedman of the conditions in which all men were born in the age before the institution of slavery appeared. On that analysis, the declaration is true, since the premise is that the natural condition of mankind is freedom.

These remarks can do no more than give a flavour of the pleasure and instruction to be derived from this wide-ranging, constantly entertaining and thought-provoking collection. These papers show Daube's mastery of language, of the ancient sources, and of their historical context. But there is more. If we stand back from the historical period to which these sources relate, there are wider lessons for the modern legal scholar or lawyer too, since all texts are in need of interpretation. First and foremost we can appreciate and try to assimilate from Daube's work the prime importance for the lawyer of close attention to language and its development, and of understanding not just the words of a text but why it is expressed in the way that it is. This is a skill relevant not just to comprehending a legal text or utterance as a matter of history but to the contemporary task of interpretation too.

David Johnston QC
Formerly Regius Professor of Civil Law, University of Cambridge
Edinburgh, 2018

Acknowledgments

Roman Law: Linguistic, Social, and Philosophical Aspects was originally published by Edinburgh University Press in 1969. The text was originally comprised of three lectures, known as the Gray Lectures, which David Daube delivered before the Faculty of Classics at Cambridge in 1966.

"'Suffrage' and 'Precedent', 'Mercy' and 'Grace'" was published in *Tijdschrift voor Rechtsgeschiedenis* 47, no. 3, (1979), 235–46.

"Withdrawal: Five Verbs" was published in *California Studies in Classical Antiquity*, 7, (1975), 93–112.

"Greek and Roman Reflections on Impossible Laws" was published in the *Natural Law Forum*, 125 (1967): 1–84.

Abbreviations

AJ	*Antiquitates Judaicae* (Josephus)
Amic.	*De amicitia* (Cicero)
An.	*Andria* (Terence)
Ann.	*Annales* (Tacitus)
Ant. Rom.	*Antiquitates Romanae* (Dionysius of Halicarnassus)
Ap.	*Apologia* (Plato)
Apol.	*Apologia* (Appuleius)
Asin.	*Asinaria* (Plautus)
Att.	*Epistulae ad Atticum* (Cicero)
Aug.	*Divus Augustus* (Suetonius)
Bacch.	*Bacchides* (Plautus)
Beitr.	*Beiträge zur Kritik der römischen Rechtsquellen*
Ben.	*De beneficiis* (Seneca the Younger)
BLL	*Biblical Law and Literature*, ed. Calum Carmichael
Bull. Ist. Dir. Rom.	*Bullettino dell'Istituto di Diritto Romano*
Caecin.	*Pro Caecina* (Cicero)
Calig.	*Gaius Caligula* (Suetonius)
CIL	*Corpus Inscriptionum Latinarum*
Cist.	*Cistellaria* (Plautus)
Claud.	*Divus Claudius* (Suetonius)
CLE	*Carmina Latina Epigraphica*
Clem.	*De clementia* (Seneca the Younger)
Cod. Theod.	*Codex Theodosianus*
Coll.	*Collatio Legum Mosaicarum et Romanarum*
Comm. Livy 1–5	*Commentary on Livy, Books 1–5*
Comm. not.	*De communibus notitiis adversus Stoicos* (Plutarch)

Curc.	*Curculio* (Plautus)
De civ. D.	*De civitate Dei* (Augustine)
De or.	*De oratore* (Cicero)
Dom.	*De domo sua* (Cicero)
Ep.	*Epistulae* (Pliny the Younger)
Ep.	*Epistulae* (Seneca the Younger)
Eth. Nic.	*Ethica Nicomachea* (Aristotle)
Fam.	*Epistulae ad familiares* (Cicero)
Fin.	*De finibus* (Cicero)
Font.	*Pro Fonteio* (Cicero)
Font.	*Fontes iuris Romani antiqui*
Fr. Vat.	*Fragmenta Vaticana*
G. Ep.	*Gaii Epitome*
G. Gracch.	*Gaius Gracchus* (Plutarch)
Gram. et rhet.	*De grammaticis et rhetoribus* (Suetonius)
Heaut.	*Heauton Timorumenos* (Terence)
HN	*Naturalis historia* (Pliny the Elder)
Inst.	*Institutio oratoria* (Quintillian)
int.	interpolated
Inv. rhet.	*De inventione rhetorica* (Cicero)
JRS	*Journal of Roman Studies*
Leg.	*Leges* (Plato)
Leg.	*De legibus* (Cicero)
Ling.	*de lingua Latina* (Varro)
LQR	*Law Quarterly Review*
Luc.	*Lucullus* (Plutarch)
Men.	*Menaechmi* (Plautus)
Merc.	*Mercator* (Plautus)
Mil.	*Miles gloriosus* (Plautus)
Mon. Anc.	*Monumentum Ancyranum*
Mostell.	*Mostellaria* (Plautus)
Off.	*De officiis* (Cicero)
Orat.	*Orator ad M. Brutum* (Cicero)
Pal.	*Palingenesia Iuris Civilis* (Lenel)
P.S.	Pauli, *Sentences*
Phdr.	*Phaedrus* (Plato)
Phil.	*Orationes Philippicae* (Cicero)

Phorm.	*Phormio* (Terence)
Planc.	*Pro Plancio* (Cicero)
Poen.	*Poenulus* (Plautus)
pr.	principium
Pseud.	*Pseudolus* (Plautus)
Quaest. Rom.	*Quaestiones Romanae* (Plutarch)
RE	*Real-Encyclopädie d. klassischen Altertumswissenschaft*
Rem. am.	*Remedia amoris* (Ovid)
Rh.	*Rhetorica* (Aristotle)
Rh. Al.	*Rhetorica ad Alexandrum* (Aristotle)
Rhet. Her.	*Rhetorica ad Herennium* (Cicero)
Röm. Staatsr.	*Römisches Staatsrecht*
Röm. Stafr.	*Römisches Strafrecht*
Rosc. Am.	*Pro Sexto Roscio Amerino* (Cicero)
Rud.	*Rudens* (Plautus)
SHA	Scriptores Historiae Augustae
Tib.	*Tiberius* (Suetonius)
Tijdschr. Rechts.	*Tijdschrift voor Rechtsgeschiedenis*
TL	*Talmudic Law*, ed. Calum Carmichael
Top.	*Topica* (Cicero)
Top.	*Topica* (Aristotle)
Trin.	*Trinummus* (Plautus)
Verr.	*In Verrem* (Cicero)
Vesp.	*Divus Vespasianus* (Suetonius)
Vit.	*Vitae Parallelae* (Plutarch)
VJR	*Vocabularium Jurisprudentiae Romanae*
ZRG	*Zeitschrift der Savigny-Stiftung, romanistische Abteilung*

ROMAN LAW:
LINGUISTIC, SOCIAL, AND
PHILOSOPHICAL ASPECTS

Part I

LINGUISTIC ASPECTS

A few years ago, when I was visiting Charlottesville in Virginia, a press-interviewer asked me: "How is it that you, as a Cambridge man, are a professor at Oxford?" I replied: "Oh, those who are not quite good enough for Cambridge are always sent to Oxford." Next day that appeared literally in the papers. I took a cutting with me and now, when my Oxford colleagues annoy me, I can show them black on white where they stand. However, once in a while you do remember your exiles, and I am greatly appreciative of your invitation to deliver these Lectures.

I propose today to make some observation on two linguistic phenomena, the agent noun and the action noun.

1

The Agent Noun*

First, for the agent noun.[1] I may bake or beg or cook or dream or see or love without being a baker, a beggar, a cook, a dreamer, a seer or a lover. That is to say, the agent noun, whether identical with the verb (cook) or formed from it by means of some ending like -er (baker from bake), often has a narrower range than the verb. This goes for Latin as well as English. The agent noun tends to be confined to the striking, it designates him who deserves to be so designated because his doing marks him, it appears to be out of the ordinary and therefore singles him out. A baker, a beggar or a cook is one who bakes, begs or cooks for a living, a dreamer dreams when he ought not to, in the middle of the road, and habitually too, a seer sees what others cannot see, a lover loves in the most important, intense and interesting way; and Latin *scriptor*, from *scribere*, signifies one who has made writing his profession, a secretary or an author.

Circumstances can make what is ordinarily ordinary, striking: in a chess match between the Perse and the School for the Blind you might divide the teams into the seers and the blind. The contrast gives the former an extra standing. Similarly, when the law looks at a person who does something, who buys, sells, borrows, lends, in that capacity, maybe as one party opposed to another, it speaks of the buyer, the vendor, the borrower, the lender. Again, a frequent application of the agent noun is where the action is introduced by some other form of the verb and

---

* To the memory of my father and brother.
1. Cf. my article in *LQR* 62 (1946): 266ff.

then there is a reference back to the agent: A man ran after a thief; said somebody to the runner. . . . By the time of the reference back, the man is in special case. The agent noun would not do in the first half: there was a runner after a thief. It is the "he ran" of the first half which, for the present story, characterizes the man sufficiently to be called "the runner" in the second.[2] In general, however, the agent noun picks out a particular remarkable division of the verb: I employ all sorts of things all the time, but it is the employment of human labour over a certain period on certain terms which makes me an employer.

It follows that if we come across a verb with an agent noun and the latter covers only a sector of the former, we must not automatically try to bring, force, the two into harmony. We must not, that is, automatically infer either that originally the agent noun must have been as wide as the verb or that the verb must have been as narrow as the noun. Yet both fallacies are common among scholars paying attention to language and, in legal history, some queer conclusions have resulted.

I shall begin with the case of the agent noun being arbitrarily inflated in order to render it coextensive with the verb.

In the sources, the noun *imperator* denotes, not anyone who gives an order, but a General. Indeed, it is mostly used of that real commander, the man who has been proclaimed General by the army itself; and, to go by the picture presented by the sources, this title borne by the leader the army has chosen precedes the more inclusive meaning General.

---

2. In this function, however, the agent noun is still very close to the participle. Not much would be lost by reformulating: said somebody to the running one. Still, if a reference back of this kind keeps recurring in the same context, it must help the development away from the participial nuance towards the proper nominal one. No doubt here is a factor (one of many—I have just mentioned another one in the text) leading to the terms buyer, vendor, *emptor*, *venditor*: a man bought a farm from his neighbour; the buyer claims that it is smaller than he was told. If this kind of discussion recurs again and again, "buyer" moves away from "buying one" and becomes a full noun. In several languages, the steps can sometimes be indicated by slight shifts in spelling or construction. In English, promiser is less advanced than promisor. A man promised his son a birthday present; when he forgot about it, they said to the promiser. By contrast: a man promised to contribute £1,000 to an insurance fund by 17 November; he failed to do so and the fund asks whether the promisor is liable for interest.

But now take Mommsen. He assumes[3] that, as *imperator* is derived from *imperare*, it originally embraced anyone holding the *imperium*. *Es scheint selbstverständlich*, he says, "it seems obvious." Rosenberg goes even further,[4] and indeed why not once the basic error is granted? He starts by declaring: *Imperator ist der Mann der imperat*, "*Imperator* is the man who *imperat*." This would include a gentleman giving an order to a servant. He cannot, of course, seriously uphold this, so, by imperceptible steps, he goes on to anyone with *imperium* and then to a *rex*. By now, manifestly, his initial statement has become rather hollow: a *rex* is not just anyone who *imperat*. Anyhow, he admits that *freilich ist in historischer Zeit der älteste, vollste Wert des Wortes imperator verschollen;* "to be sure (he says) in historical times the oldest, fullest value of the word *imperator* is forgotten"—it is restricted to a General.

All this is seen to be futile if the role of the agent noun is understood. It is perfectly normal for *imperator* to represent only a fraction of *imperare*, to be attached to the most impressive exercise of *imperium*. The evidence given by Mommsen and Rosenberg of traces of a pre-historical, unlimited scope is—as one would expect—forced. They refer to the Capitoline triad in the inscription of the Faliscan cooks,[5] Iuppiter, Iuno, Minerva, "highest *imperatores*." But surely, this triad is of good military provenance. The three are more than enough to frighten the wits out of me. There is nothing here to suggest an early indiscriminate use of the noun.

Another example of this class—the unwarranted extension of an agent noun in order to make it achieve the range of the verb—is provided by *spondere* and *sponsor*. *Spondere* means to promise, but, in the sources, *sponsor* means, not anyone who promises, but only him who promises for somebody else, a guarantor, a surety. Levy admits[6] that nowhere in extant tradition does *sponsor* denote a simple promiser. Nevertheless he thinks the word must once have been just as wide as *spondere* and, in support, quotes two texts. One of them does not contain *sponsor* at all; it mentions a *fideiussor*, and some modern authorities substitute *sponsor*.[7] The other

---

3. Mommsen, *Röm. Staatsr.* vol. 1, 3rd ed., (1887), 123.
4. Pauly-Wissowa's *RE*, vol. 9, pt. 1 (1914), s.v. "imperator."
5. *CIL* 2, 3078; Buecheler, *CLE*, vol. 1, no. 2, 2–3.
6. Levy, *Sponsio, Fidepromissio, Fideiussio* (1907), 1–2.
7. Digest 46.3.34.1, Julian *LIV digestorum*. How the text is to be reconstructed is here quite immaterial.

is a suitably emended and interpreted passage in Varro—the transmitted text is corrupt.[8]

This is poor evidence, and there will never be any better. While the verb *spondere* means to promise in general, the agent noun *sponsor* describes him whose promise stands out, who promises in support of another person's promise or possibly even in the place of another person. (Which it is, in support of a promise or in the place of somebody who does not himself promise at all, depends on our view of the early role of surety. I know where I stand but shall not here stir up a hornets' nest by deciding; in either case the surety's promise is of a most notable kind.) It is he whose promise gives him a special position, he is the promiser *kat' exochen*, the *sponsor*.

The converse method of attaining smoothness, by postulating an original narrow range of the verb, is equally doomed to failure. I am glad to report that nobody so far contends that *imperare* started by signifying exclusively the giving of an order *qua* General. With regard to *spondere* and *sponsor*, however, this line of reasoning has found favour, and with far-reaching consequences. *Spondere*, the verb, it is alleged, at first occupied the same small area as *sponsor*: it meant to guarantee, to stand surety.

This thesis has many followers; and it is a major factor in a fundamental doctrine concerning the birth of contract, first set forth by Mitteis,[9] now probably the most popular view, the doctrine that contract starts from surety.[10] How does the thesis come to play this part? *Spondere* is used of the making of an ordinary promise (with no suretyship involved) from ancient times—always remember, the sources contain no evidence of a restricted application. Actually, this ordinary promise (with no suretyship

---

8. Varro, *Ling.* 6.69: *spondit est sponsor quidem faciat obligatur sponsus consponsus.* A widely accepted emendation makes a sentence of the first three words, thus: *qui spopondit est sponsor*. And this is interpreted as covering any *spondere*. Apart from the dubiousness of the interpretation, it is surely on the cards that the words *sponsor qui dem faciat* or *sponsor qui dem faciat obligatur* belong together. By the way, the word *spondit*, which the prevalent emendation turns into *spopondit*, appears earlier on in the same paragraph: *declinatum spondit*. Here some authorities, though not all, emend it into *despondet*. Maybe it ought to be left unemended in both cases.

9. Mitteis, *Festschrift für Bekker* (1907), 107ff.

10. See, e.g. Jolowicz, *Historical Introduction to Roman Law*, 2nd ed. (1954), 290–91.

involved) is the oldest proper contract figuring in legal references and may, therefore, be regarded as the ancestor of all subsequent contracts. Now initially, it is claimed, the verb can have been no wider than its agent noun. Hence the contract by means of an ordinary promise and, with it, all subsequent contracts must descend from the contract entered into by a surety.

Whether Mitteis's idea that contract originated in surety is right or wrong I am not here concerned with; it is based on other arguments besides this one. This one, however, is utterly unconvincing since it assumes absolute, initial agreement between a verb and its agent noun to be inevitable. Language is less simple. No reason to boggle at *spondere* having the wide sense of to promise, while *sponsor* is the label for that strange man who promises by way of assistance of another man or in his stead. If I may anticipate a little, the argument I am combating receives a further heavy blow from a fact never noticed, which I shall discuss in the second part of this Lecture—namely, that the action noun *sponsio* never once signifies surety.[11]

It is amazing, incidentally, with what tenacity a beloved doctrine is carried on even when the props go one after another. Prior to the discovery of the new Gaius fragments in 1933, the advocates of the surety root of contract placed the surety phase—that primary phase when there was as yet only a promise to be liable for somebody else's debt—in the period of the XII Tables. The new fragments show that the law of that time already knew the straightforward promise to pay oneself and be liable oneself, *spondere* and *sponsio* in the wide, ordinary sense. This has, however, shaken few believers; the postulated stage when there was no *spondere* or *sponsio* but that of a *sponsor*, a surety, is simply dated further back. De Zulueta, for instance, still inclines to the surety root, though he does add:[12] "However, if in the distant past *sponsio* was nothing except a method of becoming a hostage, this had ceased to be so by the time of the XII Tables." By contrast, Levy, never really a member of this school of thought, is emphatic in pointing out the implications of the new fragments: "Extremely questionable becomes the popular thesis that *sponsio* begins by being exclusively the acceptance of liability for others,

11. De Zulueta, *The Institutes of Gaius* 2 (1955), 26ff.
12. *The Institutes of Gaius* 2 (1955), 152.

next turns into a debtor's standing surety for himself and only in the end serves to ground debt and liability in the same person at the same time."[13] Levy, however, we saw, in his turn assimilates *spondere* and *sponsor* by imputing the former's wide range to the latter.

There are close parallels to the relation of *spondere*, to promise, and *sponsor*, the promiser in support or in the place of somebody else— such as the Latin *actor* in the sense of advocate and English agent, from *agere*, or English factor and Italian *fattore*, from *facere*. *Agere* denotes any acting, *facere* any doing. But it is he who acts or does in another person's interest, or indeed he who acts or does while the person affected remains passively in the background, whom language promotes to the rank of *actor*-advocate, agent, factor, *fattore*.[14] Note also that, frequently, the man so described performs professionally. Naturally, within the compass of a verb of wide scope there may be several sectors striking enough for the agent noun to be applied. I have just adverted to *actor* in the sense of advocate, from *agere*. *Actor*, however, also signifies a player at the theatre.[15] If we adopt the reasoning of the Mitteis school in the case of *spondere* and *sponsor*, all human activity may be traced back to the stage, since *agere* must originally have been limited to the sphere of the *actor*. In reality, the noun reflects the professionalism, the artificiality, the stylized, deliberate,

---

13. Levy, ZRG 54 (1934): 299: *Schwer in Frage gestellt sieht sich aber auch die weit verbreitete Hypothese, dass die sponsio zunächst allgemein ausschliesslich Haftungsübernahme für andere, demnächst Selbstverbürgung des Schuldners und erst zuletzt Begründung eigener Schuld und Haftung gewesen sei.*

14. In Roman criminal law, factor never acquired the general sense of German *Täter* (unless we find it in the obscure Digest 48.3.7, Macer *II de officio praesidis*). Neither has English doer acquired it to this day (except in Germanizing academic jargon—my first series of *Gifford Lectures* at Edinburgh was inscribed "The Deed and the Doer in the Bible"). In a few late classical or post-classical texts (post-classical according to Beseler, ZRG 66, [1948]: 297) *factor* contrasts the person actually committing the deed with him who merely knows about it (Digest 29.5.1.21, Ulpian *L. ad edictum*) or merely does not prevent it (Digest 49.16.6.8, Arrius Menander *III de re militari*). German *Täter* is, of course, derived from the noun *Tat*, not directly from the verb *tun*. In its commonest application, as denoting an offender, it palpably singles out a very notable kind of doing.

15. In English, this meaning of *actor* seems to have come into use later than the meaning pleader, but once established it gradually ousted the latter. Throughout this Lecture, as regards the history of English words, I am guided chiefly by the *Oxford English Dictionary*.

learned quality of the acting in question; it is these features which make of the person acting thus an *actor*, single him out from the vast realm of ordinary *agere*.

We need not, then, infer from the existence of the agent noun procurer that, in England, all aid extended to a fellow man in obtaining his wants derives from the lowest of deals. The procurer is labelled as such because he procures a very special ware in a very special fashion and indeed makes a living by it.[16] But I am prepared to accept the origin of Roman contract in suretyship if my colleagues will grant me that the English contract is descended from funeral arrangements. Evidently, the undertaker must be the prototype of whoever undertakes anything. As a matter of fact, the development here is not uninteresting. The verb to undertake from the beginning embraces any kind of task. When the agent noun first appears, it singles out him who engages in a task for others—the undertaker much in the sense of its literal French translation *entrepreneur*. (Another case, therefore, somewhat comparable to *sponsor*.) Then it sticks to that particular job most readily left to a stranger, least willingly done for themselves by those principally concerned, the mourners of a near relation, and thus the meaning funeral manager carries the day. Nor is this the end of the story. In colloquial speech, from this agent noun denoting the funeral manager, the verb to undertake acquires the specialized narrow sense of to direct a burial (side by side with its ordinary, general sense). Actually, it may be followed by an accusative: you may undertake a person. In literary English this sense is extremely rare. Still, *Blackwood's Magazine* of 1900 introduces a son who "undertakes" his father. The inverted commas are in the magazine. It is not only that the usage as such is considered irregular, but in addition, in this case the normal position is reversed in that, from filial affection, a man does himself what as a rule is left to an outsider; so the verb normally in its specialized sense signifying to manage a burial for others, here refers to a burial managed by the principal mourner in person.[17]

16. The noun appears after Shakespeare only, in the seventeenth century. Shakespeare has the verb in this sense: *Measure for Measure*, 3.2.58, "does she still procure?"

17. The Latin pair *suscipere*, *susceptor* (with the action noun *susceptio*) is relevant. The development is similar—though the funeral stage is not represented—and it certainly influenced that of to undertake, undertaker, *entreprendre, entrepreneur*.

The English contractor develops in the full light of history. In post-classical times, Latin *contractor* can mean a contracting party; it is not a frequent usage, but it is well evidenced.[18] In the sixteenth century the word is taken over into English, in this general sense. Subsequently, however, in the eighteenth, it gets stuck with the master-contractor, who makes the umbrella contract for all the others, the smaller participants in the affair. The general sense now becomes obsolete. Here we simply know that the narrow noun is secondary, and the verb still retains its large range.

Sir Caspar Turnstone came down the path, propelling his little nephew before him. Even so, he was not a propeller. Micawber waited for something to turn up, yet he was not a waiter. I react strongly against some ideas of our University planners, but I am not a reactor. I refrain from multiplying examples. In deference to the current emphasis on the equality of sexes, however, I give a female illustration. *Merere* or *mereri* means to earn, *meretrix*, literally, the earneress. Was the noun at one time wide, including a schoolmistress? Or was the verb narrow and there is no profit and no merit but goes back to the example set by the call girl? In reality the noun is from the outset confined to a sector of the verb. The lady is called earneress because she makes a profession of earning, because she sets about earning in a rather special fashion, and indeed because the very fact that a woman earns is striking—there were not at the time many other ways, this kind of woman is *the* earneress.

18. Code 11.62.6.1, Gratianus Valentinianus et Theodosius, AD 384: certain possessions cannot be taken from the heirs of the holder or, indeed, from other *contractores*, i.e. persons who have acquired from him in some other way, chiefly purchase. In view of this text, I hesitate to accept Mommsen's emendation of Code 10.2.5.pr. = *Cod. Theod.* 10.16.3, Valens Gratianus et Valentinianus, AD 377. An account book of a person whose goods have been confiscated shows *nomina debitorum seu contractorum*: in default of further evidence, may the authorities enforce these items? Mommsen emends *seu* into *secum*. But *seu* is in the MSS of both Code and *Cod. Theod.* The constitution is from the same era as that considered above. And surely, we can translate "outstanding debts of borrowers (*debitores*) or such as had entered into other contracts (*contractores*)." True, the rest of the constitution contemplates loans, but these might arise from purchases, tenancies, all sorts of dealings; it was quite usual to list as "credited money" what remained unpaid, say, of a purchase price. Code 5.5.8, Zeno, AD 475, is a bit different. *Contractores* here resumes the verb *contrahere* used just before: "if unions of this kind are contracted, the contractors are to be subject to such and such consequences." This is more in the nature of the usage described above, and accordingly, this text by itself would not prove that the noun *contractor* had fully attained the sense of contracting party.

The last point is paralleled by the English noun professional as used of a woman. For a long time this signified a *meretrix*: there was no other profession for females. Nowadays they have more openings and if you hear of a lady that she is a professional, you had better enquire before you make a date or you might find yourself landed with an estate agent or a dentist. It is in fact predictable that the earlier meaning of the noun, already obsolescent, will soon have dropped out of use.

2

The Action Noun

I now come to the action noun, in the main found with transitive verbs—expel has expulsion, terminate termination, neutralize neutralization—but also with intransitive ones, hesitate, hesitation. Nearly always the noun is later: well, it is derived from the verb. Expel exists before expulsion, hesitate before hesitation. The step of forming the noun means something; a good deal or relatively little according to circumstances, but something. To put it at its lowest, there has been some reflection on the activity in question, there is some trend towards abstraction, systematization, classification perhaps, the thing is becoming more of an institution.[1]

Take neutralization. Medieval or rather Renaissance Latin has only the verb, *neutralisare*; it occurs from the fifteenth century and signifies to favour neither. French science adopts it in the form *neutraliser* and in the sense of to render neutral, about 1600 (first appearance 1611), and it takes approximately two hundred years for the action noun, *neutralisation*, to be coined (first appearance 1797).[2] English scientists borrow the verb from their French colleagues halfway through the eighteenth century, to neutralise (first appearance 1759: "I neutralized Spanish White

---

1. I shall concentrate on a comparatively late group of action nouns, formed by means of a characteristic ending. My main reason is that earlier groups are too remote for the evolution from verb to noun to be readily datable. It is easily demonstrated, however, that my considerations apply to those earlier cases as well: to this day, the action noun deed, for example, suggests a higher degree of reflection, formality, institutionalization than its verb to do.

2. For French dates I rely principally on Littré and Hatzfeld.

by fermenting it with vinegar") and the noun some fifty years later, neutralization (1808; Faraday employs it in 1827, "Neutralisations are best effected with the assistance of heat"). It is by 1800, then, that the activity has become a proper, fully recognized category in science. In connection with war and international politics, the English verb is first recorded in 1856, the noun in 1870—both, as it happens, having regard to the Black Sea. (I was so surprised by this late entry of the concept into international relations that I checked earlier sources, for example, concerning the status of Switzerland. They invariably speak, not of to neutralise, but of recognize or guarantee the neutrality.) So though by the middle of the nineteenth century science is familiar with the noun as well as the verb, international law begins all over again with the latter and the noun represents the stage when the concept is more established, elevated to an institution in the field.[3]

This kind of development is met throughout the entire realm of language, in all areas of human engagement, in philosophy, science, politics, architecture, everywhere. Its neglect vitiates or simplifies much of the intellectual history of civilization. In fact I submit that, right across the board, if we pay it the attention it deserves, a revolutionary new picture of the unfolding of thought will emerge. Just think of the difference between a simple *aequare*,[4] to be found in Plautus, and an advanced *aequatio*[5] from Cicero on; between a simple *humare*, from Varro, or *cremare*, from Cicero, and an advanced *humatio* or *crematio*, post-Augustan; between a modest Biblical *imitari Deum* and a solemn, post-Biblical *imitatio Dei*; between *iustificare*, from Tertullian, and *iustificatio*, from Augustine. In English, between to establish, second half of fourteenth century, and establishment, slowly coming in towards the end of the fifteenth, an indispensable slogan today; between to nationalize in the sense of to bring under the nation's control, first appearing in 1836 ("Neither the Arminian System nor the Nationalizing System nor the Calvinistic System exhibits the end of the

---

3. As an intransitive, denoting to steer a middle, undecided course (mostly used in a disparaging tone), to neutralize figures from as early as 1628. This sense, however never achieves an action noun at all.

4. Or *appellare, concipere, contemplari, describere, donare, inducere, introducere, mittere*.

5. *Appellatio, conceptio, contemplatio, descriptio, donatio, inductio, introductio, missio*.

sincere Gospel"), and nationalization, 1874, significantly in an explanation of the doctrine ("Nationalization of the land means that all the land in the country should be bought by the State"); between to transplant, before the middle of the fifteenth century, and transplantation, from the beginning of the seventeenth—or if we confine ourselves to the fashionable, surgical application, between to transplant, with reference to a tooth, 1786, and transplantation, with a wider sweep, including severed limbs as well as teeth, 1813. Just think of the insights to be gained by tracing, accounting for and evaluating such moves; by comparing the speed of progress of various concepts in a certain field; by comparing the speed of progress of various fields; and indeed by comparing, under this aspect, various languages and cultures. I shall here concentrate on Roman law, which, you will not dispute, is always in the vanguard of exploration.[6]

Property

Let me set out from a somewhat remote corner. It is well known that when the ancient sources refer to the appropriation of an object by seizing it, they use only the verb *occupare*, never *occupatio*.[7] At first sight this might be regarded as of no interest, a freak; but it gains in significance when we go more systematically through this branch of the law, the original modes of acquisition. *Derelinquere* in the sense of to abandon a piece of property occurs sixty times in the *Vocabularium Jurisprudentiae Romanae*;[8] *derelictio* does not occur once. (It occurs once in Cicero—in the sense of undutiful neglect, *derelictio communis utilitatis*).[9] Treasure trove is invariably spoken of as *thesaurum invenire*, never as *thesauri inventio*. Materials owned by one person being built into a house owned by another invariably as *inaedificare*, never as *inaedificatio* (a medieval word). Corn owned by one person being sown, in land owned by another invariably as *serere*, never as *satio*.[10] A's and B's things (say, two silver ingots) combining into one invariably as

---

6. *Exploro* is Plautine (*exploratum*), *exploratio* post Augustan.
7. Non-technically, *occupare* is found from Plautus, *occupatio* from Cicero.
8. Lists all occurrences of all words in the Digest, Gaius and a few other jurists; abbreviation *VJR*.
9. Cicero, *Off.* 3.6.30.
10. The noun occurs once in the Digest (7.4.10.4, Ulpian *XVII ad Sabinum*), in the

commiscere, never as *commixtio*. The making of a new thing with another man's materials invariably as *speciem facere*, never as *specificatio* (a medieval word).

If we had only, say, the two cases of *thesaurum invenire* and *inaedificare*, the absence of action nouns might be an accident of transmission; these cases are mentioned only a few times, so it might just have so happened that the verbs were preferred. However, in the case of *derelinquere*, the discrepancy between sixty times for the verb and nought for the noun is statistically significant; and when we find the noun missing in one after another of similar cases—*occupare, serere, commiscere, speciem facere*—then, though each case by itself would be too little represented in the texts to provide a firm basis for conclusions, the cumulative evidence is far from negligible. (I shall rely on this method a good deal: a cluster of even rare words, all pointing the same way, is as good as one frequent word.) It follows that, in this branch of the law at least, systematization had made far less headway in Roman times than would appear from our textbooks.

In several instances, to be sure, the action noun was reached; they are indeed particularly instructive. According to the legal situation, a man might acquire the fruits of an object belonging to another man either directly they are separated no matter by whom, or only if he gains control of, harvests, them.[11] In discussing the former alternative the sources use only *fructum separare*; there is no *fructus separatio*. In discussing the latter, however, they use both *fructum percipere* and *fructus perceptio*. This example brings out the importance an understanding of the step from verb to noun has for appreciating the relative evolution of various institutions, how advanced or backward they are, compared with one another. *Fructus perceptio* came into being when *fructus separatio* was not yet known; the latter is a medieval coinage. Here is strong and unexpected support

---

plural, denoting not a mode of acquisition, but concrete sowings which have taken place in what was originally a wood, with the result that the usufruct over the wood is extinguished by change of the object. In the language of agriculture, the farmer's activity, the nominalization of *serere* was achieved at a time when it was not yet achieved in the theory of original modes of acquisition of ownership.

11. Of course both cases are exceptional. Mostly the owner of the principal object acquires its fruits. But suppose, for example, I am *bona fide possessor* of a farm, that is to say, I cultivate a farm which I honestly think is mine, though in reality, as will emerge some day, it is yours: here the law gives me the fruits coming about while I am in possession.

for Aru's thesis,[12] probable anyhow on quite different grounds, that acquisition of fruits on separation is spurious, a post-classical intrusion into the earlier texts.[13] Making a late start, this mode of acquisition did not arrive at the action noun till the Middle Ages.

Separatio, incidentally, is not uncommon in legal literature. It may denote the separation of moveables which have been mixed.[14] The noun phrase *separatio bonorum* is familiar. Strangely, only in two texts listed by *Vocabularium Jurisprudentiae Romanae* does *separatio* mean divorce.[15] In all these—and other—cases the more systematized, established level had clearly been attained.

A few more nouns among the original modes of acquisition are noteworthy: *ferruminatio*, from *ferruminare*, *plumbatura*, from *plumbare*, *alluvio*, from *alluere*.[16] These nouns come, the first two from an artisan's craft, the third from the science of the *agrimensores*, surveyors. (Cicero mentions[17] that disputes about *alluvio* come before the centumviral court: they involved questions traditionally considered of great communal importance.) So despite their role in the law, the three nouns are not products of an internal legal development: they grew up in other branches of civilization and were taken over, ready-made by the jurists.[18] (Even so, *adplumbare* alone is represented in the sources, legal or lay; *adplumbatio*, though honoured with an entry in Pauly-Wissowa and mentioned in

12. *Bull. Ist. Dir. Rom.* 45 (1938): 191ff.

13. Typical is Digest 41.1.48 pr., Paul *VII ad Plautium*: "A *bonae fide* buyer without doubt makes the fruits his own by gaining control. . . . Finally, even before he gains control, as soon as they are separated from the land, they belong to the *bonae fide* buyer." The addition sticks out.

14. Digest 9.2.27.14, 20, Ulpian *XVIII ad edictum*; 25.1.9, Ulpian *XXXVI ad Sabinum*.

15. Digest 23.3.9.3, Ulpian *XXXI ad Sabinum*, 32.49.6; Ulpian *XXI ad Sabinum*.

16. An intransitive verb.

17. Cicero, *de or.* 1.38.173.

18. Very likely *confusio*, too, which (in addition to *confundere*) twice appears in connection with original acquisition, goes back to the language of a craft. Digest 6.1.23.5, Paul *XXI ad edictum*: "Welding brings about unification (*confusionem*), soldering does not do the same." Institutes 2.1.27: "If materials belonging to two owners combine, that entire object which comes into being through this combination (*confusione*). . . ." In neither text can *confusio* really be called a mode of acquisition, it is still a factual, industrial phenomenon. On *confundere* and *confusio* where right and duty merge in the same person I shall comment below, p. 34.

most major textbooks, is medieval. *Avulsio* also has no locus standi in ancient Roman law. It is a far later and rarer word than *alluvio*, attested from the elder Pliny on, but not found in the jurists. I suppose the rules about this contingency, though obviously classical,[19] are a later refinement to *alluvio*. It never came to a nominalization.) While in the case of *separare* and *percipere* we could gauge the relative state of progress of various legal institutions, the cases under notice give us an inkling of the comparisons which, if we are alive to the move from verb to noun and provide ourselves with sufficient material, might be possible between various provinces of endeavour—law and certain industries, law and certain crafts.

In modern expositions, *accessio* is the heading for all cases of acquisition by A of B's property as a result of the latter physically merging in A's: *alluvio*, for instance, or building on A's land with B's materials. It has long been seen that this meaning is alien to the sources. No wonder: even the verb *accedere* has not got it.[20] It is noteworthy, however, that *accessio* is used by the classics technically in several other senses: in that of a subordinate object which, in certain transactions, goes with the major one;[21] in that of addition in favour of A's usucapion of his predecessor's possession or time of possession;[22] in that of the accompaniment of one obligation, thought of as the principal one, by another.[23] In all these departments, abstraction with regard to the concept in question had gone further than in that of original modes of acquisition.

I now go on to a more basic concept. The verb *acquirere* has more than a thousand entries in *Vocabularium Jurisprudentiae Romanae*, the noun *acquisitio* has twelve. Eleven of the latter passages are in the Digest, all interpolated,[24] the twelfth is the rubric of *Ulp. Reg.* 19. But never mind about interpolation. Even if there were twelve occurrences starting from about the middle of the second century AD, the discrepancy would be staggering. In the *Thesaurus Linguae Latinae*, apart from those twelve

19. Gaius 2.71.

20. An intransitive.

21. Digest 34.2.19.13, Ulpian *XX ad Sabinum*: if I bequeath my gold, a jewel set in gold is included.

22. *Accessio possessionis* or *temporis*: Gaius 4.151; Digest 44.3.6.1, Africanus IX *quaestionum*; 44.3.15.1, Venuleius *V interdictorum*.

23. Gaius 3.126; Digest 44.7.44 pr., 4, Paul *LXXIV ad edictum*.

24. Beseler, *ZRG* 52 (1932): 42.

texts, the earliest instance of the noun is in the *Itala*. By contrast, the verb is frequent in Cicero, it is also used, for example, in the *senatusconsultum de aedificiis non diruendis*,[25] in the *Laudatio Turiae*,[26] in the edict of the curule aediles.[27] In the *Codex Theodosianus* the verb figures twenty times, in the *Post-Theodosian Novels* fifteen, the noun not once.[28]

To say that the classics preferred the verb for stylistic reasons is not enough. Style may be a contributory factor, but the phenomenon calls for a deeper explanation: it has to do with the slowness of systematizing, institutionalizing, mastery of the discipline. Beseler[29] speaks of the "aversion of the classical jurists to the noun." He instances *aequitas, captivitas, distinctio, praesumptio, ratihabitio*, all, he affirms, post-classical. It may be admitted that, though his criticism goes too far,[30] he has a point. But not a much stronger one than a future student of English writings who will be able to invoke an express recommendation of the Fowlers[31] to be sparing with abstract nouns and make for concrete expressions.

That the clue does not lie in mere elegance is easily proved. For one thing, the evolution from verb to noun is a universal one, reflected in lay literature as well as legal, and indeed to be found in literatures other than Latin. We just cannot put it down to a convention peculiar to the classical jurists. This is underlined by the fact that the *Codex Theodosianus* shows the same picture as the classical writings: twenty to nought (or, including the *Novels*, thirty-five to nought). No one would impute atticistic rigour to the *Codex Theodosianus*: it is a question of greater or lesser conceptual advance. For another thing, there are countless action nouns in the classics. In this Lecture, in order to make my point, I give prominence to cases where the action noun is conspicuously absent. But a glance at the dictionary will show that there was no conspiracy to avoid

---

25. Bruns, *Font.*, 200–1.

26. Bruns, *Font.*, 323.

27. Lenel, *Das edictum perpetuum*, 3rd ed. (1927), 555.

28. Even in the rubric of *Ulp. Reg.* 19, the noun appears in the plural, signifying the various ways of acquiring (*res mancipi, nec mancipi*); it does not represent a governing notion acquisition, though, admittedly, by this time the notion may well have been current.

29. Beseler, *ZRG* (1937): 15.

30. *Distinctio*, for example, cannot be totally thrown out. On *acceptio*, which he discusses at p. 1, see below, pp. 32–33.

31. Fowler, *The King's English*, 3rd ed. (1930), 15.

action nouns. One line of further research I am suggesting is precisely to find out in detail about their distribution; we have already seen that *fructus perceptio* is classical, *fructus separatio* medieval. Not infrequently it is indeed demonstrable that the classics themselves coined or took over from outside an action noun where their predecessors had been content with the verb. *Acquisitio* happens to be of post-classical Western origin (Western: it occurs in *Ulpiani Regulae* and the *Itala*); but we shall find that *fideiussio*, for instance, possibly came in at some point during the classical era. Moreover, once an action noun is in use, it may be about as frequent as the verb: *accusatio* and *appellatio* are examples.

There is in the case of *acquisitio* some strong, additional support for my approach: while *acquisitio* is late, *alienatio*, from *alienare*, goes back to the last century of the Republic. The verb is met in Plautus; the noun occurs in Cicero,[32] in Seneca,[33] in the praetorian edict—*alienatio iudicii mutandi causa*, somebody is about to sue you for an object, so in order to thwart him you transfer it to a mighty person or to one living in another province[34]—in the jurists, in the *Codex Theodosianus*, in the *Post-Theodosian Novels*. The contrast is dramatic. No consideration of style will account for it. It must be accounted for in terms of classification, abstraction, proceeding at a different pace in different sectors of the law.

Acquisitio is late, *alienatio* early. Why? For a long time the Roman jurists[35] produced no rules—I should say, no express, formulated rules—about acquisition as such. In the main, problems of acquisition became acute in connection with litigation about an object, with the very act of acquisition being in dispute. However, what would be controverted was not acquisition as such, but a specific way of acquiring or rather, more frequently, conveying. The party denying that the other had acquired the object would say, not "You have not acquired," but "You have not usucaped," "I have not mancipated to you," "I have made no delivery to

---

32. In the phrase *sacrorum alienatio*: Cicero, *Orat.* 144; *Leg.* 3.48. Cicero also once has *abalienatio*: *Top.* 5.28. *Abalienare* occurs in Plautus.

33. In a definition of sale: Seneca the Younger, *Ben.* 5.10.1. Here also *translatio*.

34. See Lenel, *Das edictum perpetuum*, 3rd ed. (1927), 125.

35. The Roman jurists: this is not a matter of natural law, and it would be rash to assume that, elsewhere, things might not take the opposite course, acquisition being nominalized before alienation.

you;" and his opponent would say, "I have used it for a full year," "You have mancipated, delivered." Thus the focus was all on *usucapio, mancipatio, traditio* and so forth.

By contrast, it was soon found necessary to lay down rules about alienation as such. The question of alienation arose chiefly in connection with restrictions on a man's power of disposal. Already the XII Tables knew groups restricted in a greater or less degree: women, male persons under age, lunatics, prodigals. Whatever the language of the code itself (where *alienatio* does not yet, of course, occur), magistrates and legal experts would have frequent occasion to pronounce on the position of these groups in regard to alienation in general, irrespective of any specific mode of conveyance resorted to. The evidence is unambiguous: about four-fifths of all texts containing *alienatio* belong here, deal with restrictions on disposal. Remember the edict I have just adverted to, concerning the transfer of a disputed object to a mighty person or one residing in another province. The way it was transferred would be totally irrelevant; the praetor was against alienation *tout court*.[36] In regard to alienation, then, there was far less in the way of a more thorough working out of the notion

36. Further examples. (1) The XII Tables provide (VII 12) that if an heir sells a *statuliber* (a slave manumitted "if he pays the heir so and so much money"), the latter may pay the buyer (Bruns, *Font.*, 28). According to Pomponius, Aristo (a friend of the younger Pliny), in an opinion he delivered to Celsus, argued that the word "sale" here embraced any *alienatio*: Digest 40.7.29, Pomponius *XVIII ad Quintum Mucium*. (2) The discussion of an edictal provision against alienation to defraud creditors, Digest 42.8.6.5, Ulpian *LXVI ad edictum*. (3) The discussion of a *rei vindicatio* modified by insertion of a fiction, employed where honorarian or imperial restrictions on alienation are contravened, Digest 50.16.28 pr., Paul *XXI ad edictum*. (Why VJR says this is the *actio Publiciana* I do not know, except that the *actio Publiciana* is also a *vindicatio* with fiction.) (4) The discussion of a problem arising out of a provision of the *lex Julia de adulteriis* forbidding alienation of *fundus dotalis*, Code 5.23.1, Severus et Antoninus, AD 213. (5) The discussion of a provision of the *lex Julia de adulteriis* forbidding a woman to manumit a slave within sixty days of divorce, lest he be no longer available for questioning under torture should there be a charge of adultery. In post-classical law alienation was equally prohibited: Digest 40.9.14.6, Ulpian *IV de adulteriis* (see Yaron, *Revue Internationale des Droits de l'Antiquité* vol. 2, 3rd ser. [1955], 385). (6) The discussion of an *oratio Severi* of AD 195, forbidding a tutor to alienate urban land of the ward without consent of the praetor, Digest 27.9.3.1f., 5.8.7 pr., Ulpian *XXXV ad edictum*. (7) The discussion of the *actio de peculio annalis* against him who manumits or alienates a slave, Digest 15.2.1.5, Ulpian *XXIX ad edictum*. (8) Digest 18.1.67, Pomponius

than in regard to acquisition. It is—we may conclude—in consequence of the very different settings of the discussions that the nominal stage in the case of alienation precedes by hundreds of years that in the case of acquisition.[37]

There is an illuminating corollary: *alienatio* sometimes denotes not just alienation but power of alienation. In this application, which reflects a yet further evolution of theory, the noun is often interpolated.[38] But it is represented, or at least approached, in Gaius: a ward has no power of alienation of anything without his tutor's authority.[39] In any case, no parallel signification of *acquisitio*, power of acquisition, is found either in classical or in Byzantine law. The use of *alienatio* in the sense discussed points up not only the enormously more advanced stage of this concept, but also its central area—the question of restrictions on disposal. *Alienatio* may mean the absence of a disability, the freedom to dispose.

My finding is confirmed by the synonyms of *acquirere* and *acquisitio*. The verb *parare* is very frequent, *paratio* is represented in one interpolated text.[40] *Comparare*, in the sense of to acquire, occurs two hundred times in *Vocabularium Jurisprudentiae Romanae*, the noun is rare and

---

XXXIX ad Quintum Mucium, is interesting. Originally this fragment, too, dealt with a disability: a *praedium subsignatum*—land pledged to the state—remains tied even when alienated. In the Digest, the statement is torn from its context and placed in the title *De contrahenda emptione,* with the result that a general principle emerges: throughout the private law, we are told, an object which is being alienated carries its juristic condition with it. On compilatorial generalisations of this nature see Daube, *ZRG* 76 (1959): 149–50. Note that we have to do with a "free" text (see Daube, *ZRG* 76:261ff.), a text which, by Justinian's time, was no longer otherwise applicable since the old *praediatura* was long gone.

37. Even *alienatio* as a heading in an *ex professo* treatment of modes of acquisition first appears as late as *Ulp. Reg.* 19.3,7,9; e.g. *mancipatio propria species alienationis est rerum mancipi.* The rubric, it may be recalled (above, p. 20n28) has *acquisitiones.*

38. Digest 14.6.9.1, Ulpian *XXIX ad edictum*; 24.1.3.8, Ulpian *XXXII ad Sabinum* (Thayer, *Lex Aquilia and Gifts between Husband and Wife* [1929], 131, in a criticism of Beseler, blunders about the *bona fide serviens*: this expression can indeed be applied to one who knows himself free); 42.8.12, Marcellus *XVIII digestorum*; see Beseler, *ZRG* 57 (1937): 3.

39. Gaius 2.84: if you pay a ward without his tutor's authority your debt is not gone, *quia nullius rei alienatio ei sine tutore auctore concessa est.* Moreover, there is the old precedent of *datio deminutio,* Livy 39.19.5: see below, pp. 41, 46.

40. Digest 30.39.7, Ulpian *XII ad Sabinum*; see Beseler, *ZRG* 66 (1948): 342.

mostly interpolated.[41] Professor Lawson has recently stated:[42] "In fact, throughout the ancient history of Roman law ... where we should speak of conveyancing, the Romans spoke of acquisition." In view of the absence or lateness of such nouns or noun phrases as *occupatio, thesauri inventio, acquisitio, comparatio,* and the classicality of *alienatio,* as also of *mancipatio, in iure cessio, traditio,* some reservation is surely needed.[43]

In passing—*mancipatio, in iure cessio* and *traditio* are indeed classical, but it is advisable not to be too sanguine even about their age. The verbs are ancient enough. *Mancipare* and *tradere* are Plautine; and though *in iure cedere* is first met in Varro, it is probably much older—we have to allow for the fact that this institution becomes progressively less prominent in classical law and is ignored by Justinian: our sources therefore present a strongly reduced picture.[44] The nouns are a different matter. When Paul says that the XII Tables confirmed *mancipatio* and *in iure cessio*[45] that

41. Always according to Beseler, *Beitr.* 5 (1931): 82–83. He goes too far, however; some of the passages are surely genuine. In fact, the classical usage of the noun is, I think, interestingly confined, but there is no need here to enlarge. The situation as a whole agrees with my thesis.

42. Lawson, *Boston University Law Review* 46 (1966): 185.

43. The matter is infinitely complicated. It is certainly correct that in formal transactions it was usually the person acquiring who spoke or acted; see Buckland, *Festschrift Koschaker* 1 (1939): 16ff. In a sense, this does mean "emphasis . . . placed on the acquisition of property even when it was acquired by an act of alienation by another person" (Lawson, *Boston University Law Review* 46 (1966): 185). But only in a sense; the alienor, too, played a part, if only by admitting the ceremony. And it by no means follows that the Roman jurists thought of acquisition where we think of conveyance. One distinction which is noticeable when we ponder the terminology is that the "original" modes look at the business from the point of view of the acquirer, *usucapere, occupare* and so on, the "derivative" ones from that of the giver, *mancipare, in iure cedere, tradere.* He who bases his right on an "original" mode will allege no transfer; it is his taking which will be controversial. He who relies on a "derivative" mode will usually be faced, in litigation, by the person from whom he derives his right, and while he says "You mancipated the object to me," the other will deny just this. In Jewish law, not so action-oriented, the prevailing point of view seems to be the acquirer's: *qana, qinyan.* Enough.

44. I have little doubt, however, that *in iure cedere* is younger than *mancipare* and *tradere.* The various transactions described by *in iure cedere,* I think, went on for a long time under more specific, concrete names before this expression was coined.

45. *Fr. Vat.* 50, Paul *I manualium: et mancipationem et in iure cessionem lex XII tabularum confirmat.* Cf. below, pp. 31–32, on the case of *emptio.* Very critical about *Fr. Vat.* 50, Buckland, *Text-Book,* ed. Peter Stein (1963), 234.

does not prove that the code employed the nouns. *Mancipatio* appears in Festus, *in iure cessio* in Cicero. Very likely they existed, say, by the end of the second century BC.[46] (The same is probably true of *usucapio*, first attested in Cicero.)[47] *Traditio* as a technical term may well be a little later than that. Varro mentions *emptiones et traditiones*.[48] *Venditio traditioque* also occurs in the edict of the aediles,[49] but in a paragraph hardly part of the earliest version and quite likely added towards the end of the Republic.[50] Cicero has the noun once, in the combination *traditio nexu*, signifying *mancipatio*.[51] Otherwise we know it only from the jurists of the Empire.

Still about acquisition and transfer. *Transmittere ad heredem* and the like may be found sixty times in *Vocabularium Jurisprudentiae Romanae*, *transmissio* not once; nor is it found in the *Codex Theodosianus*; nor anywhere in lay literature. Its first occurrence is in a law by Justinian.[52] An enormous amount has been written in recent decades as to whether the classics ever managed to conceive of a transfer of a right—say, a transfer of

---

46. The availability of *mancipium* may have been a factor in delaying *mancipatio*: see below, p. 35n104 and pp. 45–46.

47. Cicero, *Pro Caec.* 26.74. The form *usus capio*, with *usus* in the genitive, in *Leg.* 1.21.55, may be meant as a reminder that the XII Tables spoke of *usus*.

48. Varro, *de Re Rustica* 2.6.3.

49. Lenel, *Das edictum perpetuum*, 3rd ed. (1927), 555.

50. Lenel, *Das edictum perpetuum*, 560, notices that the items which a purchaser, to succeed in *actio redhibitoria*, must restore to the seller together with the slave are listed in a different sequence in the main edict and in the pattern formula. The former places at the head compensation for damage to the slave while in the purchaser's hands (*post venditionem traditionemque*) and then such things as offspring and profit made by hiring out the slave. The formula puts offspring and profit first and compensation after. Lenel's explanation does not convince me. I think there was development. For some time, all that was expected of the purchaser was to restore the slave plus additions. Then the need for compensation in the case of damage arose, and a clause to provide for this was appended both in the main edict and in the formula. The latter remained frozen at this stage, while in the main edict a more logical order was introduced: the slave whose quality does not come up to standard may be returned, taking account, however, of such deterioration as has been caused while the purchaser was in charge, and equally offspring, profit and so on must be restored.

51. Cicero, *Top.* 5.28.

52. Code 6.30.19.1, AD 529, dealing with the transmission of the *beneficium deliberandi* to one's successors.

ownership, *dominium*, as opposed to a transfer of the actual object; or, if they did manage, from when and how far. I shall not engage in this battle, except to observe that to discriminate between *transferre* and *translatio* would here be particularly helpful towards a more profound and accurate assessment of the development.[53]

Obligations

Here is a cluster of action nouns which astounded even myself: *sponsio*, from *spondere*, *fidepromissio*, from *fidepromittere*, *fideiussio*, from *fideiubere*, as designations of three kinds of surety. But do you want to know the truth about them?

Sponsio in the sense of the private law contract of surety simply does not exist, be it in legal sources, be it in lay. It always means the ordinary stipulation, formal promise, with no suretyship involved; or more precisely, that old variety of stipulation which was in use among Roman citizens only.[54] The reaction to this situation of Heumann and successive editors of his *Handlexikon*—Seckel among them—is remarkable. They badly feel the need to list the established meaning surety. So they quote for it Digest 1.3.1, where Papinian[55] says that *lex est . . . communis rei publicae sponsio*, "statute is . . . the common undertaking of the state." For making the evidence fit the result, this is worse than any judicial

---

53. *Transferre* is very frequent in various senses, *translatio* occurs about a dozen times in *VJR*, the texts being dubious. The noun does, however, occur in the *Cod. Theod.* Also, I may recall, in Seneca, *Ben.* 5.10.1, together with *alienatio* (above, p. 21n33). Unquestionably the notion of transfer of property in its verbal form proceeded the systematized, institutionalized, nominal form. More I shall not say.

54. To avoid misunderstandings—I do not, of course, mean that a surety might not avail himself of the form of stipulation called *sponsio*. In fact that form of stipulation did provide the instrument for the earliest surety. What I mean is that *sponsio* never specifically denotes the contract of surety as such, it always denotes the promise by means of *spondere*—to whatever use it is put. A man could give a *sponsio* by which he undertook delivery of a courtesan: it does not follow that *sponsio* signifies the promise of a courtesan. As it happens, no text is preserved using *sponsio* where a surety acts, but this, I suppose, is accidental: no text is preserved using *sponsio* where an *ancilla* is promised.

55. Digest 1.3.1, Papinian I *definitionum*.

commission. Papinian's definition is a translation of Demosthenes, who (in his speech *Against Aristogeiton*) speaks of *syntheke koine*, "a common pact"; actually, the Greek original is presented by the Digest directly after the fragment from Papinian, in Digest 1.3.2, from Marcian.[56] *Sponsio* is an apt rendering of *syntheke* in this context since a *lex*, like a stipulation, comes into operation by question and answer. Neither the Greek *syntheke* nor the Latin *sponsio* carries a trace of suretyship. All this apart from the fact that the statement is decidedly not concerned with private law arrangements.[57]

None the less Romanists are busy reconstructing texts as if *sponsio* did signify surety, and again and again where the Digest mentions *fideiussio*, this is declared to be a post-classical modernization and *sponsio* is substituted for it. I shall presently have surprising news about *fideiussio*. For the moment I would point out that it will not do to insert *sponsio* into the jurists.

Sponsus would be just possible. This is another action noun of *spondere* which, while it may function as a synonym of *sponsio*, denoting a formal civil promise in general, or at least a betrothal promise,[58] does also have the narrower sense of surety.[59] The word, however, is exceedingly rare. In general it may be assumed that if, as does happen, the appearance of *fideiussio* in a text is irreconcilable with classical law, that text must have undergone a deeper revision than the ousting of either *sponsio* or

56. Digest 1.3.2, Papinian *I institutionum*.

57. I have a feeling that Lewis and Short, too, are trying to find evidence for *sponsio* in a specialized sense when they register a series of treaties in Livy under a separate heading: agreement by giving surety. If by this they do mean that *sponsio* here denotes the undertaking of a *sponsor*, they are wrong. In all the texts they quote the noun is applied in the usual fashion; it refers to the undertaking of the principal contracting party, often a General. That his promise may be accompanied by further guarantees, such as the giving of hostages, or that there is the state behind him, does not affect the signification of the term. Mommsen has it right; see, e.g. *Röm. Staatsr.* 1, 247.

58. Varro, *Ling.* 6.71, Gellius, 4.4.2, citing Servius Sulpicius Rufus, consul in 51 BC.

59. Cicero, *Att.* 12.19.2 (the reading, however, is not absolutely certain); *Phaedrus*, 1.16.1 (the MSS have *sponsore* and *sponsum* is conjectured); Gaius 4.22. The *lex Furia* discussed by Gaius dates from about 200 BC. Whether it was characterized as *de sponsu* then or, if not, from how soon after, there is no means of ascertaining.

sponsus by *fideiussio.*[60] The older type of surety may indeed have figured, but it must have been expressed in some other fashion. The substitution of *sponsio*, a non-existent noun—non-existent in this sense—is ruled out, that of *sponsus* precarious in the extreme.

Spondere means to promise and often to promise *qua* surety. The agent noun *sponsor*, we saw, is exclusively tied to the latter, narrower sense: the surety's promise is so striking that he is the promiser *kat' exochen*. Of two action nouns, one, *sponsio*, of frequent occurrence, belongs to the general sense and no other; so the formal civil promise by means of *spondere* is an established part of the system. The other, *sponsus*, very rare, besides signifying the formal civil promise at large (or maybe its application to an engagement to be married), also has specific reference to the promise of a surety. It is—astonishingly—to this extent only that the earliest type of surety is a nominalized institution. It will be fascinating to watch how this result will be got over by those who see in *sponsio*-surety the cradle of contract.

Fidepromissio is an unmitigated artefact, not part of the real world in any sense, in any source. The *Thesaurus Linguae Latinae* has not got it. It leads a vigorous life in texts reconstructed by modern authorities who lack the insight that the road from verb to action noun tends to be arduous and may never be traversed. It might perhaps be argued that since *promittere* has *promissio*,[61] *fidepromittere* ought to have *fidepromissio*. The question, however, is not whether *fidepromissio* was logically or philologically possible—this I do not deny for one moment—but whether it did in fact materialize. There is no evidence whatever that it did. Queen Victoria

60. Take Digest 46.1.69, Tryphoninus *IX disputationum.* Lenel, Levy and others (Lenel, *Pal.* 2 [1889], 362; Levy, *Sponsio, Fidepromissio, Fideiussio* (1907), 4) are right in holding that the discussion, now about *fideiussio*, originally referred to a *sponsor*: there is release by lapse of a certain time from due day. But to replace (as they do) *ex fideiussione* by *ex sponsione* is impossible since *sponsio* at no time signified surety, and even *ex sponsu* would be too simple a remedy. The part from *item heres* to *agitur* which now contains *ex fideiussione* has suffered radical abbreviation. The classical author must have made it clear whether the lapse of time occurred during the actual tutor's life or after his death when the heir had entered. The consequences might differ accordingly, for instance, with regard to liability for *dolus* only or for *dolus* and negligence.

61. *Promittere* in Plautus, *promissio* from Cicero.

outlived the Consort. The simple verb to live goes with life. But no book has as yet appeared: "Queen Victoria, her life and her outlife."

Fideiussio may date from around AD 200; hardly from long before. Gaius does not employ it. It is indeed conceivable that it was coined, or made at home in learned discussion, by Scaevola and his pupil Papinian.[62] It is not in the *Codex Theodosianus*, though the *fideiussor* is. The *Interpretatio* to the *Codex Theodosianus* has it.[63]

Considering that such is the situation regarding *sponsio, fidepromissio, fideiussio*, the complete absence of *adpromissio* is not accidental. There is no entry in the *Thesaurus Linguae Latinae*, the word is found in no ancient source, not even Justinian. True, the verb *adpromittere* itself is rare and has been shown to be post-classical.[64] But there is no need in this case that the verb be common for significance to attach to the absence of the noun. The cumulative evidence provided by *sponsio* and so on is fully adequate: *adpromissio* is a medieval formation.

By the same token, when we look at plurality of creditors, it is highly probable that so long as *adstipulari* was a live part of the law, it never

---

62. Digest 34.3.28 pr., Scaevola *XVI digestorum* (in the question put to the jurist); 42.6.3 pr., Papinian *XXVII quaestionum*, 46.3.94.2f.; Papinian *VIII quaestionum*; 46.3.95.3, Papinian *XXVIII quaestionum*. Earlier occurrences of the noun are extremely dubious. As for the *senatusconsultum Velleianum*, Vogt is certainly right in maintaining (*Studien zum Senatusconsultum Velleianum* [1952], 2–3) that despite Digest 16.1.2.1, Ulpian *XXIX ad edictum*, the *fideiussiones* were not part of the original text. Digest 14.5.8, Paul *I decretorum*, describes a state of affairs as "so to speak *fideiussio*." By this time the concept must be fully established, but the relevant sentence does not sound Pauline. In most texts with *fideiussio* the distinction from the main debt is heavily stressed, and it would not be surprising if the noun had been coined in the course of reflection on this aspect.

63. The difference is pronounced. E.g. *Cod. Theod.* 5.13, Valentinianus, Theodosius et Arcadius, AD 392, is against *sponsores et fideiussores* for a dowry's return (yes, the *sponsores* are still in the text of the constitution though no longer in the rubric of the Code), the *Interpretatio* introduces *fideiussio* (the *sponsores* are dropped, and *sponsio* in the sense of surety is of course out of the question). Note, incidentally, that *Cod. Theod.* 5.13 speaks of the *promissiones* of the sureties *in cavenda sponsione*: the principal promise of return is called *sponsio*, and this is guaranteed by the accessory *promissiones*. Outside Roman law proper, *fideiussio* occurs first in the *Lex Romana Visigothorum* by Alaric, of AD 506, and in Cassiodorus about Gothic law.

64. Solazzi, *Bull. Ist. Dir. Rom.* 38 (1930): 1ff. He notes the absence of the action noun at p. 19. His results are approved by Buckland, *Text-Book*, 445n3.

reached nominalization. *Stipulari* is in Plautus and *stipulatio* is doubtless fairly old; it is attested from the late Republic,[65] and Cicero feels able to coin *stipulatiuncula*.[66] *Adstipulari* and *adstipulator* in the legal sense, of a subsidiary creditor added to the principal one, are extant in one jurist only, Gaius,[67] and in a very few texts from Cicero and Festus. *Adstipulatio* in this sense is not met at all prior to about AD 600. It does appear in the sense of confirmation or assent in lay literature from the elder Pliny on. Were this case isolated, we could draw no conclusion. But considering our findings in respect of *adpromissio* and so on (and also considering that the importance of contractual *adstipulari* started to decrease as early as the second century BC), it is practically certain that the absence of the action noun in the legal sense from the sources reflects its absence in fact. Apparently the *Thesaurus Linguae Latinae* finds that it ought to exist, hence accords it an entry as a technical term. But the solitary passage quoted for it, from Symmachus,[68] has nothing to do with a subsidiary creditor; the noun means confirmation, as on the ten other occasions this writer uses the noun or the verb.

It is in a lexicographical collection of Isidore of Seville that we first come across the legal, contractual *adstipulatio*.[69] This is no accident: such treatises are apt to break through to the action noun—we are given brief comparative definitions of *stipulatio, restipulatio,*[70] *adstipulatio* and *constipulatio*, the systematizing trend is unmistakable. Significantly, the last word, *constipulatio* (presented as a species of *restipulatio*), occurs nowhere else in Latin.

---

65. Gellius 4.4.2, quoting Servius.

66. Cicero, *de or.* 1.38.174: If you cannot advise a client as to the pitfalls which may lurk in a relatively insignificant promise, should he entrust you with an important case?

67. Gaius 3.110ff.

68. Symmachus, *Relationes* 10.41.3. Symmachus considers it outrageous to declare a testament invalid because one of the witnesses receives a minor legacy. Among the arguments advanced by his opponents, he writes, are "imperial rescripts setting aside the *adstipulatio*—confirmation, attestation—of one said to have furthered his own cause by his witness," *rescripta divalia quibus adstipulatio cuiusdam remota est qui suam iuvisse causam testimonio diceretur*.

69. Isidore of Seville, *Differentiarum appendix* 162.

70. Already in Cicero; also, e.g. Gaius 4.13.

Varia

Clearly, what is required is a thorough rewriting of the history of Roman Law—and other branches of history. In *Vocabularium Jurisprudentiae Romanae* as well as other dictionaries verb and action noun are often combined under the same heading, the distinction is treated as irrelevant. Yet to obtain a correct and differentiated estimate of the evolution, it is essential to note at what stage the step from verb to noun is taken. Quite a few nouns are of great antiquity, many are the result of medieval or modern preconceptions, the verb never got there while the law was alive, and the bulk lie somewhere in between.

Usus figured in the XII Tables.[71] I do not think this is true of *emptio* though it is attributed to the code by Aristo (under Trajan).[72] I would date it—and *venditio*—from the third century BC.[73] *Accusatio* is no doubt somewhat older than Cicero who provides the earliest evidence; *accusare* is Plautine. The cases of *damnatio, interrogatio* and *licitatio* look similar. Also *remissio;*[74] *remissio mercedis,* rebate of rent in tenancy, is genuinely a classical institution.[75] Also *solutio.*

71. See Bruns, *Font.,* 25.

72. Digest 40.7.29.1, Pomponius *XVIII ad Quintum Mucium: sed verissimum est quod et Aristo Celso rescripsit, posse dari pecuniam . . . quoniam lex duodecim tabularum emptionis verbo omnem alienationem complexa videretur.* This interpretation was possible even if the XII Tables contained merely the verb *emere.* Parallels abound. The edict (Lenel, *Das edictum perpetuum,* 3rd ed. (1927), 407–8) ordained *condemnatus ut pecuniam solvate,* commented upon by Paul thus: *solutionis verbum pertinet ad omnem liberationem,* Digest 46.3.54, Paul *LVI ad edictum.* Cf. also below, n. 100, Jerome's introduction of *comparatio* in discussing what he regards as a wrong use of *comparare* by his opponent Rufinus.

73. Whereas Plautus has *emere,* the noun is first attested in Varro. (In the *lex agraria* of 111 BC it is due to conjecture: Bruns, *Font.,* 75. Leo's conjecture of *emptio* in the place of *coactio* in Plautus, *Asin.* 203—*Plautii Comoediae* vol. 1, 2nd ed. [1895], 611—is arbitrary.) Still, Plautus definitely knew *coemptio,* as is proved by his use of *coemptionalis:* Plautus, *Bacch.* 4.9.52. *Redimere* in the sense of to ransom is Plautine, *redemptio* is found from Livy. As for *vendere-venditio,* the verb is Plautine, the noun occurs from the *lex agraria* (Bruns, *Font.,* 75, 82–83) and Festus remarks on an old meaning of it (of course, he may be simply indicating that the meaning became obsolete with the decay of the censorship): *venditiones dicebantur olim censorum locationes.*

74. *Remittere* in the sense of to forgive, to give up, Cicero, *Mostell.* 5.2.47. *Remissio* in this sense Cicero, *In Catilinam* 4.6.13.

75. Digest 19.2.15.3ff., Ulpian *XXXII ad edictum.*

I admit that in evaluating the evidence one has sometimes to follow hunches. *Satisficere* occurs from Plautus, *satisfactio* from Cicero; I suppose the noun is somewhat earlier than Cicero. *Satisdare* and *satisdatio* both are attested only from Cicero; the noun it may be recalled, occurs in the *lex Rubria*.[76] Surely the verb at least is considerably earlier though not nearly as early as *satisfacere*. *Satisaccipere* is Plautine—it is also met in Cato— whereas *satisacceptio* occurs only in one Digest text.[77] *Satisaccipere* was clearly subjected to less institutionalization than the other two concepts, the prevalent analysis was from the angle of performance. Remember that quite a few legal verbs prefixed by *satis* never made the noun at all: *satisofferre, satispeterei, satisexigere* and so forth.

Here a word about *acceptio* may be in place. Beseler says that, though it is Ciceronian, the classics made no use of it. Yet it would have been a suitable legal term for acceptance. Hence, he concludes, its absence must be due to rejection on grounds of style.[78] However, first, the classics did use it, though very little.[79] Secondly, Cicero himself has it once only, nor is it at all common in post-classical texts. Thirdly, its tardiness is primarily explicable by the simple fact that acceptance creates relatively few problems[80] and, therefore, is slow in becoming an institution. We may compare the well-known phenomenon that some expositions of *traditio*, the passing of ownership, stress the requirement of the transferor's intent to transfer, while silent about the transferee's will to receive.[81] The latter is rarely controversial.[82]

76. 1.15; Bruns, *Font.*, 97.

77. Digest 45.1.5.2, Pomponius *XXVI ad Sabinum*. Heumann-Seckel and Beseler, *ZRG* 57 (1937): 1, doubt the authenticity. I see little to quarrel with (apart from the concluding words *id est* and so on). *Acceptio* without *satis* occurs from Cicero.

78. Heumann-Seckel and Beseler, *ZRG* 57 (1937): 1.

79. Of the three entries in *VJR*, at least Digest 45.1.5.2, with *satisacceptio*, just considered, seems to me genuine.

80. The case discussed by Cicero, *Top.* 8.37, is not an everyday one. The Roman general Mancinus, defeated by the Numantines, concluded a treaty; the senate repudiated it and surrendered Mancinus, but the Numantines refused to accept him. It is possible to argue, says Cicero, that he was not really surrendered, since *neque deditionem neque donationem sine acceptione intellegi posse.*

81. Digest 41.1.9.3, Gaius *II rerum cottidianarum*; Institutes 2.1.40.

82. See Jörs, *Römisches Recht*, 3rd ed. Kunkel (1949), 129.

Abrogare and *derogare legem* may be found in Cato, *abrogatio* and *derogatio legis* from Cicero. That we do not come across the noun phrases in the classical jurists is chiefly, I assume, the result of the fact that the subject is so little discussed.[83] *Nuncupare* goes back to the XII Tables.[84] *Nuncupatio* is confined to post-Augustan writings. It may none the less be of Republican origin: it is part of the vocabulary of the classics in an area where they display much conservatism,[85] and the material is not plentiful. Still the interval between verb and action noun is considerable.

Here are a few action nouns which, while classical, may well not reach back into the Republic. *Evincere* is used by Alfenus Varus,[86] *evictio* first appears in Javolenus (who may have come upon it in the slightly earlier Plautus).[87] *Expensum ferre* is found from Cicero, *expensilatio* once in Latin literature, in a legal anecdote of Gellius.[88] We hear generally so little about this transaction that one's immediate inclination is to think this may be the top of the iceberg. The dates assume a certain importance, however, in the light of the fact that even *acceptilatio* is not evidenced prior to Gaius;[89] *acceptum referre* occurs from Cicero, *acceptum ferre* from the younger Seneca.[90]

The same passage from Gellius which supplies the only extant evidence of *expensilatio* also has the rare *obsignatio*, not in *Vocabularium Jurisprudentiae Romanae*,[91] indeed, first found in legal texts in two rescripts

83. *Abrogatio* is not registered in *VJR*, *derogatio* once: Digest 23.4.30, Tryphoninus *X disputationum*, *derogatio facta fideicommissi petitioni*. The passage is highly suspect; Beseler, *ZRG* 66, (1948): 277.

84. See Bruns, *Font.*, 25.

85. Look, for example, at the archaic discussion Digest 28.1.25, Javolenus *V posteriorum Labeonis*, where the verb is used.

86. Digest 6.1.57, *VI digestorum*.

87. Digest 21.2.60, Javolenus *II ex Plautio*.

88. Gellius 14.2.7.

89. Or at most Javolenus. However, Digest 45.2.2 (*III ex Plautio*) is heavily revised, and the argumentation at the end of 12.4.10 (*I ex Plautio*) also shows signs of interference (see Schwartz, *Die Grundlage der Condictio im Klassischen Römischen Recht* [1952], 196–97). It is certainly remarkable that no other first-century jurist is credited with the noun.

90. The phrase *accepti relatio*, title of a section in Buckland's *Text-Book*, 572, is non-existent. *Fr. Vat.* 329, Papinian *II responsorum*, speaks of *acceptum vel expensum ferre*. Buckland refers to Sohm, *Institutionem*, 17th ed., Mitteis and Wenger (1923), 477, but the noun phrase is not there employed.

91. Lewis and Short cite P.S. 4.6.1, but the verb alone is here used.

by Diocletian and Maxiamanus.[92] The verb is Plautine and freely used by the classical jurists. In addition, the same passage mentions *testium intercessio*, denoting the attendance of witnesses, a unique expression.[93] The accumulation of action nouns in this sentence is not accidental. Gellius tells us about his experience as a judge, when a decent man reclaimed a loan from a scoundrel. The latter denied the debt, and there was indeed no evidence apart from plaintiff's word. Defendant's advocate insisted the transaction ought to be proved *expensilatione, mensae rationibus, chirographi exhibitione, tabularum obsignatione, testium intercessione*. An impressive challenge, briefly enumerating the manifold ways to establish such a claim: lists of this kind are good soil for schematization and, hence, the action noun.

Occasionally the verb itself does not antedate the classics. *Confundere* may denote the extinction of a right and its corresponding duty or burden by union in one person; say, I become my creditor's or debtor's heir. The earliest surviving evidence for the verb dates from around AD 100, Javolenus,[94] for the noun, *confusio*, from some seventy-five years later, Scaevola or Florentine.[95] These dates, I guess, roughly correspond to reality. The later history is noteworthy. Till Diocletian inclusive, the rather sophisticated notion is common.[96] After him, we do not find it, either as verb or noun[97]—till it reappears again in Justinian.[98] All this may be accident, but I do not believe it is: it closely mirrors the fluctuations of jurisprudential capacity.

Post-classical action nouns. *Adnumerare* in the sense of to pay is ancient though not very frequent; it occurs in Plautus.[99] *Adnumeratio*

92. Code 4.54.7, 8.42.9, AD 286.

93. *Intercedere* from Plautus, *intercessio* as a helpful activity from Cicero.

94. Digest 8.6.15, *II epistularum*.

95. Digest 46.3.93.2, Scaevola *singulari quaestionum publice tractatarum*; 30.116.4, Florentine *XI institutionum*. We saw above, p. 18n18, that in the field of modes of acquisition, the institution *confusio* was attained at no period of Roman law.

96. It is found in four of his rescripts: Code 4.16.6 = 7.72.7, AD 294 (verb); 4.16.5, AD 294; 5.58.3, AD 294; 6.50.14, AD 293 (noun).

97. Varro's *Ling.* quotes *Cod. Theod.* 1.10.1, Gratianus, Valentinianus et Theodosius, of AD 381, but this is a mistake.

98. Code 6.30.22.9, AD 531 (verb).

99. According to Beseler, the classical jurists never use the verb in a sense other than that of to count out, *zahlend übergeben*: ZRG 52 (1932): 39ff.

is extremely rare. It is met in no legal source, but it is used once in Jerome's *Against Rufinus*.[100] *Adprehendere* is frequent in *Vocabularium Jurisprudentiae Romanae*, *adprehensio* does not occur in any legal source but, for example, in the *Itala*.[101] In this case, even the verb seems to become less popular with the jurists as time goes on,[102] so the tardiness in nominalization is not surprising. *Adprobare* in the legal senses of to approve and to show to be worthy of approval is far from common: about ten times in *Vocabularium Jurisprudentiae Romanae*. *Adprobatio* occurs in one interpolated passage.[103] By around AD 400 the institution of *adprobatio operis* is clearly attained: Augustine, commenting on "God saw that it was good" in Genesis 1, explains that this is *operis adprobatio secundum artem facti, quae Sapientia Dei est*.[104] *Audire* from early on may denote to hear

---

100. Jerome, *Against Rufinus* 3.6. Even *adnumeratio* in the sense of reckoning, addition, inclusion, has only a single entry in Varro's *Ling.*: *Cod. Theod.* 6.22.8.1, Theodosius et Valentinianus, AD 425. Lewis and Short give Digest 27.1.13, but the text is a Greek excerpt from Modestinus *IV excusationum*. Paragraph 2 towards the end speaks of *diarithmesis ton hemeron*, which Mommsen renders by *summa dierum*. The twelfth-century translation, however, has *adnumeratio dierum*; it is this translation which got into Forcellini's dictionary, from where Lewis and Short must have taken it. The passage from Jerome, by the way, has not so far, I believe, been properly understood. Jerome is criticizing Rufinus for treating *comparare* as a possible synonym of *emere*, whereas its only correct meaning (Jerome here alleges) is to join, to compare, to match. Rufinus had written to Jerome that he was gratuitously sending him a tract which, otherwise, Jerome would surely seek to buy, *comparare*. This usage, Jerome fulminates, is a barbarism: *cum comparatio aequalium sit, emptio pretii adnumeratio*, "since *comparatio* is a matching of equal things, *emptio* the payment of a price." That this is the point of the censure is confirmed by the continuation which dwells on another stylistic lapse. Throughout this chapter Jerome harps on Rufinus's inferiority as a philologist: "You are bilingual, you have so much Greek and Latin that *Graeci te Latini et Latinum te Graecum putant*." No doubt some of the criticisms are untenable, and were so at the time; but Jerome made them anyway.

101. John 7:30: *nondum enim venerat hora apprehensionis*.

102. Twice only in the *Cod. Theod.*

103. Digest 19.2.24 pr., Paul *XXXIV ad edictum*; the clause *quibus consequens* to the end is very badly framed.

104. Augustine, *De civ. D.* 11.21. Maybe *adprobatio* was delayed by the use— however rare—of *probatio*: Digest 19.2.60.3, Labeo *V posteriorum a Javoleno epitomatorum*; Cicero, *Font.* 8.17 (approval by the governor of road-repairs effected by the provincials). Beseler, *ZRG* 57 (1937): 41, brackets *aut improbatio* in Digest 19.2.60.3, quite unjustifiably, I think. In Digest 22.3.18.2, Ulpian *VI disputationum*, *improbatio* denotes something entirely different. It is noteworthy that *comprobare*, which starts *[continues onto next page]*

a case as a judge; the meaning is at least approximated in Plautus and is found in the senatusconsult *de Bacchanalibus* of 186 BC.[105] It is amply represented in all subsequent periods.[106] Yet *auditio* in the corresponding sense is absent not only from *Vocabularium Jurisprudentiae Romanae* but from all lay literature till the third century AD. It arrives in Tertullian.[107] As far as legal sources are concerned, we find it in two rescripts jointly by Honorius and Theodosius[108]—that is all. *Decipere*, to cheat, occurs in Plautus and is well represented in *Vocabularium Jurisprudentiae Romanae*; *deceptio* is not listed in *Vocabularium Jurisprudentiae Romanae* at all, though we find it in the *Codex Theodosianus*. The earliest evidence for it is the *Itala*.

Detentio, as is well known, has been endowed with its sophisticated meaning in the doctrine of possession in the past two centuries, and the same is true of *detinere* itself. The noun occurs once in the Digest, interpolated,[109] and in two constitutions by Justinian.[110] It is Western: we find it in the *Itala*. In the case of *detentare-detentatio*, even the verb is late and very rare. In the sense of to hold, it occurs in an imperial *Epistola* of AD 370/1 to the governor of Asia,[111] twice in the *Codex Theodosianus*, in constitutions from the beginning of the fifth century,[112] and once, about the same time, in Rufinus.[113] *Detentatio* is found in two interpolated texts

---

[note 104 continued from previous page] from Plautus and is a common verb from Cicero on, about fifty-five times in *VJR*, makes the action noun only in a solitary statement in Cicero (*Fin.* 5.22.62)—apart from the late grammarians.

105. *de Bacchanalibus* 5; Bruns, *Font.*, 165.

106. According to Beseler, *Subsiciva*, 193, 6ff., the classics avoid the sense of to accede to a request, *erhören*.

107. Tertullian, *Apologeticus* 9.150.

108. *Cod. Theod.* 11.30.67 = Code 7.62.31 pr., AD 423; *Cod. Theod.*13.5.32 = Code 11.6.6, AD 409.

109. Digest 43.25.1.5, Ulpian *LXXI ad edictum*. Ulpian is referring to Julian, whose statement is preserved in Digest 8.1.16, *XLIX digestorum*, and has *utilis petitio* instead of *detentio*. I do not believe, however, with Beseler, *ZRG* 56 (1936): 63, that *detentio* is a mere scribe's slip for *petitio*. There is an idea behind it, namely, that the pledgee is the holder of the servitude pro tem. A *utilis petitio* no longer meant much to the reviser.

110. Code 7.31.3, AD 531; Code 7.39.8.1, AD 529.

111. Valentinian, Valens and Gratian, 11; Bruns, *Font.*, 271.

112. *Cod. Theod.* 5.16.30, Arcadius, Honorius et Theodosius, AD 405; and *Cod. Theod.* 11.20.3, Arcadius et Honorius, AD 400.

113. Rufinus, *Historia Eremitica* 5.2.7.

in the Digest[114] and in two *Novels* by Justinian.[115] It is safe to conclude that the interpolations are Byzantine.

Impetrare, found in Plautus, is frequent in the jurists, in many senses; say, two hundred and fifty times in *Vocabularium Jurisprudentiae Romanae*. *Impetratio* takes a slow rise from Cicero. Its first appearance in legal sources is in the *Codex Theodosianus*, about ten times versus one hundred and thirty five for the verb. Even in Byzantine law, however, abstraction, institutionalization, went less far than modern expositions would suggest. *Impetratio actionis* is indeed known to this Code as well as Justinian's.[116] But *impetratio dominii*, nowadays current of a pledge creditor's request to the court to have ownership conferred on him, is medieval: the relevant rubric in Justinian's Code reads *de iure dontinii impetrando*.[117] *Sequestrare* comes from *sequester*. It occurs once in *Vocabularium Jurisprudentiae Romanae*, in a Byzantine interpolation,[118] and several times in the *Codex Theodosianus*. From sequestrare, again, comes sequestratio, not in *Vocabularium Jurisprudentiae Romanae*, though the *Codex Theodosianus* has it. The word hardly existed before the fourth century.

A number of action nouns make their first appearance in law, or at all, in Justinian. *Inhibere* in the sense of to restrain dates from the second century BC and is fairly common in the jurists, some twenty-five times in *Vocabularium Jurisprudentiae Romanae*, thirty in the *Codex Theodosianus*. *Inhibitio* comes up in the fourth century AD. The earliest extant legal text is a constitution by Justinian, ponderously ordaining the suppression of blasphemy and perjury in consequence of gambling losses.[119] I have already adverted to his use of *transmissio* as signifying transmission to a successor.[120] Whether or not he was the first to apply the noun in this fashion it is difficult to say. Almost certainly the expression *natalium restitutio* is his coinage. I have elsewhere written on his fascination with

---

114. 4.6.15.3, Ulpian *XII ad edictum*, 25.1.5 pr., Ulpian *XXXVI ad Sabinum*; Beseler, ZRG 56 (1936): 63.

115. Novellae 22.24, *Julian. Epit.*; Novellae 7.5.

116. Rubric *Cod. Theod.* 2.3; Code 2.57.

117. Code 8.33.

118. Digest 24.3.22.8, Ulpian *XXXIII ad edictum*; Cujas and Faber.

119. Code 3.43.2.2, AD 529.

120. Above, p. 25.

the elevation to freebornhood of a person born a slave—a fascination connected with his desire radically to sever Theodora, the woman he wished to marry, from her past as an actress. The making of a slave into, not just a free man, but a freeborn man, seemed to offer a legal precedent for total recreation; and in the legislation which, inspired by Justinian, validates the union of a senator with a redeemed actress, the cleansing of the lady is avowedly based on the analogy of the grant of freebornhood. It was Justinian himself, then, who broke through from *natales restituere* to the weightier and more institutionalized *natalium restitutio*.[121]

A few medieval or modern fabrications. *Rerum amotio. Amovere* in the sense of *furari* is frequent in *Vocabularium Jurisprudentiae Romanae*, *amotio* without entry,[122] nor does it occur in any sense in the *Codex Theodosianus* or *Codex Justinianus*.[123] *Servi corruptio*, non-existent.[124] *Dedicatio in sacrum* of a thing which forms the subject of litigation, non-existent. The Roman jurists do not go beyond *dedicare*.[125] *Defamare*[126] is post-Augustan, *defamatio* medieval and helped on by *diffamatio*, which denotes principally the spreading of an ill report. Nor did the jurists ever develop the advanced *infamatio* from *infamare*,[127] though the noun

121. See below, p. 313; and *Catholic University of America Law Review* 16 (1967): 380ff.

122. It means removal of rank in Digest 47.10.43, Gaius *III regularum*: the criminal in question will suffer *exilium aut relegationem aut ordinis amotionem*.

123. In general, *amovere* occurs from Plautus and is fairly common, about thirty times in the *Cod. Theod.*, *amotio* occurs from Cicero and is extremely rare, not at all in the Code.

124. *Corruptio* of corn supplies through age in *Cod. Theod.* 11.14.1 = Code 10.26.1.1, Valentinianus et Valens, AD 364, *corruptio usus fructus*, extinction of usufruct, in a constitution by Justinian, Code 3.33.16 pr., AD 531. In general, *corrumpere* from Plautus, *corruptio* from Cicero.

125. Digest 44.6.3, Gaius *VI ad legem duodecim tabularum*. *Dedicare* in general from the second century BC, *dedicatio* from Cicero, the verb eight times in *VJR*, fifteen times in the *Cod. Theod.*, against no entry for the noun. In the sense of to inscribe a work to somebody, the verb comes into vogue in the first century AD—Phaedrus, the elder Pliny, Martial, Statius, Quintilian—the noun only around AD 600, with Isidore of Seville's *Dedicatio historiarum ad Sisenandum*.

126. Usually in the form *defamatus*, but *defamari* in Code 7.14.5, Diocletianus et Maximianus, AD 293.

127. The verb figures in the late Republican edict *Ne quid infamandi causa fiat*:

does occur in lay writers from the early fourth century. *Sepulchri violatio,* non-existent.[128]

The process of nominalization may take place in successive, observable stages; the action noun may come up first in one sector of a verb, then in another, and it may take a long time before its use is general—if it ever does become general. A flood of light is thrown by these variations on the history of the area involved, and, obviously, the larger the area covered by a verb, the more chequered the history. Many of the nouns already mentioned furnish illustrations,[129] but let me take fresh ones. There is no such institution as *confirmatio donationis* in Roman law; at the same time, in a constitution of Marcus Aurelius,[130] we do come across *confirmatio adoptionis* denoting the imperial sanction of a defective adoption.[131] *Publicatio legis* is first found in the *Codex Theodosianus.*[132] Even the verb

---

Lenel, *Das edictum perpetuum,* 3rd ed. (1927), 401; Daube, *Atti Cong. Verona* (1948); vol. 3 (1951): 413ff.

128. *Violatio* once only in *VJR, Coll.* 3.3.1 = Digest 1.6.2, Ulpian *VIII de officio proconsulis; turpis violatio* here envisages enforced, disgraceful practice—*si dominus in servum saevierit vel ad impudicitiam turpemque violationem compellat.*

129. *Accessio, adprobatio, adstipulatio, amotio, cessio, comparatio, confusio, corruptio, dedicatio, derelictio, impetratio, inhibitio, intercessio, inventio, paratio, probatio, restitutio, separatio, traditio, translatio, transmissio, violatio.*

130. Digest 1.7.39, Ulpian *III de officio consulis.*

131. When Berger, *Encyclopaedic Dictionary of Roman Law* (1953), 407, subsumes under *confirmatio donationis* (1) a gift between husband and wife confirmed in the donor's testament and (2) a gift which, though contrary to the *lex Cincia,* is enforceable if the donor dies without revoking it, there is a further objection to be raised: even the verb *confirmare* is unsuitable for case (2). The jurists do apply it to case (1) (e.g. Ulpian speaks of the *Oratio* of Severus and Caracalla *de confirmandis donationibus,* Digest 24.1.32.1, *XXXIII ad Sabinum*), also, for instance, to confirmation by will of a previous gift to a daughter in *potestas* (*Fr. Vat.* 256a, 294, Papinian *XII responsorum*). A gift otherwise invalid is here positively insisted on by the testator (on whose death the reason for invalidity is really gone). By contrast, a gift contrary to the *lex Cincia* is defeasible only by means of an *exceptio* against which, if it is brought by the donor's heir and the donor never revoked the gift (never revoked—not: if he re-affirmed it in his will), a *replicatio* is given: *morte Cincia removetur* (Fr. Vat. 259, Papinian *XII responsorum*). No room here for *confirmare.* Beseler, *ZRG* 57 (1937): 14–15, observes that the classics were disinclined to employ *confirmatio.* He may be condemning too many texts however.

132. *Cod. Theod.* 5.3.1, Theodosius et Valentinianus, AD 434; Cf. *Cod. Theod.* 16.2.37, Arcadius et Honorius AD 404, with *publicatio edictorum.*

publicare, in the sense to publish, is post-Augustan and extraordinarily rare.[133] By contrast, verb and noun both occur from Cicero with reference to the turning of something into public property, confiscation.

A new ghost, incidentally, has begun to haunt this area. It is now being claimed that *publicatio legis* was preceded in remote times by *proquiritatio legis*.[134] However, the noun *proquiritatio* was born in 1940.[135] The verb is first found in Appuleius,[136] and there it is still closely linked to the simple *quiritare*, to cry for help:[137] Appuleius's adversary flaunts a letter to prove that the philosopher ensnared an honourable woman by magic. It is in Sidonius Apollinaris in the fifth century that we get *lex proquiritata*.[138] He refers to Theodosius's decree setting a time limit of thirty years to actions:[139] *ut fere decemviraliter loquar, lex de praescriptione tricennii fuerat proquiritata, cuius peremptoriis abolita rubricis lis omnis in sextum tracta quinquennium terminabatur,* "to speak in the language of the XII Tables, a statute was promulgated concerning a thirty years' prescription, by whose decided provisions any action drawn out into six quinquennia was abolished and terminated." From this it has long been deduced (wrongly, we shall see) that the XII Tables contained the word *proquiritare*;[140] now the further inference is drawn that they contained *legem proquiritare*; and from here to *proquiritatio legis* as an ancient Republican concept is an easy step. But, when Sidonius says that he is expressing himself in decemviral language, he has not in mind *proquiritare* at all. (Even if he

133. It occurs in Digest 9.2.41 pr., Ulpian *XLI ad Sabinum*, and 47.8.2.24, Ulpian *LVI ad edictum*, both times interpolated (on 47.8.2.24 see de Ruggiero, *Bull. Ist. Dir. Rom.* 19 (1907): 69; in 9.2.41 pr., towards the end, the two cases of destruction and recitation are unsatisfactorily amalgamated). It denotes notification of the authorities in *Cod. Theod.* 4.4.4 = Code 6.23.18, Arcadius et Honorius, AD 397, Code 8.53.30.1, Leo, AD 459, 11.59.14, Honorius et Theodosius, AD 415.

134. von Schwind, *Zur Frage der Publikation im römischen Recht* (1940), 33, relying on Weiss, *Glotta*, 12 (1923), 82–83.

135. Yes, the paternity belongs to von Schwind; Weiss was still content with the verb.

136. Appuleius, *Apol.*, ch. 82, ed. Helm, 90.

137. Attested from Lucilius; originally no doubt a cry addressed to the Quirites, the co-citizens. The noun *quiritatio* is a *hapax legomenon* in Livy 33.28.

138. Sidonius Apollinaris, *Epistulae* 8.6.

139. *Cod. Theod.* 4.14.1 = Code 7.39.3, AD 424.

140. Bruns, *Font.*, 40.

had, it would still remain a pseudo-antique usage.) He has in mind the words *tricennium* and *quinquennium*. These do not figure in Theodosius's legislation but are introduced[141] in analogy to the provision of the XII Tables respecting usucapion, which by Sidonius's time was narrowly associated with prescription: *usus auctoritas fundi biennium est.*[142] Do not think I have killed a brilliant coinage. *Proquiritatio* is in for a long life.

Another term alleged to be an early alternative for *publicatio legis* is *renuntiatio legis*. The sequence, then, is: *proquiritatio* period of the XII Tables, *renuntiatio* from the middle of the Republic, *publicatio* I suppose from the late Republic. Well, *renuntiatio* would be conceivable from Cicero on: he has, for example, *renuntiatio suffragiorum.*[143] But surely, any confidence would be misplaced. No text has *renuntiatio legis*, no text has even *renunciare legem.*[144] Evidently, theory in this matter progressed at a very moderate pace—and why not? I doubt whether, in my College, even yet a great deal of thought is given to the publication of our statutes.

Datio[145] has several meanings in addition to transfer, coming into use at different times and in different settings. But even in the sense of transfer the rise of this noun is very gradual. The discrepancy between the noun, rare, and the verb, frequent, is enormous. To be sure, the noun signifies transfer, or right to transfer, as early as 186 BC, in one of the senatusconsults following the Bacchanalian affair.[146] This does not mean that it was used wherever we today might do so.

I have grievously sinned in my courses on unjust enrichment (*condictio*) by teaching that, as a rule, an action on this ground was available to a person who had made to another person a *datio* which turned out

---

141. Something of a *tour de force*: at least the *sextum quinquennium* is far-fetched.

142. Bruns, *Font.*, 25. It is at this place, then, and not among *Fragmenta Incertae Sedis* that Sidonius should be noted. Whether *biennium* was actually in the code is here irrelevant: Sidonius thought it was.

143. Cicero, *Planc.* 6.14.

144. The doctrine is kept in life by one authority sending us to another, the sources forming a nebulous background. Von Schwind refers to Weiss; Weiss refers to Klingmüller, art. Pauly-Wissowa *RE* (1914), 600, s.v. "renuntiatio." Klingmüller does quote a series of texts, such as *Lex Malacitana*, 56–57. (Bruns, *Font.*, 150–51) where, however, we hear of *renuntiare eum*, to proclaim a man elected.

145. Beseler, *ZRG* 66 (1948): 273, holds that it is often interpolated.

146. Livy 39.19.5: see below, p. 46.

unwarranted: (This is, of course, what everybody nowadays teaches.) [147] In
point of fact, only the combination *mutui datio* is indubitably classical; [148]
and *dotis datio* may be late classical, from about AD 200, though it is not
above suspicion. [149] All the rest are post-classical or just not represented
in the sources at all. [150] *Datio in solutum* occurs in no ancient source. In

147. Even Buckland who in his *Text-Book*, 541ff., abstains from the noun, introduced
it in his lectures. Schwartz, (*Die Grundlage der Condictio im Klassischen Römischen Recht*
[1952], 196–97) lists *datio credendi causa (mutuum), solvendi causa (indebitum), dotis
nomine, ob rem, ob causam, ob transactionem, propter condicionem*; he speaks of *gestreckte,
protractive, datio* (where completed by *commixtio* etc.—*sit venia verbo*). Kaser, *Das
Römische Privatrecht* (1955), 496, writes: *Zum Tatbestand unserer Kondiktionsfälle gehört
als Ausgangspunkt eine datio.*

148. Which rather suggests that *nexi datio* in Festus 164 (quoted from Aelius
Gallus) refers to obligation, not mancipation; the question is open. *Mutui datio* occurs
in Gaius 3.90 (twice), equals Digest 44.7.1.2, Gaius *II aureorum*; Gaius 3.91; Digest
4.4.3.4, Ulpian *XI ad edictum* (itp.); 12.1.2.1, Ulpian *XXVI ad edictum* (twice, technical as
in Digest 14.6.7.3, text interfered with); Digest 12.1.2.2, Paul *XXVIII ad edictum* (quite
established); Digest 12.1.2.4 (interfered with); Digest 12.1.8, Pomponius *VI ex Plautio*;
Digest 12.1.27, Ulpian *X ad edictum* (a little dubious); Digest 14.6.7.3, Ulpian *XXIX ad
edictum* (technical, cf. 12.1.2.1); Digest 16.1.2.1, Ulpian *XXIX ad edictum* (sc. *Velleianum*,
but Vogt, *Studien zum Senatusconsultum Velleianum* [1952], 2–3, rightly rejects *mutui
dationes*, they were dodges and banned as such by the jurists, and the present text sounds
as if the women were making instead of receiving the loans). *Datio pecuniae* in Digest
14.6.3.3, Ulpian *XXIX ad edictum*, belongs here (a little dubious), though not in 35.1.57,
Pomponius *IX ad Quintum Mucium*, where a slave has to give money to be free (probably itp).

149. It is not touched by Beseler (*ZRG* 66 [1948]: 273). But it is interpolated in all
Digest texts: 15.1.47.6, Paul *IV ad Plautium*; 23.3.23, Ulpian *XXXV ad Sabinum*; 24.1.34,
Ulpian *XLIII ad Sabinum*; 50.17.23, Ulpian *XXIX ad Sabinum. Fr. Vat.* 102, Paul *VII
responsorum* maybe saves it, though it should be noted that Schulz, *Roman Legal Science*
(1946), 240, quotes this text among those in the *Fr. Vat.* which are obviously revised. In
any case the usage is not very technical. A *filiusfamilias* in his father's absence marries
and takes a *dos*. The father, returned, does not attack the marriage. Has he thereby also
consented to the *datio dotis*? This question takes up the particular act mentioned at the
beginning, it does not necessarily presuppose an institution *datio dotis*.

150. *Datio partis* in Digest 45.1.2.1, Paul *XII ad Sabinum*, probably itp. *Datio legati*
may denote the charging of a legacy, classical (see presently, in this same footnote); in the
sense of payment out of a legacy it is met only once, Digest 36.1.2, Celsus *XXV digestorum*,
itp. (I regard *id est post legatorum dationem* as an intrusion, Beseler, *ZRG* 66 [1948]: 392,
cuts out the entire discussion). *Datio* of money paid by a slave to be free Digest 29.2.74.1,
Paul *XII ad Plautium*, itp.; 35.1.57, Pomponius *IX ad Quintum Mucium*, probably itp.;
35.1.82, Callistratus *II quaestionum*, itp.; 46.3.68, Marcellus *XVI digestorum*, itp. In the

last three texts, the condition to give something (not necessarily restricted to transfer proper but including, for instance, the production of accounts) is contrasted with that to do something: this comparison no doubt encouraged nominalization. In Digest 36.1.32.2, Marcian *IX institutionum*, it is a question of *datio* by an heir to qualify, and again *dare* and *facere* are compared; *datio* is itp. No transfer, of course, is contemplated in Digest 15.1.8, Paul *IV ad Sabinum*, where the master puts something into his slave's *peculium*; none the less *datio* is itp. Again, no transfer in the case of *datio pignoris* or *hypothecae*; Digest 16.1.8 pr., Ulpian *XXIX ad edictum*, a little dubious (see Beseler, ZRG 56 [1936]: 88–89), and Digest 20.1.16.9, Marcian *singulari ad formulam hypothecariam*. Let us look at *datio legati, liberationis*, the charging of a legacy, testamentary grant of freedom. Gaius 2.243. In elementary writings, action nouns are popular. Digest 28.5.6.4, Ulpian *IV ad Sabinum*. I do not agree with Beseler's correction (ZRG 66 [1948]: 273) of *liberationis datio* into *liberationis*. The problem concerns revocation (ademption) and it will presently emerge that in this context *datio* was established in the classical era. The comparison of charge and revocation provoked analysis. Digest 29.7.14 pr., Scaevola *VIII quaestionum*, twice, in a discussion of revocation, itp. Digest 33.5.9.2, Julian *XXXII digestorum*, again practically a contrast with revocation. Genuine, *pace* Beseler. Digest 34.4.3.8, Ulpian *XXIV ad Sabinum*, revocation. Beseler rightly says it ought to be *ex neutro legato*. The text is interfered with, probably abbreviation. Digest 34.4.9, Ulpian *V disputationum*, again practically the area of revocation: a pure legacy is made conditional. For Beseler, the mere provenance from the *Disputationes* is damning. Digest 34.4.14.1, Florentine *XI institutionem*, revocation. Genuine, *pace* Beseler. This kind of statement is to be expected in an institutional work. Digest 34.4.26 pr., Paul *IX quaestionum*, comparison with revocation, itp. Digest 34.5.10 pr., Ulpian *VI disputationum*, contrast with revocation. From the *Disputationes*. The text is interfered with. Digest 40.7.2.2, Ulpian *IV ad Sabinum*. Genuine, *pace* Beseler. I suppose Digest 34.3.3.1, Ulpian *XXIII ad Sabinum*, should here be appended: a creditor on his deathbed returns an IOU to his debtor (or maybe he leaves it to him by will), the latter now has an *exceptio*, a *datio* of this kind resembling a *fideicommissum* (*liberationis*). The clause with *datio*, however, is itp. VJR takes *datio legati* four texts which ought not to be there. *Fr. Vat.* 318, Ulpian *VIII ad edictum*, *datio cognitoris*. As this is also quoted under the right heading, it is just a slip. More serious Digest 35.1.82, 36.1.32.3, 46.3.68, dealing with a slave who must give something to be free, not a legacy—all itp. anyway: see above earlier on in this footnote. In two texts *datio liberationis* envisages (or includes) grant of freedom *inter vivos*. Digest 1.1.4, Ulpian *I institutionum*. Beseler (as already Wlassak, ZRG 28 [1907]: 4) assumes a gloss. I am not so sure: the fragment is from an elementary work. (We need not even postulate that the phrase is generalized from testamentary manumission, institutional writers of the classical period are quite capable of original systematization.) In Institutes 1.5 pr., going back to this statement of Ulpian's, an alternative reading has *donatio*. I wonder whether this should not be preferred for I., *datio* being an assimilation to D. (though already represented in Theophilus: in fact we are given the Latin as well as the Greek, *datio libertatis, toutestin he dosis tes eleutherias*. The other text with *datio liberationis* among the living is Digest 40.9.20, Modestinus *singulari de enucleatis casibus*. A little dubious. *Datio* signifies a grant in Digest 37.9.1.1, Ulpian [*continues onto next page*] the *Codex Theodosianus dare* appears three hundred and twenty times, *datio* once—*datio libelli*.[151] *Reddere* is listed seven hundred and fifty times in *Vocabularium Jurisprudentiae Romanae*, *redditio* twice.[152] In neither passage does it signify re-transfer: once it stands for *redhibitio*[153] and once it refers to the return of a *pignus*.[154] May I remind you, by way of comparison, that *venditio* occurs in the *lex agraria* of 111 BC[155]—as does *deditio* from *dedere*[156]—and that *traditio* occurs in Varro and the aedilician edict.[157]

[note 150 continued from previous page] XLI *ad edictum, datio bonorum possessionis,* genuine. I shall not go into *datio* as denoting appointment of a person, *datio hominis (tutoris, cognitoris,* etc.), except to point out that, for example, *dare iudicem* occurs over forty times in VJR, *datio iudicis* in one interpolated passage, Digest 5.1.32, Ulpian *I de officio consulis.*

151. *Cod. Theod.* 13.9.6 = Code 11.6.5.1, Honorius et Theodosius, AD 412. *Datio libelli* also in one Digest text (twice); Digest 5.2.7, Paul *singulari de septemviralibus,* probably itp.

152. In general, *reddere* is found from Plautus, *redditio* from Quintilian.

153. Digest 21.1.21 pr., Ulpian *I ad edictum aedilium curulium:* "*redhibitio* is called a sort of *redditio (quasi redditio).*" Beseler, ZRG 56 (1936): 88–89, admits this as genuine, hence has to reconcile it with his thesis that the classics for stylistic reasons avoided unnecessary nouns. He remarks: *hier erzwingt der Gedanke den Gebrauch des Wortes,* "here the thought enforces the use of the word." But this is to beg the question. I suppose he means that Ulpian, wishing closely to connect *redhibitio* with *reddere,* has to introduce *redditio.* Correct. Only there might be a million other occasions when such a thought, or a different thought, might lead to a noun: it is always some thought that does it. On the other hand, had there been a classical ban on nouns, it could have been obeyed in this case as well as elsewhere.

154. Digest 16.1.8 pr., Ulpian *XXIX ad edictum,* a little dubious (see above, p. 43n150). While *datio pignoris* for somebody else's debt is intercession, *redditio* to one's debtor is not.

155. See above, p. 31n73.

156. Bruns, *Font.,* 78, 80. The verb in Naevius and Plautus.

157. See above, pp. 24–25. For completeness—*abdere, didere, indere, interdare, obdere, pessumdare* and *subdere* are Plautine, but none ever came by a noun. *Addere,* frequent, is found in the XII Tables (x 8: Bruns, *Font.,* 37) and in Plautus; *additio,* rare, first appears in Varro. *Circumdare* is Plautine, *circumdatio* attested from the *Itala. Condere* is found in the XII Tables (VIII I: Bruns, *Font.,* 29) and in Plautus; *conditio* from the *Itala. Edere* occurs in Plautus, *editio* from Cicero. *Perdere* is Plautine, *perditio* comes in about AD 300. *Prodere* with reference to a putting off is adumbrated in Plautus (*Trin.* 2.2.58), *proditio* is employed by Cato (Festus 242); the sense of betrayal is adumbrated at the verbal stage in Ennius (Festus 229) and Terence (*Haut.* 3.1.70), the noun in this sense occurs from Cicero.

The systematizing thrust of the action noun goes on after it is in existence: it is not only a sign of advance, it in turn stimulates further refinement. Such subdivisions of concepts as *stipulatio poenalis, possessio civilis, naturalis,* are not indeed impossible at the verbal stage: one might, for example, resort to verb with adverb, *naturaliter possidere.* But often it would be difficult to express the specialization simply—as in the case of *cautio Muciana.*[158] These differentiations are smoother and incomparably more frequent once a noun is available.[159] One can apply a *Gegenprobe,* a counter-test. Take the interdict *de migrando,* forbidding a landlord to prevent his tenant, when he wishes to move, from taking with him such belongings as are not pledged for the rent.[160] How different, how much wider and more fundamental, *de migratione* would sound. The Commonwealth Immigrants Act of 1962 by its very title gives itself out as a more modest, more *ad hoc* measure than if it had been called Commonwealth Immigration Act.

From the specimens I have presented it may be seen that the action noun has a particularly good chance, on the one hand, in mechanical enumerations, elementary treatises and the like, where the addressee is to be given a readily memorizable presentation; and on the other, in probing and wide-ranging reflection. We find periods of slow growth alternating with veritable action noun explosions. A notable number of juristic action nouns derive from the last hundred and fifty years of the Republic, when the foundation for an intelligible workable legal order was being purposefully laid. Even individuals stand out: when full allowance is made for the fact that Cicero certainly did not father all the words for which his work is the earliest evidence, he does remain author of a great many. The evolution is influenced by an enormous variety of factors. Among them, the peculiar linguistic position of a concept plays a not negligible part: I have the impression that *donatio* might have been formed sooner had not

158. *Cavere* with reference to promise and security in Varro, *cautio* in Cicero but unquestionably antedating him; see below, pp. 57–58.

159. To be sure, the action noun in these cases is apt to designate the result of the action rather than the action itself. On this aspect, see below, pp. 57–58.

160. Lenel, *Das edictum perpetuum,* 3rd ed. (1927), 490. In general, *migrare* Plautus, *migratio* Cicero.

donum been more or less adequate for the job;[161] *mancipium* may have delayed mancipatio;[162] *mutuum mutuatio*.[163]

It is partly because the action noun implies institutionalization, solidity, durability, that it is favoured where a particularly impressive utterance is wanted. It is hardly accidental that, while *aestimare, deferre, iudicare, petere* occur from Plautus, *aestimatio, delatio, iudicatio, petitio* first emerge in the *lex Acilia repetundarum* of 123 BC. *De ea re eius petitio nominisque delatio esto*, "in this matter let there be suit for it and report of name," does sound momentous.[164] Again, a senatusconsult of 186 BC, rewarding the freedwoman Hispala Faecenia for helping to uncover the Bacchanalian conspiracy, accorded her *datio deminutio, gentis enuptio, tutoris optio*, "power of transfer and disposal of property, of marriage outside her clan, of choice of tutor.[165]

The praetor, it seems, is more reticent. Heavy nouns in the edict do not appear to be due to deliberate solemnity. For instance, he will not in principle admit as advocate a man found guilty of *praevaricatio*: this term is practically unavoidable, a recognized category.[166] Again, in the *actio fiduciae*, defendant is supposed to act *ut inter bonos bene agier oportet et sine fraudatione*. This is demonstrably an ordinary development of the kind I am harping on, from an earlier version with the verb. In the original, oral procedure, plaintiff requested *uti ne propter te fidemve tuam captus fraudatusve sim*.[167] By the time of the written formula, *fraudare* in this domain had become an established *fraudatio*.[168] Of course, the praetor has

---

161. *Donare* Plautus, *donatio* Cicero, *donum* Plautus.

162. *Mancipare* Plautus, *mancipatio* Festus, *mancipium* XII Tables (VI I, Bruns, *Font.*, 25) and Plautus.

163. *Mutuare* Caecilius and Cato, *mutuatio* Cicero (apparently personal to him), *mutuum* Plautus. One action noun may delay another: *initium*, Ennius, versus *incohatio*, *Itala*, *litigium* (and *lis* itself), Plautus, versus *litigatio*, Lactantius.

164. *lex Acilia repetundarum* 3; Bruns, *Font.*, 59. Other notable first appearances in this statute: *praevaricatio, pronuntiato, provocatio, sanctio.*

165. Livy 39.19.5.

166. The crime of representing one side in court but really playing for the other. It is mentioned in the *Lex Acilia repetundarum*; Bruns, *Font.*, 59; also in the *Tabula Heracleensis*, 120; Bruns, *Font.*, 108.

167. Lenel, *Das edictum perpetuum*, 3rd ed. (1927), 291ff.

168. The noun is already met in Plautus, *Asin.* 257.

no hesitation to apply it elsewhere as well, as in the edict *Qui fraudationis causa latitat.*[169] In course of time, the jurists, who had to work out exactly what conduct fell under this provision, arrived at *latitatio.*[170]

Creatio is worth noting.[171] It offers an illustration of the confluence of legislative ponderosity and systematizing trend, besides posing a little puzzle as to dates.

Creare in the sense of to elect to an office is fairly frequent in *Vocabularium Jurisprudentiae Romanae, creatio* is confined to two spurious texts. The *Thesaurus Linguae Latinae*, in a listing marked as incomplete, has five hundred entries for the verb, the oldest being the *lex agraria* of 111 BC,[172] compared with a complete list of seven for the noun.[173] Of these seven, one is from Cicero, the other six are much later. The *Thesaurus Linguae Latinae* as usual is unaware of even non-controversial interpolations in the Digest and, accordingly, assumes that the earliest of the six is a fragment assigned to Papinian, about AD 200.[174] In reality, the first occurrence of *creatio* in the sense of election, after that passage from

169. Lenel, *Das edictum perpetuum*, 3rd ed. (1927), 415: hiding from creditors.

170. Digest 42.4.7.5,7,9, Ulpian *LIX ad edictum*. The noun is already used by Quintilian, *Inst.* 7.2.46, of hiding as an indication of guilt, in a passage which briefly recapitulates what a preceding chapter expounds by means of the verb *latere*, 5.10.45. Cicero, quoted by Ulpian, Digest 42.4.7.4, defined *latitare* as *turpis occultatio sui.* Beseler, ZRG 66 (1948): 337, points out that there is no other entry for *occultatio* in VJR; which, he says, corroborates his view of the gulf between Cicero, noun-loving, and the classics, noun-hating. The appearance of *latitatio* in the latter, however, should serve as a warning that we must not exaggerate; not to mention the fact that *occultatio* is missing also from post-classical law. On the other hand, it is indicative of the prevalent insensitivity to the difference between verb and noun that Heumann-Seckel list four texts under *occultatio sui*, though only the one which quotes Cicero has the noun phrase.

171. It is a sheer fluke that in learned literature it is not quite so prominent as, say, *acquisitio, denegatio, editio* and has no place, for example, in the Index to Mommsen's *Röm. Staatsr.*. It has an article, however, by Brassloff, in Pauly-Wissowa, *RE*, vol. 4 (1901), 1686ff. and an entry in Berger's *Encyclopaedic Dictionary*, 417.

172. 53; Bruns, *Font.*, 82.

173. True, it fails to register the rubrics of Code 10.68 and 10.70. By the time of Justinian, *creatio* is evidently a technical notion. Significantly, the text of the constitutions under these rubrics does not contain the noun.

174. Digest 26.7.39.6, *V responsorum*. In classical law, you do not "create" a tutor; even the verb would be out of place. The other text is Digest 48.14.1 pr., Modestinus *II de poenis*, asserting that the *lex Julia de ambitu* is out of date since [*continues onto next page*]

Cicero, is probably an enactment of Anthemius, of AD 468: "The Divine
Majesty and Our election have entrusted the full power of the Empire to
Our son."[175]

With regard to dating, obviously, if it were not for the isolated use by
Cicero, the conclusion would be that verb and action noun are separated
by some six hundred years. Cicero however, does contain the noun. At
first sight, we might become uneasy about all the other instances of a huge
time-lag in the sources: there could always be a sporadic earlier occurrence
of the noun, only the evidence is lost. Well, even suppose it were so, all
that would follow is that the evolution towards the action noun was more
gradual, irregular.

But it is not likely. In fact, Cicero's introduction of *creatio* strongly
militates in favour of my approach. The word figures in his *de Legibus*:[176]
Creatio ntagistratuum, iudicia populi, iussa vetita, quom suffragio sciscentur,
optumatibus not, plebi libera sunto, "Let the creation of magistrates, the
verdicts in popular trials, positive and negative laws; as they are resolved
on by ballot, be known to the nobles, free to the commoners." Between
138 and 106 BC a series of statutes concerning voting tablets, the *leges*
tabellariae, had for these three votes—the election of a magistrate, the
sentence in a trial and the passing of legislation—replaced the open, oral
vote by the secret, written one. Cicero would have all votes divulged to
the optumates though kept from the plebs.[177] What is relevant for us is
that in this work he avowedly resorts to formal, pompous language.[178]
Moreover, as he sees himself as the author of the ideal constitution, he
does give the electoral act more of an established, institutionalized place
than it would ordinarily enjoy: his in any case pronounced inclination

---

[note 174 continued from previous page] "the creation" of magistrates is now dependent on
the care of the Emperor and not on the favour of the people. Albertario is surely right (*Bull.*
Ist. Dir. Rom. 33 [1923]: 52) in holding this Byzantine. Should he be wrong, however, then
this is the earliest *creatio* (apart from Cicero): Modestinus is among the very latest classics,
a pupil of Ulpian's.

175. *Novellae Anthemius* 3.1.

176. Cicero, *de Leg.* 3.3.10.

177. See Mommsen, *Röm. Staatsr.,* vol. 3, pt. 1, 3rd ed. (1886), 404ff., Costa,
Cicerone Giureconsulto I (1927), 314ff.

178. Cicero, *de Leg.* 2.7.18: *Sunt certa legum verba . . . quo plus auctoritatis habeant,*
paulo antiquiora quam hic sermo est.

to systematization is here under a particular stimulus.[179] Hence *creatio* instead of *creare*.

The case brings out well what is implied in the advance from verb to action noun. For very special reasons Cicero is here far ahead of his time. I would say that if, by mischance, this passage were among the missing chapters of *de Legibus*, not only would it not affect the overall picture of linguistic development: even the view we should form of the relation of *creare* and *creatio* would remain basically—basically—correct.

To infiltrate the action noun into a stratum where it had not yet matured is a grave distortion of intellectual history. Conversely, when we do find it at a remarkably early date the presumption is that the institution was endowed with a particular status—even if (as happens) it has lost it by the time our main sources begin to run. *Ambitio*, from *ambire*, *auctio*, from *augere*, and *manus iniectio*, from *manum inicere*, are all of them old and all of them retain their standing in later periods.[180] It is different with *captio*, from *capere*, and *consultatio*, from *consultare*. While they figure among the extraordinarily small number of nouns in Plautus, signifying deception (*captio*) and deliberation as to a marriage or the like (*consultatio*),[181] they are distinctly less conspicuous in the literature of the Empire; or more precisely, in the case of *consultatio*, the ancient meaning has become rare. Evidently, the two phenomena played a greater role in archaic law and custom. Both *indicare* and *indicatio* are used by Plautus of the naming of the price in the food market. Neither is found in this sense in the classical jurists. From lay writers it may be seen that the usage continued, though the noun is uncommon. Here is an institution which, clearly important in early times, might have been taken up in earnest by the jurists, but was not.[182]

179. A certain pomposity also is a general characteristic of his. He employs *testificari* and *testificatio* instead of *testari* and *testatio*; he may well be the author of *testificatio*.

180. Though the unlawful kind of *ambitio* comes to be preferably expressed by *ambitus*; Cf. below, p. 120n109.

181. In Terence, *Hecyra* 650, the meaning is very similar: deliberation whether to take a wife back.

182. *Indicatio* occurs in one interpolated text, Digest 19.1.13.3, Ulpian *XXXII ad edictum* (see Beseler, *ZRG* 66 [1948]: 320). It denotes the statement by a seller of a slave who is a thief that the slave is reliable. If, as is very doubtful, this application of the noun comes down from the market term, we have before us one of the numerous cases of pre-classical language re-emerging (in a modified sense) in post-classical jurisprudence.

However, I believe we must distinguish. The action noun, we saw, is suitable for ceremonious, authoritative pronouncements. By the same token, it can be used to provoke mirth. Even today, an intricate pseudo-scholarly or bureaucratic monster may raise a smile: subdepartmentalization. At a time when action nouns are few and far between, here is a great opportunity for entertainers. I believe that a large proportion of action nouns in Plautus are dragged in for a joke, many even invented by him: these latter obviously reflect no established notions.

Listen to this angry, forbidding question: *Quid tibi, malum, hic ante aedes clamitatiost?*[183] This kind of address is frequent in Plautus. Another example: *Quid tibi interpellatio aut in consilium huc accessio est?*[184] It is generally held that such was everyday speech.[185] That may be so: in which case Plautus is showing up the ponderousness of people in these situations.[186] The Epilogue of the *Captivi* presents an accumulation of action nouns: *neque subigitationes neque amatio nec suppositio nec circumductio.*[187] Of these, *suppositio* was surely current. It is met in three other plays of Plautus, and we know that the substitution of a false child was a prominent theme in antiquity. *Subigitatio* and *circumductio* recur nowhere else in Plautus. *Amatio* is indeed an exclusively Plautine word. He is fond of it, employing it in five comedies. Probably he made it up; indubitably whoever made it up meant it to be suggestive and amusing. Another accumulation in the *Stichus: cavillationes, adsentatiunculae, periuriatiunculae.*[188] *Conduplicatio* and *congeminatio* signify embrace in the

---

183. Plautus, *Mostell.* 6.

184. Plautus, *Trin.* 709.

185. Lorenz, *Mostellaria*, 2nd ed. (1883), 45–46.

186. Another possibility, I suppose, is that the phrasing *quid tibi* etc. goes back to some most formal occasion and is being brought down into ordinary encounters in the comedy. It should be noted that *clamitatio* and *interpellatio* occur nowhere else in Plautus, and *accessio* only in another such exclamation, *Truculentus* 258: *Quid tibi ad hasce accessio aedis est prope?*

187. Plautus, *Captivi* 1030–31.

188. Plautus, *Stichus* 228–29. *Adsentatiuncula* and *periuriatiuncula* nowhere else in Plautus. *Cavillatio* recurs in *Truculentus* 685, where there is punning on it; see Enk, *Truculentus*, vol. 2 (1953), 156. Another accumulation in the pimp's list of his mistakes, *Rud.* 502: *quid mihi scelesto tibi eras auscultatio, quidve hinc abitio quidve in navem ascensio?* The noun is nowhere else in Plautus.

Poenulus, surely artificial formations at the time.[189] When poor Sceledanus continues his watch, his words are weighty and ridiculous: *certum est nunc observationi operam dare.*[190] Mock-firmity is conveyed by a line in the *Poenulus: ita negotium institutum est, non datur cessatio.*[191] Admittedly, it is not always possible to be confident whether a noun is to strike the public as unusual or not.[192]

The fact that an action noun is the product of the Middle Ages or even more recent times does not make it any less interesting, to me at any rate. Only we must get things straight, both for the previous phase and for the new one. I have pointed out a fair number of such cases.[193] The first step is negative: not to project them back into the Roman law from the XII Tables to Justinian. But there remains a second, constructive task: to discover exactly when and why they were wanted, since, at certain moments. Some grew out of the continuing practice of Roman law, some are the work of students. Whether in one category or the other, they are illuminating as to the state of thought behind them.

Let me exemplify by a sizeable group of modern creations which is curiously revealing. *Denegatio actionis* may serve as typical. The noun *denegatio* occurs in no ancient legal source in any sense, and the earliest lay evidence is Servius on Virgil, about AD 400.[194] That the jurists do not speak of *denegatio actionis,* only of *denegare actionem,* was actually seen by Wlassak,[195] but this has not diminished the popularity of the

189. Plautus, *Poen.* 1297: *sed quid hoc est? quid est? quid hoc est? quid ego video? quo modo? quid hoc est conduplicationis? quae haec est congeminatio?* (Cf. Plautus, *Pseud.* 1245, *corpora conduplicant*). The nouns of course nowhere else in Plautus, neither has he *duplicatio* or *geminatio.* He must be the inventor.

190. Plautus, *Mil.* 485. *Observatio* nowhere else in Plautus.

191. Plautus, *Poen.* 925. *Cessatio* nowhere else in Plautus.

192. *Coactio* in Plautus, *Asin.* 203 is probably not by itself funny (on Leo's emendation, see above, p. 31n73). *Altercatio* in Plautus, *Aulularia* 486 is hardly a fresh coinage, though perhaps meant here to sound slightly pompous. Nor, I daresay, is *velitatio* in *Asin.* 307 and *Rud.* 525 due to Plautus; whoever coined it, though, intended it to sound elaborate.

193. *Adpromissio, accessio, amotio, confirmatio, corruptio, datio, dedicatio, defamatio, derelictio, fidepromissio, inaedificatio, inventio, occupatio, proquiritatio, publicatio, renuntiatio, satio, separatio, specificatio, sponsio, violatio* are all medieval or modern, altogether or in one of the senses attributed to them.

194. The verb is found from Plautus. *Negatio,* too, is missing from *VJR.*

195. *Festgabe Pfaff* (1910), 45, now reprinted: *Labeo,* 13 (1967), 262.

noun phrase. The latter is not merely the result of the scholar's urge to bring the material before him up to his own standard of systematization. It appeals to the nineteenth and twentieth-century admiration for strength. The noun phrase is more powerful. How sombre-splendid the sound of *damnatio memoriae*. Vittinghof, who knows that it is modern, and even establishes a rather pedestrian meaning for *damnare memoriam*, immediately substitutes *abolitio memoriae*.[196] But *damnatio memoriae*, *abolitio memoriae*, *rescissio actorum* are all Wagnerian images; only the verbal constructions are found in the texts.[197] Similarly with *laudatio auctoris, nominatio auctoris, editio actionis*.[198]

These elevations are not without consequences: the way you speak of a thing influences your ideas about it. For example Pliny writes to Trajan[199] about litigation *de natalibus restituendis*, cases where a man is alleged to be wrongly considered a slave or a freedman: he was really born free, and the object of the suit is to get this native freedom restored. According to the prevalent interpretation, however, Pliny is referring to the grant of freebornhood to persons of servile birth. This is an anachronism, such grants were not yet made in that period, and even later they were made by the Emperor, not a proconsul. When we ask how it is that so gross a misunderstanding is universally shared, the answer must include (among other factors) the noun phrase *natalium restitutio* regularly used by those who discuss Pliny. The phrase, I may recall, is first met in an enactment by Justinian, where it does signify a grant of freebornhood: he thinks of Theodora's redemption as comparable to it. Pliny, however, soberly puts *natales restituere*. The momentous-sounding *natalium restitutio* is far more likely than a modest *de natalibus restituendis* to conjure up in the historian's mind the discretionary promotion to freebornhood by an act of state. Again, the commanding *denegatio actionis* not only makes you feel good, it also leads you on in a certain direction. It has been depicted as flowing from the *königliche, später prätorische Machtvollkommenheit*, "the

---

196. Vittinghof, *Der Staatsfeind in der römischen Kaiserzeit* (1936), 12–13, 47, 64ff.

197. *Rescissio* altogether only four times in *VJR*, always, it appears, interpolated: Beseler, *ZRG* 56 (1931): 31.

198. *Editiones* (without *actionum*) occurs in one interpolated passage, Digest 2.13.1.2, Ulpian *IV ad edictum*.

199. Pliny the Younger, *Ep.* 10.72. See articles quoted above, p. 38n121.

royal, subsequently praetorian omnipotence."[200] Whether this is right or wrong—*denegare actionem*, which alone appears in the sources, implies less institutionalization and less majesty than the noun phrase and, proceeding from it, one is bound to be more hesitant.

The achievement or non-achievement of the action noun is no less significant in non-legal areas of culture than in law: nor is it a peculiarly Roman phenomenon. Biblical law knows the verb *shamar*, to guard, to keep, *custodire*, but it is only in post-Biblical law that we get *shemira*, *custodia*. The verb *ya'ash*, to despair, is found in the Old Testament and in Tannaitic sources; *ye'ush*, abandonment of property, is an Amoraic institution.[201] Greek *katecho*, to hold, and *tithemi*, to set, are met in Homer and Hesiod, *katoche* from Herodotus, *thesis* from Pindar; *lytroo*, to release for ransom, occurs in Plato, *lytrosis* first appears in the *Septuagint*. While *verpfänden* is Middle-High-German and *übereignen* sixteenth century, *Verpfändung* and *Übereignung* are both seventeenth. An English example: to bail—to begin with used in the French shape, *bailler*—precedes by a considerable time its action noun bailment, which latter comes in only in the seventeenth century.

In English law, the position is indeed complicated by the interplay with Latin and French or Norman-French. Still, it is perfectly possible to investigate it from the point of view from which I have looked at Roman law, and just as vital for a proper appreciation. After all, at Rome, in many cases, the history of a concept is influenced by a Greek precursor, though I have refrained from expatiating on this aspect. Here are a few English illustrations of how borrowing may upset the normal sequence verb—action noun. The noun cession was taken over into legal language before the verb to cede, compensation before to compensate,[202] inhibition before to inhibit, naturalization before to naturalize.[203] In another case, extradition, the noun alone was imported from French, 1839, the verb to

200. Broggini, *ZRG* 79 (1962): 384.

201. *Ḥazaga* in the technical sense of prescriptive acquisition is post-Biblical. Levy, *Wörterbuch über die Talmudim und Midraschim*, 2nd ed., vol. 2 (1924), 30, regards the Hiphil *heḥeziq* in this sense as derived from the noun—surely that is unlikely.

202. Though to compense—now obsolete—was adopted about the same time as compensation: this may have delayed to compensate.

203. Though with reference to adaptation of a practice, the verb considerably precedes the noun.

extradite being made up twenty-five years later (what philologists call a
back-formation). In fact, in French itself, which had only *tradition* but no
corresponding verb *trader*,[204] the noun *extradition* came first and *extrader*
a little later (both second half of eighteenth century).

To peep outside the law, *maṣa'*, to find, and its passive *nimṣa'*, to
be found, to exist, are common in the Old Testament; the noun *meṣi'a*,
denoting the act of finding or the object found, is Talmudic, the noun
meṣi'uth, existence, is medieval. Similarly, the Old Testament again and
again reminds us of how the children of Israel went forth from Egypt
and how God brought them forth, *yaṣa'*, *hoṣi'*, *mimmisraim*. The noun
phrase *yeṣi'ath miṣraim*, the exodus from Egypt, is post-Biblical.[205] It may
be indebted to the Greek noun *exodos*, which occurs in the *Septuagint*, the
Apocrypha, the *Epistle to the Hebrews*,[206] Philo and Josephus. Again, the
Old Testament knows people that hate without cause, *sone'e ḥinnam*.[207]
It is in post-Biblical ethics that hatred without cause, *sin'ath ḥinnam*,
becomes an important category[208] Both the Old Testament and the
New have to imitate, follow after, become like, an exemplary figure, God,
Christ: *mimeisthai*, *akolouthein*, *homoiousthai*. The nominalization is
confined to subsequent elaborations of the Scriptures. In the case of the
Old Testament the time lag is big. Our first evidence of the action noun is
Philo, writing in Greek and obviously influenced by Platonic philosophy.
He uses *mimema* and *exomoiosis*. There is a far shorter interval in the case
of the New Testament: here expositors like Clement, from the outset, had
the noun ready at hand in Greek literature. One might indeed differentiate
further and inquire which of the various suitable nouns is preferred in
any given period or milieu. Again, it would be interesting to go into the

---

204. I am discounting here the far earlier *trahison* and *trahir*.

205. See Daube, *The Exodus Pattern in the Bible* (1963), 33–34. "It marks a decisive
step from thinking about that event in concrete terms towards a historical-theological
concept. Awareness of the step is indicated by the fact that, though the Old Testament
offers several nouns which might have done, a new one was chosen."

206. Heb. 11:22.

207. Ps. 35:19, 69:4: "they that hate me without cause are more than the hairs of
mine head."

208. E.g. *Babylonian Shabbath* 32b, *Yoma* 9b, *Authorised Daily Prayer Book*, ed. by
Singer (1891), 261. See below, pp. 113–14.

growth of these concepts in Greek and find out by what steps the Platonic action nouns were reached.

That there is a substantial difference between the stage of a mere *imitari Deum* or *Christum* and that where one may speak of *imitatio Dei* or *Christi* is surely undeniable. Actually, German scholars deplore the lack in English of a noun from to follow after. In German there are nouns both from *nachahmen*, to imitate, namely *Nachahmung*, and from *nachfolgen*, to follow after, namely, *Nachfolge*. As English forms a noun only from to imitate, imitation, English scholars tend to make this do for *Nachfolge* as well as *Nachahmung*. Which, the Germans rightly maintain, leads to serious muddle. Seeing that English has two perfectly good different verbs for the two nuances, this is a remarkable tribute to the importance of the action noun. It is not without irony that, while it is absolutely correct that the ideas of following after a person and imitating a person must be kept apart, the introduction of the noun *Nachfolge* is none the less a falsification of the beginnings of Christian thought on the subject—more so than the noun *Nachahmung*, imitation. The Greek for the latter, *mimema* or *mimesis*, is met, though not in the Bible, yet in such ancient writers as Philo and Clement. The Greek for the former, *akolouthia*, *akolouthema*, *akolouthesis*, does not in this context appear in the earlier theological authorities at all.

Needless to say, different languages offer different facilities—some better, some poorer—for creating an action noun or, maybe, finding a substitute. In English, in an extraordinary number of cases, the action noun is simply the infinitive substantivized—a make from to make,[209] a pull from to pull.[210] A language's potential in this respect is in itself a pointer to the mode of thinking in that civilization, and, I ought to add, at that moment, for we come across amazing expansions and contractions. It is essential not to neglect the particular historical circumstances of a language. When one crosses over from Latin to Greek, one's first impression is that the latter took far less time in equipping itself with a full complement of action nouns; and by and large that may be the truth.

---

209. The verb ninth century, the noun fourteenth.

210. The verb about AD 1000, the noun three-hundred years later. We must, of course, be careful. The verb to man (first half of twelfth century) is derived from the noun man (first half of ninth).

Some allowance, however, must be made for the fact that the earliest major works in Greek preserved to us—Homer, Hesiod, Aeschylus and so on—in many respects reflect a more advanced stage than their Latin counterparts. The development which, at Rome, takes place under our eyes, in Greece largely lies back of the sources. Anyhow, what is called for is nothing less than a complete overhaul, within each civilization, of the histories of its several territories, law, philosophy, religion, science, paying attention to the progression from the verbal phase to the nominal. Then will follow a comparison of these several areas. Then a comparison of the various civilizations.

I must confess, however, that in dwelling on the move from verb to action noun I have presented only the basic, roughest distinction. A fuller study would have to take note of subtler gradations. Even within the action noun there are significant shadings. In legal Latin, especially, an action noun sometimes denotes not the activity as such but the right to undertake it. I mentioned earlier on *alienatio* and *datio deminutio* in the sense not of disposal but of power of disposal.[211] *Testamenti factio* may denote the power to make a will; Cicero has it,[212] and it is common among the jurists. Indeed, in course of time, the expression so much recedes from the actual making of a will and concentrates on the capacity in this connection that post-classical idiom extends it to the right to take under a will—whence the *testamenti factio passiva* from the late Middle Ages.[213]

It is probable that, as a rule at least, this meaning, the power to act, is secondary compared with the act itself. In the case of *alienatio* the evidence definitely points this way, the meaning power of alienation not being attested before Gaius. Similarly, *factio* denotes conduct in Plautus,[214] and *testamenti factio* the actual making of a will in a statement of the late Republican jurist Aelius Gallus.[215] In the case of *datio*, the assumption

211. See above, pp. 21, 41, 46.

212. Cicero, *Top.* 50; *Fam.* 7.21.

213. Krüger, *ZRG* 53 (1933): 505ff. *Electio, nominatio, optio* may signify the right to elect, nominate, choose. English option and choice also may mean the power.

214. *Quae haec factio est?*, "What sort of conduct is this?": Plautus, *Bacch.* 843; *Rud.* 1371.

215. Festus 165: *nexum est, ut ait Gallus Aelius, quodcumque per aes et libram geritur . . . quo in genere sunt haec, testamenti factio, nexi datio, nexi liberatio.*

216. In the senatusconsult of 186 BC, above, pp. 41, 46, the meaning is power to transfer; and in the *lex agraria* of 111 BC, above, pp. 34–37, the meaning is power (and duty) to set up a court and judges.

that it meant transfer before it meant power to transfer is an act of faith, but I am prepared to make it.[216]

Another nuance to be considered is the action noun in the sense of the result of the activity. Performance, from to perform, may mean not only a doing ("Besides her walking and other actual performances, what have you heard her say?"),[217] but also a piece of work ("He published lives of Saints and other performances").[218] Once again, we can formulate a presumption: the reference to the activity antedates that to its result.[219] Admittedly there are exceptions. But the main trend is clear enough, and of no small relevance to a grasp of the history of concepts.

Three Latin specimens. *Aratio*, from *arare*, must have signified the result of ploughing, a plot farmed, before Plautus, since he uses it—and, indeed, *aratiuncula*—in a transferred, obscene sense.[220] As on a previous occasion, we find agriculture in the forefront of terminological evolution. *Cautio*, from *cavere*, is first attested by Cicero.[221] But already here it may signify not only the contract but also the instrument.[222] Which agrees with what one would suspect from other considerations—that the term as

217. Shakespeare, *Macbeth* 5.1.13.

218. Garrow, *History and Antiquities of Croydon*, 59.

219. To perform fourteenth century, performance as activity fifteenth, as the result sixteenth. The step from activity to result is found even with action nouns formed by means of the suffixing. Clearing denotes the action from the late fourteenth century, while the sense of a piece cleared in a forest is American (New York) frontier speech around 1800: "There was what in the language of the country was called a *clearing*, and all the usual improvements of a new settlement" (Cooper, *The Pioneers*, [1823], 5, with *clearing* in italics. The action is supposed to take place towards the end of the eighteenth century). The noun holding occurs from the first half of the thirteenth century; it denotes tenure of land from the first half of the fifteenth; and land held in tenure from the first half of the seventeenth. Here, too, there are exceptions to the sequence activity—result, but some are apparent rather than real. Building has the sense of edifice (late thirteenth century) before that of erecting one (late fourteenth). But, then, the earlier sense may derive from the (now obsolete) intransitive usage of to build, i.e. to build in the sense of to reside—as dwelling derives from to dwell.

220. Plautus, *Truculentus* 148–49: *aratio* of a boy, *aratiuncula* of a girl. The verb is used obscenely in *Truculentus* 149, *Asin.* 874. Cf. Shakespeare, *Antony and Cleopatra*, 2.2.227: "Royal wench, she made great Caesar lay his sword to bed, he ploughed her and she cropt."

221. See above, p. 45n158.

222. Cicero, *Fam.* 7.18.1.

denoting the contract was established well before that date. *Possessio*, from *possidere*, already in the *lex agraria* of 111 BC signifies both the possessing of land[223] and land in possession.[224] The latter usage is combated in a definition of the term by Aelius Gallus, at the end of the Republic,[225] and even Labeo's definition, at the beginning of the Empire, till sticks to the possessing.[226]

Three English examples. Satisfaction. Latin *satisfactio* is confined to the active meaning, what a debtor or offender performs. It comes into English (via French) around 1300; and it is only in the second half of the fifteenth century that we find it expressing a state of mind of the recipient—"the greatest richesse is satisfaction of the heart."[227] Exhibition, in the sense of displaying to the public, occurs from the second half of the seventeenth century; in the sense of articles displayed from around 1800.[228] Inhibition—Latin *inhibitio* is invariably active, a check. So was English inhibition from the second half of the fourteenth century to quite recently. In the late nineteenth century psychology availed itself of the word, to describe a check on thought or action by the unconscious will. Popular speech is now about to turn it into a state; something like unaccountable disinclination.[229]

Forgetting about these subtler differentiations—the English action noun, like the Latin, has periods of gradual advance as well as moments of proliferation: the Renaissance belongs to the latter. Formal language

223. E.g. *lex agraria* 16, Bruns, *Font.*, 76.

224. E.g. *lex agraria* 9, 93, Bruns, *Font.*, 75, 88. This meaning is also found in Festus 241: *possessiones appellantur agri*, "possessions are such and such fields."

225. Festus 233: *possessio est ut definit Gallus Aelius usus quidem agri aut aedificii, non ipso fundus aut ager*, "possession is the use of a field or building, not the farm or field itself."

226. Digest 41.2.1 pr., Paul *LIV ad edictum: possessio appellata est, ut et Labeo ait, a sedibus quasi positio, quia naturaliter tenetur ab eo qui ei insistit, quam Graeci katochen dicunt.*

227. Anthony Woodville, Earl Rivers, *Dictes and Sayings of the Philosophers*, 7, a translation of the French version of a Latin work. The development in French is quite similar.

228. The noun show signifies the action from 1300, the passive side from two-hundred years later. As a synonym of exhibition in the sense of display on a large scale it dates only from the first half of the nineteenth century.

229. I could go on indefinitely. So much so that it may be well to note that many action nouns have kept to the action—demolition, for instance, beautification, fumigation.

Here are a few more examples of action and result. (1) Publication in the sense of issuing a book occurs from the second half of the sixteenth century, in that of a book published from the second half of the eighteenth. (2) Revision denotes the action from the early seventeenth century, the product from the mid-nineteenth. (3) Plantation in the active sense occurs from the mid-fifteenth century, in that of the result from the mid-sixteenth. (4) Vegetation signifies the process from the second half of the sixteenth century, concrete plants some two-hundred years later. The noun, incidentally, was taken over from French before the verb. French *végéter* figures from the fourteenth century, *végétation* from the sixteenth; English vegetation from the sixteenth, to vegetate from the early seventeenth. (5) Coalition did not reach the sense of united parties till the mid-nineteenth century, "government by coalition," 1866. Up to then it meant the process of uniting, "towards a coalition," 1715. Latin *coalescere*, to grow together, is common of the uniting of men in the historians, Sallust, Livy, Tacitus. *Coalitus*, rare, occurs from about 300, always with reference to the process. Neither *coalescentia* nor *coalitio* is found in ancient Latin, but the latter appears in the Middle Ages, still signifying the process: *coalitionem instituentes.* In English, to coalesce and coalescence are launched simultaneously by sixteenth-century medicine, referring to the process. Coalition follows in the seventeenth, going outside science, but still denoting a growing together. To coalesce and coalescence first enter politics in the second half of the eighteenth century, "coalescing parties" 1783, "Fox's party will propose a coalescence" 1788. Coalition in this field is earlier: "an essay towards a coalition of parties" 1715. And it outlasts the other two which have become obsolete. A verb to coalite, however, derived from coalition (a back-formation) about 1735, barely made it through the eighteenth century. (French *coaliser* has endured.) Chesney, *A True Reformer*, 3 (1873), 99, distinguishes coalition, as an alliance from expediency, from coalescence, a genuine union in a crisis: "not a coalition in any sense, rather a Constitutional Coalescence." But he has his tongue in his cheek. (6) *Démoraliser* is a term of the French revolution, meaning to corrupt, and *démoralisation*, the act of corruption, is barely younger; though, significantly, the verb was admitted by the Académie in 1798, the noun in 1878. The verb was Englished as early as 1793: Noah Webster himself coined to demoralise. The noun first appears in Southey, 1809. In the sense of to destroy the stamina, English uses the verb from the middle of the nineteenth century. A little later, demoralization may signify a state as well as the action: "his army (the Turkish commander's) is in a state of utter demoralisation and disorganisation," *Daily News*, 5 November 1877. (7) No discernible gap separates the sense of action and that of result, e.g. in the cases of afforestation and generation. *Afforestare* is used in medieval Latin from the thirteenth century, to afforest appears in the early sixteenth, afforestation a hundred years later—denoting both the act of afforesting and the resultant state. Generation comes into English from Latin and French in the late fourteenth century, with a large variety of meanings acquired in the course of a long previous history. The verb to generate is adopted from Latin in the second half of the sixteenth century: French has no *générer*, only *engendrer*. (8) Anyone wishing for examples of inordinately chequered development might pursue the fortunes of institution and representation from Cicero to the present day.

favours it. To cancel dates from before the middle of the fifteenth century, but it is a statute of 1553 which introduces the noun: "The said Chancellor shall have power to make cancellation of such leases and letters patents."[230] In worship, "we make supplications,"[231] and we praise God who stirred up "the mind of Henry Chichele, for the relief of the distressed and the increase of learning and godliness."[232] English satirists are no less alive than their Roman forerunners to the opportunities offered them by this style wigged, robed or gaitered. Primers, lists of definitions, glossaries are fertile soil for the action noun today as they were at Rome, and we must now add advertisements and the like. Journalists seem generally attracted by its crisp and systematizing character.[233] As at Rome, the nominalization may affect only a sector of the verb. To electrify is first attested in a letter by Benjamin Franklin, 1747, electrification in the *Philosophical Transactions* 1748. Four years later Chesterfield uses the verb in a transferred sense: "You will not be so agreeably electrified as at Mannheim." But even today, one could not speak of the electrification of Professor Daube by the appearance of Marlene Dietrich at his lecture."[234]

Frequently the emergence of the noun illumines what goes on in that province. To fraternize, early seventeenth century; "they gave the kiss of fraternisation to negros" 1792, French revolution and Wilberforce. To mechanize, second half of seventeenth century; the noun 1839, in a complaint by Sterling about "the mechanization of the mind." To enlight, tenth century, and to enlighten, late fourteenth; Milton and Butler first use

230. Act 27, *Henry VIII*, xxvii. *Cancellare* is not used by the classics according to Beseler, *ZRG* 56 (1936): 32; *cancellatio* is exclusively technical of the fixing of boundaries.

231. The noun was taken over into English (late fourteenth century) before the verb (early fifteenth).

232. To relieve in this sense from 1375, relief from 1400; to increase early fourteenth century, the noun late fourteenth.

233. To subsidise in the sense of to support by grants goes back to the first half of the nineteenth century, subsidization is first met in the *Daily Chronicle* of January, 1907. While getting this Lecture ready for publication, I found the noun in an editorial of the *Daily Californian* of February 22, 1967, 1, discussing a letter from a professor. The letter is reproduced on page 13: it speaks of subsidising, not subsidization.

234. Wrong. From the *Supplement* to the *Oxford Dictionary* I see that since the last quarter of the nineteenth century electrification has indeed been employed figuratively; e.g. "her electrification by Mr Belport's proposal." I doubt, however, whether this usage is represented in good writers.

the verb of instruction, and it is at the same time that there enters the noun enlightenment, which later, in the second half of the nineteenth century, becomes a rendering of *Aufklärung*. To measure, fourteenth century; measurement starts in architecture in the middle of the eighteenth. The work of Gartner and Darwin is reflected in to hybridize 1845, immediately followed by hybridization in 1851.[235] To disinfect, seventeenth century; "On the influence of oxygen in the process of disinfection" 1803, Andrew Duncan, Professor of Medicine at Edinburgh. To atomize, in the sense of to reduce to tiny particles, occurs before the middle of the nineteenth century; atomization marks the introduction in the seventies of that century of the therapeutic inhalation of a spray. To motorize in the sense of to furnish with a motor 1918, motorization 1929, mostly with reference to a collective.[236]

By now so many English verbs have action nouns that the birthrate is low. In another sense, however, the growth is more rapid than ever: a new verb usually gets its noun with hardly any delay—which means that the existence of the noun is correspondingly less significant. Even so, nominalization is far from universal. To botanize as an intransitive is second half of eighteenth century—"they will botanize charmingly"[237]— and as a transitive a hundred years later—"to botanize the islands thoroughly"—yet it has not come to botanization. Again, though many of us commute between the town where we reside and that where we work, to the best of my knowledge the phenomenon is not yet described as commutation. In this case, however, it is a safe bet that we shall see the noun before long in some planning report or sociological monograph. I

235. There was a craze: "By the acquisition of this species, a new field for the hybridist is thrown open" 1849. The notion of mongrel also received a fresh impetus from Darwin. To mongrelize 1629, mongrelization 1889.

236. But at least in facetious speech the verb is coming to be applied to a person: "Are you motorized?" meaning "Have you your car with you?" The noun contraception is not, of course, derived from a verb. Actually, contraceptive seems slightly earlier, end of last century, based on conceptive, mid-seventeenth century. Then, in the first quarter of the present century, contraception was coined, thought of as the opposite to conception. I guess that when the verb arrives (back-formation), it will be not to contraceive but to contracept, sounding less passive, more energetic, a bit like to intercept.

237. Not so charming: "Philosopher!—a fingering slave, One that would peep and botanize Upon his mother's grave." Wordsworth, *A Poet's Epitaph*, 19 (1799–1800).

have not the heart to withhold from you the history of this concept, more zigzag than one might expect. The verb *commutare*, to change, to exchange, occurs in Plautus, *commutatio* in Cicero. English takes them over in the sixteenth century: to commutate or commute and commutation. They are frequently used where it is a question of, say, substituting a down payment of 100 for twelve annual installments of 10. In the second half of the last century American railways introduced reduced fares for passengers doing the same journey every day and buying a ticket for a fortnight or a month. In consideration of the undertaking of regular travel a lower price was substituted for what the several journeys would normally come to. Hence the name of such a ticket: commutation ticket. There was indeed deliberate emphasis on this aspect, deliberately weighty, formal nomenclature, since it was this quid pro quo, the undertaking of multiple travel for a reduction, which exempted the ticket from a law prohibiting alterations in fares. The holder of a commutation ticket was at first called a commutation passenger. Soon, however, he became a commuter, and the verb to commute accordingly came to denote this kind of travel. In course of time the connection with cheap tickets evaporated; thus what remains in the States as well as English-speaking countries to which the usage has spread is the daily displacement. Note that even now it must in principle be a move between two towns, i.e. railway stations. Within the same town, however great the distance between home and office, one rarely speaks of commuting. So we have *commutare* first, then *commutatio*; in the nineteenth century the commutation ticket in the sense of substitution ticket; then to commute signifying to travel on such a ticket—and I trust you appreciate my broadmindedness in ending with a case where the verb follows the action noun, instead of the other way round; finally to commute signifying to travel routine-wise from home to office and back. Or not quite finally, for the action noun to this meaning is yet to come, and is sure to come. For the moment I suggest commutation for dinner to our respective Colleges.

Part II

SOCIAL ASPECTS

There is no doubt that the Romanists of today are more alive to social and economic questions than their predecessors of fifty years ago.[1] Even so, the systematic coherence and conceptual smoothness of the law they are concerned with are so seductive that the temptation to forget about the rugged realities behind the façade is far greater for them than, for instance, for an English legal historian. I shall devote the first and major part of this Lecture to some typical illustrations of this danger. In the second part I propose to point out a few remarkable consequences of the close-knit character of the upper class at Rome, and in particular to call attention to an area of legislation and jurisdiction which almost deserves a name of its own.

1. See, e.g. Kelly, *Roman Litigation* (1966).

3

Economic Realities

Damages under the *Lex Aquilia*

Damage to property was regulated by the first and third chapters of the *lex Aquilia*, from the middle of the Republic. The first chapter ordained that a man who killed another man's slave or *pecus*—ox, cow, horse—should pay the highest value in the past year; whether the killing was deliberate or merely from negligence made no difference.[1] The original scope of the third chapter is controversial. What is agreed is that, in classical and later law, it covered all damage not falling under chapter one, hence the injuring (without killing) of a slave or *pecus* and the destruction as well as the damaging of an inanimate object or an animal not *pecus*, a dog, a cat, a chicken. And, of course, again whether deliberate or just negligent.

Now where a man merely injures (as opposed to killing) another man's slave or *pecus*, or merely damages (as opposed to destroying) another man's inanimate property or dog, one would expect him to have to pay not the full value but only the difference between that and the reduced value after interference; plus expenses for cure, repair and the like. This is indeed what in the opinion of some scholars, myself included, classical and later law did make him liable for under the third chapter; and I have written several studies tracing in detail the not uninteresting route by

---

1. Though one could plead justification, the statute speaking of killing *iniuria*; see, e. g. Digest 9.2.4 pr. (Gaius *VII ad edictum provinciale*) and 5 pr. (Ulpian *XVIII ad edictum*) on self-defence.

which the sensible, generally applicable solution was reached.[2] However, the prevalent view is different. It is—believe it or not—that once you damaged somebody's slave, beast or inanimate object, however partially, you had to pay him the full value. Remember that it is not primarily a case of criminal wrongdoing: negligence sufficed. Schulz writes as follows:[3] "If a thing only suffered deterioration and was not completely destroyed, the offender had to pay the full value of the thing. Thus the penalty was the same when a dog was killed and when he was only wounded."

At one time I was tempted to publish an article acknowledging the error of my ways and describing how, by at last embracing the reigning doctrine, I had a veil removed from my eyes and many perplexing facts never before understood had become explicable to me. Take, for a start, the disturbingly large number of names Romans used to bear: Gaius Octavius Tidius Tossianus Lucius Javolenus Priscus—that is what a jurist was called. The reason, we now realize, is that children inevitably passed through countless families. There is no child that does not at some time or other scratch a letter or two, or even four, on the wall of a house. At Rome, on the basis of the prevalent view, the father would have to pay for the entire estate—not just the house, but the grounds as well. Damage worth threepence, estate worth 25,000 pounds: he had to pay 25,000 pounds— unless, indeed, he was prepared to surrender the child to the owner. In most cases he would not be able to afford not to surrender. Let it not be said that *de minimis non curat lex*. A scratch is not a *minimum* if any damage however slight is to be made good by paying the total value of the thing; a scratch, under such a rule, is worth what the thing is worth. Some texts tell us expressly that the third chapter applies even where there is absolutely no diminution in the value of the slave—who was, say, bumped into—but medical costs were incurred.[4] So we must clearly not invoke *de minimis*. According to the current doctrine the owner was entitled to the full price of his healthy slave. If it was my child who knocked against

2. See, above all, Daube, *Studi Solazzi* (1948), 93ff.

3. Schulz, *Classical Roman Law* (1954), 590. At least he has the courage of his conviction. Quite a few authors hedge.

4. Digest 9.2.45.1, Paul *X ad Sabinum*, and the—hardly intact—second half of Digest 9.2.27.17 (Cf. *Coll.* 2.4.1), Ulpian *XVIII ad edictum*; see Rotondi, *Scritti Giuridici*, vol. 2 (1922), 458, 476.

him, I would be a fool not to hand over the child rather than paying, since, on the one hand, sooner or later I should have to part with the child owing to this Aquilian liability in any case, and on the other, I should keep receiving other people's children instead. Children, unless totally disabled, were never more than transient members of a family: Gaius Octavius Tidius and so on, and so on.

Another feature of Roman life that had always puzzled me is the inordinate amount of lending and borrowing carried on. Now I see: it was so common because there was really no private property. If I negligently turn round on my swivel-chair and your slave falls and sprains his ankle, or let us even suppose he loses a tooth, I must pay for him in full. If he is one of a performing troop of twelve you keep together, I must pay the full value of the whole troop though he goes on performing: I should have to do that if I killed him, so I must do it also in the case of partial damage.[5] If he happens to be instituted heir by a friend of yours, I guess I pay for the inheritance as well. Moreover, if I defend the action, I pay double.[6] That in a society governed by this kind of regulation nobody will be rich or poor for long is evident.

That—at first sight—most paradoxical arrangement of Roman procedure, that the judges were laymen, is finally accounted for: they did not need to know the law because it did not matter. Nothing mattered when all material life became a joke through the third chapter of this statute, which equated damaging with destruction. Ah, there was one difference, which made the regulation even more playful: the first chapter spoke of the highest value in the past year; the third, in the past month. Accordingly, if you ran over your neighbour's cow and she perished, you paid, say, 250 pounds, highest value in the past year; if she only got a bit lame, you paid a mere 235, highest value in the past month. Remember that for inanimate objects and animals not *pecus*, always the past month alone was considered. Thus, if you dropped some cigarette ash in my orchard and the orchard, with the summer house on it, went up in flames, you paid 15,000 pounds even if three months before it would have come to 16,000. And also, of course, if the ash did nothing beyond scorching a

5. Gaius 3.212, referring to killing.
6. Gaius 3.216; Digest 9.2.27.24, Paul *XXII ad edictum.*

branch with a few apple blossoms—damage amounting to half a crown—you paid 15,000 not 16,000.[7]

The magistrates of the Republic were anxious to intimate to their people—and maybe they had posterity in mind as well—that the Aquilian edifice was not due to ineptitude but was set up with tongue in cheek. So they issued a series of edicts which demonstrated that the Roman mind was perfectly capable of conceiving of compensation adjusted to the loss inflicted. An edict by the praetor dealt with things thrown from a dwelling into the road and damaging your belongings—your clothes, a slave of yours, a dog of yours. The householder's liability was strictly in accordance with the harm in the individual case: he had to pay you a double indemnification. If a free man was hit, a clear distinction was drawn between death and lesser harm: in the former case a considerable fixed sum was payable, in the latter an amount equitable in the circumstances.[8] The aediles promulgated an edict exactly analogous, concerning the case where you kept a wild animal by the wayside and it attacked property or a free man: double indemnification for damage to property, varying with the actual harm done, a fixed sum in the event of a free man's death, an equitable amount in the event of injury to a free man.[9] These edicts go back to pre-classical times: Servius knew them.[10] It is obvious that the way the jurists operated the third chapter of the *lex Aquilia* was a real hoax. Doubtless some results were found particularly amusing. If I allowed my bear to escape and he broke a finger of your slave or a leg of your dog, a careful calculation was made of any permanent deterioration as well as your expenses, say, 10 pounds in the case of the slave, 5 shillings in that of the dog, and, by way of warning to keep better guard over a dangerous animal, the edict made me pay twice that figure, 20 pounds for the slave, 10 shillings for the dog. By contrast, if I inadvertently let slip a case I was carrying and it broke a finger of your slave or a leg of your dog, under the

7. Gaius 3.210, 218. If, however, it was a freshly planted tree which had not yet taken root, you paid for the tree: 1 to 2 pounds, Gaius 2.74. Law was fun.

8. Lenel, *Das edictum perpetuum*, 3rd ed. (1927), 173–74.

9. Lenel, *Das edictum perpetuum*, 566. Why 50,000 sesterces for death in the praetor's edict *de his qui deiecerint* and 20,000 in the aedilician edict *de feris* I am not going to discuss.

10. Or the former at least: Digest 9.3.5.12, Ulpian *XXIII ad edictum*.

lex Aquilia I had to pay the total price of slave or dog, say, 300 pounds for the slave, 3 pounds for the dog—for, as Schulz says, "the penalty was the same when a dog was killed and when he was only wounded." It certainly paid to keep a bear rather than carry a load.

Such, then, is the outline of the article I once planned but never got around to. To return from this wonderland of Lewis Carroll—I hold that there are numerous texts in flagrant conflict with the prevalent doctrine. Moreover, not a single one raises any of the problems which would flow from such a weird regulation. This latter point is admitted even by its advocates. Surely, in this case, the argument from silence is overwhelming. Again, quite a few decisions are concerned with the accurate distribution of borderline cases between the first chapter and the third: for example, one which lays down that if I injure your slave and, though the wound in itself is not fatal, he dies from neglect, I am liable only under chapter 3.[11] Would these scrupulous distinctions really be meaningful if it were only a question whether I pay the highest value in the past year or in the past month?[12]

Buckland did notice the waste of resources which must take place under the system assumed by the current view: there would be no inducement whatever for a person who had caused some slight damage not to finish the job.[13] This result would indeed be inevitable; and to make a brief re-entry into the world of Alice—the many fires at Rome should no longer surprise us. If my chariot ran into a corner of your house, doing 7/6 worth of damage, I might just as well get a can of petrol and have the pleasure of seeing the whole building go up in a glorious blaze, since I must pay for it anyway. No difference between a tiny blemish and radical elimination, nor—that was the beauty of it—between inadvertence and malice. The law discouraged half-measures.

11. Digest 9.2.30.4, Paul *XXII ad edictum.*
12. In fact, even the first chapter was not carried to unreasonable extremes. If you kill my slave while it is open to me to acquire an inheritance through him, you will have to pay me its value; but if you kill him after I have acquired it through him, you need not pay for it—though, strictly, *quanti in eo anno plurimi fuerit* ought to include it. Gaius 3.212: *antequam cerneret.* Cf. De Zulueta, *The Institutes of Gaius* 2 (1953), 211.
13. Buckland, *Text-Book* (1963), 586.

But even apart from this particular consequence, my submission is that no economy could go on for a fortnight with the regulation ascribed to the Romans by the orthodox school; maybe it would not be viable for one day. Gerke has attacked my dissent in *Studia et Documenta Historiae et Juris*,[14] charging: *Er verkennt das pönale Element der Klage*, "he fails to appreciate the penal side of the action." Some penal side!

The Have-Nots

The Horror of Intestacy

I now want to say something about a major cause of historical distortion: failure to take account of the have-nots. They are apt to be forgotten because the sources, the legal ones in particular, concentrate on the haves; it is they who occupy the centre of the stage while the have-nots appear on the fringe, as delinquents or the like. Scholars too readily identify with the viewpoint fed to them.

A glaring example is the horror of intestacy attributed to the Romans.[15] The colourful expression is Maine's.[16] His thesis is taken over by one author after another: at Rome, not only when it was still a small community, but long after it had expanded into an Empire, it was an exception for a man not to make a will.[17] Far-reaching conclusions are drawn regarding the make-up of the Roman psyche, eager to dominate its individual sphere even beyond death. Indeed, the most terrible curse (Maine alleges) one Roman could utter against another was to wish on him that he should die without leaving a will.

A moment's reflection on the economic realities should reveal the fantastic nature of this universally held theory. Take the stretch of 250 BC to AD 250. Why or how would the poor chaps who slept under the bridges of the Tiber make a will? They had nothing to make a will about, nor the wherewithal to engage the cheapest lawyer to draw it up. The

---

14. Gerke, *Studia et Documenta Historiae et Juris* 23 (1957): 79.
15. See Daube, *Tulane Law Review* 39, (1965): 253ff.
16. Maine, *Ancient Law*, ed. Pollock (1920), 233.
17. E.g. Costa, *Cicerone Giureconsulto*, vol. 1 (1927), 215.

current misconception is due to the enormous role played by wills in the legal writings. But these writings reflect the doings of a tiny fraction of the population. Actually, I am convinced that even among the haves will-making was no commoner than it was, say, in Victorian England. Certainly the have-nots, the vast majority of citizens, were right out of it.

The view I am combating is bolstered up by evidence which, on closer inspection, turns out to be worthless. Let me present the three chief arguments.

The first is that the XII Tables designate a person who has made no will by the negative word *intestatus*,[18] hence this must be an exception. The conclusion, however, is far from cogent. The primary function of a word is to call attention to the striking, the uncommon. At the early stage of legal Latin in the time of the XII Tables, the likelihood is that a word for to make a will, *testari*, is coined precisely because the act is anything but ordinary. There is, then, a positive label, *testatus*, attaching to that remarkable figure who has made a will, which leaves the negative *intestatus* for the usual case.[19] When we call the world unredeemed, it does not follow that redemption is an everyday affair. What implications the prevalent argument has as to the conduct of the young Roman ladies, considering the term *virgo intacta*, I need not spell out. Incidentally I often hear Englishmen observe with pride that their language has no equivalent to the German *Schadenfreude*. The pride might be misplaced: maybe the emotion is too common here to attract notice and call for a term whereas the Germans are so sweet that if, on a rare occasion, it does occur, it stands out. Anyhow this argument from *intestatus* is no good at all.

18. V 4, Bruns, *Font.*, 23: *si intestato moritur.*

19. To be sure, the negative itself comes into use where the negative situation starts being remarkable or for some special reason requires extra consideration. To begin with, *confiteri* is a notable act and *confessus* designates him who has acted in this notable fashion. Much later, *inconfessus* is coined, when (in certain circles and on certain occasions at least) it is unusual not to have confessed. *Damnare* is manifestly a rare act, *damnatus* signifies a person affected by this rare act; and it never becomes an ordinary thing. *Indemnatus* is an epithet objectively applicable to the vast majority of people in all periods; but, as a historical fact, it is coined to describe the case where this quality acquires special importance, namely, where a person is charged with a crime but not (yet) sentenced in due form. Cf. below, pp. 98–99, on the case of *indotata*.

The next piece of evidence is a statement by old Cato that he made three mistakes in his life:[20] he told a secret to his wife,[21] he paid for a boat when he could have walked it, and he spent an entire day *adiathetos*—which is translated "without a will." To base on such an utterance by an eccentric one's estimate of the *mores* among, say, the tailors or carpenters or even the bankers of Rome is surely indefensible. The same Cato, let me remind you, remarked[22] that he never made love to his wife except during a thunderstorm. Are we to generalize this too? Why not? There is, however, another little flaw in the argument under consideration: *adiathetos* does not mean "without a will" at all, it means "without serious, planned work." As we know from Cicero, Cato preached the principle that a statesman ought to make constructive, rational use of his free time as well as his hours of official business.[23] So one of the three sins he committed in the course of his life is that he once spent a day without being purposefully engaged; his statement has not the remotest connection with wills. To be sure, there are plenty of references to the importance of wills. Cicero sees a proof of the immortality of the soul in man's concern about what will happen after his death, a concern shown in "the procreation of children, the propagation of the name, the adoption of sons, the care taken about wills, the very burial monuments and epitaphs."[24] But the end gives him away as speaking for his class. Paupers may procreate, because that costs nothing, but wills and monuments are a different matter. This second argument, then, for the horror of intestacy goes the way of the first.

We thus come to the third, which is the one that inspired Maine to coin this phrase. In one of Plautus's comedies the lover wants to summon a captain to court. For this, some formality before witnesses is required, called *antestari*, but the captain refuses to cooperate. The young man shouts at him "live unsummoned, unattested, then, *intestatus vivito*, I

20. Plutarch, *Vit.*, *Cato Maior* 9.6.

21. On the advisability of this course opinion was divided. Nicostratus holds that a husband keeps nothing from his wife but communes with her as with another self: Stobaeus, *Floril*, ed. Meineke, vol. 3 (1856), 69–70.

22. Plutarch, *Vit.*, *Cato Maior* 17.7.

23. Cicero, *Planc.* 27.66; see Nicolai, *Saeculum*, 14 (1963), 215.

24. Cicero, *Tusculanae Disputationes* 1.14.31: *procreatio liberorum, propagatio nominis, adoptiones filiorum, testamentorum diligentia, ipsa sepulchrorum munimenta, elogia.*

can go through the formality with somebody else."[25] There is also a very obscene *double entendre* which Plautus's audience apparently loved, for it recurs several times in his work,[26] but which is not fit for an audience like you. Maine, it is clear, did not suspect it. For him, and all the many writers on the subject following him, here is evidence that there was no more fearful curse in Latin than to say to a man he should die without a will. The passage has absolutely nothing to do with a will. The enraged lover is not a bit interested in the ultimate destiny of the captain's property, such as it is, nor could that wretch care less. "Go to blazes,"[27] that is what it means, "live unattested (and without testicles)."

In the forties BC the number of recipients of free grain in the city of Rome was 320,000; as only adult males were eligible, the figure does not include women and children in this class. On the other hand, ancient historians tell us that "well-to-do residents were presumably not numerically significant."[28] In these circumstances, if there were anything in the orthodox view, the normal Roman will should run: "Let my three sons Titius, Maevius and Sempronius be my heirs. I leave them my entire possessions, consisting of the shirt and the sandals I am wearing, in equal parts, with a usufruct for my widow for life." But not one will of this kind has come to light anywhere in the Empire. The most modest wills extant at least involve a house or something of comparable value.[29] The younger Pliny, in a letter, tells a friend about one Domitius Tullus who appeared to be the kind of man that would leave his estate to worthless flatterers; but,

---

25. Plautus, *Curc.* 621ff. The someone else is the willing Curculio. It is also possible to interpret "may you live without being able to call witnesses when you need them" or "may you live incapable of being called as witness, infamous"; see my article quoted above. My thesis is quite unaffected: none of the renderings conceivable can be brought into association with a will. I now much prefer the translation proposed in the text, which seems to me simplest and most in accordance with the situation. Moreover, it would fit also in *Curc.* 695, where the pimp objects to being dragged off for punishment *indemnatus atque intestatus*, "unsentenced and unsummoned."

26. Once more in the same play, *Curc.*, 30, another time in Plautus, *Mil.* 1417.

27. *Iuppiter te perdat.*

28. Brunt, *Past and Present*, 35 (1966), 8–9.

29. Except for the *testamentum porcelli*: below, pp. 75ff.. This is not to deny that, say, among a panicked army there may be an outbreak of will-making: see Caesar, *Bellum Gallicum* 1.39.

surprisingly, he distributed it dutifully among deserving relations, thus
refuting "the general notion that wills mirror people's mentality."[30] Well,
well. Domitius Tullus was a multi-millionaire. Wills mirror the mentality
of the well-to-do, others do not make them. The have-nots are invisible:
die im Dunkeln sieht man nicht. But they do exist and a history of law
which discounts them is apt to go wrong.

The Filiusfamilias

A fundamental Roman institution, the complete incapacity of a
filiusfamilias to own property, can be adequately explained only by bearing
in mind the have-nots. If you were a Roman citizen and your *paterfamilias*
was alive, you could not own anything.[31] Age or rank made no difference.
Suppose the head of a family was ninety, his two sons seventy-five and
seventy, their sons between sixty and fifty-five, the sons of these in their
forties and thirties, and the great-great-grandsons in their twenties, none
of them except the ninety-year-old Head owned a penny. If the seventy-
five-year-old senator or the forty-year-old General or the twenty-year-old
student wanted to buy a bar of chocolate, he had to ask the *senex* for the
money. This is really quite extraordinary. Had it been so only in very early
times, in the fifth and fourth centuries BC, when Rome was a compact
settlement of peasants and craftsmen, it would be understandable. But
it was still the law in the time of Caesar or Hadrian, when Rome was
the capital of the Western world and full of foreigners under no such
restraints. An adult Greek or Jew could buy, sell, borrow, lend, keep
horses, go to the pictures, send flowers to his lady, even if his father or
grandfather was still around. His Roman contemporary was unable to
do any of these things unless he succeeded either in persuading the old
man to support him or in finding somebody willing to extend credit to
him in the hope that he would outlive his elders and eventually, when
a *paterfamilias* himself, settle his debts with the addition of a generous
bounty. From Constantine onwards, in the fourth century AD, the system

----

30. Pliny the Younger, *Ep.* 8.18: *quod creditur vulgo, testamenta hominum speculum
esse morum.*

31. Buckland, *Text-Book* (1963), 280.

was dismantled. Mostly the books (if they are interested in social or economic aspects at all) ask why this happened. The foremost question to put is surely how the system could go on for so long.

From a cursory reading of the literature one might gain the impression that already Augustus carried out a radical reform; but this is definitely not the case. He ordained that a *filiusfamilias* serving in the army might dispose by last will of what he had acquired by way of soldier's stipend and booty.[32] Obviously, this affected only a tiny group and even that only in a marginal way. So long as a soldier managed to escape death, in practice, whatever the law, stipend and booty had always been his. Even before the Augustan decree no *paterfamilias* could run after his son or grandson fighting the Pannonians on the Danube if he took his pay, as well as the ring taken from a slain enemy, to the local beauty queen. When in the early Empire this camp property, *peculium castrense*, was officially recognized as freely available to the soldier, that was no more than legalization of an inevitable state of affairs. Augustus did go just a little further: a *filiusfamilias*-soldier was to be able to make a valid will about stipend and booty.[33] We can imagine how his popularity with the troops increased when he took the line that the last wishes of one who fell in battle should be given effect, and his possessions go to the comrade or girl he named. But remember that a *filiusfamilias* lost this privilege as soon as he left the service: prior to Hadrian, a *filiusfamilias*-veteran had no property to leave, and even if he had made a will in the army, it lapsed, since everything was now again fully in his father's or grandfather's hands. It cannot be said that Augustus's measure had the slightest impact on the position of a *filiusfamilias* in general.

There is preserved a *testamentum porcelli*, a will of a piglet,[34] which has been neglected by Romanists because it infringes most of the rules about the drawing up of a will and therefore looks devoid of legal interest. But it is a will of a soldier—the piglet is about to perish under

32. Institutes 2.12 pr.

33. The legal recognition of *peculium castrense* in the *filiusfamilias*-soldier's lifetime was undoubtedly speeded up by this measure of Augustus concerning disposal *mortis causa*.

34. Haupt, *Opuscula*, vol. 2 (1876), 175ff.; now easily accessible in Buecheler, *Petronii Saturae*, 6th ed., ed. Heraeus (1922), 346–47.

the butcher's knife—and a soldier's will was exempt from formalities.[35] Indeed, the piglet is evidently disposing of his *peculium castrense*: his father is still alive and actually among the beneficiaries.[36] St. Jerome, around AD 400, knew this will;[37] it was concocted, we learn from him, by Thracians[38]—Thracians were prominent in the Roman armies. The will, then, is prior to Jerome, considerably prior since it was a popular joke by his time. The *terminus post quem* is Augustus's concession of will-making in respect of the *peculium castrense*. The piglet is on active service, so the will might—though it need not—antedate Hadrian, who extended the concession to veterans. On the other hand, the piglet seems to dispose not only of what he acquired while a soldier but also of objects given him for the purpose of service when he joined up: exactly from when such objects were recognized as part of the *peculium castrense* we cannot say.[39]

35. Gaius 2.114. A sketchy history in Digest 29.1.1 pr., Ulpian *XLV ad edictum*. Institution of several persons as heirs *certarum rerum* is admitted in Digest 29.1.17 pr., Gaius *XV ad edictum provinciale*.

36. Examples in the Digest of fathers as beneficiaries in this case: Digest 29.1.17.3, Gaius *XI ad edictum pronvinciale*; 49.17.17.1, Papinian *II definitionum*; 49.17.20, Paul *singulari ad regulam Catonianam*. Juvenal (16.51ff.) counts it among the privileges of soldiers that "they alone have the right to make a will in the father's lifetime, for it has been decided that what is obtained by military labour should not be included in the bulk of the property whose absolute control is with the father." He goes on to introduce a decrepit father legacy-hunting, courting his successful soldier-son with a view to inheriting his valuable decorations. It is noteworthy that the piglet, though doing something in his will for father, mother and sister, makes no mention of a wife: in the first two centuries of the Principate soldiers could not marry.

37. In the Preface to chapter 12 of his *Commentary on Isaiah* he observes that more people appreciate light stories than Plato; the *testamentum porcelli* is recited by crowds of laughing schoolboys; as for himself, he is content with the praise of the superior few. In *Against Rufinus*, 1.17 he is running down Rufinus's Latin style (Cf. above, p. 35n100); of course, he remarks, there are the simple multitudes who enjoy the unlearned and nonsensical, such as the *testamentum porcelli*. Editors of the *testamentum* and others (Friedlaender, *Sittengeschichte Roms*, 9th ed.; Pauly-Wissowa, *RE*, vol. 1 [1919], 177) have concluded that the will is the work of schoolboys. This does not follow at all. The imagery smacks of the barrack-room. I see no reason not to take Jerome's *Bessorum* seriously: see the next footnote. It matters little.

38. *Bessi*, a leading Thracian tribe. See also below, p. 79n53, on Tergeste, Triest.

39. Fully recognized, for example, in Digest 49.17.11, Macer *II de re militari*; Macer wrote in the first half of the third century. See Jörs, *Römisches Recht*, ed. Kunkel, 291–92.

As there is no translation into a modern language, let me read it to you.

"M. Grunter Hyena the piglet has made this will. As I cannot write myself,[40] I have dictated it.[41] Butcher the cook said: 'Come here, destroyer of the house, digger up of the soil, runaway, piglet, and today I take your life.' Hyena the piglet said: 'If I have done anything, if I have sinned in any way, if I have broken some little vases with my feet, I petition you, master cook, I ask my life, grant it to the petitioner.' Butcher the cook said: "Come here, boy, hand me the knife from the kitchen[42] in order that I may make a bloody end of this piglet."[43] The piglet is seized by the assistants, led off on the fifteenth day before the first of the Herbal Month,[44] when herbage is plentiful, in the consulship of Roastingtin and Peppersauce. And as he saw that he was going to die, he asked for an hour's reprieve and petitioned the cook in order to be able to make a will. He called for his parents,[45] in order

40. *Potui* as a present, I cannot, occurs again further on, *in cuius votum interesse non potui*; see below, p. 78n48.

41. Dictation of a military will, e.g. in Digest 29.1.40 pr., Paul *XI responsorum*.

42. On *cocina* instead of *coquina* see below, n. 44.

43. I would not press details. Lest it be argued, however, that the piglet seems to be executed by his commander for his military crimes rather than killed in battle, and what about the right to make a will in such circumstances, I draw attention to Digest 29.1.11 pr., Ulpian *XLV ad edictum*: "Those soldiers who are sentenced to death for a military crime may make a will only in respect of *bona castrensia*." The passage may have suffered interference, but I think the gist is classical.

44. Haupt says there is no trace anywhere of *kalendae lucerninae*: it is just facetious. This is correct, but at least the approximate meaning of *lucerninae* can, I think, be established. I connect it with English lucerne in the sense of clover (or something like it), which is known from the seventeenth century, and French *luzerne*, known from the sixteenth, apparently most at home then in the Provence and Languedoc. The dictionaries have no etymology, but I consider it very likely that here, in the vulgar *testamentum porcelli*, the root is present. It should be noted that, as Haupt points out, *cocina* for kitchen (see above, n. 42), also unique, is a precursor of Spanish *cocina*, Italian *cucina*, French *cuisine*, German *Küche*, English *kitchen*. The strongest support for my interpretation, of course, comes from the following clause, *ubi abundant cymae*, "when herbs (or vegetables, cabbage) abound" (*ubi* in temporal application).

45. Even in the case of a military will somehow the intent to make a will had to be demonstrated. It was not enough, for instance, to tell a beneficiary privately: "You can have such-and-such a thing of mine." The calling together of witnesses was an almost necessary step: *convocatis ad hoc hominibus*, Digest 29.1.24, Florentinus *X institutionum*; Institutes 2.11.1, quoting a rescript of Trajan.

to apportion to them[46] something from his provisions. He declares: "To my father Hoggy Lardy I give and bequeath to be given 30 pecks of acorn, and to my mother Reverend Sow I give and bequeath to be given 40 pecks of bearded wheat,[47] and to my sister Gruntress, whose wedding I shall be unable to attend,[48] I give and bequeath to be given 30 pecks of barley. And of my organs I shall give and donate to the cobblers my bristles, to the brawlers my head-armament,[49] to the deaf my ears, to the pleaders and prattlers my tongue [it is exactly the kind of will our transplanting surgeons wish everyone of us to leave behind] to the sausage-makers my entrails, to the stuffing experts my thighs, to the women my loins, to the boys my bladder, to the girls my tail, to the sodomites my bum, to the runners and hunters my heels, to the robbers my claws.[50] And to the unmentionable cook,[51] I apportion as bequest the soup ladle and pestle which I brought with me[52] from Trevest right to Triest; he may wear

46. *Dimittere* in the sense of "to leave something" is met in Gaius 1.195 and *G. Ep.* 2.7.8.

47. Laconian wheat is bearded, hairy; Cf. Pliny the Elder, *HN* 18.20.93, and (for *arista* used of human hair) Persius, 3.115.

48. *Potui* again in the sense of I cannot: see above, p. 77n40.

49. *Capitina*; the translation is my guess.

50. Haupt aptly quotes Plautus, *Pseud.* 852, where thievish cooks have *ungulae*. Vom *Schwein wurde alles vermendet*, says Orth, "no part of a pig went unused"; Pauly-Wissowa, *RE*, vol. 2 (1923), 810, s.v. "schwein."

51. *Nec nominando coco.* In Digest 28.2.3 pr., Ulpian *I ad Sabinum*, a father disinherits his son, calling him *non nominandus*. We also, however, find testators insulting beneficiaries. Digest 28.5.49.1, Marcian *IV institutionum, filius meus impissimus male de me meritus heres esto*; Digest 32.37.2, Scaevola *XVIII digestorum, Maevio liberto meo de me nihil merito dari volo lagynos vini vetusti centum quinquaginta*. In Digest 28.5.9.8, Ulpian *V ad Sabinum, non tamen eo quod contumeliae causa solet addi* shows that Ulpian gave a ruling about these cases; but it was the opposite of that before us, and the reviser betrays himself by the most inelegant way the clause is squeezed into its present position. (Digest 30.54. pr., Pomponius *VIII ad Sabinum*, traditionally adduced as concurring with 28.5.9.8—e.g. Biondi, *Successione Testamentaria e Donazioni*, 2nd ed. (1955), 210—deals with an entirely different situation.) It is just conceivable that the piglet omits the proper name of the cook, *Magirus* (Butcher, see above, p. 76), in order not to do him too much honour. Even in an ordinary will the beneficiary's name is not essential, it is enough to designate him in unmistakable fashion: Digest 28.5.9.8.

52. *Quae mecum attuleram.* Surely these were gifts of military objects made to him when he enlisted. If the pluperfect may be pressed, it is: which I had brought with me. Cf. Digest 49.17.4 pr., Tertullian *singulari de castrensi peculio: Miles praecipue habere debet quae*

them on a cord tied round his neck, that's best.[53] And I want a monument inscribed with golden letters—M. Grunter Hyena the piglet lived 999½ years; had he lived another half year, he would have completed 1000 years. My very good friends and consuls of my life, I ask you that you deal well with my body, season it well with good condiments of nut, pepper and honey, in order that my name be honourably mentioned for all time. My masters and relations, you who are attending this making of my will, let it be signed.' Bacony signed. Morselly signed. Spicy signed. Sausagelump signed. Porkrind signed. Charles Lamb signed.[54] Weddingpig signed."[55]

This *peculium castrense* meant nothing to the mass of *filiifamilias*. How was it possible, then, for the position to remain virtually unchanged till Constantine? An essential part of the answer is that, for the bulk of the population, these rules did not operate at all. In the urban areas at least, the vast majority of residents were have-nots, with not much to litigate about and certainly lacking the means to litigate with. In theory, if a beggar's son hired out his services, the wages paid him belonged to his father; so did the cigarette stubs he picked up from the gutter. The reality was totally different, he would never be bothered. Among the have-nots,

tulit secum in castra concedente patre. In the edition by Buecheler and Heraeus, incidentally, *attuleram* is followed by a colon; that is to say, *de Tebeste* and so on is connected with *liget* and so on, "from Tebest to Triest he may wear them." This is not impossible, but I prefer to take *de Tebeste usque ad Tergeste* with *attuleram* and start a fresh clause with *liget*.

53. Trying to reproduce the jingle in the Latin: *Tebeste—Tergeste—de reste.* An alternative: from Reeds to Leeds, he may wear them from his neck, as beads. The piglet has come from Tebessa in North Africa: Numidian auxiliaries were esteemed in the Roman army. He ended up at Triest, which city may conceivably have been chosen by someone who shared the notion that it was Thracian (see above, pp. 75–76, regarding Jerome's description of the *testamentum* as of Thracian origin). Istria (where Triest lies) is represented as Thracian by both Apollodorus and Skymnos; see Oberhummer, Pauly-Wissowa, *RE*, vol. 11 (1936), 395, s.v. *Thrake.* But I am almost tracing the piglet's peregrinations as if he were Gaius.

54. *Celsinus.* Haupt refers to Apicius, *De Re coquinaria* 8.7.12, giving the recipe for *porcellus Celsinianus*, sucking-pig à la Celsinus. I think Charles Lamb's essay on the origin of roast pig has earned him the honour of being Celsinus's English counterpart.

55. Maybe the pig to be used for the wedding-cake *mustaceus*, into which an enormous amount of lard was put; see Orth, Pauly-Wissowa, *RE*, vol. 2 (1923), 809; and Pauly-Wissowa, *RE*, vol. 11 (1922), 2092, s.v. "kuchen." A soldier's will would have been valid even if not signed by seven witnesses; but who would want to miss out any of these funny names?

whatever your status in the family, the little you acquired was yours from the age you had sufficient wits to acquire anything. In the slums, there was no distinction between a citizen and a Greek or Jew. Poverty is a great equalizer.[56]

The texts bear out what commonsense suggests. It suffices to recall the money distributions made by the Emperors. "To each member of the plebs of Rome I paid out 300 sesterces under my father's will; in the twelfth year of my tribunate I gave to each 400 sesterces for the third time. These distributions never reached less than 250,000 people"—so Augustus informs us in the account of his reign.[57] The younger Pliny, in his eulogy of Trajan, praises the Emperor for making provision for those among the poor whom illness or absence might prevent from collecting on the appointed date, "so that none of the Roman plebs, when you bestowed largesse, should feel himself a mere man rather than a citizen."[58] They did not sort out *patresfamilias* and *filiifamilias*; and the thought that the former might lay hands on what was doled out to the latter simply did not enter their minds. That whole system did not apply to this class.

It follows that our question is to be re-formulated far more narrowly: how to account for the long-lasting propertylessness of a *filiusfamilias* in the small, well-to-do stratum of Roman society? The prospect a *filiusfamilias* had of some day not only being rid of his seniors but also lording it over others was a help—more so than it would be today, since expectation of life was shorter. By the time you were thirty, statistically there was a good chance that your forebears were all gone. But in many cases, of course, they were not,[59] and it must have been precisely in the better off circles that people tended to live longer than average. Again, Roman law admitted emancipation, the dismissal of a son from paternal power, so that he achieved the status of a *paterfamilias*. But this remedy

56. So is wealth, but more on the level of choice than that of necessity.

57. *Mon. Anc.* 3.7ff., ch. 15.

58. Pliny the Younger, *Panegyricus* 25: *ne quis e plebe Romana, dante congiarium te, hominem se magis sentiret fuisse quam civem.* Nowadays, in such a context, to feel oneself a man would be considered more desirable than to feel oneself a citizen; except, I suppose, in France.

59. When the figures for expectation of life are not broken down, they include infants, among whom mortality was highest. But infants had no children. A *filiusfamilias* was interested in the mortality of those above the age of fifteen.

was in the discretion of the father; it was, moreover, no unmixed blessing for the son; and it remained rather uncommon.[60] I shall come back to it.

Another mitigating factor was the custom—manifestly confined to the haves—of letting a *filiusfamilias* administer and live on a special fund, *peculium*. Too much, however, should not be made of this. For one thing, the *paterfamilias* might reduce or completely recall it at any moment. For another, even while it operated, the *filiusfamilias* was not normally entitled to use it for any liberality. He might buy, sell, hire and so on, but not (unless specially authorized by the *paterfamilias*) make a gift, manumit a slave, leave anything by will. Even with respect to the *peculium*, that is, he lacked true independence. It is significant that, as I mentioned a moment ago, when Augustus courted the sympathies of the troops, it was a liberality, the bequeathing of stipend and booty, which he allowed them. Conversely, Tiberius, from the moment of his adoption by Augustus, conducted himself like a good *filiusfamilias*, which meant that "he neither made gifts nor performed manumissions."[61] No doubt the *peculium* he had[62] enabled him to transact any business necessary to his comfort. But liberality was open only to a *paterfamilias*, which he no longer was and in fact wanted to demonstrate that he no longer was.

Liberality—connected with *liber*, free—is the ultimate test of power, whatever the rules of a system. The parable of the two sons in Luke is set in a non-Roman world, where a son is not legally debarred from having

60. Digest 37.12.5, Papinian *XI quaestionum*, tells us of a father who behaved outrageously to his son and was forced by Trajan to emancipate him. When the son died, the father claimed his possessions as *parens manumissor*. I am happy to add that he ran into difficulties.

61. Suetonius, *Tib.* 15.2: *Nec quicquam postea pro patrefamilias egit . . . nam neque donavit neque manumisit.* The notice implies that, had he overstepped the rights of a holder of a *peculium*, he might have got away with it: his was, of course, an exceptional case. Suetonius goes on to record that even inheritances and legacies left to him Tiberius accepted only as additions to the *peculium* (Cf. Digest 15.1.7.5, Ulpian *XXIX ad edictum*, quoting Labeo). Again, he might have got away with treating them as independent property. As is well known, it was only Justinian who finally made such gifts the property of the *filiusfamilias* (and even then with a usufruct for his *paterfamilias*): Code 6.61.6, AD 529. It is interesting how early, in very special circumstances like those of Tiberius, the idea could be entertained.

62. Mentioned by Suetonius, *Tib.*; see the preceding footnote, on the matter of inheritances and legacies.

property of his own in his father's lifetime. The elder brother, however, stays at home on the farm, as a member of his father's household, working with him, being fed and clothed by him. No reason to doubt that he participates in all business of the farm—yet when it comes to liberality he has no standing. "Lo," he complains to his father, "these many years I serve thee, and yet thou never gavest me a kid that I might make merry with my friends."[63] Aristotle defines things owned as things I have power to alienate, and he adds specifically that by alienation he understands gift as well as sale.[64]

I think that this concentration of liberality in the Roman *paterfamilias* has enormous implications. Jolowicz in his section on *patria potestas* writes:[65] "One limitation there was ... *Patria potestas* has no concern with public law, and a son under power could vote and hold a magistracy just as freely as a *paterfamilias*." In a formal sense this is correct, like the proverbial saying that anybody may stay in the Ritz. Realistically, however, the private law restrictions on a *filiusfamlias* could not but carry over into the public, political domain. It is not only that, up to a point, a *paterfamilias* might give his *filiusfamilias* direct orders to embark on or refrain from a course of action. We must consider the overall effects of the legal setup. Say, a *filiusfamilias*, in the late Republic, wished to campaign for a magistracy. An ordinary *peculium* was not enough. He needed money, a great deal of it, to give away as largesse: which means, he needed the specific support of his *paterfamilias*. Admittedly there were unlawful ways of enrichment. Verres was a *filiusfamilias* with a *peculium*[66] and no doubt, at the start of his career at least, his father had conceded him the privilege to make gifts; but he soon managed to mobilize independent—and necessarily illicit—resources. But not everybody was as unscrupulous. In general, even in public life, a *filiusfamilias* remained rigidly controlled by his *paterfamilias*, who held the purse strings. It is difficult to conceive of a more powerful brake on any deviation from traditional family politics or, indeed, on any

---

63. Luke 15:29; see Daube, ZRG 72 (1955): 329ff.

64. Aristotle, *Rh.* 1.5.7.

65. Jolowicz, *Historical Introduction to Roman Law*, 2nd ed. (1952), 118. He quotes Digest 1.6.9, Pomponius *XVI ad Quintum Mucium*: *Filius familias in publicis causis loco patris familias habetur, veluti ut magistratum gerat, ut tutor detur.*

66. Cicero, *Verr.* 2.1.23.61, assigns importance to the *tabulae patris.*

tendency to detract in a thorough going way from the old-established scope of *patria potestas*. The means for such a platform would not be forthcoming. In a sense it was precisely in the public sphere that even a *filiusfamilias* with *peculium* was most fettered. Present day demands for student power arise out of the increased economic independence of the youthful bourgeois; they would be impossible without it.

Here it may be worth while to remind ourselves that the—from the political point of view—most important fruits of liberality were withheld from foreigners; above all, the Roman *cursus honorum*, open to a *filiusfamilias*—if supported by his *paterfamilias*. In his own state, of course, a foreigner could attain office, and do so whether or not his father was alive. Another example of containment in regard to liberality: a foreigner, by releasing a slave, made him free but could not make him a Roman citizen.[67] A *filiusfamilias*, indeed, owned no slave; he was propertyless. It is highly doubtful whether, in classical law, he could manumit a slave in his *peculium* even with his *paterfamilias*'s authority.[68]

The principal explanation of the tenacity with which the Roman upper classes —for it is only a question of that minority—stuck to these incredible rules is that they saw them as expressing, and safeguarding, their innate superiority over the foreign rabble and probably, in course of time, also over the rabble at home. There is no limit to the hardship people will bear for the sake of status, national or sectional. Here lies the clue, and if only we look, the sources contain a good many corroborative hints. Gaius, for example, repeatedly stresses that *patria potestas* is more exclusively Roman than other institutions which, under Roman law, apply to citizens only: it is found, he declares, among practically no other men.[69] Hadrian himself attached great weight to the exclusiveness of the institution.[70] In this feeling a *filiusfamilias*, however inconvenient his condition, was united with his Head. The rarity of emancipation, adverted to above, certainly has something to do with this. The better citizens were proud of this grotesque family structure.

67. Buckland, *The Roman Law of Slavery* (1908), 534, 594.
68. Buckland inclines to consider it possible: *The Roman Law of Slavery* (1908) 458–59, 718ff.
69. Gaius 1.55, 189; Cf. Gaius 1.9.2; Digest 1.6.3, Gaius I *institutionum*.
70. Gaius 1.55, 93–94.

The old English Public Schools, Eton, Charterhouse, Winchester, furnish a close analogy. Future historians will be hard put to it to understand how it was that, in the first half of the twentieth century, the boys attending these establishments would put up with strict hours, corporal punishment, fagging for seniors, no girls, no pictures, when all the time they could watch their contemporaries at the High School next door leading a jolly life. We have to do with the self-imposed discipline of an elite; rules, the original function of which is gone, but which are retained religiously for the sake of their present, almost more important function—to symbolize and strengthen the select and noble over against the common. If you think that I am over-emphasizing this aspect of the Public Schools, you are right. But there are amazing parallels. For instance, the Roman system of *patria potestas* evoked the admiration of certain foreigners, as do the Public Schools today. Dionysius of Halicarnassus, who was more Roman than most Romans, who sympathized with the senatorial party and who advocated statutory limitations on the manumission of slaves because he considered them an undesirable addition to the citizenry,[71] characterizes *patria potestas* as one of the points in which Rome is vastly superior to Greece; and he especially singles out the life-long power of the Head, his power over sons who are adults, married men, high magistrates.[72] The only major Public School founded in Britain in the past thirty years was founded by Kurt Hahn, a refugee from the Nazis on account of his race, who had previously directed a school on the English model in Germany.

There are other areas in Roman law which may be compared or contrasted. The laws imposing restraint on feminine luxury were often defended as protectors of native high-mindedness against alien vulgarity. On the other hand, it is clear that the Roman women, many of them, longed for that vulgarity. Livy represents a speaker against such a statute as pointing out that, while it might prevent jealousy between Roman women, they were all resentful at seeing their foreign rivals attractively decked out. A grievance of this nature, he adds, must weigh more heavily on women than it would on men who have offices, priesthoods and so on to make

---

71. Dionysius of Halicarnassus, *Ant. Rom.* 4.24; Cf. below, p. 91n9, pp. 114–15.
72. *Ant. Rom.* 2.26.1ff.

up for amenities foregone.[73] Once again, of course, we move in affluent company. The wives of the poor were affected neither by the enactment of a luxury-limiting measure nor by its abrogation, nor did their husbands hold offices and priesthoods. In the end, the women—the rich women—did get the restraints removed. The *filiifamilias* remained under the old-fashioned regime for many more centuries. But then, in the circles where it was of realistic significance, they as well as the *patresfamilias* might aspire to those honorific posts which rewarded hardship and which, remember, were closed to foreigners; and the old-fashioned rules, as I have explained, underlined the distinctiveness of the higher breed.

I would now, however, add a further point. From as early as the second century BC, the system of absolute propertylessness of a *filiusfamilias* developed the most unpleasant creaks. Sons wished their fathers dead, and more and more frequently the wish was father to the deed. No use shutting one's eyes to it. The references in literature must be taken seriously. In the comedies, naturally, the grimness of the situation is apt to be given a humorous coating. In Terence, a father is furious that his son, in his absence, allowed a court to sentence him to take to wife a poor pretty girl though he could have got out of it by providing her with a dowry and marrying her off to somebody else. The young man admittedly had not enough cash for the transaction but he could have raised it, the father exclaims, from the usurers. This argument, however, is countered by a slave who is in league with the son: "Who would lend him while you are alive?"[74] The audience would laugh, but the nasty implication is obvious. Another play of Terence's contains a rather tragic monologue of a father in the course of which he says in so many words that his sons are just waiting for his death.[75] The laughter quite ceases when we turn

73. Livy 34.7.5. The speaker is the tribune Lucius Valerius, advocating the abolition of the Oppian statute in 195 BC. Cf. below, p. 118n102. By the way, Sage, in Loeb Classical Library, *Livy*, vol. 9 (1953), 439, mistranslates 34.7.11. The *scilicet* introduces two rhetorical questions: "If you repeal the Oppian law, will it not still be in your discretion to forbid (if you so wish) what now the law forbids? Will your daughters, wives, even sisters be less *in manu* (subject to your control)?" The thought in 13 connects up with this: "They prefer their luxury to be in your discretion rather than in the statute's."

74. Terence, *Phorm.* 302–3.

75. Terence, *Adelphoe* 874: *meam mortem expectant.*

to serious literature. Cicero's earliest speech in a criminal trial was in defence of a man accused of murdering his father.[76] Suetonius comments on how different early Emperors viewed the terrible penalty prescribed for parricide: one would approve, another would be put off. There were enough cases of the crime for a ruler to develop his own style of dealing with it.[77] Seneca praises a father who did not cut the allowance of a son who had plotted his death.[78]

A *filiusfamilias* resorted to manifold devices to improve his lot. Prior to a senatusconsult of the first century AD, one of them was to go to the usurers who would lend him money, repayable when *patria potestas* came to an end, i.e. when great-grandfather, grandfather, father had passed on. It was an extremely risky business for a usurer: if the *filiusfamilias* died before becoming *sui iuris*, the money was lost.[79] Obviously, a usurer would try to get as much security as he could, by methods necessarily questionable. He could hardly enquire into the provenance of an article of value which the *filiusfamilias* handed him as pledge. Indeed, he might not mind it if the *filiusfamilias* thought of means of hastening the departure of a long-lived father. A senatusconsult about the middle of the first century AD had the definite, avowed aim of protecting a *paterfamilias* from the peril to his life if his son got into the hands of money lenders. It was called, the sources tell us, *senatusconsultum Macedonianum*, after a *filiusfamilias* Macedo who, in this situation, had killed his father; and it laid down that henceforth a person who lent money to a *filiusfamilias* could not sue for repayment even when the debtor became *sui iuris*.

In the eighteenth century the traditional account was declared apocryphal: the dastardly crime must have been perpetrated by the moneylender in the case, not the *filiusfamilias*. This theory, which so well chimes in with the romantic picture of ancient Rome, has become fairly fashionable; so much so that in the leading Latin dictionaries—Lewis and Short, Georges—Macedo is entered as the name of a Roman usurer. Another theory is that no murder took place at all. Most scholars, rejecting the account given in the sources, identify *filiusfamilias* with young

---

76. Cicero, *Rosc. Am.*

77. Suetonius, *Aug.* 33; *Claud.* 34; Cf. Seneca the Younger, *Clem.* 1.23.

78. Seneca the Younger, *Clem.* 1.15.2.

79. Cf. the remark quoted above, from Terence's *Phorm.*: "Who would lend him while you are alive?"

man—a fallacy which, on the subconscious level, underlies a good deal of thinking about the *filiusfamilias*, "child" in English, *Haussohn* in German. The senatusconsult, they believe, was designed to safeguard a young man from his improvidence: he should not waste his prospective wealth. But a *filiusfamilias* might be a mature statesman. As late as around AD 200 Ulpian writes that the regulation covers a *filiusfamilias* who is a consul.[80] Or take a citizen *sui iuris* who promises repayment of a loan to be made to him, then he is adopted by another citizen who thereby becomes his *paterfamilias*, and now he receives the loan. The senatusconsult, the jurists decide, does apply: the loan will never become actionable.[81] Conversely, if a *filiusfamilias* promises repayment of a loan to be made, then becomes *sui iuris* and now receives the loan, the senatusconsult does not apply, he can be sued.[82] It is not youthful extravagance which is the criterion, but solely the debtor's status as *filiusfamilias* and the resultant danger to him who stands between him and independence. It has been argued that a *filiusfamilias* heavily in debt would never commit parricide; on the contrary, as the usurers could proceed against him only when he was *sui iuris*, he would wish his *paterfamilias* many years of good health. But this is to look at the rules in a vacuum, totally disregarding what actually happens in these circumstances. I wonder whether the holders of this view have ever read the plays of Plautus. Once a *filiusfamilias* was involved with moneylenders, the latter, if he did not satisfy them, were in a position to blackmail him mercilessly. They could withhold further support of the grand life he was by now used to. Worse, they could threaten exposure of his loans, of the manner in which he had spent them, of the embezzlements and other offences he was guilty of in connection with them. At any rate, this is how the Romans saw it: from the speech of Cicero I just mentioned it may be gathered that heavy debts and a zest for high living ranked as standard motives for parricide in the trials.[83] I am afraid (as I have demonstrated

80. Digest 14.6.1.3, *XXIX ad edictum*.
81. Digest 4.6.6, Scaevola *II quaestionum*.
82. Digest 14.6.3.4, Ulpian *XXIX ad edictum*.
83. Cicero, *Rosc. Am.* 14.39: *Luxuries igitur hominem nimirum et aeris alieni magnitudo et indomitae animae cupiditates ad hoc scelus impulerunt*, "Doubtless, then, it was riotous living, the enormity of his debts and unbridled passions which drove the accused to this crime?" Cicero finds it easy to deal with these hypothetical imputations since his client lived quietly in the country.

in greater detail elsewhere)[84] the repulsive information transmitted concerning the occasion for the *senatusconsultum Macedonianum* is true.

There were indeed other awkward complications caused by the *filiusfamilias*'s disabilities. Say, a *filiusfamilias* studying at a place distant from home lends his allowance to a friend or has it stolen from him. Repayment or restitution is owing to his *paterfamilias*: the allowance remains the latter's property. So, in strictness, if the friend or the thief does not settle, the *filiusfamilias* has no action. Difficulties of this kind are discussed by several jurists.[85] The point to bear in mind always is that the parties involved belong to the comfortable fraction of the population; those on the right side of the case at least—not, necessarily, the thief.

84. Daube, *ZRG* 65 (1947): 261ff. On 308ff. I argued that a date under Claudius is likelier than one under Vespasian. I should have mentioned two of the texts quoted above, Suetonius, *Claud.* 34, and Seneca the Younger, *Clem.* 1.23, as lending support to my suggestion.

85. E.g. Digest 5.1.18.1, Ulpian *XXIII ad edictum*; 12.1.17, 44.7.13, Ulpian *I disputationum*. On how Cicero financed his son's studies at Athens, see Kroll, *Die Kultur der Ciceronisclen Zeit*, vol. 1 (1933), 118–19. A father's dishonest management of an estate left to him with a *fideicommissum* in favour of his son could be ended only by the Emperor's intervention: Digest 36.1.52, Papinian *XI quaestionum*; see Daube, *Studi in memoria di Emilio Albertario* (1950), 445ff.

4

Roman Society

Altruistic Dodges

I come to the second part of this Lecture, devoted to some hitherto neglected results of the compact nature of upper Roman society. It is well known that the mutual duties among the group went far beyond what would be expected nowadays. Recently, I did some work on evasions of law, dodges, at Rome and particularly on their social and economic setting.[1] One conclusion which emerged, and which I think is valid far beyond Roman law, was that dodges were the preserve of the well-to-do: the poor break the law, the rich get around it (or at least try to).

However, this is not what I want to enlarge on here. What I want to talk about is a specifically Roman phenomenon, anything but universal: an inordinately high proportion of dodges reported in the sources are operated from altruistic motives, in order to assist a friend or a relation in need, or even an inferior provided he is attached to you, a loyal slave, for instance, or a freedman.[2] For Cicero, when he inquires at length whether

1. A summary is printed in Daube, *Proceedings of the Classical Association*, 61 (1964): 28ff.

2. When I speak of altruistic motives, I am aware how vulnerable a notion this is. Psychoanalysts tell us that I may help you because I hate you; even orthodox psychology knows of the association of charity and self-satisfaction; and the instances of benevolence I am going to discuss are confined to those inside the group—my very point. Nevertheless I am undeterred, using the term altruistic in its naive signification, of that action which the ordinary person affected would describe as a good turn done to him.

one may or ought to do wrong for the sake of a friend, this is more than academic speculation; it is an acute problem.[3]

His answer is in the negative, but as the experts remind us,[4] as far as his own conduct is concerned, we often find him sailing near the wind. He would, for example, write to a judge before whom a friend is to be tried, saying that of course right must triumph, but the judge might wish to know that in Cicero's opinion the man is a splendid, upright citizen. I feel sure that Cicero knows what he is doing. He must not directly infringe the moral or legal code; but anything short of, that in the interest of a friend in trouble, is permissible or, indeed, obligatory. In a letter to his brother he expresses the view that the latter—who was then governor of Asia—had gone too far in interfering with the course of law on behalf of a friend. "In some matters," he writes, "there is no room for favours," "in some matters," so in general there is room.[5]

The Insolvent Debtor

The Digest tells us of a strange dispute among Republican lawyers.[6] I owe you 50 pounds and pay you 5. You return the five-pound note to me, by way of gift, and I immediately hand it to you again; and so on, till I have given you the same note ten times. Question: Have I paid you 5 pounds or 50?

At first sight it looks like one of those legendary riddles: Achilles and the tortoise; or Epaminondas, the Lacedaemonian, says, all Lacedaemonians always lie—can this, then, be true? But there, the old jurists are serious about this five-pound note, and it is finally the great

---

3. Cicero, *Off.* 3.10.43; *Amic.* 10.35ff. The problem has a long history before Cicero.

4. Kroll, *Die Kultur der Ciceronischen Zeit*, vol. 1 (1933), 60ff.; Kelly, *Roman Litigation* (1966), 56ff.

5. Cicero, *Epistulae ad Quintum fratrem* 1.2.10: *Via iuris eiusmodi est quibusdam in rebus ut nihil sit loci gratiae.* The point is noticed by Kroll, *Die Kultur der Ciceronischen Zeit*, vol. 1 (1933), 65. I shall not conceal the fact that Cicero's censure followed a visit paid him by the man hurt by the governor's action, and that this man was then praetor-designate.

6. Digest 46.3.67, Marcellus *XIII digestorum*; see Daube, *Proceedings of the Classical Association*, 61 (1964): 30; Watson, *The Law of Obligations in the Later Roman Republic* (1965), 208ff.

Servius whose decision is accepted: I have paid you 50. The explanation is that in ancient Rome infamy befell an insolvent debtor not only if it came to an auctioning off of his goods, but also if he got his creditors to be satisfied with less than the full amount, if *cum eis pactus est se soldum solvere non posse*.[7] In the case of the same note or coins being shoved to and fro, what happens in reality is that the creditor consents to an arrangement: he takes a portion of the debt and calls it quits. It is only in a formalistic sense, by way of fake, that he receives all. Why this jugglery? Because if the poor debtor is to be saved from infamy, the reality has to be covered up, and—here I come to my point—the creditor is prepared to help in this. From the fact that the question is taken up by a number of writers it looks as if this circumvention of the rigorous treatment of insolvency had been resorted to more than once; maybe in certain circumstances it became the thing to do. Legal opinion prior to Servius seems to have been prevalently against condoning it: the truth being that the debtor *pactus est se soldum solvere non posse*, he must suffer accordingly. From Servius on, the dodge is admitted and a creditor can avert infamy from the debtor who pays only part of what he owes.[8]

Slaves and Freedmen

Slaves and freedmen, too, "belong," and a generous master or patron will go to great lengths to nullify obstacles the law puts in the way of rewarding them. When, in 2 BC, Augustus restricted the number of slaves a man could free in his last will,[9] with such certainty were attempts at

---

7. *Tabula Heracleensis* 114–15; Bruns, *Font.*, 108. That the provision, or the gist of it, figured in the *Edict* is shown by Lenel, *Das edictum perpetuum*, 3rd ed. (1927), 79. He does not, however, refer to the text under notice. By the way, infamy on account of theft, assault or dolus befell a man not only if he was condemned in an action but also if he had compromised: Greenidge, *Infamia* (1894), 25, 130–31. The equation, as far as infamy is concerned, of a debtor's arrangement with a total seizure of his goods reveals a suggestive affinity of insolvency with those contemptible delicts.

8. For a dodge to help a man who needs a surety, Digest 12.6.18 (Ulpian *XLVII ad Sabinum*), see below, p. 116n96.

9. Legislation of this nature had been recommended by Dionysius of Halicarnassus some five years before: see above, p. 84, and below, pp. 114–15.

evasion anticipated that the statute itself contained a clause invalidating transactions designed to get around it.[10] It did not stop people from trying; of course not, since one could always contend that the transaction in question was no fraud on the law but within it.

For instance, an owner of four slaves, who was allowed only to release two, would bequeath the other two to an acquaintance, with a direction to free them. It seems that this stratagem was tolerated by the classics.[11] They did not tolerate another one. The statute provided that if a testator manumitted more than the permissible number, the gift would be valid for those named first, up to the limit. One master who wished to give freedom to more than he was entitled to wrote all their names in a circle, so that each could claim to be the first. Alas, the decision was that none would be free.[12]

Again, a freedman's patron was entitled to services, and furthermore he had a limited right of succession. It was permissible, however, for a freedman to buy off these burdens. There is evidence of a friendly dodge in this connection: the parties went through a fictitious redemption, that

10. Gaius 1.46: *lex Fufia Caninia quae in fraudem eius facta sint rescindit.*

11. Digest 35.1.37, Paul *singulari ad legem Fufiam Caniniam.* The legatee's role was not entirely shadowy: he did obtain the advantage of patronage. *E contrario,* I suppose that if a man appointed his son heir, directing him to manumit the supernumerary slaves, this would not have been approved since the son-heir would obtain nothing by manumitting them that he would not have obtained had the testator conferred freedom directly.

12. Gaius 1.46; see Daube, *LQR* 80 (1964): 225ff. The device was thought up by one who knew of the Delphic oracle which, to the question how the Seven Sages were to be ranked, had replied that their names should be arranged in a circle—each of them was first. The same legend inspired the idea of the Round Table by means of which King Arthur settled the quarrels about precedence among his knights: it is one more instance of the transplanting of a classical motif into medieval material. Significantly, the Round Table appears relatively late in the tales of King Arthur: it was in Ausonius's *Ludus Septem Sapientium,* popular in the France of the Middle Ages, that the romancers found the oracle. From King Arthur's Round Table derive not only all round table conferences and similar uses of this kind of seating but also the round robin of the fleet, the demands of mutineers signed in a circle in order to make it impossible to single out (and string up) the ringleaders. Occasionally nature might seem to write in a circle. Digest 1.5.15, Tryphoninus X *disputationum,* discusses the case of a slave-woman manumitted if and when she had borne three children. Evidently a fourth child would be born free. But there was a complication: this woman gave birth first to one child and then to triplets. Cf. Digest 1.5.16, 34.5.10.1, Ulpian VI *disputationum.*

is to say, a figure was named but the understanding was that the patron would never exact it. In this case, while the classical lawyers refused to cooperate, under Justinian's law it was no longer necessary to have recourse to a dodge since he allowed the gratuitous remission of the freedman's obligations.[13]

Fideicommissa

The whole institution of *fideicommissa*[14] came into existence as a device to leave your estate or some of it to a person the law said you could not leave it to. Under the law of the late Republic, you could not name as heir or legatee an alien, anyone who was proscribed, outlawed, or, if you belonged to the wealthiest class of the census, a woman. So a testator who wished his possessions to go to his Greek teacher would institute a Roman friend his heir, adjuring him to pass them on to the Greek. The nominal heir was under no legal compulsion to carry out the testator's desire; what force the latter had was founded entirely on religion and trust. Augustus legalized (and in the process, I shall argue, tamed) the procedure. Before that, however, it was manifestly a dodge of the type I am here concentrating on, for somebody else's benefit.[15]

Cicero reports the case of a rich citizen with a daughter.[16] He appointed a friend his heir and, in the will, mentioned that he had requested the heir to hand over the estate to his daughter. For Cicero, a father taking this course was asking what he was morally obliged in his daughter's interests to ask, *quod rogare debuisset.* The heir, however, not only denied that the request had ever in fact been put to him, but also expressed doubt as to whether, even had it been put, he could have complied. Why? It was contrary to the statutes (the *lex Voconia*

13. Digest 18.1.36, Ulpian *XLIII ad edictum;* Code 6.4.3, AD 529. See Daube, *Studi Arangio-Ruiz,* vol. 1 (1952), 192ff.; Daube, ZRG 76 (1959): 177ff.

14. Buckland, *Text-Book* (1963), 353ff.

15. The machinery is interesting. Moral pressure is substituted for legal, and also use is made of an interposita persona: the heir stands in front. See Daube, *Proceedings of the Classical Association* 61 (1964): 29.

16. Cicero, *Fin.* 2.17.55.

in particular) which, as a magistrate, he had sworn to uphold;[17] and he retained a large part of the estate.[18] Cicero clearly does not believe in the honesty of the man's scruples. But whether honest or not, they do illustrate the tension I referred to above between your duty within your circle and the more general dictates of rectitude.

The same tension dominates an affair brought up by Cicero against Verres; in fact the moral issue was here rather more complicated.[19] One Publius Trebonius wanted to provide for a proscribed brother. The method he chose was, if not exactly *fideicommissum*, something quite similar.[20] He appointed a number of friends and a freedman joint heirs, directing that each of them should bind himself by an oath to see that at least half of what he got would reach the proscribed Aulus Trebonius. On Publius's death, the freedman did take the oath. The others went to Verres, then *praetor urbanus*, who did two things for them. First he let them off the oath, so they could keep their portions without sharing with Aulus. Of this part of Verres's handling of the case Cicero more or less approves: after all, a *lex Cornelia* expressly prohibited any aid to an outlaw. But, secondly, Verres punished the freedman by depriving him of his portion, thus making it accrue to the portions of the others. This, according to Cicero, was motivated solely by Verres's contempt for the lower orders: he could not stand seeing a freedman come into a large fortune. There was no genuine good reason, Cicero holds, for this measure. The freedman could be blamed neither for obeying an instruction of his dead patron Publius

17. Cf. Cicero, *Off.* 3.10.43: *neque contra rem publicam neque contra ius iurandum ac fidem amici causa vir bonus faciet,* "neither contrary to the public good nor contrary to an oath and faith will a good man act for his friend's sake."

18. Not, it seems, all of it. He seems to have followed the advice of a number of persons he consulted, to the effect that he should let the woman have "no more than would have gone to her under the *lex Voconia*." I take this to mean one of two things: either that he should hand over only as much as would fall into a lower class of the census, or (see, Gaius 2.226) that he should hand over only half. Surely it does not mean—a possibility suggested by Rackham in the Loeb Clasical Libarary (Cicero, *Fin.* [1921], 142)—that he hand over nothing.

19. Cicero, *Verr.* 2.1.47.123f.

20. As *fideicommissum* was not yet at the time incorporated in the legal system, higher degree of variability is only natural; and it is perhaps somewhat unhistorical to confine the term to such arrangements as were recognized by the jurisprudence from Augustus onwards.

Trebonius nor for standing by his present patron Aulus Trebonius, despite his proscription.[21] If, in fulfillment of his oath, he was going to infringe the *lex Cornelia*, by actually giving something to Aulus, there would then be the time for a charge under that statute.

I shall not probe Cicero's argumentation, having said enough, I think, to demonstrate the role of those pre-Augustan *fideicommissa* as altruistic dodges—altruistic, that is, within the group. But I will add a word about subsequent developments. Augustus's recognition of *fideicommissa* was designed not only to support these arrangements (though I am not doubting for one moment that the official motivation is part of the truth) but also to control and indeed restrain them; at least it did have this effect. It is well to note that he left the heir free to destroy a *fideicommissum* by refusing the inheritance and thus creating intestacy.[22] As far as *fideicommissa* of single objects are concerned, this is not perhaps remarkable: it merely put them on the same level as ordinary legacies, which were equally gone if the heir of the will declined. But it was, of course, precisely in the case of a *fideicommissum hereditatis*, where the fideicommissary is to receive the estate in toto, that an heir was most likely to abstain. It was not till AD 73 that a senatusconsult (*Pegasianum*) ensured the operation of such a *fideicommissum*. By that time, *fideicommissa* had been thoroughly domesticated, generosity undesirable from the government's point of view suppressed.

Let us look at women, aliens, and persons out of step with the family legislation of the Principate. Women, it is true, had their position bettered: they could obtain even a large fortune by way of *fideicommissum*. But this was part of a general change of attitude in the question. They were rapidly becoming capable of being made heirs without restriction. We have the testimony of Gellius that by the middle of the second century at the latest the *lex Voconia* was quite obsolete.[23]

21. It would seem that the freedman was originally released by the father of Publius and Aulus. When the father died, the two sons became joint patrons.

22. True, if he himself was the person that would inherit on intestacy, he might get into difficulty with the praetor when claiming under the latter head; see Lenel, *Das edictum perpetuum*, 3rd ed. (1927), 363–64. What happened if he was a *suus* is controversial.

23. In Gellius 20.1.23 he represents Africanus as listing it together with other archaic statutes which, sound in their day, were totally obliterated. *[continues onto next page]*

As for aliens, I would distinguish four states. Augustus shrewdly entrusted jurisdiction in this matter to the consuls. No citizen in his senses would provide for an alien unacceptable to them, and if he did it would be useless or worse.[24] Though in special cases, say, that of an important foreigner who befriended Romans abroad, a *fideicommissum* would be upheld.[25] Then, second stage, came a period of more laxity— small *fideicommissa* were supervised by praetors—and for a while a *fideicommissorum* in favour of an alien was generally actionable.[26] Third stage: actionability was removed.[27] Which as one might expect, led to

---

[*note 23 continued from previous page*] When Gellius wrote this work, Africanus was already dead (Kunkel, *Herkunft und soziale Stellung der römischen Juristen* [1952], 172). Gaius was still alive, yet in Gaius 2.274 he speaks of the *lex Voconia* as in force: one of the numerous instances of mechanical copying from an older work—see below, pp. 262–63.

24. As is well known, under Augustus there was a proposal to suppress the free expression of opinion about the Emperor in a will. I suppose the sanction would have been forfeiture of the estate. Anyhow Augustus set his face against the measure: Suetonius, *Aug.* 56.1. This does not mean, however, that people did in practice feel free. Suetonius also tells us, *Aug.* 66.4, how anxious Augustus was to receive generous bequests from his friends, and they had to be flatteringly worded too (though he was not greedy—confirmed by Tacitus, *Ann.* 2.48). From Tacitus, *Ann.* 6.38, and Dio Cassius 58.26, we learn that Fulcinius Trio abused Tiberius in his will; Trio's sons concealing the will, Tiberius, who had got to know of it, ordered it to be divulged to the senate. But Emperors did not as a rule act this way, else the incident would not have been carefully recorded. What was generally expected is shown by the fact that Trio's sons were frightened. Tacitus, *Ann.* 3.76, mentions Tiberius's civil reaction when a prominent wealthy lady made bequests to anybody who was somebody, omitting him. Under Nero, if you left him too little, you ran the risk of forfeiture to the fisc because of ingratitude: Suetonius, *Nero* 32.2. If you perished in disgrace, institution of the Emperor as chief heir and eulogies might save something for your family: Tacitus, *Ann.* 14.31.11, 16.11.2, 16.19.5. Domitian, after a more promising beginning (Suetonius, *Domitianus* 9) ended up by being not much better than Nero: Tacitus, *Agricola* 43. Lucian, *Nigrinus*, 30, represents the philosopher as remarking that Romans while alive flatter their superiors and reveal the truth only in their wills when they need no longer dread the consequences. This seems to me a general criticism, with no special reference to the Emperor.

25. Gaius 2.285: *et fere haec fuit origo fideicommissorum*; Institutes 2.25 pr., primarily about codicils, with stress on Romans finding themselves abroad.

26. This stage is represented by the opening part of Gaius 2.285: *ut e peregrini poterant fideicommissa capere.*

27. Gaius 2.285: *sed postea id prohibitum est.*

testators once again going outside the law and asking an heir, though the request was not enforceable even as a *fideicommissum*, to show his loyalty by voluntarily giving so-and-so much to such-and-such an alien friend That this happened is apparent from the fourth and final move: Hadrian ordained that a *fideicommissum* for an alien was forfeited to the fisc— ruthlessly stamping out all evasion, all extra-legal benefaction.[28]

Fideicommissa for unmarried persons or persons married but childless went through a similar evolution, only, as the Emperors had here far more at stake, the end of the road was reached sooner. Augustus himself was the spiritual father of the legislation which, in order to promote marriage and improve the birthrate, placed enormous obstacles in the way of these recalcitrant groups getting inheritances or legacies. At first sight it looks as if *fideicommissa* for them had been valid, enforceable. This, of course, would have made hay of his laws, which might just as well—or almost as well—not have been enacted at all. The problem is so perplexing that most authorities look the other way.[29] To solve it, we must again realize that, to begin with, no express ban on *fideicommissa* was needed. In Augustus's reign, a testator would hardly try to achieve by means of *fideicommissum* what he could not achieve otherwise; he knew that a *fideicommissum* fell in the competence of the consuls, who would react strongly against anything the Emperor disapproved. But here, too,

28. Gaius 2.285: *sed nunc . . . senatusconsultum factum est ut ea fideicommissa fisco vindicarentur.* Hadrian had wide sympathies. At the same time, as we saw above, he was jealous of the old Roman institution of *patria potestas* and there are indications that he had his reservations about things foreign. For example, "he diligently cultivated Roman religious observances, but despised foreign ones": SHA, *Hadrian* 22.10. His eradication of *fideicommissa* for aliens belongs to this side of his thinking. I have received no assistance from historical works Henderson (*The Life and Principate of Hadrian* [1923], 206) cursorily refers to legislation about "technical questions such as inheritance and bequest," but he finds it of no interest: "Hadrian's rescripts concerning these must be left to the appreciative enthusiasm of the professional student."

29. De Zulueta is one of the very few to draw attention to it: *The Institutes of Gaius* 2 (1953), 115. Kniep, *Gai Institutionum Commentarius Secundus* (1913), 430, indeed draws the conclusion that the admission of *fideicommissa* for *caelibes* and *orbi* was the price Augustus had to pay for getting passed their exclusion from inheritance and legacy; so his victory, Kniep urges, was of a formal nature, these groups could in reality obtain most testamentary benefits. At least this theory is a genuine, courageous attempt to come to grips with the problem. But it is utterly incredible.

there followed a laxer period when a *fideicommissum* was actionable, or more probably, the jurists argued that it might be.[30] This phase, however, did not last long. The senatusconsult of AD 73, which I have already mentioned, once for all put a stop to any attempt at circumvention: a *fideicommissum* for a person against whom these laws were directed was to be no more actionable than if he had been named heir or legatee,[31] and indeed, like an ordinary inheritance or legacy it would go either to other, worthy beneficiaries under the will or, if none existed, to the treasury.[32] So here, already Vespasian closed the loophole which, with regard to aliens, was closed only by Hadrian. What is relevant for us is that such extreme measures were required to prevent testators favouring people contrary to the spirit of the laws.

The Undowered Bride

My last illustration will be dodges to make a dowry appear larger than it is or indeed to simulate the existence of a dowry where none has been given. I shall delineate the background somewhat more fully than is strictly necessary, first because the figure of the *indotata*, the undowered bride, is rather touching, and maybe I can induce somebody to write her history, in life and in literature; and secondly, because the case is instructive as to the very special complications which are apt to affect our legal evidence as distinguished from all the rest. One difference which strikes one right away is that whereas historians, playwrights, orators and so on from early times pay considerable attention to the *indotata*, prior to the Byzantine period she plays a negligible part in the writings of the lawyers.

---

30. Gaius 2.286, 286a. Note that whereas in 2.285, concerning aliens, we are told that *poterant capere*, in both 2.286 and 286a, concerning *caelibes* and *orbi*, we are told that *videbantur capere posse*.

31. Gaius 2.286a: *capere posse prohibiti sunt*, with the same meaning as in 2.285 quoted above.

32. Gaius 2.286a: *eaque translata sunt ad eos . . . aut ad populum*. This clause corresponds to *sed nunc* etc. in 2.285; except that in the case dealt with in 2.285 there was an interval between the establishment of non-actionability of a *fideicommissum* and its penal redirection, while in that dealt with in 2.286a the one senatusconsult declared a *fideicommissum* non-actionable and a *caducum*.

The ideas voiced about her in general literature are strongly influenced by Greek models. The word itself is doubtless a translation of *aproikos*, maybe also of *anekdotos*. We find it in the comedies of Plautus and Terence, in comments on the advantages of an *indotata* and equally— regardless of the inconsistency—on the magnanimity of him who takes one. It should be realized, however, that the very concept *indotata* presupposes a well-to-do society where a dowry is the rule: you speak of a girl as *indotata* only because *au fond* her situation is not what one would expect. Among the proletariat the fact would not be worth noting.[33] The truly prevailing attitude peeps out even in the comedies in the—Greek— sanction that the ravisher of a girl must marry her without a dowry; so this is, after all, unpleasant. The daughters of Fabricius Luscinus and Cn. Scipio, as their fathers were too devoted to public service to provide for them, were dowered by the state.[34] Appius Claudius (who dedicated a book to Cicero) never forgot that his father left him in such straitened circumstances that he had to give away a sister without dowry.[35] Horace advises Scaeva not to beg from his benefactor too flagrantly, by saying "my sister is *indotata*, my mother destitute";[36] and Martial mocks a father embarrassed to scrape together a dowry for an overaged daughter.[37] Evidently, a dowry is highly desirable.

The word *indotata* is not met in good classical prose; presumably it is not yet quite incorporated in Latin.[38] In the rhetoricians, the Greek rule just mentioned, with some modification, grows into a favourite theme: the girl at her father's bidding may choose whether her ravisher is to suffer

33. Cf. above, p. 71n19, on the formation of negatives: *confiteri, confessus, inconfessus. Dotare* is coined in an era when it signifies a striking act, and the *dotata* is an exception. Indeed, when we look at the Roman population as a whole, she never ceases being that. But, in the upper stratum where a giving of dowry becomes the thing to do, it is the omission which may receive notice—hence the appearance of the term *indotata.*

34. Valerius Maximus 4.4.10; Appuleius, *Apol.* 18.

35. Varro, *de re Rustica* 3.16.2.

36. Horace, *Epistulae* 1.17.46.

37. Martial 7.10.14: *poscit iam dotem filia grandis.*

38. Cicero once uses it in a tropical sense: the civilian Scaevola's art was *indotata et incompta*, "undowered and unadorned," whereas Crassus enriched her with *dote verborum*, "a verbal dowry" (*de or.* 1.55.234). This looks a deliberately decorated, "dowered" way of putting it.

death or to marry her.[39] Not surprisingly, the alternative death—marriage is so stark and dramatic that in course of time the quality of the marriage as undowered recedes into the background: in the elder Seneca we still find the attribute *indotata* in the law, in Quintilian it has dropped out.[40]

The classical jurists rarely, if ever, use the verb *dotare*;[41] and they never describe a woman as *indotata*.[42] In fact, the adjective is confined to Justinianian statements. It does not occur in the *Codex Theodosianus*. Of the four constitutions in the *Codex Justinianus* which contain it, three are from Justinian and the fourth, though ascribed to Alexander, some three hundred years before, is falsified.[43] Similarly, though it is found over a

---

39. *Pace* Bonner, *Roman Declamation* (1949), 89ff., this is Greek. Code 9.13.1.2, which he adduces in support of a Roman setting, is very late, from Justinian, AD 533, and directed against Hellenistic-Oriental practices. Jewish law, for instance, knows of circumstances where the man guilty of rape or seduction must marry the woman who, however, may refuse him: *Babylonian Ketuboth* 39b; Philo, *De Specialibus Legibus* 3.71.

40. The cases under the law are amusing. 1. The father delays producing his daughter for the purpose of choosing, thus keeping the ravisher on tenterhooks. 2. The ravisher flees, the father gives his daughter to somebody else, the ravisher returns, and now the father claims that his daughter may still opt—it being virtually certain in the circumstances which way. 3. The girl chooses marriage but the ravisher denies the deed, he is convicted in a trial, and now the girl claims to have a free option again. 4. A twin is ravished and hangs herself. The father produces the other twin who demands that the ravisher be executed: as nobody notices the substitution this is done. The substitution is discovered and the father charged with causing the young man's death. 5. A man ravishes his absent brother's fiancée. At their father's intercession she chooses marriage. Later the ravisher-husband catches the returned brother in adultery and, though their father again intercedes, kills him. He is disowned by the father. 6. A rich man asks a poor girl's father for her hand and is refused. Father and daughter are shipwrecked and find themselves on the suitor's land. He again entreats the father, who silently weeps. He marries her. Returned, the father wishes his daughter to exercise the option—in which direction is obvious. 7. A married man ravishes a girl. She chooses marriage. He divorces his wife, who charges him with unjust, groundless divorce. 8. A young man in one night ravishes two girls. He is condemned to death by one, to marriage by the other. Here are the sociable aspects of Roman law for you, if you have done with the social ones.

41. Beseler, *ZRG* 57 (1937): 35–36, says never, and he may well be right.

42. Levy, *Der Hergang der römischen Elzescheidung* (1925), 12.

43. Code 5.17.1, Alexander, AD 229. It is a pity that Varro's *Ling.* takes no note of this fact, which was already seen by Mitteis, *Römisches Privatrecht* (1908): 70, and naively gives 229 as the date.

dozen times in the Digest, all the passages are spurious and probably all due to the compilers.[44]

Why no *indotata* in the classics, and why does she crop up in later dicta? Under the classical regime, technically, she raises no problem: there is no enforceable duty to provide a dowry,[45] and moral or humanitarian considerations are accorded little room in the discussions. Things change as time goes on. The concern not to have a decent girl undowered finds more expression, sentiment is allowed to intrude, and besides, the father's discretion is gradually curtailed: by Justinian, dowry has become a legal or at least semi-legal obligation (for the well-to-do, it goes without saying: in this matter, too, the traditional expositions of Roman law tend to generalize what in reality applied to a tiny fraction of the population). It is as a result of this development that quite a few old decisions are revised

---

44. Take Digest 21.2.24, Africanus *VI quaestionum*. This connects up with fragment 22.1, Pomponius *I ex Plautio*: a woman buys land and hands it over as dowry, a third party claims to be owner and is successful in his action, the woman may proceed on the ground of eviction at once (without waiting for the marriage to end) *quasi minorent dotem habere coepisset, vel etiam nullam si tantum maritus optulisset quanti fundus esset,* "since she has a reduced dowry from this moment, or also none if the husband paid as much as the land was worth." The portion from *vel etiam nullam,* "or also none," is interpolated. Besides being (or trying to be) over-meticulous, it gets a great deal wrong. It assumes that the land is all the dowry there is, whereas that may or may not be so; and it distinguishes between the case where, as a result of the third party's action, the dowry is merely reduced because somehow or other the husband managed to pay less than the full value of the land and the case where the dowry is wiped out because he had to pay up. None of this, of course, is envisaged by the classical author: his argument was simply that the eviction had an immediate adverse effect on the dowry, justifying immediate regress by the woman-buyer of the land (an eminently practical decision). It should also be observed that the interpolation reckons with simple damages whereas the classic was no doubt thinking in terms of double the price. If we now go on to Digest 21.2.24, we are told that if the husband himself proves to be the owner, then, as there has been no eviction by means of an action (but a sort of automatic self-eviction), the legal situation is different *quamvis aeque indotata mulier futura sit,* "though the woman will equally be going to be without dowry." Whether or not other bits of this fragment are spurious, the words quoted, it is clear *(aeque,* "equally"), refer back to that interpolated clause in 22.1 which remarks on the possibility of elimination of the dowry. They must have been inserted when this section of the Digest title was put together—by the compilers.

45. Except, it would seem, in special cases from Severus and Caracalla, about AD 200: Digest 23.2.19, Marcian *XVI institutionum.*

and the word appears. Some of these interpolations were spotted as early as by Faber in the seventeenth century. Ulpian, for example,[46] puts this case: I hand over an object to someone contemplating marriage, on the terms that ownership is to pass for the purpose of dowry if and when the event takes place. I die before it takes place. As at this moment my heir becomes owner and—this is important—as there is no binding contract to which he would succeed, the arrangement falls to the ground. So far the text makes sense. Now follows an appendix: "But it is more benign to impose on the heir the necessity to consent in order that the woman should not be *indotata*."

One fragment, though it does not contain the word, very much reflects the new trend. It is attributed to Paul and constitutes something of a proclamation in the Digest title on dowry: "It is in the public interest that women should have their dowries safe, on account of which they can marry."[47] No classic could have written that they can marry because of their dowries. In its original context the fragment had to do with privileged creditors, who, when an insolvent debtor's goods are auctioned, need not share with the rest but, as far as possible, are satisfied in full. Dowry was privileged (as was, for example, a ward's claim against his tutor): if a husband's goods were auctioned, his wife got her dowry entire, before other creditors took their dividends.[48] Already we have arrived at a far more circumscribed and sober range of the dictum.

We can, however, establish exactly what Paul wrote. He dealt with the case of a girl taken to wife before she had attained marriageable age. The man went bankrupt. Was she a privileged creditor? On the one hand, there was no legal marriage, hence no valid dowry; on the other, if the two stayed together, a legal marriage would ensue and the dowry would come into operation.[49] Paul held that she was privileged, and it was in arguing

46. Digest 23.3.9.1, *XXXI ad Sabinum*; see Buckland, *Text-Book* (1963), 230n7. Varro's *Ling.* is unaware of the position.

47. Digest 23.3.2, Paul *LX ad edictum*: *Rei publicae interest mulieres dotes salvas habere, propter quas nubere possunt.*

48. Lenel, *Pal.*, 1(1889), 1078; Lenel, *Das edictum perpetuum*, 3rd ed. (1927), 429.

49. Digest 12.4.8, Neratius *II membranarum*, is relevant. If a dowry was given where a couple were under marriageable age, Servius had allowed *condictio* at once. Neratius was prepared to leave the matter in suspense: *condictio* would lie only if and when they separated before reaching marriageable age, but for the moment there was no *condictio* since, if they

this decision that he said: "For it is in the public interest that this girl, too, should obtain her full claim, in order that on reaching marriageable age she can be married to the man." We actually have this explanation preserved in another part of the Digest.[50] The compilers, by a method they employed in many other cases,[51] generalized the statement[52] and accorded it a prominent place in a basic title, where it now says something quite different, in accordance with the new philosophy.[53]

The *indotata*, then, is absent from the classical evidence. Yet this is just the consequence of the technical preoccupation of the jurists. Socially and economically she played her role in that period no less than later, and, at times, even in reading the legal discussions we can sense her

---

stayed together, the relationship would become marriage, with the dowry valid, and the interval was no more intolerable than where a dowry was given by a fiancée prior to her wedding.

50. Digest 42.5.18, Paul *LX ad edictum: Interest enim rei publicae et hanc solidum consequi, ut aetate permittente nubere possit.*

51. Daube, ZRG 76 (1959): 176ff.

52. They cut out *enim* and the reference to age, they replaced *solidus* by *salvus*, and they turned the singular *haec* into the plural *mulieres.*

53. As usual, the revision has been somewhat clumsy, not thorough enough. Strictly Digest 23.3.2 advocates the safe restitution of a dowry with a view to remarriage. It is true that the unambiguously final *ut possit* of 42.5.18 is replaced by the vaguer *propter quas possunt.* But at first sight the text still appears to contemplate what restitution of the dowry will enable a woman to do in the future. That is of course not what the compilers mean: they mean generally that dowries make possible marriages, first marriages. In the original version, there was indeed restitution with a view to a future marriage, namely, that which would come about once the girl reached the requisite age.—Digest 24.3.1, Pomponius *XV ad Sabinum*, opening the Digest title on restitution of dowry, has undergone a similar fate. "The cause of dowries always and everywhere takes precedence; for it is also in the public interest that dowries should be preserved for the women since it is extremely necessary that females should be dowered for the procreation of offspring and the populating of the state with children," *Dotium causa semper et ubique praecipua est; nam et publice interest dotes mulieribus conservari, cum dotatas esse feminas ad subolem procreandam replendamque liberis civitatem maxime sit necessarium.* The generalization is betrayed right away by "always and everywhere". These words and the portion from "for it is also in the public interest" are spurious. (Beseler, ZRG 57 [1937]: 36, rejects the entire fragment, which seems too radical.) Exactly what case Pomponius discussed, it is impossible to say. It could have been that surviving in Digest 23.3.24, from the same book (it follows 24.3.1 in Lenel, *Pal.*, 2 (1889), 120); but one could think of any number of others—like 42.5.18, quoted above, or 24.3.66.2, Javolenus *VI ex posterioribus Labeonis.*

standing in the background. In this connection the stratagems adverted
to in introducing this topic are significant: a woman with no dowry will be
represented as bringing one, or a woman with a small dowry as bringing
a large one. Already the Republican jurists examined such legacies by
husbands as "On account of the money given me by way of dowry, let
my heir pay out fifty" when, in reality, less or nothing had been given as
dowry; and they held that the figure named was payable—a doctrine
carried on by the classics, confirmed by Severus and Caracalla and
adopted by Justinian.[54] Modern authorities mostly take it for granted that
the testators must have slipped up.[55] It is far more likely, however, that
at least some were conscious of the discrepancy; and that they acted as
they did because they cared not only for the woman's financial prosperity
but also for her and her family's reputation. If so, that would have greatly
facilitated the decision to recognize these bequests.[56]

In an allied case, from Celsus,[57] we are expressly told that the testator
knew. Here a dowry had been given but the husband had returned it to

54. Digest 33.4.6, Labeo *II posteriorum a Javoleno epitomatorum*, quoting Servius,
Cascellius, Alfenus Varus and Ofilius; 33.4.1.8, Ulpian *XIX ad Sabinum*; Institutes 2.20.15.

55. E.g. Riccobono, *ZRG* 43 (1922): 280; Beseler, *ZRG* 53 (1933): 17. By contrast,
Voci, *Diritto Ereditario Romano*, vol. 2, 2nd ed. (1963), 326, does not confine the doctrine
to error. Riccobono adduces stipulations taking place after divorce, but these are not
necessarily perfect parallels. E.g. Digest 45.1.21, Pomponius *XV ad Sabinum*, considers
a promise, made after divorce, to return so-and-so much that was given as dowry when,
in reality, nothing or less had been given. Admittedly the promiser seems to be in error.
But, then, the setting of a promise *divortio facto* is utterly different from that of a legacy
left *constante matrimonio*. In the former, we shall hardly look for a dodge resorted to by
the ex-husband in order to procure his ex-wife a special advantage material or in respect
of reputation. In the case of a legacy during marriage, such devices make sense. Actually, I
wonder whether, if a legacy of the kind under review could be definitely proved to be the
result of error, it would not be ineffective.

56. It would have facilitated it whatever its technical basis. The latter, incidentally,
varies in different periods and with different jurists. It was certainly not just *falsa
demonstratio non nocet*.

57. Digest 31.21, *XX digestorum*. I agree with Levy, *ZRG* 46 (1926): 419 (against
others, e.g. Schulz, *Einführung in das Studium der Digesten* [1916], 49) that while *hoc tamen
praetextu usus esset* is spurious, the clause *quasi dotis reddendae nomine eam summam legaret*
is an essential element in the presentation of the case. As for *hoc tamen . . .*, the testator
needs no pretext in order to make a bequest. As for *quasi dotis reddendae . . .*, this is the
point: he leaves the money as if it were owing as dowry.

his wife during marriage. In full awareness he left her a legacy of forty by way of repayment of dowry. The legacy was upheld. In general, in Celsus's time, the return of a dowry during marriage was an invalid gift of *vir* to *uxor*. It was valid, however, in exceptional situations, say, the wife had pressing debts.[58] We may assume that in the present case such a situation had occurred, but the husband gallantly covered it up by his misleading phrasing of the legacy. That some greedy heir, unwilling to pay it out, exposed the scheme was not his fault.

We can unearth a dodge which the jurists did not allow. The Digest contains an extract from Julian,[59] in its present form quite incongruous. The main part is a long rigmarole, that if I make you a gift of money on the understanding that you should lend it to me, it is neither gift to you nor loan to me. Then comes an appendix reminiscent of one cited above: "It is more benign that it should be gift and loan." Indeed, why ever not? Why ever should I not be able to make you a gift of money even though for the moment I need the cash and take it back as a loan from you? In another part of the Digest a decision admitting such an arrangement is actually preserved,[60] and it is obvious from the details that the decision was needed not because of any difficulty of principle but because of a complication of the particular case, having to do with the *lex Cincia*.[61]

58. Digest 23.3.85, Scaevola *VIII digestorum*; 24.3.20, Paul *VII ad Sabinum*; see Wolff, *ZRG* 53 (1933): 324ff., without reference, however (unless I have overlooked it) to 31.21.

59. Digest 12.1.20, *XVIII digestorum*.

60. Digest 39.5.33.1, Hermogenian *VI iuris epitomarum*.

61. That statute rendered a gift above a certain amount unenforceable; that is to say, once the gift was fully carried out it could not be attacked, but so long as the donee had to go to court for it, the donor had an *exceptio*. (The statute was directed against bribery. The idea—a not unreasonable one—was that the moment the man from whom you wanted favours had definitely cashed in, he was free again and in a position to act for or against you as he thought fit. In connection with the purchase of votes we know that candidates often deposited the monies with a *sequester*, who was to pay voters if and only if they had done what was expected of them: this method gave security to both parties, the candidates and the voters; see Mommsen, *Röm. Strafr.* [1899], 869.) In the case in question a money gift exceeding the statutory limit was made, on the terms that it should be lent to the donor. This produced a neat problem: when the loan was reclaimed, could the borrower—donor say that he was being sued contrary to the *lex Cincia*, i.e. that plaintiff was going to law for the gift? Or if the borrower-donor had promised *[continues onto next page]*

The puzzle is solved if we take note first of the provenance of the fragment—it goes back to Julian's discussion of restoration of dowry[62]— and secondly of a rescript by Severus and Caracalla dealing with a related case.[63] It emerges that Julian was concerned with a prospective husband giving his fiancée money on the understanding that he would receive it back as dowry: evidently in order that she should not be without a dowry or with too small a one.[64] This transaction was not recognized, neither his transfer to her nor hers to him; which meant that on termination of the marriage, she could not claim this sum as her dowry. The text doubtless suffered some interference before it reached the compilers. But it is most probably they who resolved to generalize it, lift it from its specific

---

[note 61 continued from previous page] repayment of the loan (a frequent type of promise), could he avail himself of the *exceptio in factum* (Lenel, *Das edictum perpetuum*, 3rd ed. (1927), 513) "*si non donationis causa promisi me daturum*," i.e. could he maintain that he had made the promise with a view to gift? The verdict, however, went against him: his original transfer of the sum to the donee had fully completed the gift, and when he received the money back by way of loan that was a new, different affair no longer falling under the statute. Some critics have taken exception to the fragment, the diction of which is below classical standards. But Schulz is right (*Roman Legal Science* [1946], 223): Hermogenian is so late as to be practically post-classical, hence there is no point in purifying the text, he just did not write like a classic. As for the substance of the ruling, I see no reason to assume that it differs from the classical position. Even if it did differ, my argument would remain valid: the transaction would have been rejected only for the sake of a scrupulous (over-scrupulous) adherence to the *lex Cincia*, not because of anything inherently wrong with transfer of money as gift followed by re-transfer as loan.

 62. *Soluto matrimonio*; see Lenel, *Pal.*, 1 (1889), 369.

 63. Code 5.3.1, about AD 200, quoted by Lenel, *Pal.*, 1 (1889), 369. The Emperors reject a Greek mode of creating a dowry, namely, by means of a fictitious acknowledgment of receipt of a dowry on the part of the husband (without even the formality of transfer and re-tranfer). Much literature on *donatio in dotem redacta* and allied topics; see, e.g. Mitteis, *Reichsrecht und Volksrecht* (1891), 270ff., 297–98, 476ff.; Meyer, *Klio*, 6 (1906), 437–38; Rabel, *ZRG* 28 (1907): 29–30; Jones, *Law and Legal Theory of the Greeks* (1956), 176. Betti's discussion of 12.1.20, incidentally, in *Bull. Ist. Dir. Rom.* 42 (1934): 322ff., by disregarding the palingenesia of the fragment, completely misses the point (as does Kaser in following him, in *Das Römische Privatrecht*, vol. 2 [1959]: 57). As a result, he also misconstrues the relation between this decision and Code 5.3.1. He overlooks, too, the special reference of Digest 39.5.33.1 to the *lex Cincia*.

 64. Very likely, once again the purpose was not purely practical, to provide for her—or it could have been attained by an appropriate stipulation—it was also to make her look a better match.

application to dowry, suppress all mention of this institution and thus fit it for inclusion in *De rebus creditis*, their basic title about loan, where it would figure as a rule about that contract.[65] To suit the new scope, however, the original decision had to be turned into its very opposite, rejection of the transfer and re-transfer had to become recognition— hence the "benign" ending (in conformity with the decision concerning the *lex Cincia*) by which gift and loan are both validated.

Here, then, we come upon a case from the classical epoch where the husband himself attempted, unsuccessfully, to dower his bride: an altruistic machination, whether his primary object was to secure her materially or to save her from disgrace or to do both. There could hardly be a better illustration of the extraordinary intricacies presented by our legal sources. Let me remind you that while the classics display incomparably less interest in the *indotata* than does Justinian, in the text before us it is the latter who has eliminated the dodge in favour of a poor girl. That problem is no longer directly exhibited in this passage, and it is only by a critical analysis that we can establish its occurrence in the older, classical work on which Justinian draws.

Many hundreds of years later, in the *Chartreuse de Parme*,[66] the Marquis Crescenzi is about to marry Clelia Conti. Her father, Fabio Conti, is shocked to hear her called *une fille sans dot*. He purchases an enormous estate, with the Marquis's money, to serve as dowry. Stendahl tells us that the Marquis however, an *être eminemment logique*, regrets the expense of the transaction.

I cannot resist the temptation, before leaving the subject of marriage, to introduce an episode from early Roman history, the dispute about the maid of Ardea,[67] which enshrines a motif recurrent in countless variations in many literatures: the girl between two suitors, one of her own humble class, the other higher up. As far as I can see, the motif has not so far been

---

65. It is noteworthy that even now the text does not use the unambiguous technical term for "to make a loan," *mutuo dare*, but throughout operates with the wider notion *pecuniam credere or in creditum dare* which one could imagine to have figured in Julian's dowry case. That the compilers were adepts at generalizing classical utterances and diverting them to different topics I have repeatedly observed: see above, p. 22n36, pp. 102–3, p. 105n61, and below, p. 116n96.

66. Chapter 23.

67. Livy 4.9.

isolated; it does not figure in Stith Thompson.[68] Yet we meet it constantly, in folksong and elaborate poetry, in fiction and plays; not to mention reality. Think of little Em'ly in *David Copperfield*, courted by Ham, her cousin, and Steerforth; of the film *Le jour se lève*;[69] of the feeling of the immigrant group in *West Side Story* that their young women should take "one of their own kind." The girl may be enticed by the glitter or be loyal to her pal; or the latter may represent an inferior life unworthy of her, while the prince is to raise her to the status she deserves. One of the two may take her against her will. Again, she may find her choice opposed by her family, or indeed some of them may urge her one way and some the other. Often it is the mother who favours the ambitious match. Not always, however: in the memorable quarrel between Sancho Panza and his wife concerning their daughter's future, it is the wife who represents sturdy, vulgar commonsense while he insists that only a grandee will be good enough. Of course, they need not have become so excited since no grandee has as yet asked for Mary Sancha's hand.[70] There are all sorts of combinations. The two rivals may be one, or virtually one: the lowly one, for example, may test the lady by disguising himself as a person of consequence, or by commissioning such a person to propose to her. *Così fan tutte* comes to mind.

About the middle of the fifth century BC there lived at Ardea, a Latin community not far from Rome, a fatherless girl of the plebeian order, whose beauty was the cause of a public disaster. She was wooed by a plebeian and an aristocrat. Her mother, wishing her a splendid alliance, directed her to accept the nobleman. Her guardians, on the other hand, were biased in favour of their fellow-plebeian and bade her marry him. She herself was not asked, it seems, and we do not know what her preference was. The controversy was submitted to the magistrates, who decided for the mother. Thereupon the plebeians abducted the girl by force. The nobles counterattacked. The plebeians, driven out of the city, besieged the latter and sacked the farms belonging to their enemies. These now invoked the aid of Rome, with which Ardea had a treaty. As the plebeians turned for help to the Volsci, a veritable war ensued. (It

68. Thompson, *Motif-Index of Folk-Literature*, 6 vols. (1955–58).
69. I believe the superb, original version can no longer be seen.
70. Cervantes, *Don Quixote*, pt. 2, bk. 3, ch. 5.

sounds very modern.) In the end, the Romans defeated the Volsci and subdued the plebeians.

It has recently been claimed[71] that the anecdote was invented (or, insofar as historical, preserved) in order to inculcate the gist of the *lex Canuleia*, the Roman statute of around 445 BC which rendered plebeians eligible to marry patricians. But whatever lesson may be aimed at, it cannot be this. Quite apart from the fact that the events are laid at Ardea, not at Rome[72]—if they were intended to exemplify this pro-plebeian reform, the girl would have to be a patrician and her tutors against her stooping to a union with a plebeian; or alternatively, she could be plebeian, but in that case the resistance to the union ought to come from her patrician suitor's people; or yet again, she could be a plebeian on whom a haughty member of the upper order had illicit designs—one remembers Virginia (or even Lucretia)—so her guardians would object to misuse and demand honourable wedlock. Any of these versions would do, but not that before us. If you want a story to celebrate academic integration, you will not put the case of a negro's advisers forbidding him to register as a student at a wide-open, welcoming university; your case must be that of the university authorities forbidding the secretary to enroll him. It is most unlikely that the anecdote purposes to convey anything at all concerning the *lex Canuleia*. But if it does, it refers to a kind of Black Power movement, an ultra-radical section among the plebeians who deplored the statute and advocated abolition of the *conubium* between the orders introduced by it. I cannot believe this.[73]

71. Ogilvie, *Latomus*, 21 (1962), 477ff. The main conclusions of this interesting article are summarized by Ogilvie in *Comm. Livy 1–5* (1966), 547–48.

72. Volterra in *Studi in onore di Antonio Segni* (1966), 3ff., gives strong reasons for rejecting Ogilvie's assumption that Ardean marriage law is here thought of as identical with Roman.

73. Besides the innovation of the *lex Canuleia*, there are two more provisions, according to Ogilvie, which the anecdote is designed to bring out: namely, that marriage might be without *manus*, and that marriage without *manus* might be entered into by a woman *sui iuris* against the will of her guardians. However, again quite apart from the precarious identification of Ardean law with Roman, first, it is incredible that either of these provisions of the internal law would be illustrated by means of an incident leading to a war. Secondly, the possibility of marriage without *manus* surely did not need to be illustrated at all. Thirdly, it is extremely doubtful whether, in the [continues onto next page]

Really, the existence of *conubium* between the plebeians and aristocrats of Ardea is taken for granted by the narrative; there is not the faintest indication of a problem in this respect. The narrative is in fact antiplebeian, or at least against the plebeians of Ardea, declared to be inferior to the Roman ones who, when they seceded from their city, deliberately refrained from ravaging the farms.[74] The noble suitor of the maid is praised for being attracted by her beauty alone, without looking for the usual advantages of a match. Whereas the mother has the girl's welfare at heart and is happy about her chance, the plebeian guardians are depicted as motivated by sheer party interest. We must not forget that Livy is professedly recounting the episode as a warning of what a terrible thing the jealousy between factions can be. It is the plebeians who, instead of abiding by the verdict of the court, resort to violence. (That the magistrates themselves, who are presumably most if not all of them aristocrats, may not be quite free from prejudice is not noted by Livy, though the plebeians would no doubt be alive to it.) It is the plebeians who call in an outside power (the Romans, appealed to by the nobles, are at least allies of some sort); and it is they with whose discomfiture the affair terminates.

I shall attempt no deductions from the narrative as to the law of Ardea respecting the conclusion of marriage, and especially as to whose consent was required. *A fortiori* I shall not inquire whether the result would illumine ancient Roman law—it might do so either if the two systems were in fact close, or if, though they were not, the tale assimilates the Ardean to the Roman. The episode, however special and arresting, furnishes a nuance of the popular theme of the two suitors. This does not mean that it cannot have happened or at least contain a nucleus of historicity. A motif may be ubiquitous precisely because it is true to life.

[note 73 *continued from previous page*] fifth century BC, a woman *sui iuris* could generally marry without *manus* against the will of her guardians; if she could, this narrative which pitches the mother (and a court), not the girl herself, against the guardians would fail to illustrate the point. Fourthly and most conclusively, there is in the anecdote not the vestige of an allusion to the distinction between marriage with *manus* and marriage without *manus*.

74. Livy 4.9, *nihil Romanae plebi similis*. For the restrained conduct of the Roman *plebs* during the first and second secessions, cf. Livy 2.32.4; 3.52.3.

As far as the dissension within the girl's circle is concerned at any rate, we find a very similar one assigned for decision to a provincial governor at the end of the second century AD.[75]

The Protection of the Non-Tipper

The rest of this Lecture I shall dedicate to legislation and jurisdiction for the protection of the non-tipper. In the typical case, the law in appearance restrains a man from harming himself by an excess of generosity, while in reality it is designed to come to the aid of him who has no wish to be over-generous.

We might start from a situation familiar to all of us. Many clubs have a rule against tipping. (I mean here tipping at discretion, not regulated

75. Code 5.4.1, Severus et Antoninus, AD 199: "When it is a question of the marriage of a girl and there is no agreement between her guardian and her mother and her relations as to the choice of her future husband, the verdict of the governor of the province is needed." The affinity of this situation and its handling with Livy's story has long been seen. Ogilvie (*Latomus*, 481–82) tries to brush it aside: "the dispute here (Code 5.4.1) was not concerned with the giving of consent to a marriage but with the choice of a husband where the girl did not have or had not voiced any preference." As for the girl's attitude, however, neither are we told in Code 5.4.1 that the ruling contemplates a girl who is indifferent; nor, in Livy, that the maid of Ardea did reveal her feelings. And as for the former half of his statement, I do not see what else than consent to the marriage might be in issue. Ogilvie urges that if Code 5.4.1 were thinking of the guardians' consent, "by the same argument it could be maintained that the consent of the mother and the relations was required—which is palpably untrue." But it is not palpably untrue by any means: see Buckland, *Text-Book* (1963), 113–14. From just about that period (probably in connection with tendencies to impose a duty to provide a girl with a dowry—see above, pp. 101–2.) such controls came to be recognized here and there; cf. Code 5.4.20, Honorius et Theodosius, AD 408–9. Ogilvie wants Code 5.4.1 out of the way for two reasons. First, it should not be mixed up with the serious constitutional trial at Ardea, where he thinks *conubium* was at stake. Secondly, he is contending, it may be recalled, that at Ardea—standing for Rome—a girl *sui iuris* needed no consents for marriage without *manus*, yet unless Code 5.4.1 is somehow explained away, it does require consents. As a matter of fact, though his thesis is untenable, he need not have been inconvenienced by this text: there might have been ever so many changes in the rules in the course of six-and-a-half centuries. It would indeed be surprising if the system presupposed in Code 5.4.1 fully or even to a high degree coincided with that presupposed in the ancient anecdote.

things like 15 per cent on the bill or the Christmas box.) Admittedly concern for the dignity of the personnel may be one of the reasons, but another is that the system is easy on the member who is unwilling to tip (whether from lack of funds or from meanness) and would otherwise feel pushed. (Don't try to dispute this, for I have sat on committees charged with this matter and moved by just this consideration.) Again, when a Fellow of my College marries, the Bursar sends round a note asking for money to buy a corporate wedding present and he adds that contributions are not to exceed so-and-so much, say, two guineas. At Rome, in the late Republic and Principate, with the then prevailing strict notions of *officium*, of what was owing to one's friends and retainers, the problem of pressure was far more serious, so serious that it could not be left to convention. There is in fact a whole, so far unisolated, corner of jurisdiction and legislation dealing with it. It is this branch "for the protection of the non-tipper," which I am going to characterize by a few examples.

I have already mentioned that a freedman could buy off the rights his former master retained over him and his estate, but that when a liberal patron went through a *proforma* sale, undertaking not to claim the price, the lawyers would not have it. There is more evidence of resistance against gratuitous renunciation of a patron's rights,[76] which was indeed not admitted till Justinian.[77] Why? It is not enough to reply that the *Edict* spoke of a buying off. That could have been interpreted less rigorously, or even changed. Surely, among the considerations in favour of an unbending attitude was this, that if gratuitous waiver was allowed, even a patron not so inclined might feel constrained to proceed that way. Decency is dangerous, a sort of plague. If one patron is kindly to his freedman, others will be, but what is worst, in the end the disease will belong to the *bon ton*, you cannot exclude yourself. So it is up to the law to prevent the infection.[78]

---

76. Digest 38.2.47.2, Paul *XI responsorum*.

77. Code 6.4.3, AD 529.

78. Regard for the patron's children certainly did play a part, but it alone would hardly account for the obstinate insistence on a price: after all, there was nothing to stop him from wasting the money received from his freedman or from bequeathing it to third persons not his children. Moreover, from Digest 38.2.47.1 just cited, it looks as if a patron's son also could not in classical law let off the freedman without charge.

Gratuitous waiver—the very word "gratuitous" may teach us something. In English, as in French, "gratuitous" means either "free of charge," "liberal," or "groundless" in a bad sense: *acte gratuit*. Both meanings already exist in Latin. The pleasant one occurs as early as in Plautus, the unpleasant one is first met in the younger Seneca:[79] "Hatred is the result of a hurt, *ex offensa*, or groundless, *gratuitum*." One factor in the rise of the latter may well be the fact that more and more frequently what purported to be given free, as a liberality, was in truth enforced by the social code. The element of active good-will was absent; what remained was the feeling of giving something for nothing. People still described such acts as done by way of grace and gratitude, "gratuitous,"[80] but what they meant was that they were done *sine causa*. From here to the bad sense is no far cry. Gratuitousness and duty are associated in numerous texts. Cicero writes that generosity, *liberalitas*, is not mercenary; it is *gratuita*, exercised for the sake not of reward, *fructus*, but of duty, *officium*.[81] Similarly, in his opinion, the dying Epicurus showed his *probitas gratuita* by such fine acts as remembering the children of a disciple: *tanta officia*.[82]

What is (to me) fascinating is that the Hebrew adverb *ḥinnam*, derived from *ḥen*, "grace," "graciousness," has exactly the two meanings, "without recompense," "freely," on the one hand, "without cause" in the bad sense on the other.[83] To be sure, the Old Testament world is not that of the Roman *officia*. Nevertheless the development is very comparable. Among the earliest extant Biblical laws are directions as to when a slave obtains his freedom "gratuitously" whether the master likes it or not.[84] Again, there are traces of an ancient legal custom according to which a junior member of a family was to serve the Head "gratuitously."[85] So here,

---

79. Seneca the Younger, *Ep.* 105.4. Disregarding adumbrations in Livy.

80. *Gratuitus* derives from *grates* and is related to *gratia*.

81. Cicero, *Leg.* 1.18.48.

82. Cicero, *Fin.* 2.31.99.

83. Indeed, the oldest instance of the latter meaning is "people that hate without cause," strikingly reminiscent of Seneca's *odium gratuitum*. The noun phrase, "hatred without cause," however, is post-Biblical: see above, p. 54.

84. Exod. 21:2, 11.

85. Gen. 29:15; see Daube and Yaron, *Journal of Semitic Studies* 1 (1956): 60ff.; Daube, *The Exodus Pattern in the Bible* (1963), 62–63.

too, the compulsory graces may have contributed to a degradation of the notion.[86]

Once we are awake to the importance of this aspect of Roman legal life, other illustrations come readily to mind and, indeed, a number of puzzling features become explicable. Take Augustus's law of 2 BC, quoted above, which limited the number of slaves a man might release by testament. A few years before, Dionysius of Halicarnassus, favouring the senatorial party—what would nowadays be called the Right—had recommended legislation of this nature.[87] One of his arguments was that more often than not a master who released his slaves in his last will was actuated by the unworthy desire for posthumous reputation: people would notice the new freedmen among his cortege and acclaim his benevolence. Now for one thing, it can be proved that this unworthy motive was far from general. As we have seen, a method (one of many) resorted to evade the statutory restriction was to bequeath a supernumerary slave to a third party, on the terms to manumit him.[88] Evidently, that slave could not grace the testator's cortege as a freedman: it was the third party who, on carrying out the terms of his legacy, would become his patron. In any case, the very fact that a testator who manumitted his household *en bloc* could look forward to leaving behind a name for magnanimity shows how the bulk of citizens viewed such conduct.

Dionysius's strictures, however, are revealing. It is a commonplace in moralistic instruction—we come across it in Cicero[89]—that munificence should not be overdone and that where it is, frequently the purpose is ostentation. This sounds simple, until we ask what, in any relationship,

---

86. The semantic history of "gratuity" is in full flow. The word signifies (1)favour, attested from 1523; (2) money-gift, from 1540, often in return for services; (3) more particularly a money-gift by a superior to an inferior, a servant, from the nineteenth century (3a) a bounty on discharge or retirement, from the beginning of that century, (3b) a tip, from the middle. Up to this point, it can all be found in the *New English Dictionary*, vol. 4 (1901). Recently, however, the term (or one conspicuous application at least) is moving away from gift altogether. It more and more comes to signify a payment firmly expected on a certain occasion, maybe even enforceable at law; and even the amount is less and less in the discretion of the payer.

87. Dionysius of Halicarnassus, *Ant. Rom* 4.24.

88. Digest 35.1.37, Paul *singulari ad legem Fufiam Caniniam.*

89. Cicero, *Off.* 1.14.44.

is overdoing and what is ostentation. To this, different traditions, classes, value systems will manifestly give different answers. But there are some constant determinants, among them a powerful resentment against those who threaten to establish standards beyond what we could happily comply with: we want to see them restrained, and in the society with which Dionysius was concerned it might be necessary to restrain them by law. The statute here discussed, needless to say, had several objects. The sources, in addition to repression of the lust for posthumous popularity, mention the stemming of the influx of inferior elements into the citizen body.[90] That the *colluvio servilis sanguinis*, however, cannot have been a supreme consideration comes out in the fact that the Augustan marriage legislation, while encouraging a freeborn woman to have three children, encouraged a freedwoman to have four.[91] (Then, as today, more child-bearing might be expected from, *zugemutet* to, the females from the lower mass.) One object we must not overlook is the protection of the non-tipper, i.e. prevention of a state of affairs when an owner of slaves, not to be despised as mean and forgetful of what a good guy ought to do, had no choice but to ordain wholesale release in his will.

If we look at the legislation from this angle, clearly if involuntarily indicated by Dionysius, as a curb on intolerable liberality, we become aware of a distinct affinity with the sumptuary laws, directed against the intolerable display of wealth. I shall say something about them in a moment. Before, however, let me refer to a *lex Cornelia*, probably of Sulla, which provided that no one might be surety for one man to one man in the same year for more than 20,000 sesterces.[92] There is a long-standing puzzle attached to this statute. It is generally thought that it was combating the irresponsible assumption of risk: why, then, did it forbid only to go beyond 20,000 for one man? Which left you perfectly

90. Dionysius of Halicarnassus, *Ant. Rom* 4.24.; Suetonius, *Aug.* 40.3; Dio Cassius 56.33; Gaius 1.13ff. They mention also the safeguarding of legacies: Gaius 2.228. If an estate was too depleted by manumissions, the debts might equal if not exceed the assets, the heir might refuse it and this would kill the testament including legacies and, indeed, manumissions—except, perhaps, if he was a *suus*; what happened in that case is controversial, the texts are far from telling a clear story.

91. *Ius quattuor liberorum*: Gaius 3.44; *Ulp. Reg.* 29.3; Buckland, *Text-Book* (1963), 167.

92. Gaius 3.124.

free to ruin yourself by standing surety for fifty. But the statute was not combating recklessness. Its purpose was not to prevent you from risking as much as you liked, it was to shield him who was averse to getting involved in other people's debts—he was provided with a means of keeping such items down without ceasing to count as a gentleman.[93] But for the intervention of the legislator, in the late Republic and early Empire it was next to impossible to refuse a friend's or dependant's request to guarantee an obligation. How routine a service this was may be gathered from a series of letters of Cicero's where he cannot remember whether or not he made himself liable for a certain acquaintance;[94] while the way Horace declaims on the hatefulness of these demands[95] is direct proof that they were widely resented—which is not inconsistent with the fact that a well-meaning friend of a person in need of a guarantor might do his best, by means of one of those altruistic dodges discussed above, to defeat the statute.[96]

93. The statute also forbade only to go beyond 20,000 to one man; so you could exceed the sum for the same man if he had several creditors. According to Appleton (ZRG 26 [1905]: 42) this laxity was inevitable since one of several creditors might not know that another had already taken a guarantee from you; hence it would have been wrong to deprive him of the security your promise gave him. There is much to be said for this explanation. But even this part of the statute might reflect the main purpose as I see it (which does not force us to drop the factor pointed out by Appleton). There was no reason to discourage an enthusiastic benefactor from going around with his protégé and helping him with dozens of sellers of goods, estate agents and moneylenders. But except in very special circumstances, a request for such multiple support was hardly *comme il faut*; a non-tipper could normally avoid it, he was sufficiently protected by the statutory limit on an undertaking to one creditor. Appleton, incidentally, quotes Cuq for the view (drawing support from Cicero, *Pro Murena* 34.7) that the *lex Cornelia* primarily contemplated the intercession of a mighty person for his client. If this is correct (or to the extent to which it is), the measure belongs to the same kind of climate as the opposition to gratuitous renunciation of a patron's privilege.

94. Cicero, *Att.* 12.14.2, 12.17, 12.19.2. True, the transaction would have taken place over twenty-five years before.

95. Horace, *Satirae* 2.6.23ff., esp. 27.

96. Digest 12.6.18, Ulpian *XLVII ad Sabinum*, says that if premature payment is made by one who owes under a condition which must materialize, there is no *condictio*, whereas if it is made by one who owes under another condition of which it is doubtful whether it will come to pass, there is *condictio*. A strange formulation. A condition which must materialize is *dies*: I promise you on a Sunday to pay so-and-so much if tomorrow

It all flowed from the tight togetherness of the club. In the second century BC a law (*lex Apuleia*) provided that if one of several sureties paid more than his portion, he could recover from the others.[97] This shows the spirit in which such arrangements were treated. The several sureties may have made no agreement between them; for the lawgiver, the mere fact that they guaranteed the same debt unites them into a body where none ought to have an advantage over the other. What is as illuminating as the

---

will be Monday, *dies certus*, I promise you if X will die, *dies incertus*. Yet the text calls it *condicio* and goes on to speak of a real condition as *alia condicio*. The fragment comes from Ulpian's discussion of *adpromissores* (Lenel, *Pal.*, 2 (1889), 1184), from where indeed we have a further dictum with the curious formulation, Digest 46.2.9.1: "he who takes a promise under a condition which must materialize is held to take an unconditional promise." Lenel connects the two statements with the rule (Digest 46.1.8.7, Ulpian in the same book, Gaius 3.126) that a surety's position may be less but not more stringent than the principal debtor's; in particular if the principal debt is conditional, the surety's may not be simple, though the converse is allowed. This is possible, but I am not satisfied because it leaves totally unexplained the surprising concept of "a condition which must materialize"; it looks as if it had surprised Ulpian himself who, in 46.2.9.1, denies it any force. I believe the statements are connected with the *lex Cornelia* which, Gaius tells us, 3.124, covers "any money certain to become due, i.e. contracted for without any condition; therefore even such money of which we are promised that it will be paid at a certain date—*in diem certum*—falls in this category, because it is certain to become due." A conditional debt, then, was clearly not covered. To get around the statute, an unconditional debt had to be dressed up as conditional, had to be provided with "a condition which must materialize," as when I promise if a boat will be seen in Ostia harbour within the next three months. The jurists, however, did not pass this dodge. 46.2.9.1 lays down that such a "condition" is not a condition. 12.6.18 explains that it does not count as a condition in the matter of *condictio*: premature payment by a debtor under such a "condition" gives him no *condictio* though he has one under a real condition. In the original Ulpian, together with these passages, there must have been the verdict rejecting this "condition" as a means of circumventing the *lex Cornelia*. It is not preserved: Justinian was no longer interested in this lex. Incidentally, I have shown elsewhere (*ZRG* 76 [1959]: 167ff., though I had not yet gained clarity on 12.6.18) that Celsus was the first jurist, in the use of premature payment of a debt, to restrict *condictio* to condition and refuse it not only for *dies certus* (where it had been refused before him) but also for *dies incertus* (where it had been admitted). Gaius in 3.124 still treats *dies incertus* as on a level with condition: the *lex Cornelia* does not apply, he represents *dies certus* as illustrating its remarkable range. Whether this reflects a widely shared view or whether, as often, he takes over an out-of-date detail from his source I leave open.

97. Gaius 3.122.

regulation itself is its subsequent interpretation: Gaius conceives of the law as establishing between the sureties a sort of partnership, *quaedam societas*. A *societas* between persons whose bond is neither kinship nor *consensus*, but participation in the same *officium*.[98]

The *lex Cornelia* seems to have formed part of Sulla's sumptuary laws.[99] This would suit my thesis very well, for the protection of the non-tipper is an aim of most anti-luxury measures; it definitely played an enormous part in the Roman ones which got under way towards the end of the third century BC.[100]

One form of extravagance, namely, at burials, had been legislated against far earlier, in the XII Tables, and indeed, Roman tradition has it, by King Numa. Those early provisions may have been inspired by religious beliefs, and in particular by hostility to Etruscan ritual. By 200 BC, though an anti-foreign slant persisted, the enemies of high living appealed chiefly to the simplicity of the past, to the virtue of moderation or even frugality and to egalitarianism (of a sort—as far as appearances were concerned). It would be a mistake to dismiss these sentiments as altogether spurious. But surely, behind them or side by side with them there was at work the wish to put down the prodigals whose style set the tone and forced their parsimonious brethren to emulate them or be out of the swim. Many people's lives (among the upper crust) were overshadowed by the fear of being thought a miser, to judge by the frequent mention of it in literature.[101] Lavish spending would be a way out; but a cheaper one was to have laws which, by prohibiting lavishness, made the miser undetectable.

Sometimes the cat is let out of the bag. When a statute limiting female luxury was to be repealed,[102] old Cato spoke for its retention—

---

98. We must not press the comparison, but I am not convinced that, say, in the classical period, in an action under this law, defendant may not have enjoyed *beneficium competentiae*.

99. Westrik, *Adnotationes ad loca Gai Institutionum de sponsoribus, fidepromissoribus et fideiussoribus* (1826), 37, 49–50; quoted by Voigt, *Das Jus Naturale*, vol. 4 (1875), 425.

100. For a general account see Kübler, art. *Sumptus*, in Pauly-Wissowa, 2nd ser., half-vol. 7, 4A:1, (1931), 901ff.

101. E.g. Horace, *Satirae* 1.2.1ff., depicting the dilemma when you want to be called neither a miser nor a spendthrift.

102. The Oppian statute, repealed in 195 BC: Cf. above, p. 85n73.

of course—and one of his arguments addressed to the women (the rich women) who clamoured for its abolition was this: "For while it is perhaps natural to feel shame or anger when what is denied to one of you is granted to another, with the dress of all made alike what is there which any of you need fear will render her less conspicuous? What one is most ashamed of is stinginess and poverty: the statute relieves you of either since you do not have what you are not permitted to have."[103]

A *lex Licinia* passed some time before 100 BC is traditionally entitled *de sumptu minuendo*,[104] which would indicate that it was intended to curb expenditure. From Macrobius we hear[105] that it was the aristocratic party who had pressed for it. From which Kübler infers[106] that it must have relaxed the provisions of a prior *lex Fannia* and that we should replace *de sumptu minuendo*, "concerning expenditure to be reduced," by *de severitate legis Fanniae minuenda*, "concerning the austerity of the *lex Fannia* to be mitigated." This, however, is to forget about the non-tippers who, at times, may form an influential lobby precisely among the highest circles where a few *bon viveurs* can make things dreadfully uncomfortable for everyone else. Gellius transmits a speech[107] apparently delivered in support of the *lex Licinia* and vehemently attacking extravagant entertainments: this can scarcely be squared with anything but "expenditure to be reduced."

There were, let me observe, certain types of munificence openly fought on behalf of such as were unwilling or unable to compete. The most interesting is *ambitus*,[108] the effort of a candidate for high office to win votes by the display of costly array, the distribution of gifts, the arrangement of public games, the banqueting of friends. Throughout the Republic one law after another tried to keep *ambitus* in check. Sulla probably sponsored one.

---

103. Livy 34.4.12. It is immaterial for my purpose whether or how far the speech is genuine. All that matters is that here is a source preserving an express reference to the interests of the stingy.

104. Chapter heading of Gellius, 15.8

105. Horace, *Satirae* 3.17.7.

106. Kübler, in Pauly-Wissowa's *RE*, 2nd ser., half-vol. 7, 4A:1, (1931), 907, s.v. "Sumptus." The discrepancy between Macrobius and Gellius in respect of details of the statute is open to several explanations; at present none of them can be more than guesswork.

107. Gellius 15.8.

108. See Mommsen, *Röm. Strafr.*, (1899), 865ff.

The main reason the object of protecting the non-tipper was here freely admitted is that the tipper in this case did not act, barely pretended to act, from generosity. Everybody knew what he was after, he was "ambitious" (related to *ambitus*);[109] in fact he was doing business, he was buying, and buying,[110] moreover, a commodity which ought not to be for sale. Hence, in this case, the non-tipper was beset by no feeling of inferiority. There were other elements in the situation to boost his confidence. *Ambitus* often involved an unworthy degree of self-ingratiation with the public. Columella in the first century AD prefers to look after his land rather than "to purchase the honour and power of the insignia at the price of dishonour, by abject servility, let alone the dissipation of his property."[111] Again, recourse to *ambitus* showed that the man could not succeed by virtue of his and his family's reputation and real qualities (I mean what orthodoxy deemed the real qualities). According to Livy, the first law against *ambitus* in the fourth century BC was made because of the mode of canvassing of *novi homines*, upstarts.[112] No doubt the old set felt not only that this was wrong but also that it would be unpleasant to have to compete. Note the emphasis on expense at the end of Columella's observation.

Mutatis mutandis the old considerations still apply to our modern treatment of electioneering expenses; nor am I sure that our control is significantly more effective than was the Roman. As for the latter, Mommsen remarks on the irony of the fact[113] that the term *candidatus*,

109. *Ambire*, "to go around in villages and hamlets among the electorate," conduct prohibited by a law of 358 BC: Livy 7.15.13. (A candidate for election to the Académie Française has to call on every member.) Of the two nouns *ambitus* and *ambitio*, the former came to be confined to an unlawful mode of canvassing, the latter was less technical and acquired the sense of "ambition," whence the adjective *ambitiosus*, "ambitious,"; see Mommsen, *Röm. Strafr.* (1899), 866; and cf. above, p. 49n180.

110. Columella, 1 praef. 10 speaks of *mercari*; I shall quote the passage in full presently.

111. Collumella, 1 praef. 10; see the preceding footnote.

112. 7.15.13, cited above, n. 109.

113. Mommsen, *Röm. Strafr.* (1899), 866. An interesting monograph on a problem concerning American elections comes my way while I am proofreading: Epstein, *Corporations, Contributions, and Political Campaigns: Federal Regulations in Perspective*, (1968).

"candidate," taken literally, designates a person guilty of ostentation prohibited by an early law: it means "dressed in shiny white."

Dress, male and female, is indeed a means of social differentiation in all ages, whether major, between high and low, or subtle, between high and a little higher. It must have been irksome for a respectable citizen who would not or could not waste money to watch another becoming the talk of the town by his splendid attire. No wonder quite a few sumptuary regulations give relief to the former by obstructing the latter. Down to this day the feelings of the non-dresser can be a factor in the adoption of a fixed group apparel, say, by a religious order or a school. I am not saying that it is present in all instances, nor that, even where it is, other considerations may not be of weight: identity of outfit may give expression to genuine egalitarianism; it may enhance separateness from the outside world, solidarity and allegiance on the inside; it may serve such mundane purposes as easy mutual recognition, smooth administration, reduced cost, rapid equipment. It is these other considerations which predominate in the most notable case of all, the armed forces—though as soon as we enter the officers' mess, for example, we are again likely to come across conventions taking account of the member who cannot afford a silver cigarette étui.

Incidentally, in the matter of dress, the rather abstract concept "uniform" was introduced, it seems, by Louvois, under Louis XIV, in the course of his reorganization of the French army: very fitting it should come from that powerful, centralizing, rationalizing reign. Au fond, the term still has its main base in the military domain. It entered English towards the middle of the eighteenth century. About the first, if not the first, English writer to transport it to outside its original sphere was Dickens, when he designed the uniform of the Pickwick Club.[114] For the readers of the time, the joke must have been far more amusing than for us who are accustomed to hearing of the uniform of nurses, of a gang, of the City.

I conclude with the history of the Jewish funeral.[115] An orthodox Jewish funeral is very simple: everybody gets a plain, white linen shroud.

---

114. In 1837: "the proposed uniform, sir, of the Pickwick Club." See New English Dictionary, vol. 10, pt. 1, U (1926), 223.

115. See Kohler, Jewish Encyclopedia, vol. 3 (1902), 432ff., s.v. "burial."

No doubt the idea that at that ultimate stage all are equal plays a part, as it did in Roman thought: Cicero, commenting on the disapproval of funeral pomp in the XII Tables and in Solon's legislation, declares it "assuredly in accordance with nature that differences in wealth are ended in death."[116]

Ah, if only the Talmud did not preserve the account of how the austere practice came to be established! By the beginning of the era, social convention required funerals so gorgeous that the non-tippers, people who had not the necessary means, or thought they had not, would leave relatives unburied and stealthily move to some other place. So the great and rich Gamaliel about AD 90, in order to remedy the situation, had himself buried in the most modest way. I can tell you from what I have seen in California that there is need there for a Gamaliel, in fact not only among men but also among beasts. When the dog I keep at San Francisco dies, I shall certainly take the next plane to Europe. Gamaliel's good deed had a little *Nachspiel*.[117] It was usual for the mourners, after committing the corpse, to forgather for some wine. The reform initiated by him was so popular that a toast in his honour was added, and in the end the drinking became so excessive that once again the Rabbis stepped in and abolished it altogether.[118]

---

116. Cicero, *Leg.* 2.59: *tolli fortunae discrimen in morte.* French undertakers advertise *pompes funèbres.*

117. *Babylonian Ketuboth* 8b.

118. Cf. the ban on *circumpotatio*, round drinking at a funeral, promulgated by the XII Tables—Cicero, *Leg.* 2.60.

Part III

PHILOSOPHICAL ASPECTS

Whenever one considers the philosophy of Roman law, the relation to Greece is bound to come up. Roughly, while Greece furnished the great ideas, it was the Romans who transmuted them into something of practical applicability. Of this process there are many familiar examples, to which many more could be added. The apostle Paul affirms that among those who have become Christians, there is neither Jew nor Greek, neither bond nor free, neither male nor female.[1] With this may be compared a series of three Jewish thanksgivings of the period: a man expresses his gratitude for not being created a heathen, an ignoramus, a woman. (I always think this is very chivalresque, for how could one adore women if one were not created a man?). A triad attested from the fourth century AD, and even closer to Paul, still forms part of the orthodox daily morning prayer: thanks for not being a heathen, a slave, a woman.[2] Again, the dying Plato praised his guardian angel for being created a man, not an irrational animal, a brute; a Greek, not a barbarian, a foreigner; in the time of Socrates instead of in any other.[3] The third part, "in the time of Socrates," we may assume, elegantly takes the place of something more usual.

Clearly, there was floating in the Mediterranean world in those centuries a threefold division of the basic human condition, with all

---

1. Gal. 3:28; see Daube, *The New Testament and Rabbinic Judaism* (1956), 80, 442.

2. *Authorised Daily Prayer Book*, ed. Singer, 5–6; see Daube, *Theology* 69 (1966): 517.

3. Plutarch, *Vit., Marius* 46.1.

sorts of variations adapted to different circumstances; and one of these variations, I suppose, was the Roman trichotomy of *capitis deminutio*, change or loss of status, according as it affected a Roman's liberty (*capitis deminutio maxima*), citizenship (*minor* or *media*) or membership of a family (*minima*).[4] Very reminiscent of the other triple groups, but the practical twist is unmistakable.

Here we really know so little that such a suggestion is easily made: it is vague and harmless. Often we know just slightly more, and then we run into troublesome problems. I shall present two cases: first, certain grounds of liability or freedom from liability, and second, a mode of reasoning met in the legal sources.

---

4. Gaius 1.159ff. Schulz, *Classical Roman Law* (1951), 72, is probably right in attributing the classification to Q. Mucius. The rest of his discussion of the institution, however, is not wholly convincing.

5

Standards of Liability

Dolus, Culpa and *Casus*

Roman law is much admired for its three standards of liability: *dolus*, evil intent, *culpa*, negligence, and *casus*, accident.[1] I deliberately ram your car with mine: *dolus*. I bump into your car from lack of care: *culpa*. A sudden tornado thrusts me into your car: *casus*. There was a time when this classification was looked upon as a characteristic achievement of the Roman legal genius.[2] Nowadays scholars seem inclined to follow Kübler,[3] for whom it is a direct borrowing from Greece. This thesis, however, is at least an exaggeration. The truth is far more complicated.

The three standards are not, of course, met anywhere in Plato. But Kübler detects them in the *Rhetorica ad Alexandrum* and in Aristotle.

---

1. I am aware that my renderings are inadequate approximations.

2. E.g. Binding, ZRG 39 (1918): 5ff. By the way, it is in this article, it seems, that Binding coined the word *Interpolationenjagd*, "interpolations hunt" (p. 10: *wie ich mich scherzhaft ausgedrückt habe*, "as I have jokingly expressed myself"); and the man whom he accused of it was none other than Lenel who, seven years later, in ZRG 45 (1925): 17–18, published an article under this title against Beseler. Kalb had paved the way by his essay *Die Jagd nach Interpolationen in den Digesten*, "The hunt for interpolations in the Digest" (1897).

3. Kübler, "Der Einfluss der griechischen Philosophie auf die Entwicklung der Lehre von den Verschuldensgraden im römischen Recht," *Rechtsidee und Staatsgedanke, Festschrift für Binder* (1900): 63ff., apparently approved by Kunkel, *Römisches Recht* (on the basis of Jörs), 3rd ed. (1949), 179.

He is wrong. But this is not his fault. It is largely due to a long-standing serious misinterpretation of Aristotle.

We must begin with the earliest relevant work, the *Rhetorica ad Alexandrum*. It recommends[4] that the accused in a criminal trial adopt one of the following positions: I did not do it, did not kill the man; I did it but it was lawful—say, killed him in self-defense; I did it but there were mitigating circumstances. Kübler's thesis is based on what the ancient writer has to tell us about mitigating circumstances. Prominent among them are *hamartema* (or *hamartia*) and *atychema* (or *atychia*), and these are opposed to *adikia*, deliberate evildoing, unmitigated. *Hamartema* is defined as harm inflicted as a result of ignorance; *atychema* as harm you do not intend, your intention is all right and things go wrong not through yourself but through other people or misfortune, bad luck. Kübler, sharing a common misunderstanding which finds its main expression in commentaries on Aristotle, translates *hamartema* by "negligence." With *adikia* corresponding to *dolus*, and *atychema* to *casus* (I shall presently have to make a reservation to the latter identification), this gives him the three standards of liability: *dolus*, evil intent, *culpa*, negligence, *casus*, accident.

The flaw is that the *Rhetorica*, in explaining *hamartema*, makes no reference whatever to negligence, lack of care or the like. It emphasizes ignorance, lack of knowledge, lack of information; and what it contemplates is the traditional situations of this type—for example, the killing of a friend in battle, intentionally but from error, mistaking him for a foe. (The Draconian inscription exempted this case from punishment.)[5] In contradistinction to *atychema*, accident, where for instance the spear with which you practice hits a bystander or the catapult you are demonstrating goes off, in *hamartema*, these disasters from ignorance, you do have the harmful intention—you do aim at that soldier, Oedipus did go for the old man who barred the way—only it is owing to a misapprehension, you believe that soldier to belong to the enemy, Oedipus, was unaware the old man was his father. This has nothing to do with negligence. Whether the ignorance was inevitable or whether more scrupulous examination could and should have prevented it is immaterial. Similarly, negligence as such plays no part in *atychema*, accident. This embraces all unintended mishap

---

4. Aristotle, *Rh. Al.* 4, 1427a, 23ff.
5. Demosthenes, *in Aristocratem* 53.637.

whether blameless in our (the Roman) sense—the bystander suddenly moves into the playing field, there is a hidden fault in the catapult—or not—you are careless in throwing the spear, in handling the engine.

The classification is essentially incommensurate with the Roman one, it is the outcome of totally different historical and dogmatic antecedents. Negligence has no part in it. To equate the two tables is to distort at least one of them. Even *atychema*, which at first sight looks the same as *casus*, is not quite the same, precisely because it includes unintended harm even if caused negligently, a wide sector excluded from the Roman *casus* which is opposed to *culpa*. If I bump into your car from lack of care, from the point of view of the *Rhetorica ad Alexandrum* it is *atychema*, but in the Roman system it is *culpa*, not *casus*.

Let us now look at Aristotle, and first at his *Rhetorica*,[6] very close indeed to the *Rhetorica ad Alexandrum*. Once again we are advised that the accused, though he has done the deed, need not be guilty of *adikema*, an unmitigated crime. He has available two equitable pleas in extenuation, *atychema* and *hamartema*. Except that *adikema* replaces *adikia*, the terms are exactly those of the *Rhetorica ad Alexandrum*; and though, in expounding them, Aristotle strikes out on his own, they are employed in exactly the sense which they have in the older treatise. Indeed, it is the very purpose of the fresh elements appearing in his definitions to bring out that sense more clearly. *Atychema*, he explains, happens unexpectedly, *paralogos*, and is not due to wickedness, *mochtheria*. *Hamartema* does not happen unexpectedly, *paralogos*, and yet it, too, does not originate in vice, *poneria*. By contrast, *adikema* does not happen unexpectedly and is indeed the product of viciousness.

As in the *Rhetorica ad Alexandrum*, we find distinguished *atychema*, the unintended mishap, where the harm occurs unexpectedly; and *hamartema*, where it does not occur unexpectedly, where you do intend it—and none the less you act without viciousness, *poneria*, because your motives are all right: your action springs from ignorance. It is quite unjustifiable to turn the latter category into negligence. If you shoot a member of your platoon who looks like an enemy, this killing in error is not, on the basis of the work before us, to be assigned to different classes

---

6. Aritotle, *Rh.* 1.13.15f., 1374b 1ff.

according to the degree of circumspection applied: it is *hamartema* even
in the absence of negligence, even, that is, if you are as conscientious in
ascertaining the facts as is feasible in the circumstances. On the other
hand, what for us are typical cases of negligence—you are incautious in
practising with a spear, in demonstrating a catapult, in driving your car—
fall under *atychema* no less than the same situations where the accused
is free of fault, say, an abnormal gust of wind diverts the spear, a safety
catch of the catapult breaks, the steering wheel of the car jams. Aristotle's
use of *paralogos* is most helpful in stressing the element of the unplanned,
or even contrariness to plan, in *atychema*: I aim my spear at a board, the
next moment, as a result of some coincidence, I find myself the cause of a
man's death. This element is equally there whether or not I exercise proper
care; and it is it which distinguishes the class from both *hamartema* and
adikema, where there is nothing *paralogos* about the man's death—only,
in *hamartema*, my decision to do him in is excusable when note is taken
of the fallacious assumption underlying it. And let me repeat: there is no
thought of marking off the avoidable, careless fallacy from the unavoidable
one.

When we proceed to the *Ethica Nicomachea*, we are, it is true,
confronted by a novel development; but even here it is wildly anachronistic
to import the Roman standards. I shall deal with three sections.

The first[7] is devoted to the distinction between voluntary and
involuntary acts, for the purpose of adjudging moral responsibility. It is
not surprising in this context to find deeds committed through ignorance
labelled as involuntary.[8] What is new is the wide scope of ignorance, the
subsumption under this heading of both the *hamartema* and the *atychema*
of the earlier works; in other words, of both the case where you mistake
a fellow soldier for an enemy or, like Oedipus, your father for a stranger,
and that where your spear is diverted from your aim, where you give a
lesson in catapulting and the missile goes off or where your car runs into
another. All these latter mishaps are now under deeds from ignorance.

This is a terrific attempt at reduction; and though somewhat forced,
it is by no means irrational. After all, it is quite correct that even in the case
of accident you are lacking some vital information, possession of which

---

7. Aristotle, *Eth. Nic.* 3.1.13ff., 1100b 18–19.
8. I omit the requirement of compunction after the deed.

would make you act differently. In a way, the disaster may be attributed to the fact that you do not know what diverts your spear or makes the missile go off or makes your car bump into another.

Curiously, notwithstanding an enormous dissimilarity in background, a comparable trend is discernible in the *Pentateuch*, in the Priestly Code.[9] Priestly legislation started making allowance for ignorance in the field of levitical commerce where countless actions, innocuous in themselves, became illicit if done by or to a person or object belonging to a special category. It was all right to eat an ox or enter the sanctuary, but an offence to eat an ox dedicated to the temple or enter the sanctuary in a state of uncleanness. An offender unaware of the dedication or his uncleannesss was provided with a routine mode of atonement; and the law had a technical designation for this kind of error, *sheghagha*,[10] evidently corresponding to *hamartema* as used in the classifications I have presented: you do intend the deed—to eat the ox, to enter the sanctuary—and nevertheless you are guilty of no ill will, you act from a misapprehension. The remarkable thing is that, ultimately, the notion of *sheghagha* was transferred to the regulation of homicide[11] and there referred to *atychema*, accident, unintended killing, say, by an unfortunate throw of a weapon. So here, too, "error" became the overall heading for involuntary harm, to the confusion of posterity—from the Rabbis of the Talmud to the Old Testament specialists of the present day—seeking to make one whole of the various strata of evolution.

Before leaving this section of the *Ethica Nicomachea*, an important point must be noted—important not only for its own sake, but also because a proper appreciation of it will make us less prone to the current misunderstanding of the following sections. Aristotle, we have seen, conceives of both the old *hamartema* (you mistake a friend for a foe) and the old *atychema* (your spear takes the wrong course) as involuntary since they are the result of ignorance. By an express proviso, he excludes from this heading crimes perpetrated in drunkenness, in a rage or in passionate

9. Some preliminary remarks of mine may be found in *Revue Internationale des Droits de l'Antiquité* 2 (1949): 208, 211–12; a fuller discussion is given in Daube, "The Deed and the Doer in the Bible," *Gifford Lectures*, ed. Calum Carmichael.

10. E.g. Lev. 5:18.

11. Num. 35; Josh. 20.

desire.[12] These deeds are voluntary, for, though you act "not knowing" (*agnoon*) what you are doing, you do not act "from ignorance" (*di' agnoian*). Your action, he contends, is not, as in the other cases, due to lack of information concerning a specific circumstance (that the soldier you aim at belongs to your side, that a movement you make or a gust of wind is going to deflect your spear). It is due to your very drunkenness, anger or lust, and when you say that "you do not know" what you are doing, what we mean is that you are unaware, not of a specific circumstance, but, more generally, of the nature of your deed, you are forgetful of the restraints incumbent on a decent citizen. In fact, "you do not know" in much the same sense as an offender in cold blood: even he is ignorant in this wider sense, even he acts insensitively to his true interests, to the right end of man. Unlike Socrates, Aristotle refuses to accept this moral error as abolishing responsibility.[13] If we apply the categories of the rhetorical works, what you perpetrate in drunkenness, in a rage or in passionate desire is *adikia* or *adikema*; we shall presently find this conclusion borne out by further statements in the *Ethica Nicomachea*. There is so far, of course, no trace of anything resembling *culpa*, negligence.

Next, a section[14] where Aristotle is concerned to prove that virtue and vice are voluntary, within our power. Society at any rate proceeds on this basis, he observes. It metes out punishment to those who cause harm—except if they act under compulsion or from ignorance—and honours those who do nobly, thus repressing the former type and encouraging the latter. It would never exhort us to do anything involuntary, for instance, not to feel heat or hunger. Again, the argument is largely directed against the Socratic doctrine that, all wrong flowing from ignorance, no one sins voluntarily. For Aristotle, it may be recalled, wrong flows from ignorance only where you are mistaken as to a particular fact; while if your error is of the general, moral kind, about your calling, about the good, you admittedly act "not knowing," but not "from, as a result of, ignorance"— you do will your deed.

That society is with him, he goes on, comes out impressively in two cases. First, you may be held to account precisely for "not knowing." Your

<hr>

12. Aristotle, *Eth. Nic.* 3.1.14f., 21ff., 1110 25ff., 111a 22ff.
13. Cf. Daube, *Sin, Ignorance and Forgiveness in the Bible* (1960), 21ff. [BLL 384ff.]
14. Aristotle, *Eth. Nic.* 3.5.7ff., 1113b 21ff.

very blindness to right and wrong, that is, may be punishable if you are clearly seen as answerable for it. Thus the great lawgiver Pittacus (tyrant of Mytilene at the beginning of the sixth century BC) increased the ordinary penalty where a crime was committed in drunkenness. We have already seen that, in Aristotle's view, a drunkard's action is voluntary, it is *adikia* or *adikema*, his "not knowing" is essentially the same as that of a criminal who is sober. We now learn that what is notable about drunkenness is that our responsibility for "not knowing" what we are doing is more evident than in sober crime; so evident that it may attract an extra penalty.

It is hardly necessary to point out—but I must, in view of Kübler's thesis—that this treatment of a deed in drunkenness is fundamentally different from that which would bring it under *culpa*, negligence, as something midway between *dolus*, intended harm, and *casus*, harm caused by accident. If we are to correlate at all, in Aristotle's system the deed in drunkenness falls under *dolus*, and he quotes Pittacus's legislation as shewing that it is sometimes judged even worse than the ordinary dolose deed. Negligence as a standard of liability simply has no look in.

The second case Aristotle invokes in support is punishment of a man even though he does not know a legal prohibition which one ought to know and which creates no exceptional difficulty. Here at least I can see how commentators coming from the Roman scheme might arrive at the standard of negligence. Aristotle distinguishes between difficult laws and laws readily intelligible; not to bother about the latter is certainly negligence, carelessness, blameworthy lack of application. Only, in Aristotle's system, this attitude does not bring the deed down from *dolus* to a less serious class of *culpa*. On the contrary, it is precisely this lack of application which (like drunkenness) lies at the root of vice, of *dolus*. The deed to which it leads is voluntary, dolose.

Aristotle, remember, is here out to demonstrate that society's practice makes no allowance for the "not knowing" in a general, moral, Socratic sense. So he adduces a striking parallel—no allowance is made for being unacquainted with a prohibition of the positive law which is not beyond ordinary understanding. The contravention is considered voluntary, subject to the full rigour of whatever sanction is threatened. While it is easy to see how commentators got misled, the fact is that this passage no more than any of the preceding ones has to do with negligence as a standard of liability.

The analogy between an offender not knowing about the positive law he ought to know and an offender not knowing right and wrong in general is fully spelled out. Society inflicts punishment on the former: just so, Aristotle climaxes his argument, it inflicts punishment—I quote— "in the other instances where the not knowing is the consequence of unconcern, so that the person is himself responsible for his not knowing, since it would be in his power to be concerned."

This little sentence has been fatally misunderstood. What it does is to draw the conclusion from the parallel of not knowing such positive law as is easy to know. Just as in this case the wrongdoer does not get off, since his mental state is at fault, so society does not let off the wrongdoer for not knowing what he is doing in a general, moral way—he also is master of his character, he could be a better man had he applied himself. It is a fierce anachronism to turn this into a proclamation of *culpa*, negligence, as a standard between *dolus* and *casus*. Aristotle devotes a good many subsequent paragraphs to explaining how you have to train diligently to acquire the habit of right-doing and how unconcern and neglect make you prone to wrongdoing. His negligence is not placed side by side with *adikia*, voluntary crime, as another, lesser degree of guilt. It is the great factor in the genesis of crime, the soil in which the latter grows. It is the sloth, the reprehensible lack of moral fibre, which results in, and grounds your responsibility for, evil actions, actions which, in the Roman grouping, are to be assigned to *dolus*. Only a man constantly striving for perfection will remain free from evil, while evil—the dolose deed—is the ultimate outcome of lack of discipline.[15] Contrary to Socrates's teaching, sin is voluntary, the sinner's "not knowing" (which cannot be denied) his own fault, a reflection of his carelessness. We must not harmonize this with the Roman scheme.[16]

15. Considering this aspect of Aristotle's theory, I am not sure whether Kunkel (*ZRG* 45 [1925]: 344) does not assume too close a connection between the *aner spoudaios* and the *diligens paterfamilias*.

16. It is just conceivable that the clause "in the other instances . . ." refers not to ordinary crime, but to the states of mind previously paired off with drunkenness, namely, rage and passionate desire (above, pp. 129–30). If so, what Aristotle is saying is that he who acts in such a state quite obviously does not know what he is about, yet society punishes him: his not knowing what he is about is due to defective discipline, a man must from the

In Deuteronomy,[17] the idolatrous Israel is reproached: "Thou hast forgotten God that formed thee." In Roman and Roman-inspired law, forgetfulness is among the commonest varieties of negligence, the lesser guilt. But it would be wrong to think that this passage from the Old Testament is introducing the standard of *culpa* as midway between *dolus* and *casus*. Forgetfulness here means defection, rebellion, criminal sloth, it is the height of wickedness: "They are a very froward generation."[18] Similarly, the unconcern of which Aristotle speaks characterizes the criminal, it is not as if it were split off from vice as a lighter matter, but the two go together, the former being the attitude which produces the latter. The Deuteronomic forgetting and this Aristotelian remissness in the self-formation of the evil character[19] could exist in systems which never thought of opposing the deed from *culpa* to *dolus* or *casus*.

Lastly, we may look at a third section in the *Ethica Nicomachea*[20] which, while harking back to the distinction proposed in the *Rhetorica* for use in a criminal trial, at the same time incorporates the wider notion of a deed from ignorance worked out (we have seen) in a preceding part of the Ethics. The result of the combination is the appearance of *hamartema* in two senses: the narrow old one, you mistake a friend for a foe, and an enlarged one which embraces *atychema*, your spear takes the wrong course. But again, there is nothing corresponding to *culpa*, negligence: that is a foreign body introduced by later students of the work.

Aristotle begins by arguing that voluntariness is of the essence of just or unjust conduct, hence only voluntary wrongdoing can be blamed. Voluntariness is excluded by ignorance or compulsion, and the former may have regard to the person you are attacking (you do not know he is your father), the instrument you are wielding (you believe the spear has a button on it), the effect of what you are doing (you mean to prick but

---

outset strive to tame himself. My main argument remains unaffected: there is no trace of a separate standard of negligence, negligence—in the sense of leading an undirected life—is what lies behind the doing of evil and what deprives an evildoer of excuse.

17. Deut. 32:18.

18. Deut. 32:20.

19. The very way in which I put this indicates that Deut. and Aristotle's *Eth. Nic.* are widely different.

20. Aristotle, *Eth. Nic.* 5.8.1ff., 1135a 15ff.

it comes out as a grievous injury) or indeed the whole action (*ten praxis holen*, the catapult you are demonstrating goes off).[21]

This is the doctrine we found him expounding in a previous chapter: mistake, in the traditional sense, and accident are both subsumed under the one heading of ignorance. I have already pointed out that, though perhaps a *tour de force*, this compression is not without some rational foundation: if you knew that by an unfortunate coincidence what you intend as a prick will be a serious wound, or that the catapult's spring will break, you would proceed differently no less than if you knew the person you are about to strike to be your father. Viewed from this angle, harm caused by accident is construable as harm inflicted as a result of ignorance.

A few paragraphs further on,[22] Aristotle draws the consequence by affixing the label *hamartema* to the entire complex of mistake and accident. A deed springing from ignorance, he says, is a *hamartema*, and this includes the case where you do not mean to hit a man at all (say, you demonstrate a catapult) as well as that where you do mean to hit him but only because you are in error as to his identity. Within this broad area of *hamartema*, however, he goes on to distinguish—exactly as in the *Rhetorica*—between *atychema*, accident, where the harm occurs *paralogos*, unexpectedly, and *hamartema* in its narrower sense, where the harm does not occur *paralogos*, you do intend it, and none the less there is no *kakia*, badness, on your part—evidently the case where you mix up friend and enemy, father and stranger. It is interesting that, in his further elucidation of the difference between *atychema* and *hamartema*, he employs an idea which is not represented in his *Rhetorica*, though it is in the *Rhetorica ad Alexandrum*. The latter, it may be recalled, defines *atychema*, accident, as the case where things go wrong "not through yourself (as they do in *hamartema*, mistake, where, under the influence of an erroneous assumption, the harm is intended) but through other people or a mishap." Aristotle explains that in the case of *hamartema* the origin of the train of events (*arche tes aitias*)[23] lies in you, in the case of *atychema*, outside.[24]

---

21. Of the examples in brackets, the first is found in *Eth. Nic.* 5.8.3, 1135a, 30, the third in 5.8.6, 1135b, 15, the second and fourth in 3.1.17, 1111a, 10ff.

22. Aristotle, *Eth. Nic.* 5.8.6, 1135b, 11ff.

23. The popular emendation of *aitias* into *agnoias* is, of course, quite unjustified.

24. The sequence *hamartema—atychema*, too, is the same as in the *Rh. Al.*

In contrast with *hamartema* in the wider sense—mistake and accident—is the deed perpetrated knowingly: *adikema*. There is no need here to go into the division between an offence committed in a passion, especially in a rage (and, more especially, under provocation), and a premeditated offence. In the former event, though guilty of a wicked deed, the doer need not be wicked, whereas in the latter he is.[25]

Kübler quotes this chapter of the *Ethica Nicomachea* for his thesis—*adikema* equals *dolus*, intentional wrongdoing, *hamartema* equals *culpa*, negligence, and *atychema* equals *casus*, accident. He is anticipated by Maschke, for whom "Aristotle is the creator of the Greco-Roman and modern doctrine of liability."[26] Note the "and modern." Throughout his discussion, Maschke attributes to Aristotle not only the establishment of the standard of negligence[27] but even highly specialized teachings of the early twentieth century.[28]

However, neither Kübler nor Maschke could have fathered the Roman scheme on Aristotle had the latter not been considerably Romanized long before. His transformation began as early as some fourteen hundred years ago. Gauthier and Jolif, in their masterly commentary on the *Ethica Nicomachea*, like everybody, identify *hamartema* with negligence, and they offer the example of a man who, practising with a weapon on a road, hits a passerby; the same disaster on land duly assigned to such practice would be *atychema*. As the example is found in a work on the *Ethica Nicomachea* possibly dating from the sixth century AD, they believe it to be about as

25. Aristotle, *Eth. Nic.* 5.8.8ff., 1135b, 20ff. Incidentally, it is generally held that the three types of injury Aristotle declares to exist in 5.8.6, 1135b, 11, are *hamartema*, *atychema* and *adikema*. This is possible, but it would make his arrangement awfully clumsy. I regard it as far more probable that the three types are *hamartema* in the extensive meaning (subdivided into *atychema* and *hamartema* proper), wrong committed in a passion, and wrong premeditated.

26. Maschke, *Die Willenslehre im Griechischen Recht* (1926), 123.

27. Proceeding from the traditional misinterpretation of the sentence cited above, "in the other instances where the not knowing is the consequence of unconcern," 3.5.9, 1114a 1, he remarks, p. 154, that *damit ist eine generelle Diligenzpflicht in gewissem Umfange statuiert.*

28. The entire treatment of 5.8.6ff., 1135b 11ff., on pp. 156ff., is vitiated by radical Romanization cum modernization.

good as if it were from Aristotle himself.[29] But a great deal had happened in the intervening eight hundred years in the law and legal thought of the Mediterranean world. The Roman jurists had indeed brought the category of *culpa* to bear on cases of this sort: if you prune your tree and kill somebody's slave passing by, in principle you are liable only if he was walking on a public road, yet given certain conditions you may be guilty of *culpa* even if it all takes place on your property.[30] Or again, if, playing at ball, you push over and injure the caddie, it is *casus* rather than *culpa*.[31] On the basis of the authentic Aristotle, if, while practising, you unwittingly hit a passerby, it is *paralogos*, unexpected, *atychema*, accident, no matter whether you are in the gymnasium or on a highway. Interestingly, Clement of Alexandria, about AD 200, who heavily draws on Aristotle, is not yet Romanizing at all.[32]

By the way, there is a significant time lag in the Romanization of Aristotle between the commentaries, the translations and the indexes. The commentaries are the first to bring him up to date—I have just mentioned a (possibly) sixth-century one—and they have little difficulty in going as far as they like. Gauthier and Jolif affirm that *hamartema* is *l'homicide par imprudence de notre législation*.[33] Translations are naturally more resistant. For instance, in the sixteenth and seventeenth centuries,

29. Gauthier and Jolif, *Aristotle, L'Ethique à Nicomaque*, vol. 2, pt. 1 (1959), 401, referring to Heylbut, *Eustratii et Michaelis et Anonyma in Ethica Nicomachea Commentaria* (= *Commentaria in Aristotelem Graeca*, ed. Prussian Academy, 20), (1892), 238.

30. Digest 9.2.31, Paul X *ad Sabinum*; cf. Institutes 4.7.3; I omit details. See Watson, *The Law of Obligations in the Later Roman Republic* (1965), 238ff.

31. Digest 9.2.52.4, cf. 10.3.26, Alfenus II *digestorum*. In Antiphon's *Second Tetralogy*, where a boy is killed picking up the javelins in the gymnasium (3.6), the problem is conceived chiefly as one of causation; the prosecution holding that the person who threw the weapon caused the death, the defence that it was caused by the boy himself since he ran into the path of the weapon. See Maschke, *Die Willenslehre im Griechischen Recht* (1926), 73ff.

32. Clemens Alexandrinus, *Stromateis* 14–15, 60.1ff. There is, needless to say, much deviation from Aristotle. For example, according to 15, 62.2, it is *hamartema* to lead a dissolute life, *atychema* to strike a friend believing him an enemy, *adikema* to violate a tomb. But the standard of negligence does not yet intrude. In 15, 64.4, he says—quite in the spirit of Aristotle—that readiness for education and obedience to the laws are within our power.

33. Gauthier and Jolif, *Aristotle, L'Ethique à Nicomaque*, vol. 2, pt. 1 (1959), 401.

paralogos, the quality characteristically attaching to *atychema*, accident, and not attaching to *hamartema*, ignorance, is still correctly translated *inopinato* or *praeter rationem*. A reader not misled by commentaries could still reach the right understanding: whereas in *atychema* the harm is unintended, comes about contrary to all calculation, in *hamartema* it is intended, by no means unlooked for (it is *nec inopinato* or *nec practer rationem*)—only the intention is formed in reliance on a false premise, friend is taken for foe. An unbiased reader, that is, would hardly import the criterion of care or carelessness. By contrast, Rackham, the translator of the *Ethica Nicomachea* for the Loeb Classical Library, renders *paralogos* not by "contrary to expectation," but by "contrary to reasonable expectation"; so if you are careless, unintended harm, though it is unexpected, is not reasonably unexpected and therefore falls under *hamartema*. The standard of negligence is here smuggled into the very text, though even here with a certain restraint, and a footnote is still needed to make the modern meaning quite explicit.[34] The translations by Ross and others are *au fond* equally faulty. I cannot possibly list even a fraction of the distortions due to the fundamental flaw in this matter common to all students of Aristotle. Yet in the indexes of editions, whether in Greek or in another language, invariably we look in vain for entries under a heading "Negligence" or the like. To this day, there has been no thorough, comfortable amalgamation of the misconception with the system as a whole.

The texts invoked by Kübler, then, cannot have furnished the model for the Roman standards. Should we make such a fuss about them? Since Freud we know we must do with *dolus* alone; there is definitely no *casus*. If I accidentally break my toothglass, it is either because I dislike it, or because I like it and want to punish myself, or indeed because I neither dislike it nor like it but substitute it for something else which I either dislike or like. . . .

---

34. Rackham, *Aristotle, The Nicomachean Ethics* (1956), 300–1: "*atychema*, accident or misadventure, an offence due to mistake and not reasonably to be expected, and *hamartema* in the narrow sense, a similar offence that ought to have been foreseen." In 3.5.9, 1114a, 3, incidentally, Rackham, p. 147, misparaphrases: "as he could have taken the trouble to ascertain the facts." As demonstrated above, the passage (literally, "as he had the power to be concerned") does not envisage harm inflicted negligently in the sense that the doer ought to know more about the particular situation. It envisages lack of application as the source of dolose wrongdoing: "as he could have taken the trouble to discipline himself."

Kübler, however, claims that he has direct evidence of the take over he alleges, namely, a reference by Paul—preserved in the Institutes of Justinian[35]—to *culpa quam Graeci adikema dicunt,* "culpa which the Greeks call *adikema.*" But for one thing, Paul, writing at the beginning of the third century AD, is a poor witness of what would have taken place two-hundred-and-fifty years earlier. For another, he associates *culpa* with *adikema*; not *hamartema* at all. So Kübler considers emendation, the substitution of *hamartema.* To this, however, he realizes one may object because the reading *adikema* is confirmed by Theophilus's *Paraphrase of the Institutes.* He says one should not be put off too much: maybe the authors of the Institutes themselves replaced *hamartema* by *adikema* since they were no longer familiar with Aristotle's classification.

Well, *hamartema* is not there. Worse, even if it had the meaning attributed to it by Kübler, it would be the wrong word and *adikema* the right one. Paul is thinking of the *culpa* which grounds liability under the *lex Aquilia,* concerning damage to property. He represents it as synonymous with *iniuria,* the term occurring in the *lex.* It comprises *dolus* as well as negligence—anything not accident.[36] *Hamartema* would be out of the question even if it signified negligence. I do not think I need go on with this text.[37]

---

35. Institutes 4.4. pr. Pauline provenance is more or less guaranteed by *Coll.* 2.5.1, *libro singulari de iniuriis,* though the clause is part of a bit which has dropped out of the *Coll.*

36. This is rightly stressed by Kunkel, ZRG 49 (1929): 163, 171. Whether, as he considers possible, the classic wrote *damnum culpa datum* where we now find *culpa* may be left open. Schulz, *Roman Legal Science* (1946), 196, upholds the present version, *culpa.*

37. Still, a note on a further argument of Kübler's. In the following part of the text, Paul mentions another application of *iniuria,* namely miscarriage of justice, *iniquitas et iniustitia,* for which the Greek, he says, is *adikia.* Kübler urges that as *adikia* is used in this very bad sense, *adikema* could not be used for the far milder *culpa;* here, he concludes, is support for his replacement of *adikema* by *hamartema.* However, first, as *culpa-adikema* in this passage embraces both negligence and *dolus* (which fact Kübler overlooks and has to overlook), the sense is not quite so mild. Secondly, in Greek writings *adikema* is often met as denoting or at least including an unintentional offence; Philo speaks of "voluntary and involuntary *adikemata*" (*De Posteritate Caini* 13.48). Thirdly, *adikema* and *adikia* are, after all, two different nouns and a writer may well endow them with different nuances. Fourthly, *non constat* that Paul's two definitions of *iniuria*—as *culpa-adikema* in the area of the *lex Aquilia,* as *iniquitas et iniustitia-adikia* in that of miscarriage of justice—go back

Among the reasons for the difference between the Greek scheme and the Roman is this, that the former is primarily concerned with a criminal law trial, the latter with a claim for payment of damages.

The Greek scheme proceeds from the trial of a crime, indeed, from homicide. According to the Greek experts, the defence has three possibilities. (1) It can deny the deed: the accused did not kill at all. (2) It can admit the deed but maintain that it was lawful: for instance, the accused killed in self-defence. Or (3) it can admit the deed but raise special pleas—such as ignorance or accident, the accused did not know the man belonged to his own army, the accused was only demonstrating the catapult which went off. In this scheme, if negligence were to be given a place, its chief role would be that of a counter-plea to accident. The prosecution would be able to reply: Yes, the catapult went off unexpectedly, but you could and should have been more careful, so though you are less blameworthy than a real murderer, you are not free of blame. In antiquity, however, the need for this counter-plea is not too pressing. Were it not for rather novel features of our civilization such as wholesale surgery and, above all, road traffic, negligence would not be very prominent in criminal law. "In modern times," say Cross and Jones, "most cases of manslaughter by criminal negligence . . . arise in connection with the driving of a motorcar by the accused."[38] In other words, in ancient criminal law, once allowance is made for the unwitting character of a deed, little urgency attaches to the splitting off of negligence as something between accident and *dolus*.

The deed from ignorance, let me remark—I mistake the man for an enemy soldier—has an enormous fascination for the ancients, an incomparably greater one than accident. If we survey homicide in Greek lay literature, accident is rare but error of all kinds abounds. Oedipus kills his father unaware of their relationship; the daughters of Pelias kill theirs expecting Medea to bring him back rejuvenated; Prokris is killed by her

---

to a single source; so the postulate of absolute consistency is hardly justified. It would be dubious even if the definitions did come from the same source. *Hamartema* itself is a good illustration of the lack of rigour in such matters. In his *Rh.* 2.22.7, 1396a, Aristotle understands by it an evil deed, without any mitigation. The verb *hamartanein* in *Eth. Nic.* 5.8.8, 1135b, 23, refers to an offence committed in a passion.

38. Cross and Jones, *An Introduction to Criminal Law*, 5th ed. (1964), 152. I like the "by the accused." As careful legal writers, they point out that the dead are not called to account before our tribunals.

husband who mistakes her for a doe; Pentheus is torn to pieces by his mother and other Bacchantes who think he is a lion; Aktaeon is hunted to death by his own dogs and friends who see a stag in him; Theseus fatally curses his son Hippolytos whom he believes to have seduced Phaedra; Kreon, misjudging his authority over against the higher laws of heaven, sentences Antigone to death. Similarly, in the Biblical narratives, Old Testament and New, there is only one case of accidental homicide, and it is so insignificant *qua* homicide, this aspect is so little made of, that you will never think of it: I offer a third of my Gray Lecturer's stipend—the whole fee for this Lecture—to whoever can name me the case at the end of the next quarter of an hour. By contrast, homicide from ignorance plays a considerable part, up to the putting to death of Jesus by them who know not what they do.

Of the three postures of the defence, (1) the accused did not kill at all, (2) he did kill but lawfully, (3) he did kill but he has an excuse such as ignorance or accident, posture (1) is least interesting from a philosophical point of view. It involves a simple question of fact, a matter for the police to clear up. The literary genre representing this posture is the detective story, opening with a number of suspects each of whom professes innocence, "I did not do it," and going on to pick out the culprit. An author may excel in psychological finesse and style; nevertheless, considering the essentially flat theme, it is understandable that this branch of writing ranks relatively low.[39] It is postures (2) and (3) which furnish material for the magnificent, searching works of the Greeks and Hebrews. Antigone insists that her transgression of the king's command was lawful, dictated by a superior principle. Oedipus invokes his total ignorance of the relevant circumstances. The Amalekite who slew Saul mistakenly thought his deed would be agreeable to David.[40] In Jonah, the sinful people of Nineveh are pardoned because they cannot discern between their right hand and their left hand—a consideration foreshadowing Jesus's prayer for forgiveness for his enemies. Here lie the worthwhile puzzles for those who ponder human ways: where it is a question of the justification of a prima facie wrongful deed, and, above all, where it is a question of an agent under the influence of error.

39. I love it.
40. 2 Sam. 4:10.

Accident, however, though it falls under the same heading of special pleas as ignorance, defence no. (3), is found far less deserving of deeper study. The deed in error is felt to be the real problem of man as man, as a thinking being; error—where things proceed not unexpectedly, not *paralogos*, not *praeter rationem*, but on the contrary as intended, everything goes according to plan, in the language of Aristotle you are the author of the train of events—and yet it is all flawed by ignorance, misapprehension, misjudgment, when the desired result is finally achieved, when you have killed the soldier you aimed at, it turns out to be a calamity. The accidental deed does not show up the defective nature of man at his highest level, the level of thought. Essentially it is just an expression of that subjection to fate which is common to all that exists: men, beasts, even inanimate objects. If the javelin with which I practise hits an onlooker, that is no different, *au fond*, from his being hit by lightning—except that heaven has used me as instrument instead of an electric current. It has nothing to do with my rational self.[41] It is highly relevant that, for Aristotle, tragedy is characterized by that peculiarly human plight, where the rational design is carried out and then proves to have been disastrous. A person accidentally smashing his toothglass is not tragic, in Aristotle's sense.[42]

Here I would note that the current misinterpretation of his *Rhetorica* and *Ethica Nicomachea*, which turns *hamartema* into negligence, quite overlooks the close link with the theory of tragedy set forth in his

41. To be sure, to the religious mind even the accidental deed did pose a worrying problem: why is this particular man used as fate's instrument? Philo and the Rabbis answered, because of a previous sin he must have committed: see Daube, *Vetus Testamentum* 11 (1961): 267 [BLL 425-26]. In that article I left it undecided whether the idea reached Philo from the Rabbis or the Rabbis from Philo. (Independent development is ruled out by the strikingly similar way in which the idea finds expression in the two.) I would now accord priority to Philo, for the idea occurs (as I had not noticed) in Antiphon's *Second Tetralogy* 3.8 (see above, p. 136n31, and below, pp. 156ff.). The prosecution argues that if the stain of unwitting killing falls upon a man from heaven for his impiety, it would be wrong to impede this visitation and acquit him. So Philo is drawing on his Hellenistic education.

42. From the moment that, as in the *Eth. Nic.*, the accidental deed is subsumed under ignorance and consequently becomes *hamartema* in an extended application, it does partake of the nature of the tragic, it does represent a flaw in reasoning. But Aristotle's theory of tragedy is based on the narrower meaning of *hamartema*, be it that he worked it out before he arrived at the wider meaning, be it that only a theory based on the narrower meaning did justice to the actual tragic material before him.

Poetics. The tragic hero, he explains, is overthrown not through badness and wickedness, *kakia* and *mochtheria*, but through some great error, *hamartia megale*; and it is his discovery of his error, his passing from ignorance, *agnoia*, to knowledge, which fully completes his tragedy.[43] The terminology is too similar to that in the *Ethica Nicomachea* to warrant the assumption of two utterly disparate lines of thought. But surely it is impossible to bring negligence into the *Poetics*. Aristotle instances Oedipus and Thyestes as typifying his tragic hero. Are we to impute negligence to Thyestes because he did not examine the meat set before him by his brother in order to make sure that it was not his own son he was eating? Was that the essence of his tragedy? Would the myth of Oedipus really be the same if Oedipus had taken a corner with more haste than caution would demand, and had bumped into his father—whom he knew—so that the latter succumbed? For that matter, would it make no difference to the story of the New Testament if Jesus had died being struck by a tile which fell from a roof as a result of the carelessness of some Jewish and Roman workers engaged on repair?

I am far from denying that, in certain areas of the law, the Greeks did fairly early make (or come near to making) negligence into a standard of liability—for instance, in connection with the holding of offices, but in other contexts too. There are advances in this direction in Antiphon's *Tetralogies*; under Plato's regime a guardian of an orphan is subject to a penalty if guilty of negligence or knavery (*amelein* or *kakourgein*).[44] Aristotle was of course familiar with all such developments.[45] My point is that not only do they occupy a very subordinate place in myth, saga, drama, but, above all, they are simply not reflected in the passages which I have reviewed as relevant to Kübler's thesis, that is to say, in the threefold

43. Aristotle, *Poetica* 11, 1452a, 29–30, 13, 1453a, 7ff., 14, 1453b, 30–31, 1454a, 3–4. Discovery as conceived by Aristotle has a wide range; it can, for example, take place in time so as to prevent the horrible deed. There is no need here to enlarge on this topic.

44. Plato, *Leg.*, 928B.

45. The lawgiver, when regulating education, must start with procuring the most promising material, hence the most suitable parents: "he must first bestow diligence (*epimelein*) on marriage," Aristotle, *Politica* 7.14, 1134b, 31. Note, however, that this is one of those numerous recommendations of diligence which cannot be said to create a technical standard: there is no court to conduct an inquiry into diligence or negligence in any given case and render its verdict in accordance with the result.

scheme of the *Rhetorica* and *Ethica Nicomachea* from which he affirms that the Romans took their division.

Whether or not Roman law was influenced by those cases where Greek philosophers, orators and jurists approached or achieved the standard of negligence, I shall not discuss; I think some influence is highly probable. What chiefly accounts for the Roman classification *dolus*, evil intent, *culpa*, negligence, *casus*, accident, as distinct from the Greek one, is that its root is in civil law, concerned with compensation, rather than in criminal law or, more narrowly, the law of homicide, concerned with retribution.

In the latter, as I have just argued, at a time when there are not large numbers of negligent killings, to protect from retribution, or excessive retribution, the unwitting doer, the man actuated by no *dolus*, is good enough; there is no urgent need to refine and exclude negligence from this protection. In disputes about compensation, however, such an arrangement would not do. Neither in delict (you damage my boat) nor in contract (you fail to deliver the merchandise promised) would it make sense generally to relieve of accountability everyone but the deliberate offender. In some relationships, no doubt it is all right to allow a claim only on the ground of *dolus*, for example, where you gratuitously execute a commission for me. As a rule justice, it is felt, requires that he who causes loss or disappointment, with or without intent, should make it good— unless indeed events were beyond his control: the book you borrowed from me perishes in a conflagration.

It is this latter limitation which is a vital factor in the Roman scheme. At a primitive stage, when the sifting of evidence as to the precise situation and conduct of a party presents huge difficulties, recourse may be had to fixed external criteria; say, a borrower is free if the object disappears as a result of fire, earthquake or armed robbery. This objectively based liability will work fairly, in the vast majority of cases, though admittedly a less dramatic occurrence may exceptionally be as overwhelming as one of the recognized acts of God, while some other time it may be possible to save a book even from a fire. In course of time the courts tend to dispense with these rigid criteria and go by the merits of any given case. (The development is neither uniform throughout the entire legal order nor irreversible. For a variety of reasons the past fifty years have seen a revival of strict liability in many branches of the law.) Once the subjective attitude of each individual defendant is gone into, the Roman classification is a plausible one to emerge: the defendant will assert that he could not help things, and that plea will collapse not only if he displayed *dolus* but also if he displayed negligence.

Even in Greece, let me repeat, in quite a few cases negligence is recognized as grounding liability. But it does not figure in a system of standards comparable to the Roman, most definitely not in the chapters from Aristotle we have considered.

The Roman rhetorical works show an intriguing mixture. The basic structure, borrowed from the Greek predecessors, is still largely dominated by the criminal trial; but the cases discussed have shifted to lesser crimes and even near to private law, and blameworthy behaviour other than sheer *dolus* plays a considerable part.[46] Thus we are told of a Rhodian decree under which a ship with a ram entering the harbour will be confiscated: what is to happen to a ship driven there by a storm? Prima facie, this is an instance of accident, act of God. But the decision, we learn, is not so easy. It will depend on whether the necessity could have been avoided, the storm foreseen, on whether there was *inertia, neglegentia, fatuitas*. What in Antiphon is adumbrated in speeches about a peculiar mishap and in Aristotle is confined to a few contexts mainly to do with public or semi-public office,[47] has become articulated and generalized, an established component of forensic theory. It is now possible to raise the question of negligence wherever accident is invoked to escape from a fine or the like. Maybe some of this advance already goes back to late Hellenistic writings lost to us; but I should be surprised if a good deal of it were not genuinely Roman.

When did the Roman jurists start speaking of *culpa* in connection with negligence—be it that the term meant fault in a wide sense, whether *dolus* or negligence (this usage seems to have come up first), be it that it meant negligence as such, specifically?[48] In the field of the *lex Aquilia*,

---

46. Cicero, *Rhet. Her.* 2.16.23ff.; *Inv. rhet.* 2.31.94ff.

47. And, of course, in ethics, sloth is the root of all evil; but this, as I have tried to demonstrate, does not make it into a legal ground of liability.

48. I am simplifying: even by the end of the classical period there were few cases in which *culpa* was fully synonymous with *neglegentia*. For the purpose of my argument, however, these finer points may be disregarded.

concerning damage to property, the date is relatively early, about 100 BC. Quintus Mucius Scaevola employs *culpa* in a decision quoted above, about a man who prunes trees and kills a slave passing by, and Alfenus Varus, some sixty years later, is obviously familiar with the concept; one of the cases where he works with it I have also adverted to already—the ball player pushing over and injuring a caddie.[49]

For other fields, the earliest evidence is found in Servius, who flourished about 50 BC, between Mucius and Menus. He declares that in respect of objects received by way of dowry, a husband is liable for both *dolus* and *culpa*. (He would be liable under the latter heading, for example, if he allowed a fine house to deteriorate.) It is generally believed that this was laid down already by Publius Mucius Scaevola, father of Quintus Mucius—so that *culpa* would have operated, or at least would be attested, in dowry one generation before it operated, or is attested, in damage to property, instead of one generation after.

However, Publius Mucius went less far than Servius. His niece was married to C. Gracchus. In 121 BC there was a riot, Gracchus was pronounced a public enemy, his house plundered by the mob, he himself killed and his property confiscated. The authorities resolved, however, to let the widow have back her dowry. It was then that her uncle contended that this ought to include everything she would have got had she reclaimed the dowry from her husband; hence it ought to include compensation for dotal objects destroyed in the riot, since the latter had been caused by her husband's *culpa*. Not surprisingly the authorities did not accept this advice.[50]

If we do not let ourselves be blinded by later developments, it emerges that, basically, Publius Mucius still adhered to a husband's liability for

---

49. Digest 9.2.31, Paul *X ad Sabinum*; 9.2.52.4, Alfenus *II digestorum*. The case of the pruner illustrates the precedence of negligence in private law. Mucius is concerned with the monetary claim of the owner of the slave killed. A *lex Cornelia* of Sulla, imposing severe punishment on the killing of a man free or unfree, is applicable to the deliberate deed only. In Digest 48.8.7, Paul *singulari de publicis iudiciis*, we are expressly told that a pruner who does not call out, thus causing the death of a passer, does not fall under the statute—though, admittedly, P.S. 5.23.12 adds (no doubt on the assumption that the pruner would be of low status) that nevertheless he will be sentenced to work in the mines.

50. Digest 24.3.66 pr., Javolenus *VI ex posterioribus Labeonis*; Plutarch, *Vit.*, *C. Gracch.* 17.5; Appian, *Bella civilia* 1.3.26; see Daube, *Studi Biondo Biondi* I (1963): 199ff.

dolus alone. Certainly he did apply the term *culpa*; not, however, in the sense of negligence but in that of reprehensible activity leading to an unfortunate result. (One might compare, also from the law of dowry, the notion of a divorce which, though effected by one spouse, yet is brought about by the *culpa* of the other.)[51] Again, he did unquestionably extend liability: the husband's wrongdoing had no specific relation to the dowry, it was not as if Gracchus had committed *dolus* in dealing with the goods brought in by his wife, his misconduct merely caused the incident, the sedition, in the course of which they perished. The jurist, then, was moving in the direction of inclusion of negligence. But it was Servius who took the decisive step in establishing the wide scope of a husband's liability: *dolus* and *culpa*, dolose behaviour and negligence. That is, after all, why this rule is associated with his name. Very probably he invoked the opinion of Publius Mucius Scaevola in support, and later jurists— Labeo, Javolenus—saw that opinion as anticipating his statement.[52] This should not make us overlook the gap between the two—a typical one: in those three-quarters of a century between Publius Mucius and Servius there was much evolution of this kind, from carefully groping first steps in a particular case to fully formulated principle.

What is of special interest is that Servius was able to exploit an opinion using *culpa* in the sense of dolose, criminal activity for his rule that a husband is answerable not only for *dolus* but also for *culpa*— signifying negligence. The oscillating character of *culpa* remains important throughout Roman law. Earlier on in this discussion I cited Paul referring to *culpa* as a condition of liability in damage to property, *culpa quam Graeci adikema dicunt*: here *culpa* covers *dolus* as well as negligence, anything not *casus*.[53] All this renders it even more unlikely that the triad *dolus-culpa-*

51. E.g. *Fr. Vat.* 121, Papinian *IV responsorum*; see Bonfante, *Corso di Diritto Romano*, vol. 1 (1925), 256. From the field of the *lex Aquilia*, cf. Digest 9.2.52.1, Alfenus *II digestorum*. Somebody removes a lantern in front of a shop; the shopkeeper runs after him; the fugitive strikes him with a whip; in the ensuing scuffle the shopkeeper puts out one of the man's eyes. No damages, Alfenus holds: *culpam penes eum qui prior flagello percussit residere*, "culpa rests with him who first struck with a whip."

52. Digest 24.3.66 pr.: *Dolum malum et culpam eum praestare oportere Servius ait; ea sententia Publii Mucii est.*

53. Institutes 4.4 pr.; cf. *Coll.* 2.5.1, Paul *libro singulari de iniuriis*.

casus represents a simple transfer into Roman law of a ready-made Greek classification.[54]

Differentiation in Life and Differentiation in Law

Negligence

I wish to make some remarks to dissociate myself from a widespread fallacy.[55] Historians often fail to distinguish between the idea that application is desirable and negligence to be avoided—an exceedingly old idea—and the operation of diligence or negligence as a legal standard in the sense that a court's decision will turn on whether defendant has acted as he ought to—a far later phenomenon. For that matter, as I shall elaborate below, they often fail to distinguish between the condemnation of *dolus*—very old—and *dolus* as a standard in the sense that the verdict in a trial will depend on whether or not the individual accused has behaved dolosely—not always so old.

In early Roman law the tutor of a person under age, or the curator of a lunatic, could be proceeded against only if his conduct was dishonest, dolose.[56] This does not mean that a tutor was not from the beginning expected to *tueri*, "guard his charge," a curator to *curare*, "look after him": a great deal more than abstention from embezzlement. It would be as wrong to infer from their exclusive liability for *dolus* that the duty to do a decent, diligent job was not seen, as it would be to infer from the designation "tutor" or "curator" that any remissness in *tueri* or *curare* would lead to judicial accountability. Again, there is an aedilician edict imposing a substantial fine on you if an animal you keep by the wayside escapes and kills somebody or does damage. You must pay up no matter how careful you may have been: strict liability.[57] Yet it would be foolish

54. By the way, I wonder whether the English "guilt" may not be etymologically related to *culpa*. I am not saying that it is probable, but neither does it strike me as impossible.

55. Cf. Daube, *Vetus Testamentum* 11 (1961): 246ff [BLL, 72, 73].

56. E.g. *actio de rationibus distrahendis*, Buckland, *Text-Book* (1963), 163.

57. Digest 21.1.40.42, Ulpian *II ad edictum aedilium curulium*, 1.4.9.1.

to deny that circus owners were unaware of the need for and usefulness of scrupulous precautions. A General may be answerable for treachery only, or for treachery and carelessness, or for any defeat, even an inevitable one. Whichever system prevails, people know that a General had better exercise care and foresight. These reflections stand to reason, but they are apt to be forgotten. Let me be more specific.

Frequently it is thought that, because in a certain matter diligence is recommended or a warning against negligence given, that must be the technical standard applied by the courts. However, it need not be. I shall give one typical example of such a mistaken deduction, which then serves as basis for a major historical judgment: Goodenough's attribution of this standard to the Jewish practice at Alexandria around New Testament times.[58]

According to Biblical law, if a man kindles a fire on his land and it spreads to that of his neighbour, he is obliged to compensate the latter. His liability is absolute: there is no clause to restrict it to the case where there has been negligence on his part.[59] Tannaitic law, that is to say, the early Talmudic law of, say 100 BC to AD 200, still adheres to this regulation.[60] Goodenough claims that Philo, however, writing at Alexandria in the first third of the first century AD, depicts a more progressive state, with the standard of negligence fully recognized: so Alexandrian Jewish practice is in advance of the Rabbinical one of the same period.

What is this claim founded on? On a series of admonitions by Philo which, while accompanying the precept in question, are anything but a part of it. Philo in his work on Biblical law, modeling himself on Plato who held that laws should be supported by reasons, usually gives detailed comments on a provision, setting out its function and making us appreciate Moses's wisdom in promulgating it. With regard to fire,[61] he begins by enlarging on the danger of this element and the desirability of the utmost caution. Then he goes on to state the regulation, and he states

---

58. Goodenough, *The Jewish Courts in Egypt* (1929), 163–64.

59. Exod. 22:5.

60. *Mekhilta on Exodus* 22:5; *Misnah Baba Qamma* 1.1, 6.4ff.

61. Philo, *De Specialibus Legibus* 4.6.26ff.; Exod. 22:5 is also mentioned in Philo, *Legum Allegoriae* 3.89.248ff. where fire stands for the irrational impulse which, with the help of the passions, consumes virtue and so on.

it exactly as it appears in the Bible and early Talmud: if a fire you kindle on your land escapes, you must make restitution—no proviso that the judge should probe and let you off, for instance, if the wind turned in a way you could not foresee. Finally he returns to the theme of his introduction, adding that the offender, having to make amends, will learn to be more careful in future.

What Goodenough does is to mix Philo's socio-moral advice and the law into one—an unwarranted procedure. All that Philo says about the importance of being careful with fire must have been known to Prometheus, let alone Moses or the Tannaitic Rabbis. If they none the less ordain strict liability, exacting compensation even if the damage is the result of accident, it is chiefly because, in their age, it would be too difficult to get the evidence for each individual case. In general if your fire spreads, it is due to negligence; so in general the precept is fair—the occasional exception just cannot be provided for. But neither does Philo provide for it. He takes if for granted that if your fire does harm you are at fault—the fine, he remarks, will make you more careful—which is by no means the same as saying that you need pay only if you are at fault in the actual case. As many of us know to our cost, quite a few modern traffic laws fine you for the act, making no allowance for the case where, exceptionally, you are free from negligence. A future historian will err if, from a newspaper article which says that traffic laws are needed because of young people speeding to their amorous engagements, he concludes that you are let off if you can prove you were on the way to a meeting of the College Council.[62]

62. I incline to regard Plato's law about fire as essentially identical with Philo's and, indeed, a probable source of inspiration for the latter's presentation. In Plato, *Leg.* 843Cff. neighbors are exhorted to take care (*eulabein, dieulabein*) not to commit unfriendly acts against one another and, above all, not to encroach on one another's land. There follow several laws which seem to envisage dolose trespass, and then one to the effect that if a man in burning down his waste does not take care and the fire spreads to the adjoining field, he shall pay a fine to be fixed by the officials. At first sight this looks like liability for negligence: negligence is mentioned, not as in Philo in the exposition, but in the law itself. I greatly doubt, however, whether even Plato intends to make negligence by the particular defendant a condition of the fine. The reference to lack of care, it seems to me, simply reflects his concentration on the normal situation, his assumption (shared by Philo) that the spreading of such a fire must be due to negligence: the exceptional case just does not enter into consideration. Even here, that is, liability is absolute *[continues onto next page]*

Goodenough's erroneous conclusion unfortunately has major consequences, since it is among the vital props of the thesis to which the book in which it occurs is devoted. His argument runs as follows. Early Talmudic law does not use the standard of negligence. First century Roman law does. First century Alexandrian Jewish law does. Ergo—his main thesis—in weighty matters the Jewish courts in Egypt follow an independent line, looking not to the Rabbis but to Rome.

Only the first step of the argument is correct: Tannaitic law does not work with the standard of negligence. The second step is wrong. When Goodenough asserts that the first century Roman law regarding fire marks off negligence from accident, he is basing himself on utterances of second and third century jurists, and even in this material the distinction is not genuine but interpolated by later hands.[63] On the third step, referring to Alexandrian practice, I have said enough.[64] Clearly, as Philo

---

[note 62 continued from previous page] and all the officials have to do is to adjust the fine to the nature and extent of the damage. Exod. 21:36 is very similar. While ordinarily, if A's ox kills B's, the two owners share the loss, if an ox is known to be wild "and his owner does not guard him," the law ordains full reparation. This does not mean an inquiry in the individual case whether A did in fact guard the beast. The lawgiver takes it for granted that he did not, else no damage would have been done—which is true of the generality of cases. "And his owner does not guard him" for practical purposes equals "and the ox kills another ox." See Daube, *Zeitschrift für die alttestamentliche Wissenschaft* 50 (1932): 153. To be sure, in course of time, in the hands of subsequent exponents, such *obiter* phrases are apt to be reinterpreted and become part of the substantive rule.

63. See Kunkel, ZRG 45 (1925): 331ff. In passing, from texts like Digest 47.9.9, Gaius *VI ad legem duodecim tabularum*; Digest 49.19.28.12, Callistratus *VI de cognitionibus*; Pss. 5.20.1ff. (*Coll.* 12.2.1; 2.4.1; 5.1.2), *Coll.* 12.5.1f.; Ulpian *VIII de officio proconsulis*; 12.6.1, Paul *singulari de poenis paganorum*, it seems to me that the XII Tables distinguished between the ordinary case of making a fire on your land and its spreading to your neighbour's and the case of making a fire on your land just next to your neighbour's dwelling so that it burns down. In the former case you must make restitution, strict private law liability. The latter case falls under criminal law, like the direct setting fire to a house. The code threatens capital punishment, though only if you are guilty of evil intent, *dolus*; presumably in the absence of *dolus* the obligation to compensate will take over, but we cannot be certain. There may well have been a time when, if you made a fire near a dwelling, *dolus* was assumed.

64. Or, if not, let me add that other passages from Philo adduced by Goodenough are even less in his favour than that about fire. See, e.g. below, p. 152n70, regarding the liability of a depositee.

does not introduce the standard of negligence into the Biblical ruling, and as neither he nor anyone else in Egypt could get it from Roman law where by this time it does not yet operate, the thesis of the book collapses.

The converse fallacy is equally common: the belief that where a legal system does without negligence as a standard of liability, negligence cannot yet be thought of or at least its role not yet be appreciated. But it may be fully appreciated: there are plenty of reasons, apart from lack of understanding, for not making it into a standard.

I have already argued that a rule prescribing compensation if your fire spreads to another's field is based (partly at any rate) on the realization that, in most cases, some carelessness does come in. It would be impracticable to ask the courts to find out about the presence or absence of fault behind each incident. So the thing to do is to generalize, to resort to strict liability—which, in a sense, is liability for negligence, namely in the sense that it is negligence which the lawgiver is out to repress: only he objectivizes it, treats it as established by the very spreading of the fire. This is not mere speculation: Philo, we just noticed, in expounding the strict rule makes it quite clear that what it is directed against (at least as he sees it) is irresponsible conduct.[65] He makes it so clear, in fact, that Goodenough is misled into ascribing to negligence the function of a standard, with each decision depending on whether the particular defendant was at fault or not.

The Biblical shepherd must replace an animal which he loses to an ordinary thief but need not replace one taken by an armed gang.[66] A similar distinction is made in many ancient laws. Surely one important consideration is that, in general, with sufficient diligence he can prevent ordinary theft. From this angle, once again we may speak of liability for negligence in that special sense, negligence objectivized.[67] A shepherd's moral duty to do his best and, say, take what measures he can to keep his flock away from the route of an armed gang will be recognized even though the courts go by rigid, external criteria.[68] The law had not basically

65. Plato mentions this aim in the rule itself; see above, p. 149n62.

66. Exod. 22:9ff.

67. There are other factors. For example, ordinary theft leaves little trace: one would largely have to accept the shepherd's word for it. By contrast, the presence of an armed gang in the region will normally receive wide notice.

68. Cf. 1 Sam. 17:34.

changed by New Testament times; yet "the good shepherd giveth his life for the sheep."[69]

Or take a depositee, a person who gratuitously guards an object you entrust to him. In Biblical and Tannaitic law, as in a number of other ancient systems, he is liable only for *dolus*.[70] But it can be shown that, in religion and ethics, he is expected to watch scrupulously over your property. Josephus, in introducing the relevant paragraphs, compares the custody of a deposit to that of a sacred object.[71] The Hebrew *shomer*, "keeper," "guardian," which is used of a shepherd and a depositee, is used of countless other varieties of keepers, some liable absolutely, some for *dolus* only, some not at all. Always a degree of care is envisaged: the very word implies it (as does Latin *tutor* or *curator*). "Behold," says the Psalmist,[72] "he neither slumbereth nor sleepeth, the guardian of Israel."

Intent

It is bad enough to deny the ancients insight into the nature of negligence. But over large and important areas they are deemed incapable even of grasping *dolus*.

The commandment "Thou shalt not covet"[73] again and again puts Biblicists off. Ancient courts deal with facts, theft, robbery and

---

69. John 10:11.

70. Exod. 22:6ff. and *Mekhilta* on this section. It is only later, in Amoraic law, that liability is extended to negligence; see Daube, *Festschrift Schulz* I (1951): 124ff., and *Libro Jubilar de Belaunde (Mercurio Peruano)* (1963): 231ff., reprinted in *Juridical Review* 76 (1964): 212ff. Goodenough, *Jewish Courts in Egypt*, 169, 227, contends that Philo thinks of negligence as the basis of action in deposit: the Alexandrian Jewish courts had imported that standard from Rome. But for one thing, by Philo's time this standard had not yet entered the Roman law in this domain (it never entered it apart from one text about *culpa in concreto*). For another, in Philo's exposition, a depositee who alleges that the object was stolen from him must take an oath that he has not misappropriated it (*nosphisasthai*), nor colluded with the thief (*koinopragesai*), nor been telling an utter lie when pleading theft by a third party (*holos synepipseusasthai klopen*). This is manifestly a denial of *dolus*, a kind of oath which would be senseless if there were liability for negligence. Goodenough says Philo is not writing a Digest, there must have been further formulas. Well . . .

71. Josephus, *Antiquitates Judaicae* 4.8.38.285.

72. Ps. 121:4.

73. Exod. 20:17; Deut. 5:21.

the like, not with thoughts. So the conclusion is drawn that either this commandment is late, or *ḥamadh* for once denotes not "to covet" but "to misappropriate."[74] But the commandment is not meant to come before the courts; it is addressed to the conscience. Certainly courts get busy only when a theft has been committed and, indeed, it must be a provable theft.[75] This does not imply that they did not know, from the time of Adam and Eve in paradise, that theft—like many another sin—springs from coveting. In fact a man who, say, could show that he had been loaned his neighbour's plough would never be sentenced for theft—from the outset *dolus* is an essential ingredient. There is absolutely no reason why a collection of warnings should not, even in the earliest period of the Old Testament, contain "Thou shalt not covet," with no need to give the verb a more concrete sense than it has.

Let me go on to a more dramatic illustration. It is a dogma that, in dealing with homicide, not only does early law equate the unwitting doer with the witting, but this course is taken from blindness or indifference to what separates the two. In reality, full equation occurs much more rarely than the prevalent view has it, and where it does occur it is a *pis aller*, resorted to because of the insurmountable practical obstacles in the way of determining which side of the line a given case falls: by treating as a murderer, say, anyone who kills by a direct blow or anyone who kills with a piece of iron, justice is done in the vast majority of incidents though, now and then, an innocent person gets trapped. The alternative would be for the law to abdicate altogether.

In the *Pentateuch* both stages—death to whoever kills by a direct blow and death to whoever kills with a piece of iron—are preserved.[76] The latter statute is part of a legislation avowedly concerned with confining the rigour of the law to those who deserve it. But the former too is designed to get at *dolus*—the *dolus* being objectivized, established by the external situation.

---

74. E.g. Noth, *Exodus*, transl. Bowden (1962), 166.

75. How narrowly circumscribed provable theft was at some stage in Biblical legislation I have shown in *Studies in Biblical Law* (1947), 89ff.: a man was found guilty of theft of an animal only if he had slaughtered or sold it.

76. Exod. 21:12; Num. 35:16—in their original setting, as yet unprovided with the reservations which in the text before us modify them.

Latte in his authoritative article in Pauly-Wissowa[77] affirms of early
Greek law: "Murder (*phonos*) is a unitary concept, determined by the
result; he who kills a man is a murderer, intent or other circumstances
being quite immaterial; *es herrscht reine Erfolgshaftung*, there prevails pure
liability for the outcome." He quotes two stories. One is from the *Iliad*:[78]
Patroclus recounts how, as a young man, he killed a chap in wrath over
the dice. He willed it not, he says, *ouk ethelon*, he was in a fury. He had
to go into exile. The other is found in Hesiod and Pausanias.[79] Hyettus
surprised his wife with a paramour, son of a mighty person. He slew the
adulterer and he, too, was exiled. These two were lucky they lived when
they did. Some *Erfolgshaftung* indeed. In England, the latter, since 1671 at
least, would have his charge reduced to manslaughter. The former, prior to
1957, could have been hanged; and even between then and quite recently
that might have happened to him if he shot his victim. Otherwise—
for example, if he strangled or knived him—from 1957 he could get
only life imprisonment. And that, I must warn any of you who may be
thinking of imitating either of those bravoes, you could still get now: life
imprisonment.

There is not a single case in the whole of Greek literature—myth,
saga, history—or, for that matter, in the Bible, of a man who killed without
intent being put to death, be it in the course of self-help, blood-vengeance,
be it by public authority; and this although there are laws which (as I have
just remarked) objectivize dolus and impose the death penalty, say, on any
killing by a direct blow. Not a single case: let that fact sink in.

It is true that exile—honourable exile as a rule—may be inflicted.
Foremost among the factors accounting for this practice is the attitude
of the victim's family and friends who, then as today, will be slow to
accept explanations. Nor, in judging their reaction, must we forget that,
even in the absence of intent, homicide is hardly ever purely accidental,
nearly always negligent—to which feature the ancients are fully alive.
It is also true that even the unwitting doer may feel guilty, unworthy,
singled out as a source of disaster.[80] But such feelings are not unheard

77. Latte, Pauly-Wissowa's *RE*, vol. 16, pt. 1 (1933), 280–81, s.v. "mord."
78. Homer, *Iliad* 23.86ff.
79. Hesiod, fr.144 (Rzach); Pausanias, 9, *Boeotia*, 36 (4).
80. Cf. above, p. 141n42, about a doctrine found in Antiphon, Philo and the Rabbis.

of in the 1960s. Adrastos, having unintentionally killed his brother, was exiled and hospitably received by King Kroisos. It appears that he was accidentprone, for, at a hunt, he unintentionally killed the son of his host. The latter forgave him, but he could not forgive himself and committed suicide. Far from lumping together witting and unwitting homicide, this story reveals a perfect awareness of the difference. Had Adrastos acted with intent, on the one hand Kroisos would not have forgiven him and on the other, paradoxically, he would not have killed himself but have been quite happy to live on.

A word about the violent end of Antinoos in the *Odyssey*, the interpretation of which has suffered much from the prejudice I am combating.[81] Odysseus, returned but as yet disguised as a beggar, sits in his hall among the feasting suitors who resent his uncouth presence. He boasts that he can handle Odysseus' (his own) bow: none of them can. They tell him that he is drunk and should leave it alone, and that if he persists he will only do terrible things with it and draw dire punishment upon himself, much like that abominable centaur who, having imbibed too much wine at a wedding, raped his host's bride and had his nose and ears cut off. Of course, Odysseus takes the bow. He starts by some preliminary display of prowess, then announces that he is going to aim at a novel target and shoots an arrow into the throat of Antinoos, the most prominent member of the company. The suitors at this moment do not yet realize that he perpetrated the deed with full deliberation, but attribute it to his drunken raving. Yet murder it is. They run for their weapons, vowing that they will make him pay with his life.

It is widely held that the suitors at this stage believe Odysseus to have killed Antinoos without any intent, by a shot that went wrong. As they nevertheless threaten him with death, we have before us a mode of thought—it is inferred—to which the distinction between *dolus* and accident is alien. But an unbiased reading shows that they believe him to have acted not without intent but (as I have described it) without set purpose. That is to say, they do attribute intent to him; but intent the result, not of rational planning, but of a drunken fit. Just note these points: as Odysseus is about to seize hold of the bow, what he is likely to do is

---

81. Homer, *Odyssey* 22.1ff.; see, e.g. Maschke, *Die Willenslehre im Griechischen Recht* (1926), 6.

compared to the crime of a drunken monster who committed rape. Again, just before he slays his hated enemy, he proclaims in so many words his resolve to hit a target of an unusual kind. Further, as soon as Antinoos falls dead, the suitors, we are told, run for their shields and spears: why, if they are under the impression that the deed was unwitting? A mere accident is unlikely to be repeated, and these people are not given to nervous fears. Lastly, the phrase used to inform us that they as yet look on the killing as not fully deliberate is the same as characterizes Patroclus's killing of a friend in a gambling dispute. There is intent in both cases. What there is not is rational reflection: it is ruled out by uncontrolled anger in the case of Patroclus, by drunken wildness (the suitors believe) in that of Odysseus.

However, even if we conceded that the suitors at this moment deem the killing entirely unintentional, due to a shot which went wrong—it would be utterly mistaken to think of them as blind to the difference between *dolus* and accident. Unless we expect them to follow some doctrinaire academic line, how are they to behave in this situation? What kind of accident is this? A worthless tramp interferes where he has absolutely no business and, despite the most insistent warnings, recklessly causes a noble young man's death. It is only natural that they should be fiercely enraged at what later Roman law would call *culpa lata*, *lascivia* or the like.[82]

John O'Hara writes in the America of the mid-twentieth century. In his *Hope of Heaven*[83] a dubious character, long estranged from and despised by his family, returns and inflicts himself on his son and daughter. He always carries a revolver around with him and there is no love lost between him and his son. Still, it is by accident that the revolver goes off and the son killed, and his grief is genuine. None the less, as he departs for good, his daughter's fiancé refuses to shake hands with him.

A common failing of modern research into ancient law is the inclination to primitivize the sources, to press the naive side of any statement or custom and overlook the element of sophistication which is often quite strong. I cannot here pursue this vast subject and confine myself to a very few illustrations.

---

82. E.g. Digest 48.8.4.1 (*Coll.* 1.11.1), Ulpian *VII de officio proconsulis*.
83. O'Hara, *Hope of Heaven* (Panther, 1960), 87.

The Hittite laws define accidental homicide by the phrase: "only his hand transgresses."[84] From such a formulation modern authorities will take it that full responsibility for the result was seriously assigned to the organ. It is obvious, however, that the construction must not be taken too literally: the Hittite laws do not provide that if a man kills unwittingly, his hand—the transgressor—should be cut off. That would indeed be small comfort to its owner.

At Athens, proceedings might be instituted against a weapon which caused a death. Plato, Aristotle and Demosthenes agree in restricting them to two cases: where no person had handled the weapon, and where somebody did do the killing with it, but escaped undetected, leaving it behind.[85] Instead of deducing from the narrow field of this trial that people were alive to its precarious, second-best character, Maschke argues that they must have regarded the weapon as the exclusive cause even where the person who had killed with it was available, provided his killing was accidental. So in this case, too, no matter what the sources say, there must have been proceedings against the instrument. I need hardly remind you that there are many early systems (such as the Biblical, the Hittite, the Babylonian) without a trace of such proceedings, a fact which should give pause to those who would see in them a crude, naive stage.

My third and last illustration is Antiphon's *Second Tetralogy*, like the other tetralogies a model debate, an exercise, not a series of speeches meant for an actual trial. Listen to how Maidment, the editor-translator in the Loeb Classical Library characterizes it in his Introduction:[86] "*Tetralogy II* . . . is concerned with the case of a boy who was accidentally killed by a javelin—cast in the gymnasium. Now it might be expected that . . . the author would make the prosecution take the line that the victim met his death as the result of a deliberate intention . . . or else as the result of criminal negligence; while the defendant would reply . . . that death occurred by misadventure. But instead both sides admit from the start that the death was purely accidental, because for the writer it makes no difference. A life has been lost by violence . . . (the thrower) will have to

84. Hittite Laws, I3f.

85. Plato, *Leg.* 8.873Ef.; Aristotle, *Athenian Constitution* 57.4; Demosthenes, *Against Aristocrates* 76.

86. Maidment, *Minor Attic Orators*, vol. 1 (1953), 39–40, 45.

make reparation with his life. . . . It is hardly necessary to point out how extraordinarily primitive are the beliefs which lie behind this conception of blood-guilt. They have their roots in the dim past. . . . Homicide, whatever the circumstances in which it is committed, is punishable with death." Maidment fully realizes that already Dracon—and, indeed, pre-Draconian law—distinguishes between intentional and unintentional killing, and he admits that he cannot explain the discrepancy with this *Tetralogy*. But he sticks to his guns.

Well, after this, we are prepared for a quick, crass, gory exchange. What do we get? An argument so subtle and daring, especially on the side of the accused, that the latter himself is represented as apologizing for upsetting accepted commonsense notions and directing attention away from appearances to the deeper truth.[87]

The case put is simple: a man throws a javelin in the gymnasium, and the boy who picks up the thrown javelins runs into the path of the weapon and is killed. Under the Attic law of the time, such misadventure in the course of a contest or practice for a contest would have been *phonos dikaios*,[88] killing within the law, a justifiable deed—hence exempt from punishment. The *Tetralogy*, for the purpose of its discussion, assumes a law which does not confer automatic exemption.[89] The defence pretends to be able to prove that, even in the absence of a special proviso, the javelin thrower must be let off: he did not kill at all, it was the boy who, moving into the way, brought about his own death. The prosecution argues that the boy conducted himself correctly, so cannot be held responsible. Moreover, even if it were granted that his movement was a cause of the result, at least the javelin-thrower by his action became a joint killer: he should be sent into exile.

There is here a most searching, disturbing analysis of a certain variety of misadventure, yet the editor thinks that "both sides admit that

87. Antiphone, *Tetralogy*, Speech 2, pt. 2.

88. It is immaterial whether this terminology was used in statutes or not, sufficient that it is found in the orators.

89. This is the sense of the law invoked in Antiphon's *Tetralogy*, Speech 2, pt. 9, and Speech 3, pt. 7, and forbidding "to kill unjustly or justly." Its artificiality, its *ad hoc* nature, stares one in the face. Of many impossible comments that of Maschke, *Die Willenslehre im Griechischen Recht* (1926), 53, is perhaps the most impossible.

the death was accidental because it makes no difference." So the *Tetralogy* would need no modification if the boy had been murdered by a jilted lover; accident is chosen simply, I suppose, because it makes a good story. But preconceived opinion has led to more distortion. "A life has been lost," the editor says, "the thrower will have to make reparation with his life." The fact is that at no point in the *Tetralogy* is there a request for the death penalty: the deed (if a deed at all) is accidental, exile is all that may be demanded.[90]

To return to Maschke, this is what he says[91] about the early Greek epic: "Intent (*Vorsatz*) has no legal relevance because it has no ethical relevance. The Homeric Greek feels a deed by which he is hurt to be the doer's fault, guilt (*Schuld*), without asking in the least about imputation or even causation: guilty, *aitios*, is anybody from whom harm comes." In evidence he cites an altercation between Achilles and Agamemnon. The former says he joined the war because of the wrong done by Paris and his people to Agamemnon and Menelaus, not for anything they did to

90. Besides several references to exile (e.g. *Tetralogy*, Speech 1, pt. 2), for good measure a direct contrast to the death penalty is drawn in that part (Speech 3, pt. 10) where the prosecution argues that, even if the boy's movement were deemed a cause of the disaster, the javelin-thrower furnished a joint cause. The boy, the prosecution continues, incurred harsher punishment than an unwitting killing warrants: he died. It would be unfair, therefore, to allow the joint killer to escape scot-free, scil. to be spared even the proper punishment, exile. Maidment (p. 45) quotes Speech 2, pt. 9, as mentioning the death penalty for any kind of homicide. This must be a misprint. Probably he has in mind Speech, 3, pt. 9. Here the prosecution urges that the defence ought not to invoke the javelin-thrower's honourable life as a consideration against rigorous punishment: the poor victim who lived just as honourably was punished with death! There is nothing in this clever rhetorical flourish to warrant the conclusion that the accused, if condemned, would face anything worse than exile. Towards the end of the *Tetralogy* (Speech 4, pt. 9) the defence warns the court of the bad conscience they will have if the accused *diaphtharei*, "perishes," "is demolished," "is found guilty." Maidment (p. 113) translates "is put to death." That would be the connotation if it were a trial for murder. On this occasion the meaning is "sentenced to exile." As the genuineness of the *Tetralogy* is controversial, I draw only subsidiary support from the *Choreutes*, a speech composed by Antiphon for an actual trial of unintentional homicide, where once again exile is the punishment envisaged in the event of condemnation (pt. 4). On the sophisticated idea thrown up by the prosecution in the *Tetralogy* (3.8) that an unwitting homicide must be a sinner—that is why heaven makes him the cause of the disaster—see above, p. 141n41.

91. Maschke, *Die Willenslehre im Griechischen Recht* (1926), 6–7.

him personally—they did not drive away his cattle nor ravage his lands: "the Trojans are in nothing at fault, *aitioi*, against me."[92] I can detect here no vestige of liability without imputation or causation: the driving away of cattle and the ravaging of lands are dolose acts of banditry, and so, of course, are Paris's abduction of Helen and his fellow countrymen's obstinacy in protecting and abetting him. Against Agamemnon and Menelaus, it is implied, they are indeed at fault, *aitioi*; but what they did does not strike me as exactly an act of God.

All this talk about *reine Erfolgshaftung*, intent without legal significance since without ethical significance, is nineteenth-and early twentieth-century mythology. It is really, come to think of it, just fantastic. Think of Greek and Hebrew insight into, and preaching against, hatred. Think of—outside homicide—Greek *hybris* and *klope*, Roman *iniuria* and *furtum*, old delicts with evil intent a primary element in them. Actually, the Homeric Greek does not ask only about causation and imputation and intent. He is sensitive to different kinds of *dolus*—of course. Had Hector killed Patroclus unintentionally, by a stone thrown into the air for fun, Achilles would not have maltreated his corpse. Had he been a vulgar robber who killed Patroclus in order to sell his armour, Achilles would not have honourably returned his corpse to his father. Yet that *reine Erfolgshaftung* is almost universally accepted—and this prompts a question. There must be something very special about a theory which, though so totally absurd, so totally without evidence, indeed contrary to it, could gain such wide credence. What is it?

The answer is that it satisfies two very deep divergent desires or needs, both of them exceptionally powerful in the last century and the first decades of the present (for it is in that period, not in the dim past, that those extraordinarily primitive beliefs have their roots): on the one hand the belief in steady progress—which enables us to look down on those childlike creatures of the beginning, who had no conception of the subjective data behind the visible ones, and to whom we are far superior and constantly more so in evaluating motivation and the like—and on the other hand the romantic notion of the heroes of antiquity as lapidary, classical figures whom we can only look up to, figures *aus einem Guss*,

92. Homer, *Iliad* 1.153.

monolithic, dealing with facts and not, like the miserable bourgeois, with sentimentalities, hitting back without asking questions, true elemental forces of nature. (It does not need a psychoanalyst to guess why this latter half of the picture would have a special appeal to the scholar cooped up in his study.) I am not siding with those at the moment fashionable anthropologists who make the Papuan headhunters into avant-garde thinkers, preferably á la Teilhard de Chardin. But that dog of mine which I shall leave unburied at San Francisco[93] notices whether I kick him in anger or from inadvertence.

As for the havoc that the prejudice I am opposing causes outside classical and Biblical studies, I will submit just one minor example on which I hit recently. In *Beowulf*[94] King Hrethel's second son unintentionally kills his elder brother with an arrow, a deed—the romancer tells us—for which the father can impose neither a fine nor other, sterner punishment. Commentators agree that it is only because of the relationship that retribution is ruled out; had the king to do with a stranger, it would be exacted in full.[95] Indeed, the episode, thus interpreted, is constantly used to prove the premise of its interpretation—that accidental homicide in Germanic law ranked as a serious crime or even as murder.[96]

What a method! I very much doubt whether Hrethel would remain (or whether the storyteller thinks he would remain) equally passive had the shot been aimed with murderous intent. The narrator compares Hrethel to a man whose son has been hanged, i.e. executed, and may not be avenged. This comparison is particularly apt if meant to put justified killing by way of execution on a level with unwitting killing: in both cases the character of the deed demands that hostility to the doer be kept under control. (It would be somewhat reminiscent of the Greek scheme of defence, with the pleas of lawfulness and accident.) That the king

---

93. See above, pp. 121–22.

94. *Beowulf* 2435ff.

95. Klaeber, *Beowulf and the Fight at Finnsburg*, 3rd ed. (1936), 213; Sedgefield, *Beowulf*, 3rd ed. (1935), 139; Wrenn, *Beowulf*, 2nd ed. (1958), 220–21.

96. Brunner, *Deutsche Rechtsgeschichte* 2, 2nd ed. Schwerin (1928): 820; Liebermann, *Die Gesetze der Angelsachsen* 2, (1903–16): 265, 717. On p. 265 Liebermann dissociates himself from the extremists by suggesting that, whatever we may find in legal regulations, the ability to discriminate between intended harm and unintended harm is as old as mankind (*uralt-menschlich*) seeing that even the higher domestic animals acquire it.

considers his hands tied by the inadvertent nature of the killing rather than the relationship is corroborated by a detail conveniently overlooked in the literature: though resentful and, indeed, dying from grief, he leaves his second son his share in the kingdom."[97]

I repeat: the sources—Oriental, Greek, Roman—offer not one example of an unintentional killer being killed. I do not, of course, count the cases where the prevalent doctrine says, Ah yes, but he would have been killed were it not for such-and-such special circumstances. I want to be shown one instance where he is killed: surely a modest request. If the prevalent view is right, there ought to be hundreds. Even where an unwitting killer goes into exile, he is likely to find friendly hospitality— the case of Adrastos is typical—and the same goes for a slayer from intent, provided his motive is one people can sympathize with: remember Patroclus who murdered in a gambling quarrel and Hyettus who murdered an adulterer. There is displayed in these reactions enormous sensitivity to the subjective nuances of a deed.

I observed above that the ancients are less intrigued by the accidental deed than the deed committed in error. Even so they know or at least divine a good deal about the former. Nowadays if a lover inadvertently pushes his rival over a cliff, we pride ourselves on considering the possibility of unconscious volition. Perseus, by an unfortunate throw of the discus in the games, killed his grandfather, thus inheriting the kingdom. No version of this old myth mixes it up with murder. Nevertheless, while in some accounts he is represented as merely sorry—for he was fond of the old gentleman—others, perhaps earlier, make him seek a kind of exile and

---

97. Miss Whitelock, cited with approval by Wrenn, *Beowulf* (1958), 220–21, is the first to have noticed that the hanging contemplated is that of a criminal, which does not entitle the family to start a feud; and she is absolutely right in regarding this legal obstacle as the *tertium comparationis*—Hrethel too must not give rein to what resentment he may feel. As to why he must not, however, even she still thinks exclusively of his being the killer's father and pays no attention to the element of accident. I ought to add that the relationship may still be relevant as far as the exclusion of a fine is concerned: a stranger, that is, might well be forced to make some payment. But the poem seems to place special emphasis on the impropriety also of other, severer measures (they are in the foreground precisely in the verses which introduce the comparison), and it is here that the lack of *dolus* appears the decisive consideration. Of the explanations of the comparison prior to Miss Whitelock's, one was more far-fetched than the other; nor is Taylor, *Leeds Studies in English*, 7/8 (1952), 51ff., convincing.

renunciation, by swapping countries with another king. Why does he do so? Because, we are told, "he felt ashamed on account of the mutterings about his killing."[98]

Now it is time to ask whether anyone got the only Biblical case of accidental homicide? Good, nobody. Remember the two whores who brought their dispute before King Solomon?[99] They shared a room and each had a baby. One of them overlaid hers in the night and, when she noticed it, crept across to her colleague's bed, put the dead baby there and took the live one back with her. Next morning the mother of the live one discovered the fraud and demanded that the exchange be undone, but the thief denied that anything wrong had occurred. Well, all the King is concerned about is that the true mother of the live baby should be established. Not the flicker of a thought is devoted to the overlaying, the unintentional killing. Today there would be a terrific fuss; there would be an inquest, and all sorts of disagreeable things might happen.

98. Pausanias 2.16.3; Cf. Apollodorus 2.4.4.
99. 1 Kings 3:16ff.

6

Reductio ad Absurdum

Reductio ad absurdum in the Roman jurists.[1] For a start let me present two cases from Labeo, who flourished under Augustus.

A husband in his will bequeathes to his wife the utensils for beautification, the toilet articles. Under this legacy, it is held, she gets only what objects had been set aside for her use, not, for example, a mirror in his study. Otherwise—here we come to the *reductio ad absurdum*—if he happened to be a manufacturer of such articles, she would practically dispossess the proper heir. Again, I sell you a major piece of land, say, for 50,000 pounds, reserving for myself the quarries, the beds of stone, on it. Some time later a quarry we had not known of when we concluded the contract comes to light.[2] Held, finally, that you may keep it since, otherwise, if the whole estate turned out to rest on beds of stone, you would just lose the full price of 50,000 pounds, and I remain with the land.[3]

---

1. On this subject I have given extensive documentation in two addresses, one in English (*The Use of* "Reductio ad Absurdum" *by the Roman Jurists*), delivered at the joint meeting of the Societies for Roman Studies and for Hellenic Studies at Cambridge, 1958, and one in French (*Le raisonnement par l'absurde chez les jurisconsultes romains*), somewhat less full, delivered at the Institut de Droit Romain, Paris, 1958. The French address, with discussion, was cyclostyled and circularized by the Institut.

2. That sort of thing happened: it is discussed for usufruct in Digest 7.1.9.3, Ulpian *XVII ad Sabinum.*

3. Digest 34.2.39 pr., Javolenus *II ex posterioribus Labeonis*; 18.1.77, Javolenus *IV ex posterioribus Labeonis*; see Daube, *University of Ceylon Law Review* 1 (1958): 1ff.

Beseler regards all *reductio ad absurdum* as foreign to classical law; where it appears in classical writings, it is due to Byzantine revisers steeped in Greek ideas.[4] I dissent. His main evidence of Greek provenance is the use of the future tense for the objectionable consequence: otherwise it will come to pass, *fore*, that the proper heir is dispossessed, that the entire estate is reserved for the seller. But he must have been content to look at a very narrow selection of Greek texts. Having gone into the Greek *reductio ad absurdum* I find that its formulation is highly varied, definitely not such as would have suggested to a translator into Latin a peculiar association of this argument with the future tense. In fact, the latter is not employed in a large number even of Roman *reductiones*.[5]

Anyhow, the *reductio ad absurdum* is universal. Admittedly the Greeks made a fair analysis of it and the Romans learned a great deal from them. But the argument is so frequent in Cicero, Livy and precisely the classical jurists of the first century AD that what borrowing there was— and there was, indeed—must by and large have been early. Of course there are interpolated *reductiones*: there are interpolated *a fortioris*, analogies, anything. This does not alter the picture as a whole. In fact it would be a pity to subject the history of *reductio ad absurdum* in Roman law to simplifying distortion; for it furnishes yet another illustration of Greek thought being demonstrably influential, yet undergoing characteristic modification in the direction of pragmatism. It is interesting to watch the Roman jurists applying the *reductio* in just that manner and within just that range which are of maximum service to their specific purposes.

The usual philosophical definition of *reductio ad absurdum* is the establishing of a syllogism by showing the contradiction of its conclusion to be inconsistent with its premise. We must, however, distinguish between the logic of is (as opposed to ought) and mathematics on the one hand, and normative reasoning, the making of decisions, on the other. In the logic of is and mathematics, where premises and conclusions are

---

4. Beseler, *Beitr.* 4 (1920): 16; Beseler, *Tijdschr. Rechts.* 8 (1928): 293; and Beseler, *Tijdschr. Rechts.* 10 (1930): 202–3; Beseler, *Studi Bonfante* 2 (1930): 72; Cf. Schindler, *ZRG* 74 (1957): 226–27, against wholesale rejection of all texts with *absurdum*.

5. Beseler himself, in *Tijdschr. Rechts.* 10, divides the Roman material into two sections, with and without the future. The latter group, however, is condemned no less than the former.

unambiguously stated, the argument (the ideal one) is quite exact and reliable. It is really a *reductio*, not *ad absurdum*, but *ad impossibile*, in Greek *adynaton*. If A is true of no B and B of some C, A is not true of some C since if it were true of all C, B would be true of no C—against the premise that B is true of some C. If laziness is never found in a law undergraduate, and some Cambridgemen are law undergraduates, some Cambridgemen at least are not lazy since, if all of them were, none of them would be a law undergraduate—contrary to the premise that some Cambridgemen are law undergraduates.

Even with regard to this strict *reductio*, Aristotle in his *Topica* enjoins caution. He urges that, in public dialectic disputation, where you put your conclusion as a question inviting your opponent's assent, you should—unless the impossibility you point out is absolutely obvious—refrain from this argument and give preference to others (*a fortiori*, analogy). For, thanks to the rather involved structure of a *reductio*, your opponent might deny your conclusion and get away with it, have the audience on his side.[6]

In his *Rhetorica* he explains in precisely what exceptional conditions dialectic *reductio* might avail a debater, and he illustrates it by a defeat that Pericles, who was a rationalist, inflicted on the soothsayer Lampon. Lampon refused to enlighten Pericles about the secrets of the Demeter cult: they were not for the ears of the uninitiated—and, of course, only women were initiated. So Pericles asked Lampon whether the secrets were known to him and Lampon replied that they were. "How so," was Pericles's parting question, "seeing that you are uninitiated?"[7] Another example quoted by Aristotle is Socrates's refutation of the charge of godlessness. His accuser Meletus himself had in his indictment mentioned Socrates's belief in entities inspirited (*daimonia*). Socrates shrewdly did not ask for confirmation of this: he did not need it, it was manifest, and a question about it might have given Meletus an opportunity for wriggling out. What he did ask was whether spirits were not either the offspring of gods or

---

6. Aristotle, *Top.* 8.2, 157b, 34ff.

7. Aristotle, *Rh.* 3.18.1, 1418b i.f., 1419a 1ff. Whereas in the passage from the *Top.* the adjective is *adynaton*, in the *Rh.* it is *atopon*. The latter is often used, as here, with reference to *reductio ad impossible*, though the former is not extended to *reductio ad absurdum* in the field of ought.

something pertaining to gods.[8] Which Meletus admitted. There followed the concluding question: "Is there, then, a man who believes in offspring of gods but not in gods?"[9]

When we come to normative logic, decisions (including legal ones), the argument mostly assumes a far less rigorous character, though it is not quite so lax and insubstantial as one might think at first sight. At first sight one might think of it as the propping up of a decision by showing the alternative to be inconsistent with what is desirable, reasonable, fair, lawful; in short, with the wider aim to which a person deciding feels called on to conform. We are in the realm of ought, and the *reductio* is not *ad impossibile* or *adynaton*, but merely—in accordance with the familiar phrase —*ad absurdum*, in Greek *atopon*. Take an umbrella with you when it rains since, otherwise, you will get wet. A buyer must pay since, if he does not, he goes counter to a binding contract.

If we proceed from this model, however, clearly almost any reasoned decision is a *reductio ad absurdum*, at least by implication: any decision is chosen in preference to the opposite, less acceptable one. I never quarrel about nomenclature, and you are welcome to call it *reductio ad absurdum*. Only it is not what the Romans understand by it; and in general we, too, mean something more pregnant.

8. Question of definition: Aristotle, *Rh.* 2.23.8, 1398a.

9. Cf. Plato, *Ap.* 15, 27bff. There are differences, but according to the *Ap.* as well as the *Rh.*. Socrates, instead of asking Meletus whether entities inspirited did not form part of his, Socrates's, teaching, simply reminded him that the indictment acknowledged that much. It must be added, alas, that the text of the passage from the *Rh.* is doubtful. Especially if we compare Aristotle's *Sophistici Elenchi* 15, 174b 8ff., 38–39, it appears possible that Aristotle's point is that, at times, a way out of the precariousness of dialectic *reductio* is to relax the rules of disputation and put the final conclusion in the form, not of a question, but of a statement. On this basis, Socrates's conclusion should be translated: "There is, then, a man—if we follow up your contentions—who believes in offspring of gods but not in gods—you must be joking." That, grammatically, *estin hostis oietai* may denote an affirmative "there is a man who believes" is certain: see, e.g. Sophocles, Frag. 354 (*The Fragments of Sophocles*, vol. 2, ed. Pearson [1917], 26), *eisi d'hoitines ainousin anoson andra*, "there are those who praise a healthy man." It cannot be objected that in Plato and Aristotle the phrase generally implies a question: we have (on this alternative interpretation) to do with a deliberate deviation from normal practice. In Plato's *Ap.*, 15, 27Df., the final upshot of the debate is definitely summed up by Socrates without further attempt to make Meletus concur.

When do we, or the Romans, speak of conduct, a course person has decided on, as absurd, with any precision? One application is where conduct is not just ill-considered but strikingly incongruous, in conflict with the conspicuous professed purpose of the agent. Not if you simply go out without an umbrella, but if a valetudinarian who takes an umbrella in a drizzle goes out without one in a downpour. Not if a buyer does not pay, but if a man who charitably buys from an impoverished friend in order to assist him does not pay. A particularly clear instance is self-defeating conduct where by going to extreme lengths in one direction you land at the other end, achieve precisely the reverse of your plan. Appeasement may be so viewed. Or *summum ius summa iniuria*: by over-meticulous, too anxious striving for justice you bring about the worst injustice, say, you give judgment for a general who, having concluded a truce for three days, attacked in the second night—a "night" not falling under "days."[10] Evidently, there is affinity between the absurd and the ridiculous or downright foolish. In Greek, *geloion* is a frequent synonym of *atopon* and in Latin *ridiculum* of *absurdum*—it occurs even in juristic texts; and, incidentally, while I do not think the Romans needed the Greeks for hitting on *reductio ad absurdum*, the particular epithet *ridiculum* does look to me a rendering of *geloion*.

It is possible, then, to redefine *reductio* in the sphere of ought more closely, as the propping-up of a decision by showing the alternative to be in striking contrast to the declared specific objective of the enterprise. Naturally, even within this narrower *reductio* there are degrees of absurdity (as there are not of impossibility), so even after redefinition the range of the argument remains considerable. I shall in due course isolate a yet more circumscribed variety.

Before going on, however, I would draw attention to a little feature that relates to what I have propounded so far, i.e. to *reductio ad absurdum* (in the realm of ought) as the exposure of a specially notable incongruity. We shall see that the argument is apt to be put in a somewhat strident tone; above all, far more often than, say, in the case of an argument a *fortiori* or from analogy do we find the point made by means of a rhetorical question—"What can be less charitable than to raise the hopes of an

10. Cf. Cicero, *Off.* 1.10.33.

impoverished friend by buying from him and then not pay?," "What will encourage an aggressor more than appeasement?"

The Digest[11] brings a longish section from Ulpian on legacies of wine, in the course of which he introduces a testator leaving his "old wine." At this point an extract from Hermogenian is interposed, with the decision that the legacy refers to such wine as the testator used to treat as old. If this cannot be established—and here the Digest returns us to Ulpian, whose verdict is that any wine not new counts as old, even last year's. Now comes a fragment from Paul, a *reductio*: "On another ruling, what end or beginning of old wine could be assumed?"

Evidently, the compilers found no such *reductio* in Ulpian, otherwise they would not have switched to Paul. By the same token, it is clear that they did not make up this bit: if they had, they would have given it as part of Ulpian's discussion, not split it off as belonging to Paul, under a special, fictitious inscription.[12] Ulpian and Paul were contemporaries, beginning of the third century AD, Hermogenian is considerably later, practically post-classical.[13] Ulpian's decision—any wine not new is old—was rather drastic. Paul, however, seems to have concurred: he supported it by pointing out that, if one rejected it, the result—as the line could be drawn at no other point—would be worse than a less satisfactory decision: it would be no decision at all. That of course would mean destruction of the legacy, very deplorable: legacies were to be upheld at almost any cost. (In some modern systems the legacy might indeed be unenforceable for lack of determinability.) Hermogenian, later than Ulpian and Paul, did hit on

---

11. Digest 33.6.9.4, Ulpian *XXIII ad Sabinum: Item si vinum vetus sit legatum;* 33.6.10, Hermogenian *II* (should be *IV*, Lenel, *Pal.*, 1 [1889], 273) *iuris epitomarum: ex usu testatoris legatum aestimabitur, id est quot annorum vino pro vetere utebatur; quod si non appareat;* 33.6.11, Ulpian *XXIII ad Sabinum: vetus accipietur quod non est novum, id est et anni prioris vinum appellatione veteris continebitur;* 33.6.12, Paul *IV ad Sabinum: nam aliter observantibus quis finis aut quod initium veteris vini sumeretur?* See Daube, *ZRG* 76 (1959): 258–59. The case doubtless comes from Sabinus: both Ulpian and Paul are commenting on him. The problem of "old wine" arose in other connections, e.g. *mutuum*, Digest 12.1.3, Pomponius *XXVII ad Sabinum*, where the solution must have been quite different.

12. And a correct one, too, for in Paul *IV ad Sabinum* there is a portion concerning legacy of wine or oil: Lenel, *Pal.*, 1 (1889), 1261. Such tiny fragments, broken off pieces, are rarely a fabrication of the compilers; see Daube, *ZRG* 76 (1959): 257ff.

13. Cf. above, p. 105n61.

a subtler answer: the testator's habits were to be the criterion, "old wine" meant what he had treated as old.[14]

The *reductio* must be earlier than Hermogenian. Once his solution existed, it was no longer necessary to apologize by saying that the drastic course advocated was better than no course.[15] We may take it, therefore, that the *reductio* is not only not due to the compilers but stood in Paul's work.[16] Indeed I suspect that he took it over from Sabinus. In any case, it supplies a good example of a repulsive alternative—no decision—presented in a high-pitched modulation.[17]

One thing is common to all *reductio* of the normative kind: a dependence on value judgments and, with it, uncertainties of many sorts. Admittedly the same goes for any reasoning as to ought, such as *a fortiori* and analogy; only the qualitative element as distinct from the quantitative is more obtrusive in a decision based on *reductio ad absurdum*. We all know how readily the conclusion is open to attack. The valetudinarian may retort that he catches cold more easily in a drizzle than when properly

14. Ulpian and Paul got over the ambiguity by contending that a different verdict *multo minus commode fieri posse*, Hermogenian by deriving his interpretation of the testator's words *ex factis, dictis, animo atque vita eius*: Cicero, *Inv. rhet.* 2.40.117f.

15. True, Justinian does incorporate the argument. But it is one thing to construct it and another to quote it once it is constructed. The final part of frag. 10, by the way, *quod si non appareat*, contemplating the possibility of Hermogenian's method proving impracticable, may well not come from him but be inserted by the compilers, with a view to combining this answer with the older one by Ulpian: see Lenel, *Pal.*, 1 (1889), 273.

16. Incidentally, it uses not the future, but the imperfect subjunctive, *sumeretur*, a normal form in an "irrealis."

17. Here may be the place for a note on the opposition of the Proculians to assigning barter to sale. What they found fault with was the undecidability of all barter cases, which this classification, in their view, implied. Their argument runs more or less as follows: if the aim of classification of contracts is to determine the respective duties of the parties, and if sale involves delivery of an object for payment of a price, then barter must not be subsumed under sale since, if it is, each party's performance is to be treated as at once delivery and payment—absurd, it means a complete muddle with regard to their duties. The *reductio* sounds more cogent than it is; it can be attacked on various grounds. In fact Gaius, who records it (3.141), also records the rejoinder of a Sabinian that there are cases of barter where it is possible to distinguish between one party as seller, obliged to delivery, and the other as purchaser, obliged to payment—namely, if I clearly initiate the business by offering an object for sale and we then agree that you give me another object for it.

drenched. It is precisely justice at its highest, it might be contended, which rewards outstanding prowess and therefore upholds the sly general who attacked in the night. The hoary semi-utilitarian argument that you must not lie because, if everybody lied, belief would die out and you would be frustrated—well, the liar knows better: he will cross that bridge when he comes to it.[18] If the widow-legatee obtains virtually the whole estate, the testator being a manufacturer of cosmetic utensils, what harm is done? The heir still has the satisfaction of the compliment of being nominated in the will. In the case of a quarry being discovered after conclusion of the sale, the late Republican jurist Tubero did adhere to the strict wording of the reservation and adjudge the quarry to the vendor.[19] To Labeo's *reductio* that, on this basis, if all land turns out to be quarries, the vendor gets paid and yet keeps all, Tubero might have replied that this was no more than right: the buyer entered into precisely this contract. Failure to delimit "old wine" would invalidate the legacy. Good: maybe the testator just wanted to tease the parties and their lawyers. We saw that Aristotle regards even the strict *reductio ad impossibile* as a *pis aller* in disputation because it might not convince. His reserve must surely embrace the *reductio ad absurdum* for the purpose of decisions.

The oldest mathematical *reductio* known to me is by Democritus.[20] This type *ad impossibile* alone is represented in Euclid and Archimedes, as also in Aristotle's *Analytica Priora* and *Topica*.[21] But already Plato is full of both the strict—is—type and the laxer—ought—type, several

18. Kant had good reason for preferring to condemn lying as an annihilation of the dignity of man: at least this stand is apodictic.

19. A colleague of mine from English law prefers this unbending solution. By saying "unbending" I am already expressing sympathy with the buyer: a highly subjective sentiment.

20. Reported by Plutarch, *Comm. Not.* 39. It is a twofold *reductio*, a neat puzzle: if a cone is divided into segments—if each segment is of the same extent as the next, the cone will not (as it does by definition) taper to a point, yet if each segment differs from the next, the cone will have distinct steps. The emerging position is described by the superlative *atopotaton*, "most absurd," perhaps in order to call attention to the impasse where both the conceivable alternatives can be refuted.

21. Russell is wrong in affirming (*The Listener*, 59, 1506, 6 February 1958, 255, also *Encounter*, 64, January 1959, 6) that Euclid would say "which is absurd" of the denial that you know you have visible eyes.

varieties of them, and so are other writers, early and late. It would be wrong to assume that the strict type, because first analysed and defined, is historically older in life and then softens into the laxer type. (Die-hards swearing by the logic of is would presumably speak of deterioration rather than softening.) The laxer, popular type is just as old as the strict, maybe older. Abraham, told by God that the city of Sodom will be wiped out, insists that God must not destroy the righteous with the wicked: "Shall not the judge of all the earth do justice?"[22] If an ordinary chap leaves his umbrella at home in a downpour, it may be unwise; it becomes laughable if the person so acting is a valetudinarian. A man in his frailty will often do injustice: he will be simply wrong. But if the judge of all the earth does injustice, it is absurd. Note the rhetorical question, typical of *reductio ad absurdum* even in Genesis: should the judge of all the earth not do justice? A character in Cicero, defending a seller's right to keep quiet about defects of the object, argues: what would be so absurd as for an auctioneer at the owner's behest to cry, Here's an unsanitary house for sale?[23] Again, the conduct described as absurd involves a flagrant, more than ordinary incongruity: the owner pays an auctioneer in order to achieve the most effective advertisement possible, at the same time asking him to run down the object. And again, the rhetorical question—what would be so absurd?

Frequently, as the *reductio ad absurdum* must bring out a striking, foolish contradiction, it concentrates on the secondary results of the decision combated: the latter itself may not be so glaringly inconsistent with the premises, hence it is its consequences which are dragged in as revealing the absurdity. According to Livy, the decemvirs were advised not to restrict speech within the senate-house, otherwise more dangerous speech would ensue outside.[24] Appius Claudius warned the populace that if he were summarily arrested, what humble plebeian would be safe? Rhetorical question.[25] If a master was assassinated by one of his slaves, the law required all slaves in the house to be put to death. Under Nero a prefect, owner of four hundred slaves, was murdered. There was a suggestion to relax the law, but Gaius Cassius Longinus, head of the

22. Gen. 18:25.
23. Cicero, *Off.* 3.13.55.
24. Livy 3.39.6.
25. And *fore*, the future I discussed above. Livy 3.56.13.

Sabinian school, squashed it:[26] "Whom may his rank defend if it did not help the prefect of the city? Whom may the number of his slaves keep safe if four hundred did not protect Pedanius Secundus?" Rhetorical questions again. The *edictum Carbonianum* provided that if, on the death of a *paterfamilias*, a person below age, below puberty, set up as heir, was attacked as not being among the children, the suit might be postponed till he came of age. This protection was extended to the case where the young person was attacked as being a slave since, otherwise, scoundrels would be induced to make the graver allegation.[27]

In this form, the argument is often related to "this would open the door to . . ." By the way, the outrageous secondary result need not be anything in the material world, it may be an unbearable thought. In his speech for Caecina Cicero argues that, if the interdict in question were to be understood in the way adverse to him, the forefathers who drew it up would emerge as a most inferior lot. Once again, the conclusion is put forward as a rhetorical question: if the interdict is inapplicable, what could be said to be more negligent or stupid than the work of our forefathers?[28]

A subspecies of this *reductio*, looking to secondary results of the course to be avoided, is common in the Roman jurists: what is claimed to be outrageous is not just any results of that alternative, but that alternative pursued to its utmost intrinsic consequence.[29] The two opinions with which I started are examples. If a widow to whom the toilet articles are bequeathed were to receive more than those which had been assigned to her use, say, a mirror in her husband's study, then, if her husband had been a manufacturer of toilet articles she would be entitled to the bulk of the estate. If a vendor of land who reserves for himself the quarries were to succeed in a claim to a quarry discovered after the contract, then, if the

26. Tacitus, *Ann.* 14.43. His stern character, however, also impelled him to actions which must command admiration: see Daube, *Festschrift Leibholz* 1 (1966): 311ff.

27. Digest 37.10.1.5, Ulpian *XLI ad edictum.*

28. Cicero, *Caecin.* 14.40.

29. Strangely, in the *Concise Oxford Dictionary*, under "reduction to absurdity," apart from the loose application "pushing of a principle to unpractical lengths," this is all that is listed: "proof of the falsity of a principle etc. given by producing a logical consequence of it that is absurd." According to the large *New English Dictionary*, too, this is the one meaning of reduction to absurdity—entered under "Reduction 9, conversion into a state, b." However, the strict *reductio* (above, pp. 165–66) does appear, under "Reduction 7, logic."

entire land turned out to be quarry-land he would pocket the price without giving anything in return. The objectionable decision is objectionable because it would commit you to an absurdity in a hypothetical extreme case. In itself it is perhaps just tolerable, but it is spun out to what might follow on an unbending, "logical" application, and it is the end-stage which damns it. The term *reductio ad absurdum* here often refers less to the exposure of the course to be rejected as incongruous than to this thorough spelling out of what it "logically" involves; and, significantly, writers are apt to substitute *deductio ad absurdum*—the wrong decision is pursued, brought down, "deduced," to its ultimate, unhappy implications. In a way, Labeo's interpretation of *morbus*, "ailment," belongs here.[30] Under the aedilician edict, if a slave you bought in the slave-market proved to have a *morbus*, you had the right to return him. According to Servius (consul in 51 BC, friend of Cicero's), you could return him even if he lacked a tooth. Labeo (under Augustus) said no. If *morbus*, he explained, which denoted an abnormal state, *contra naturam*,[31] were extended to so normal a disability, babies would be born ailing because born without teeth.[32]

There is affinity not only with "this would open the door to . . ." but above all with the warning of the thin end of the wedge. We do, of course, meet this variety outside the law, for instance, when it is said that the hydrogen bomb is the *reductio ad absurdum* of warfare. Warfare is designed to settle a conflict to one's advantage; it cannot, however, but lead to nuclear fighting; in which extreme case it will be found self-

30. Gellius 4.2.12. His argument is taken over, with modifications I shall touch on below, p. 176n37, in Digest 21.1.11, Paul *XI ad Sabinum*.

31. To be exact, such a state *contra naturam* as diminished usefulness: Gellius 4.2.3. Labeo's definition is largely adopted by Sabinus and subsequent jurists: Digest 21.1.1.7, Ulpian *I ad edictum aedilium curulium*.

32. The argument is vulnerable, like most of these *reductiones*, but no more than the rest (see below, p. 176n37). It has, however, been grossly misunderstood. Labeo is usually represented as maintaining that if a quality—like lack of a tooth—is a defect in an adult it must also be one in a baby; hence if a baby is not defective for lack of teeth, neither can an adult be. This is of course stupid reasoning: it would apply to walking and talking, a paralytic or dumb adult would be sound. But it is definitely not the reasoning of Labeo. He proceeds from *morbus* as an abnormal state; and he contends that if you treat as ailing an adult with a perfectly normal disability, then indeed you ought so to treat babies who have no teeth—nor walk or talk; while if you do not so treat them, you must not so treat an adult with no more than a normal disability. Manifestly, with this position, the

defeating, the quickest route to self-extinction. I need hardly remark on the vulnerability this *reductio* shares with most in the area of ought.[33] At Cornford's University everybody knows everything about the wedge in academic government:[34] "The *Principle of the Wedge* is that you should not act justly now for fear of raising expectations that you may act still more justly in the future." He even saw the character of the argument as a last resort, a *Notbehelf:* "A little reflection will make it evident that the wedge argument implies the admission that the persons who use it cannot prove that the action is not just. If they could, this argument would be superfluous."

Why are the jurists keen on the thin-end-of-the-wedge *reductio? Reductio ad absurdum* counted as a second-best argument. Hence it tended to be employed in rather nearly balanced questions, where you would show up as unacceptable not so much the alternative course itself as its secondary results. And whereas in lay reasoning any consequences would do, the jurists, concerned with the building up of a system, a coherent or coherent-appearing body of rules, inclined to think of the consequences threatening from a rigorous extension of the inferior decision; or to put it differently, it was consonant with sound juristic technique to base the rejection of the alternative on its own internal "logic," on what would happen if one kept going on in that direction.

---

attribution of *morbus* to a paralytic or dumb adult is quite consistent: it is a question of states *contra naturam*. From the point of view of *Wissenschaftsgeschichte*, it is interesting to note the attitude of different scholars to the—as they see it—silly argument. Most of them keep mum. Buckland sturdily concludes that even a great classic is capable of nonsense (*Yale Law Journal* 33 [1924]: 347). Riccobono thinks (*Bull. Ist. Dir. Rom.* [1893]: 6, 146) that Labeo joked, and he refers to Gellius 13.10.3; but that passage is far from saying that Labeo made jokes. Beseler (*Tijdschr. Rechts.* 10: 206) claims that, in Gellius 2.12, the section *et absurdum admodum est* and so on is Gellius speaking, not Labeo— flagrantly a special plea and simply untenable considering Gellius's customary manner of presenting his material. Even if it were Gellius speaking, he must draw on a juristic treatise since, as already indicated, the idea reappears in Digest 21.1.11. Beseler condemns this text as interpolated, unjustly in my view. Anyhow, whether genuine or interpolated, it ultimately derives from the same early classical legal source as Gellius's account.

33. It may be retorted that war is conducted for the sake of a principle, not for advantage; that it need not lead to the hydrogen bomb; that if it should, it will be time enough to desist; that even a nuclear war could not destroy us; etc.

34. Cornford, *Microcosmographia Academica* (1908).

The second-best character of *reductio ad absurdum* (I mean the fact that the ancients judged it second-best) comes out in a further way: the argument is apt actually to figure as a second one, added to another principal one, to tip the balance where the first one alone may not be quite sufficient. No doubt once you do have another argument as well, the assignment of second place to *reductio* has also to do with the general rule for a forensic address, that you should put your positive considerations first, and the demolition of your opponent's case after.[35] But the phenomenon of *reductio* as a makeweight extends far beyond legal texts. I remember no instance where *reductio* leads, to be followed by another argument.[36]

I mentioned above that one of the characters in Cicero's *De officiis* defends by means of *reductio ad absurdum* the right of the seller of a house to keep quiet about its pestilential condition. The *reductio* is preceded by several other arguments. There is no coercion on the buyer. The buyer knows that the seller dislikes his house. Now an argument *a fortiori*: a seller is not accountable for certain express misstatements, puffery, such as "well-built villa for sale" when it is not so well-built, *a fortiori* he must not be condemned for silence. It is only after all this, by way of termination, that the speaker turns to the absurdity of your auctioneer shouting "Come and buy an unsanitary place."[37] Similarly, Labeo, in dealing with the lack of a tooth, begins by urging that this is not *morbus*, not an abnormal state, seeing that most people find themselves in it. Apparently he feels that this consideration might not be enough to overthrow Servius's verdict, so he

---

35. E.g. Cicero, *Rhet. Her.* 1.3.4; Cicero, *de Inv.* 1.14.19, 2.40.116ff.; *Partitiones oratoriae* 38.133. *Confutatio* in *Rhet. Her.* does not, as suggested by Caplan (Loeb Classical Library (1954), 32 n.b), correspond to *elegchos* in Aristotle's *Rh. Al.* 7 and 13. The latter serves both to build up your own case and to demolish your adversary's; it is one of seven kinds of proof, several if not all of which are destined for both purposes. It is indeed the *tekmeria*, 7 and 9, which seem to be used by way of refutation only.

36. In my writings, this would not mean the same—I am in the habit of putting my strongest point last; the ancients, and particularly the jurists, were not.

37. As usual, the ought reasonings are very precarious. In fact Cicero himself comes down on the other side: whatever the law, at least from the moral point of view he definitely disapproves of a vendor who does not disclose defects. See Stein, *Fault in the Formation of Contract in Roman and Scots Law* (1958), 9, 33.

adds the *reductio*: if *morbus* covers even normal disabilities, humans are born ill.[38]

In the quarries case, the first argument against the vendor's claim to a quarry discovered after the contract is from analogy plus definition. I cannot sell non-existent things[39] and, similarly, cannot reserve such things in a sale (analogy), and quarries not known are non-existent (definition). The *reductio ad absurdum*, taking the form of a *deductio* to the extreme, where all the land finally turns out to rest on stone, comes second.[40] Again, take the decision that the *edictum Carbonianum* is to cover the allegation that a person under age set up as heir is a slave. As first argument we are given an *a fortiori*: if the law sees to it that nobody should be unfairly denied his status as child, it must all the more see to it that nobody should be unfairly labeled as slave.[41] It is then that the *reductio* is added, pointing

---

38. To which one could reply, for instance, that to subsume under *morbus* some normal disabilities need not mean to subsume all. In Digest 21.1.11, incidentally, Paul *XI ad Sabinum*, the babies serve as material for an argument from analogy and the *reductio* refers to old men. There are now three arguments. The first is that lack of a tooth is not *morbus*, is not an abnormal disability, since many people are minus some tooth. The second, from analogy, is that though we are born without any teeth, we are not therefore suffering from *morbus* till the teeth appear: it is a normal stage. Third, the *reductio*: otherwise—i.e. if *morbus* were to cover normal disabilities—no *senex* would be sound (*esset*, imperfect subjunctive). Why the miserable normal no longer is preferred for the *reductio* to the hopeful normal not yet I am not going to discuss. As stated above, Beseler assumes interpolation. Among his main objections to the text is this, that some old men do have all their teeth. I suppose, according to him Paul ought to have written: disregarding an exceptional case here and there, no *senex* would be sound. But, then, there are infants born with teeth: Merlin and Richard III, for example.

39. Digest 18.1.8 pr., Pomponius *IX ad Sabinum: Nec emptio nec venditio sine re quae veneat potest intellegi.* Buckland, *Text-Book* (1963), 482, prominently quotes Digest 45.1.97 pr., Celsus *XXV digestorum*. That text is about stipulation and not here relevant. As a matter of fact, there is nothing against a stipulation without a physical object: I may, for example, promise you a service. Digest 45.1.97 pr. turns on impossibility. I promise you a possible service (a service!) and, should I fail to perform it, a hippocentaur. The decision is that the first part of the stipulation stands as if the second were not there at all.

40. I have already pointed out that it is deemed far from conclusive by English lawyers; they wonder whether Tubero was not right after all.

41. This consideration was presumably helped by the fact that the edict spoke of a controversy whether the person was *inter liberos*, "among the *liberi*" (Lenel, *Das edictum perpetuum*, 3rd ed. (1927), 348). Though *liberi* here primarily *[continues onto next page]*

to the undesirable consequence of the opposite decision, the premium it would put on the more dangerous allegation.

A good example occurs in the discussion of a *lex commissoria*,[42] an agreement between the seller and buyer of a farm that if payment is not made by a certain date, the farm *inemptus sit*, literally, should be unbought. Obviously, the seller may cry off if not paid in time. The problem arises whether the buyer may avail himself of this term against the seller's will: may the buyer say, I have not paid in time, in which event our pact provides for automatic lapse of the contract, so I regard it as off?

The answer is, No. It is supported by two arguments. First, a reasoning from the purpose, meaning, of the agreement: it is entered into for the seller's sake, designed to strengthen his position. Then a *reductio ad absurdum*, with that typical intrusion of a hypothetical extreme: otherwise, if the farmhouse burned down, the buyer could not only get out of the contract but also, by so doing, shift the risk normally on him. Normally, from the moment of sale, destruction or deterioration of the object is the buyer's loss (unless the seller is at fault). Hence, in the absence of a *lex commissoria*, or even in its presence if he paid in time as he undertook to do, there would be no question of relief for him because the house burned down. It would be monstrous, the *reductio* implies, if he did not pay in time, to reward him by conceding that the sale was automatically cancelled so that he could save his money.[43]

We have before us a neat illustration of the use of *reductio* in a fairly balanced case. To present-day civilians the rule of this text as to the effect of the pact may seem self-evident. But it was far from self-evident in the period of Sabinus, from whom in essence the fragment may be considered as deriving. No doubt the pact—a usual one long before him—had from the outset been conceived in the exclusive interest of the vendor. The firm phrasing *ut fundus inemptus sit*, "the land should be

---

[note 41 continues previous page] denoted "children," it could be easily pressed to denote "free children." The *a fortiori* argument, then, to some extent included an argument from definition, interpretation of an ambiguous term.

42. Digest 18.3.2, Pomponius *XXXV ad Sabinum*.

43. One might, of course, retort that he relied on the phrasing which, so long as the seller did not actually sue him for payment, enabled him to keep his options open. My friend from English law does incline to reject the *reductio*. The latter, by the way, uses the future tense, *futurum*: "It would be in the buyer's power."

unbought," was to be a threat to the buyer; when it became customary, it did not occur to people that it might be invoked by the buyer contrary to the vendor's wishes. However, there came a moment when it was, and it must have been hard indeed to frustrate this manoeuvre. The words of the pact—automatic lapse—were against the seller; and as he himself had formulated it, his request for a very loose interpretation was further weakened.[44] Accordingly, the first argument, from purpose, though highly important, was not by itself conclusive. Nor would even a reference to the result of a verdict against the seller in a simple case have been quite sufficient. It would not have been sufficient, that is, to point out that it would be unfair, generally, to allow a buyer who did not pay in time to treat the contract as null. That in itself would not have been a crying iniquity (though in modern expositions this is how the *reductio* always appears[45]— understandably, from a modern point of view, as the argument from the spirit of the agreement is now dominating and accepted as fully adequate). It is the *reductio*, or *deductio*, revealing where the alternative course might "logically" lead to which supplies the additional push needed, the picture of a fire in which the house on the land perishes and a non-paying or slow-paying buyer backs out unscathed, leaving the seller with the ground and the ruins. That, Sabinus argues, would surely be intolerable. Beseler declares the *reductio* superfluous, even annoyingly so, coming as it does on the heels of what he deems an absolutely cogent argument—that the *lex commissoria* is intended to help the vendor.[46] This is an unhistorical approach, it is to base early first-century law on presuppositions not current till some hundred-and-twenty years later.

My impression is that the *reductio ad absurdum* had its hey-day in the early classical era. Naturally, it did go on afterwards, but not, it looks to me, in the same degree. There are many reasons. One of them may be that the early classics were nearer to rhetorical thought; which means that they had a sound schooling in, and a heightened sense for, the variety of

44. See Digest 18.1.21, Paul V *ad Sabinum*, 50.17.172 pr., Paul V *ad Plautium*. This consideration may indeed have been a factor in Labeo's decision against the vendor in the quarries case, Digest 18.1.77: see above, pp. 164, 173–74, 177–78.

45. E.g. Buckland, *Text-Book* (1963), 496: "It was not void *ipso iure*, as this would enable the buyer to cry off, if he did not like his bargain, by not paying the price."

46. Beseler, *Tijdschr. Rechts.* 8:293: *Nach dem durchschlagenden Argumente des quia-Satzes, ist nam rell. Überflüssig und ärgerlich.*

possible reasonings and their respective appropriateness for different uses. Another point to consider is that the *reductio ad absurdum* more than other arguments, such as a *fortiori* or analogy, has something of an antithetical, combative flavour. It is always against, and that rather suits the early classics. Their predecessors, the late Republican jurists, had produced some general order and *Übersicht* in the law; they had done the most urgent analysis and synthesis, definition of concepts and classification. The ground-work was thus laid for further systematic, thorough development. The early classics availed themselves of the opportunity; and—again, maybe, to some extent under the influence of rhetoric—they proceeded to work out right and wrong often by establishing where they differed from those who had gone before and from one another. There was a certain polarization of positions, as shown by the setting up and keeping up of the two well-known schools. In this climate not surprisingly the *reductio* flourished. In course of time, jurisprudence flowed in a more unified stream of broad consensus, with a corresponding recession of the adversative argument.

Some years ago, when Alcatraz was given up as a prison, I hoped that All Souls would buy it to have a *dépendance* in that beautiful bay. I am glad now this did not happen, for I hear that one of the theological Colleges at Cambridge is up for sale. . . .

LEGAL CONCEPTS
AND
SOCIAL CONVENTIONS

Part IV

LINGUISTIC VARIATIONS

7

"Suffrage" and "Precedent,"
"Mercy" and "Grace"*

Mod legalese in Shakespeare

A cute little piece in the *Chronicle* by W. Safire on the latest trendy expressions[1] includes "basically" as a replacement of "I mean, uh" or "actually," and "to track a development" instead of "to monitor" which, in turn, long ago superseded "to follow." Such fads are always significant. "Basically" reflects the thirst for the handful of down-to-earth essentials. "To monitor" evoked the radio-engineer's efficient reading of signals. Its successor "to track" is not, as an Oxonian might like to think, a harking back to safari and hunt, but space age lingo. No doubt the testtube baby just born will inspire a few chic neologisms.

In my lectures, occasionally I throw in such a phrase. "Don't trivialize me." I have long ceased being ashamed of keeping my class awake by any device that does it no harm, and I am fortified by a discovery I made many years since in Shakespeare—my favourite reading next to the Bible: he was very quick in picking up and putting to use new words or new meanings of words. (Not the same as independent coinage for which he is justly celebrated). He might even show off a little with them.

---

*To Charles Kingsley and Margaret Barrett, in gratitude.
1. W. Safire, *San Francisco Chronicle*, July 26, 1978, AA–1.

This is hardly surprising. He was, after all, not just a writer but also an actor and—more importantly—a producer, intensely concerned to captivate a large and varied public; and he knew "that all with one consent praise newborn gawds, and give to dust that is a little gilt more laud than gilt o'erdusted."[2] Remember that in the *Winter's Tale*, one of his last and most soulsearching plays, he brings a bear on the stage, apparently availing himself of an opportunity offered by the bear-pit in Southwark next door to the Globe.[3] The animal's brief role has to do with enormous problems respecting human responsibility, nature and fate, reason and passion, power and powerlessness[4]—yet there it is: a live bear, no doubt well trained, for low-brow, additional excitement.

By now I have a little collection of such terms, some of them legal or semi-legal. "Suffrage" and "precedent" will probably interest most readers.

The former is, of course, the English version of Latin *suffragium* which originally, like "suffrage," meant "vote" or "right to vote." I say originally, for some twenty-five years ago Geoffrey de Ste. Croix drew attention to the entirely different sense it acquired when the monarchy brought about a fundamental transformation of public life.[5] Which keywords historians choose as particularly illuminating might itself make a subject for historical inquiry. *Suffragium* clearly appeals to the present interest in the politico-social data behind constitutional law.

Before outlining de Ste. Croix's thesis, a remark about etymology. The word used to be linked to *sub-frangere*, "to break off." A literal rendering would be "a broken off piece," synonymous with *tabella*, the tablet on which you inscribed your vote. Alas, it is one of the many "obvious" derivations that are wrong. The secret, written vote, which makes things a trifle more complicated for those in power, superseded the open, oral one only in the last century of the Republic—from 139 BC on. As Kübler has pointed out, *suffragium* is much older.[6] He suggests Greek *phrassein*, "to fence," as a

---

2. Shakespeare, *Troilus and Cressida* 3.3.176ff.

3. Quiller-Couch's brilliant and plausible suggestion; see Quiller-Couch and Wilson, eds., *The Works of Shakespeare, The Winter's Tale* (1931), xx.

4. See e.g. my lecture *The Defence of Superior Orders in Roman Law* (1956), 6 [repr. *LQR* 72 (1956): 497].

5. See G. E. M. de Ste. Croix, *British Journal of Sociology* 5 (1954): 33ff.

6. See B. Kübler, in Pauly-Wissowa's *RE*, 2nd series, vol. 4A:1 (1931), 654–55.

clue: the assembly met in an enclosure. Quite plausible. I wonder whether *phrazein*, "to indicate," might be relevant.

In the Republic, then, *suffragium* signified "vote," "right to vote."[7] Perhaps the most notable, continuous exercise of the right took the form of filling the high offices of state in the people's assembly. Already then blocks of voters were manipulated from behind.[8] From the time of Augustus on, the assembly became more and more nominal, to disappear in the third century. The same thing happened in the Greek cities under Roman rule. The last known proceedings of a municipal assembly of about AD 300, on a papyrus from Oxyrhynchus, record nothing but acclamations of the resolutions naming the council: "Bravo president, bravo the city's boast, bravo Dioscorus chief of the citizens" and so forth.[9] It reminds one of certain parts of the world today.

The plums of government service are in the gift of the Emperor; more precisely, the Emperor advised by his entourage—since his first-hand knowledge of what goes on and who is available is limited. From the early second century on, we meet *suffragium* in the sense of "favourable decision" and, above all, in that of "assistance" or "influence." What you now need to advance is not victory at the polls but a friend at court. The future Emperor Vitellius, we hear, secured promotion to Legate of Lower Germany through the *suffragium* of a fellowmember of the circus-faction of the Blues, a "most mighty man," *potentissimus*;[10] you cannot here translate *suffragium* by "vote," it denotes "assistance," "influence."

By Constantine, this sense is technical, and in 338 Constantius II reinforces earlier laws against the purchase and sale of *suffragium* in connection with an appointment.[11] N.B.: only trafficking is prohibited, not free help. But, whether licit, half-licit or illicit, the trade in everything— justice, honours, privileges—is immense. As the apostle Paul invokes his status as a Roman, the military tribune in charge, a naturalized citizen, enviously remarks: "With a great sum I obtained this freedom."[12] (I once

7. E.g. Cicero, *Leg.* 15.33.

8. E.g. Cicero, *Leg.* 15.34.

9. See A.S. Hunt and C.C. Edgar, *Select Papyri*, vol. 2 [Loeb Classical Library, 1934], 144ff.

10. Suetonius, *Vitellius* 7.1.

11. *Cod. Theod.* 6.22.2, Constantius Aconio Vicario Africae.

12. Acts 22:28.

quoted this when asked why I did not re-marry.) In 394, Theodosius capitulates and lays down that you must pay what you promised for *suffragium* if you obtain the job; the decree is adopted by Justinian.[13] *Codex Theodosianus*, incidentally, is inconsistent ("schizophrenic" would be the in attribute): it still includes Constantius's ban despite Theodosius's legalisation.

Patronage is the mainspring of administration—quite generally, not at all confined to improper deals. Towns attach themselves to persons of consequence who are to be their patrons. If you want an audience with the Emperor, you must understand the intricate system of patron, his friends, their underlings and the latter's slaves. You may have to work your way up through all these echelons, any of them potentially supportive or obstructive—hoping the patron will bring you into the presence. (Lovers will understand: they must make friends with the *chien du logis*[14]). A contre-temps, to be sure, is always in the cards. Vespasian was approached by one of his ministers on behalf of a brother who desired the lucrative station as imperial cashier. This ruler was shrewd and businesslike. He noticed that the two were not really brothers and sold the post to the candidate direct, telling his attendant: "Find yourself another brother, the fellow you thought was yours is mine."[15]

From about 500 on, *suffragium* enters religion, in the sense of "intercession," and we find patron-saints. "Heaven resounds with your *suffragia*," exclaims a devotee of St. Martin.[16] The belief in heavenly advocates is indeed far older, going back to Judaism.[17] But it is now being fully worked out on the secular model. One of the terrors of the Last Day in the medieval hymn *Dies Irae* is your standing alone before the Judge, without a patron: *quem patronum rogaturus?*[18]

Another landmark reached by the early sixth century is that the word can denote "a sum of money—or another douceur—to buy influence." In

13. *Cod. Theod.* 2.29.2, Theodosius, Arcadius et Honorius Rufino Praefecto Praetorio, Code 4.3.1.

14. Molière, *Les Femmes savantes*, I, 3, v.239-244

15. Suetonius, *Vesp.* 23.2.

16. Venantius Fortunatus, *Life of St. Martin of Tours* 1.309.

17. 2 Macc. 15:11ff.

18. Effectively used by Goethe, *Faust* 1.3826.

Byzantine glossaries, *suffragium* is defined as *dosis*,"gift."[19] In 535, Justinian, as an afterthought to the permissiveness of his major codification, forbids the giving of *suffragium* for the governorship of a province.[20] A new governor takes an oath by the Father, the Son, the Holy Ghost, Mary, the Four Gospels and the Archangels Michael and Gabriel, that he has not contravened the law. If he has (thus runs the imprecation he utters against himself) he will incur the fate of Judas, the leprosy of Gehazi, the tremor of Cain—and certain legal penalties such as confiscation of property and corporal punishment. All of no use.

Thus far de Ste. Croix. I do not think he mentions that Greek *psephos*, "pebble," then "voting pebble," moved in a similar direction, though far less radically and doubtless under the impact of Roman conditions. Libanius, a friend of the Emperor Julian, speaks of a city having "a great *psephos*, influence."[21] It is noteworthy that he composed a declamation on patronage.[22]

More intriguing is the question how it is that, in contemporary parlance, "suffrage" once more has its original value. In the Middle Ages, this had practically dropped out, yet nowadays it dominates. When my brother and I were toddlers, our father used to place a hat on the table and by means of magical formulas and gestures make a live rabbit to sit under it. Before he showed it to us, however, he would say that to cause

19. *Corpus Glossariorum Latinorum* 2.191.58.

20. Novellae 8.

21. Libanius, *Orations* 18.13.

22. Libanius, *Orations* 47, cited by de Ste. Croix (*British Journal of Sociology* 5 [1954], 45n2). This address is full of actions and postures which, *mutatis mutandis*, recur again and again. Three examples. (1) Libanius writes for the good of the commonwealth. But his self-interest is obvious. Owner of a large estate, he complains not about patronage as such but about a new kind: tenants, instead of relying on their landlord's protection as heretofore, more and more look to the military who can help them not only against outsiders but also against the landlord himself. (2) The tenants are playing off the remoter oppressor against the immediate one. I remember from my time at Aberdeen that enthusiasm for an independent Scotland was more subdued there than at Edinburgh: the latter did not get away with everything so long as one could appeal to London. Among the Jewish dispersion, this method has played an enormous part. (3) The case furnishes an excellent illustration of how antisemitism is activated. For several generations, the tenants on Libanius's land had been Jews. Now that they start making claims and getting the army to intervene, he speaks of them as "these typical Jews."

a rabbit to come was easy; the real coup consisted in conjuring it away again. So some further wavings of hand and mutterings, then a lifting of the hat—and lo and behold, there was no rabbit to be seen. De Ste. Croix has succeeded in importing the meanings "assistance," "influence," "bribe." I must now get rid of them again.

First, as for the Middle Ages. The old tie with "vote," "right to vote," is virtually gone, whether in Latin, English, French or any other language. The first English-Latin lexicon, *Promptorium Parvulorum*, of the middle of the fifteenth century, offers: "suffrage or help = *suffragium*."[23] The fourteenth to fifteenth century entries for "suffrage" in the Oxford Dictionary exclusively concern "intercession," "prayer," "help," "support," "assistance."[24]

Neglect of this situation has led to an imprecision in this work. It says[25] that a "suffragan (bishop)" is so titled because he can be called on by his superior to give his "suffrage" for him, vote on his side. But when "suffragan" came up, *suffragium* or "suffrage" had not yet recovered its former territory. Du Cange is right (and he bases himself on texts) in interpreting the title as *adiutor*, Greek *boethes*, "helper."[26] (The *Concise Oxford Dictionary* is better, except for its final reference directly to the classical Latin usage *suffragari*, "to support with vote").[27]

To stay with the Church for a moment, *suffragia* signifies "intercessionary prayers," especially for the dead—as in Wyclif, 1380.[28] In liturgy, at the latest since the twelfth century there is a section devoted *ad poscendum suffragia sanctorum*, "to requesting the intercessionary prayers of the saints." These play a part in Luther's theology, from his theses on.[29] They were abolished from public worship in our time, in 1960, by Pope John XXIII.[30]

23. *Promptorium Parvulorum*, ed. A. Way (1865), 483.

24. See *New English Dictionary*, vol. 9, pt. 2, ed. C.T. Onions (1919), 111.

25. See *New English Dictionary*, vol. 9, pt. 2, ed. C.T. Onions (1919), 110.

26. See Du Cange, *Glossarium Mediae et Infimae Latinitatis*, vol. 6 (1883—1887), 649.

27. See *Concise Oxford Dictionary*, ed. H.W. Fowler (1929), 1220.

28. Quoted in *New English Dictionary*, vol. 9, pt. 2 (1919), 111.

29. E.g. theses 26ff. See J. Köstlin, *Luthers Theologie*, vol. 1 (1968), 370ff.

30. See T. Schnitzler, *Lexikon für Theologie and Kirche*, vol. 9, 2nd ed., ed. J. Höfer and K. Rahner (1964), 1149.

The pristine force is revived through the new learning. The first English evidence of "suffrage" = "vote" is More's *Comfort against Tribulation* of 1534.[31] He is invoking a passage from the Apocalypse:[32] "To him that overcomes I will give to eat of the hidden manna, and will give him a white stone—Vulgate: *calculum conditum*, Greek: *psephon leuken*—and in the stone a new name written." He translates "white suffrage" and explains that in Greece where, he reminds his readers, St. John (for him, the author of the Apocalypse) lived, "every man's assent was called his suffrage, which in some places was by the voices, in some places by hands, and one kind of those suffrages was by certain things that are in Latin called *calculi* . . . round stones." So here the long-buried meaning is quite consciously dug up.

As for his exegesis of the Biblical text, I cannot so far find it prior to him. Modern commentators leave us the choice between thinking of a ballot of acquittal in a criminal trial or an entrance ticket to paradise.[33]

The restoration of the classical "suffrage" had been anticipated across the channel. French, like English, takes off from "suffrage" in the sense of "intercession." But the original meaning here reappears as early as the fourteenth century,[34] in Bercheure—significantly, in a description of voting in the Roman *comitia*. The next evidence given by Littré is Calvin.

Bercheure, a friend of Petrarch's, belonged to the first wave of the Renaissance. No doubt More was familiar with his work. Even so, it is not absolutely certain that he depends on him.

Shakespeare first employs "suffrage" in Act I of *Titus Andronicus*, a very early piece, of between 1589 and 1592: "People of Rome and people's tribunes here, I ask your voices and your suffrages."[35] The scene is Rome; and he introduces the new-old application only after preparing the ground, furnishing the more familiar equivalent—"your voices (this is universally intelligible) and your suffrages." This half-line is typical of his skill in getting the effect he wants. A strange, academic usage unclarified would grate on the mass of his audience. With this briefest of explanations—

31. T. More, *Dialogue of Comfort against Tribulation* 3.26.
32. Rev. 2:17.
33. See e.g. J. Massyngberde-Ford, *Revelation* (1975), 399.
34. See E. Littré, *Dictionnaire de la Langue Française*, vol. 4 (1875), 2072.
35. Shakespeare, *Titus Andronicus* 1.1.218.

which, indeed, flows so smoothly it does not sound didactic at all—it becomes an elegant flourish.

In Act IV he uses the term again, this time without translating it first: "the people's suffrages."[36] Neither does he provide crutches the third and last time, in *Pericles*, one of his later plays (foreshadowing the *Winter's Tale* and *Tempest*), 1607–8: "Forbear your suffrages."[37] It should be observed that the setting is still the ancient world: to it, throughout his corpus, the term remains confined.

Some fifty-five years lie between the *Comfort against Tribulation* and *Titus Andronicus*; yet the bulk of his spectators could still be tickled with that classicism, "dust that is a little gilt." For that matter, nearly two centuries divide More from Bercheure. Today, in modern countries, owing to the media, an innovation in vocabulary becomes known in no time, and not only to a select circle but in every stratum. It would be an interesting study to find out about and compare the speed and depth of absorption of neologisms in various cultures and periods. Also their staying power: among my students, many a locution that is neat in one semester is gross in the next.

As the primary meaning of *suffragium* was being brought back, the "debased" one receded. Today, except for a few traces in the Church, it is gone. No doubt changed conditions and easy replacement account for this development.

I would add that a more general inquiry into designations for "vote" and allied matters might be worthwhile. One thing likely to emerge is the enormous power of historical association. To this day, for example, "plebiscite"—once an enactment of the plebeians as opposed to the patricians—retains a slightly rebellious flavour. It takes place in a crisis, a determined assertion of the popular will (often, of course, totally directed from above). This is not at all true of "referendum," though dictionaries frequently define it as "a kind of plebiscite."[38] The definition is correct—only it does no justice to the orderly, almost bureaucratic,

36. Shakespeare, *Titus Andronicus* 4.3.19.

37. Shakespeare, *Pericles* 2.4.41.

38. See Brockhaus, *Enzyklopädie*, vol. 15 (1972), 530. In the paragraph on plebiscite, in *Encylopaedia Britannica*, vol. 18 (1973), 42, it is stated that "unlike referendum (*q.v.*) a plebiscite is not a normal method"; but in *Encylopaedia Britannica*, 19:36, s.v. "referendum" and "initiative," the two are paired off. The *New Encyclopaedia Britannica*, *Micropaedia*, vol. 8 (1974), 39, in sketching plebiscite, omits the reference to its exceptional character; on

Swiss atmosphere. Certain questions the government, capable but merely human, neither could nor should nor even will wish to decide; they are to be passed on, "referred," to the people at large. *Volksbegehren* and *Volksentscheid* again have their own connotations. (In the constitution of the German Federal Republic the *Volksentscheid* is reduced to a very small role, because of its demagogic past in Weimar times).

No less revealing would be the opposite cases, of severance of native ties. "Voice" manifestly at the outset (in the fifteenth century) signified an open stand—like German *Stimme, Abstimmung*; so did "poll," a counting of visible heads (seventeenth century). Now they cover secret proceedings. "Show of hands" (eighteenth century) is too concrete to have been similarly extended. Yet Greek *cheirotonia*, "hand-extension," and Hebrew *hasba'a*, "finger-raising," have proved adaptable. Maybe "handshow" would have been equal to the task. "Ballot," the sixteenth-century Venetian *ballotta*, is one of the few terms originally presupposing secret machinery. Its scope, however, has also widened and one could now say: "Let us have an open ballot on this question."

The evolution of "lobby" is reminiscent of certain phases of *suffragium*. In the *Oxford Dictionary* of the beginning of this century, the noun in the sense of "frequenters of the legislature with a view to influencing it" as well as the verb are marked as peculiar to the States.[39] All entries, whether of English or American provenance, are disparaging. "The lobby and corruption are legitimate subjects for satire."[40] "American manners, American lobbyism and American corruption."[41] Even the assurance "What is known as lobbying by no means implies in all cases the use of money"[42] is hardly eulogistic. By contrast, the Webster before me notes only of the verb that it is "chiefly U.S.," and the definitions imply no condemnation.[43] Actually, the "lobbying" of lawgivers, even as a paid job, has become perfectly accepted.

---

the other hand, there is no mention of plebiscite in the entry on referendum and initiative, pp. 469 –70.

39. See *New English Dictionary*, vol. 6, pt. 1, ed. H. Bradley (1903), 376.

40. See *Century Magazine*, March 1884, 655/1.

41. See *Pall Mall Gazette*, September 6, 1883, 3/2.

42. See J. Bryce, *The American Commonwealth*, vol. 1 (1888), 556.

43. See Webster, *New International Dictionary of the English Language*, 2nd ed. (1960), 1448.

"Vote" itself has an intriguing history. It is formed from Latin *votum*, the passive participle of *voveo*, "to vow." The initial range of *votum* is "that which is promised," "a promise," "a vow," especially to a deity. ("Votary," "votive-offering" and "devotion" still reflect that stage). It is in the nature of this transaction, however, that you expect, want, something in return. Whether, over time, this aspect gains in importance or simply comes more into the open—by the early Principate, the word often signifies "a wish," "a prayer."[44] Finally, in the late Middle Ages, we arrive at "a wish," "a decision"—"a vote" as in current speech.

To go on to "precedent," the date when this noun attained its mature operation has been substantially pushed back in the past few decades—a sign of the labours bestowed on English legal history. As usual, even the best textbooks do not always keep pace. Plucknett is permanently on reserve at Boalt Hall. He tells us[45] that the first technical instance known to Sir Carleton Kemp Allen is 1557. I was puzzled, less because the *Oxford Dictionary* lists a passage from 1523[46]—the exact import of the term here is not quite certain—than because my edition of *Law in the Making* represents the usage as going back to the second half of the previous century[47] and "reappearing" in 1557.[48] On probing, I found that in the first two editions—1927 and 1930—he indeed describes the reference of 1557 as the earliest he has been able to discover.[49] A series of articles by T. Ellis Lewis, however, drew attention to fresh material,[50] and from the third edition on—1939—the revised presentation is offered.[51] Plucknett first appeared in 1929. He could have corrected the point in the third edition, 1940, but somehow neither then nor later got around to it.

In Elizabethan English, "precedent" was still around in a number of senses, such as "original draft," subsequently all to be overwhelmed by that

44. See C.T. Lewis and C. Short, *A Latin Dictionary* (1879), 2014–15.
45. See T.F.T. Plucknett, *A Concise History of the Common Law*, 5th ed. (1956), 348.
46. See *A New English Dictionary*, vol. 7, pt. 3, ed. J.A.H. Murray (1909), 1243.
47. See C.K. Allen, *Law in the Making*, 6th ed. (1958), 193ff.
48. See Allen, *Law in the Making*, 6th ed. (1958), 199.
49. See Allen, *Law in the Making*, 2nd ed. (1930), 141.
50. See T. Ellis Lewis, *LQR* 46 (1930): 207ff.; *LQR* 47 (1931): 411ff.; *LQR* 48 (1932):230ff. In *LQR* 46 (1930): 357, a case of 1459.
51. See Allen, *Law in the Making*, 3rd ed. (1939), 186ff., 192.

of "example for imitation." It signifies "original draft" in *Richard the Third*, where a scribe says of an indictment: "Eleven hours I've spent to write it over. The precedent was full as long a-doing."[52] As a specimen of "example for imitation" we may quote a line from *Titus Andronicus*: the hero calls the deed of Virginius, who killed his beloved daughter in order to save her from dishonour, his "pattern, precedent and lively warrant."[53]

The latter application of the word is indeed the more frequent one in Shakespeare. But the full juristic content appears only once or, perhaps, twice; and that use, we may assume, was young enough at the time to intrigue an audience. It is Portia, the ideal judge, who is made to introduce it, with deliberate emphasis, in the *Merchant of Venice*, of 1596. In the initial part of her intervention, when she pretends to resist those who would simply deprive Shylock of his rights, she declares: "It must not be; there is no power in Venice can alter a decree established. 'Twill be recorded for a precedent, and many an error by the same example will rush into the state."[54] Note the recording, note the setting out of the consequences that must ensue.

Two passages from *Henry the Eighth*—ca. 1613—are worth comparing. I disregard the controversy respecting the authorship of the play: the relevant sections do not sound un-Shakespearian.

In Act II, the King, by seeking impartial outside opinions on his marriage problem, is giving "a precedent of wisdom."[55] However, though legal matters of the greatest weight are involved, it looks as if we had before us the general meaning "example for imitation": there is nothing to tie it down to "judicial precedent" proper.

A closer approximation occurs in Act I. A special tax levied on Wolsey's orders is revoked by his master as illegal: "Things done without example in their issue are to be feared. Have you a precedent for this commission? I believe, not any. We must not rend our subjects from our laws and stick them in our will."[56] True, even here, at first sight, it seems merely an administrative measure for which authority in past proceedings is requisite. But Wolsey has just defended his action by pointing out

52. Shakespeare, *Richard the Third* 3.6.7.
53. Shakespeare, *Titus Andronicus* 5.3.44.
54. Shakespeare, *Merchant of Venice* 4.1.215ff.
55. Shakespeare, *Henry the Eighth* 2.2.85.
56. Shakespeare, *Henry the Eighth* 1.2.91.

that it had the "learned approbation of the judges"[57]—scil. those on the King's Council. So the censure may be directed also against their reckless advice—which would come fairly near the area of judicial decision.

Shakespeare was not above repeating a hit.[58] It is just conceivable that he is once again parading the technical function of the term, not as yet commonplace. If so, Henry's pronouncement about the institution is complementary to Portia's: she stresses the evil of a precedent flawed, he that of an arbitrary verdict lacking a precedent.

In the LSAT, the poet or his early publishers would lose marks for poor spelling; *horribile dictu*, more often than not they write "president."

The Quality of Mercy is Not Strained

Yet its lineage is not wholly noble. As is well known,[59] the word represents Latin *merces* which, from the sixth century AD on, often denotes "compassion" or perhaps better "compassionate behaviour." Previously, it denoted "reward," a sense still reflected in "mercenary." What accounts for the innovation? Not, I fear, a welling up of unselfishness.

We first come across it in Christian theology, largely conceived from the point of view of the poor masses. In the late Empire, the gap between them and the haves was tremendous. Consequently, a small labourer, a soldier or the like learned more and more to look on the pay for his services as a favour, our "mercy."

In other cases, general display of benevolence formed the starting-point, to be followed by more specific emphasis on donation: *caritas*, "charity," signified "affectionate dealing" before it signified "relief"; *eleemosyne*, "compassion," preceded "alms"; *pietas*, "piety," "pity," preceded "pittance." *Merces* commenced as "reward," "due remuneration," but, as one side became all-powerful and the other helpless, moved through "relief," "alms," "pittance," to something like "affectionate dealing," "compassion," "pity."

57. Shakespeare, *Henry the Eighth* 1.2.71.

58. E.g. the awe-inspiring ban on suicide: Shakespeare, *Hamlet* 1.2.132 and *Cymbeline* 3.4.79. See my article in *Philosophy and Public Affairs* 1 (1972): 414, (repr. in *Suicide and Life-Threatening Behaviour* 7 (1977), 159.

59. See *New English Dictionary*, vol. 6, ed. H. Bradley (1908), 351.

Shakespeare, plainly in an optimistic mood, continues his praise of mercy: "It blesses him that gives and him that takes."[60] He might have said it of grace. But it is not all that can be said.

Let us begin with him that gives. Wherever such conduct is a duty, legal or moral, he may experience resentment rather than bliss. It comes out in the semantics of "gratuitous" (in French, *gratuit*) which can signify on the one hand "free of charge," "munificent," on the other, "senseless," "absurd" (*acte gratuit*).[61]

Both uses already exist in Latin. The pleasant one is the earlier, reflecting the intrinsic nature of *gratia*: Plautus has it.[62] (*Gratis*, by the way, in fuller spelling *gratiis*, being the ablative plural of *gratia*, "with graces," was too near the root ever to turn bilious. English "gratis" is still confined to "free of charge"). The unpleasant one is first met in the younger Seneca: "Hatred is either the result of a hurt or senseless, *gratuitum*."[63] A decisive factor in this process was that more and more what purported to be tendered spontaneously was in truth enforced by the social code. Hence, frequently, in the place of genuine good-will there was the feeling of sacrificing something for nothing. People might still speak of an act as done by way of grace, "gratuitous," but mean "for no reason." From here to the really bad connotation was not a far cry.

The evidence for gratuitousness as an ought is plentiful. Cicero writes that liberality is not geared towards *merces*, "reward," or *fructus*, "profit," but is "gratuitous," in pursuance of *officium*, "duty."[64] Similarly, in his opinion, it was by performing such *officia*, "duties," as remembering the children of a disciple, that the dying Epicurus showed himself a man of *probitas gratuita*, "gratuitous probity."[65] The jurist Paul informs us that the contract of mandate is "gratuitous," having its basis in *officium et amicitia*, "duty and friendship"; and he adds that *merces*, "reward," is opposed to *officium*, "duty."[66]

60. Shakespeare, *Merchant of Venice* 4.1.187.
61. See above, p. 113.
62. Plautus, *Cist.* 740.
63. Seneca the Younger, *Ep.* 105.4.
64. Cicero, *Leg.* 1.18.48.
65. Cicero, *Fin.* 2.31.99.
66. Digest 17.1.1.4, Paul *XXXII ad edictum*. The *ergo*, "therefore," in the clause *contrarium ergo est officio merces*, is puzzling. The solution, however, lies not in emendation but in reconstruction of the longer exposition which the compilers have shortened.

These writers indeed adhere to an ethics, still widely accepted, for which not only is gratuitousness a moral duty but all moral duties are gratuitous. Gratuitousness is a sort of superelement: the exercise of no virtue is compatible with desire of gain, you must love—*amare, diligere*—justice, fairness and so on. I shall not here embark on the problems involved in making a duty of a mind-set or emotion, and love in particular.

There are comparable developments in other languages. In German, *vergebens* and *vergeblich,* "in vain," are—if we omit details—offshoots of *vergeben* in the sense of "to give away for no consideration."[67] ("To forgive" is an elevated application of this.) Presumably, the emotional link is much the same as that between the two meanings of "gratuitous."

Umsonst, literally "for thus," "for so," is worth quoting. It may denote either "for free" or "to no purpose." In this case also, the positive usage seems to antedate the negative one.[68]

The most striking analogy I can think of, however, is Hebrew *ḥinnam.* This adverb derives from *ḥen,* "grace" (as does the name Hannah); and at times it stands for "no recompense being exacted," at times for "without cause." Indeed, an old instance of the latter application is "they that hate me without cause,"[69] reminiscent of Seneca's *odium gratuitum.*

To be sure, the Old Testament world is not that of the Roman *officia.* Still, the Book of Exodus contains very ancient directions as to when a slave obtains his freedom "gratuitously" whether the master likes it or not.[70] Again, there are traces of an archaic custom according to which a junior member of a family must serve the Head "gratuitously."[71] Openhandedness is generally a quality you had better show if you care for your reputation.[72] So here, too, compulsory "graces" contributed to the degradation of the notion. The parallel is all the more valuable as any influence in one direction or the other is out of the question.

---

67. See J. and W. Grimm, *Deutsches Wörterbuch,* vol. 12, pt. 1, ed. E. Wülcker (1886), 388ff.

68. See J. and W. Grimm, *Deutsches Wörterbuch,* vol. 11, pt. 2, ed. V. Dollmayr (1913), 1155ff.

69. Pss. 35:19, 69:4.

70. Exod. 21:2, 11.

71. Gen. 29:15. See D. Daube and R. Yaron, *Journal of Semitic Studies* 1 (1956): 60ff.; also Daube, *The Exodus Pattern in the Bible* (1963), 62ff.

72. The texts with *nadhabh* and its derivatives are relevant, starting with Exod. 25:2.

Actually, the Deuteronomist is aware of the likely reaction of owners having to release a slave. In his revision of the rules of Exodus, he adds the warning: "It shall not be hard in your eyes when you let him go free."[73] It should be remarked that *ḥinnam* does not figure in Deuteronomy. The law states simply "you shall let him go free from you,"[74] not "he shall go out free gratuitously." Possibly, by that time, the pejorative "without cause" had already sprung up, so it was prudent in this context to avoid the word altogether.

It may be added that there are distinct adumbrations of a general requirement of right-doing for its own sake, with no expectation of an immediate return. The good man loves righteousness and the commandments[75] and the duty to love God is promulgated by the Deuteronomist in so many words.[76]

The de-gracing of *ex gratia* and "gratuity" is proceeding under our very eyes. When a disbursement is described as being made *ex gratia*, there is rarely any trace of sympathy: it is simply an announcement that no right on the part of the recipient or others in his situation is admitted. English law in fact now knows an enforceable promise to pay so and so much *ex gratia*.[77]

"Gratuity" signifies (1) "favour," attested from 1523. (2) "Money-gift," from 1540, often in return for services. (3) More particularly, "money-gift by a superior to an inferior, a servant," from the nineteenth century on; (3a) "bounty on discharge or retirement," from the beginning of that century, (3b) "tip," from the middle. Up to this point, all can be found in the *Oxford Dictionary*.[78] Recently, however, the term is moving away from gift altogether, towards "extra pay on a certain occasion," i.e. pay firmly expected if not enforceable at law. Even the amount is less and less in the discretion of the payer. That it is still designated "gratuity" rather than "extra pay," "surcharge" or the like may be due not only to the ordinary staying-power of traditional vocabulary but also to a certain nostalgia, a tacit understanding between payer and payee to keep up appearances.

73. Deut. 15:18.
74. Deut. 15:12.
75. Pss. 45:8, 119:47.
76. Deut. 6:5; Cf. Exod. 20:5; Deut. 5:11.
77. *Edwards v. Skyways Ltd.* (1964) *Weekly Law Reports* 1:349.
78. See *New English Dictionary*, vol. 4, pt. 2, ed. H. Bradley (1901), 372.

Turning to him that takes—we can well believe that he is happy, receiving an unearned boon (that is what "grace" properly means); but what about those passed over?

J. N. L. Myres has shewn that, in *Codex Theodosianus*, *gratia* and its derivatives almost exclusively refer to the evil of "favouritism."[79] It can indeed be paired off with *suffragium*: the seeker of a good post will make ruinous payments for "influence or the favouritism of mighty persons."[80] (Greek *charis* may be used in the same bad sense and is so used by Libanius in the address on patronage mentioned above.[81]) According to Myres, the corrupt nature of this worldly *gratia* in that epoch was a major motive behind Pelagius's teaching that divine rule was not governed by this force. Whereas Augustine thought of man as morally helpless and capable of virtue only by "the grace" of God, he preached free will and judgment according to deserts.

The implications as to the prevalent regime were not lost on its beneficiaries: a fascinating fact pointed out by Myres is that attacks on "favouritism" in *Codex Theodosianus* abruptly cease in 419, the year following the final condemnation of the Pelagian heresy. In Britain, he argues, Pelagianism contributed significantly to the overthrow of Roman sovereignty.

It might be profitable to extend his inquiry. God, magnanimous donor with no questions asked, versus God, meticulous dispenser, is a perennial conundrum, and we could probably learn a good deal by systematically looking into the relation of the manifold doctrines about it to the secular structure.

As for *ḥen*, it never descended to the low level of "favouritism." But its unpredictable wielding by heaven is stressed in Exodus—"I will be gracious to whom I will be gracious"[82]—and its erratic nature on earth in Ecclesiastes (not surprisingly)—"the race is not to the swift nor yet grace

79. See J.N.L. Myres, *JRS* 50 (1960): 24ff. On *gratia* in the Digest, see P. Stein, in *Synteleia Vincenzo Arangio-Ruiz*, vol. 1 (1964), 130ff.

80. *Cod. Theod.* 6.24.3, Valentinianus et Valens ad Severum Comitem Domesticorum.

81. Libanius, *Orations* 47.13. By contrast, *pace* H.G. Liddell and R. Scott, *A Greek-English Lexicon*, 9th ed. (1940), 1979, in Lysias 14.40, there is nothing intrinsically objectionable about *charis*.

82. Exod. 33:19.

to men of skill."[83] Hundreds of years later, the Rabbis and Paul wrestle with the problem where the former pronouncement leaves divine justice.[84] While for N. W. Ewer God's choice of the Jews is odd as, fundamentally, any act of grace must be, the repartee culminating in "he knows what's what" bases their place on the democratic merit principle. Here I shall leave the matter.

How fast modern English is swept along by currents similar to those around AD 400 is illustrated by a sentence of Myres's. (This is not to overlook notable differences). Introducing the pejorative sense of *gratia*, he writes: "*Gratia* means not so much "grace" as "favour," and not so much "favour" as "favouritism." At least for the young generation in California, the final portion—"and not so much" etc.—would no longer be necessary: "favour" by itself, certainly the plural "favours," is sufficiently icky. A survey of the use of the noun in the *San Francisco Chronicle* in the seventies would surely yield much the same result as he gives for *gratia* in *Codex Theodosianus*. His article appeared less than twenty years ago.

83. Eccles. 9:11.
84. Jerusalemite *Targum* ad loc., Rom. 9:15.

8

Withdrawal: Five Verbs

What unity these five notes have lies in their genesis. I wondered about the origin of "to recant." In the course of going into it, I became aware of other verbs with similar meanings which, by the sound of them, seemed to have an interesting history: "to resile," literally signifying "to leap back," "to renounce," which must have to do with *nuntium*, "a message," and "to repudiate," from the province of *pudor*, "shame." So I went on to do a little research on them—with no thought of propounding a thesis. The section on "to retract" was added when a reader of the rest was pleased, or least displeased, with the points I made as a Roman lawyer.

To Recant

Literally, this is "to chant again, against, back." Horace employs *recantare* in a poem[1] addressed to a beautiful young lady whom, in previous pieces, he had insulted: these now being "recanted," he hopes for forgiveness. It is universally agreed[2] that he is rendering Greek *palinodeo*. Stesichoros—contemporary with Sappho—had written an ode defaming Helen of Troy, for which blasphemy he was struck with blindness. Immediately he composed a "re-ode," "counter-ode," *palinodia*, in which he proclaimed her

---

1. Horace, *Odes* 1.16.27.
2. See E. Fraenkel, *Horace* (1957), 209.

innocent, and his sight was restored.[3] In course of time, the noun came to denote "retractation" generally—Cicero uses it thus[4]— and the verb *palinodeo* "to retract." Horace, then, is "retracting" his earlier utterances; but by putting an exact equivalent of *palinodeo*, he is alluding, too, to the original, narrower "re-ode"—his position, he insinuates, is similar to that of Stesichoros. As is well known, he compares himself to the latter also in Epode 17,[5] though in a far more mocking vein.

I wonder whether there is not even more to his choice of *recantare*. Compounds of *cantare* tend to have to do with the supernatural. *Incantare*—our "to enchant"—initially means "to chant a spell into something or somebody": *excantare* "to chant something or somebody out of their place." The XII Tables[6] condemned the "chanting in" of an evil spell, and the "chanting out" of fruits from somebody else's field or the decoying of his corn. *Incantare* at least is not confined to archaic sources. In fact, as its scope widens, it figures also in the absence of an actual chant. At the same time, it never quite loses that supernatural flavour; a trace of it lingers to this day. Horace's *recantare*, it looks, may contain a suggestion of "removal by magic."[7]

Ovid warns us[8] that the worries of love are not to be "recanted," got rid of by herbs and sulphur. (A few lines before,[9] he speaks of "crops passing from one field into another": clearly one of the untoward incidents contemplated by the XII Tables.) There are two possibilities. Either he adopted the word from Horace, who was his senior by some twenty years and whom he admired. In this case, it is difficult to imagine that he gave it a totally different sense: he must have seen in the model passage a hint at magical transformation. Or he did not borrow from Horace, but *recantare*

3. Plato, *Phdr.* 20.243Af; Isocrates 10 (Helen). 64, Pausanias 3 (Laconia). 19.13,20.1.

4. Cicero, *Att.* 2.9.1, 4.5.1, 7.7.1.

5. Horace, *Epodi* 42ff.

6. VIII 8.

7. Professor Borimir Jordan of University of California at Santa Barbara, who read the typescript of this note, suspects that even the Greek *palinodia* was here and there associated with that notion: it is called a mode of purification, *kartharmos*, in Plato's *Phdr.*. In Cicero, it is true, no magical element is noticeable.

8. Ovid, *Rem. am.* 259. See H. Fränkel, *Ovid* (1945) 62, 203.

9. Ovid, *Rem. am.* 225. Cf. Ovid, *Amores* 3.7.31, quoted in Bruns, *Font.*, 31.

as signifying "to remove by magic" enjoyed independent currency. In this case, it becomes even more probable that this meaning plays a part in Horace's expression.

"Now I would change," says the penitent wooer, "those bitter lines for sweet, wouldst thou only become my friend and give me again thy heart."[10] Here follows the phrase *recantatis opprobriis*. If my hunch is correct, though we may English it by "the offending verses being retracted" and/or "the offending verses being superseded by this re-ode," he is also looking forward to the new, unburdened life that will result: "the offending verses being spirited away." Those bad things will all be miraculously gone.

Nisbet and Hubbard in their recent commentary argue, unconvincingly, that the poem in question is not an apology for an attack at all.[11] They are indeed right in holding that the main part, a sermon against anger, has reference not to a past state of Horace's mind, but to the lady's present one. But this does not affect the traditionally accepted character of the ode. Here is a summary: the lady is encouraged to destroy the criminal outpourings; anger is about the most destructive force conceivable, so she had better relent; he too in his young days fell prey to it and penned those rash poems; "now I would change," etc. According to Nisbet and Hubbard, the lampoons enraging the lady were directed not against her, but against others or society at large. However, as they admit, besides the *recantare* at the end of this ode which connects up with Stesichoros's, there is the very opening line patterned on him: the lady is apostrophized "a maiden, fairer than thy mother fair"—a Helen *rediviva*. It seems wrong to play down the significance of these clues.

Apparently, *recantare* does not occur in medieval Latin either in the sense of "to retract" or in that of "to remove by magic." Nor is it taken over by any language other than English, where "to recant" makes its debut in the sixteenth century. Craigie,[12] therefore, is justified in representing the word as coming straight from Horace and going back, through him, to *palinodeo*. The second-oldest reference listed by Craigie is Sir Thomas

10. Horace, *Odes* 1.16.25ff. Translation by E. C. Bennett, *Horace, The Odes and Epodes* (Loeb Classical Library, 1919), 51.

11. R.G. Nisbet and M. Hubbard, *A Commentary on Horace: Odes, Book 1* (1970), 201ff.

12. W.A. Craigie, *New English Dictionary*, vol. 8, ed. by J. A. H. Murray (1910), 227–28.

Elyot's Latin-English Dictionary of 1538, s.v. *palinodeo*: "a contrary song, or retracting of that which one has spoken or written, now of some men called a recanting." What is strange is that s.v. *recantare*, we hear nothing about this sense: "to charm away, to charm out a thing, which was brought in by enchantment, as the witches (called wise women) are wont to do." Quite likely, for a while, Ovid's meaning—readily intelligible—was alone recognized by the Renaissance scholars, and they interpreted Horace accordingly. It was only when the latter's relation to Stesichoros was more fully explored that attention was paid to the role of *palinodeo*, so that *recantatis opprobriis* became "the insults being retracted." The new insight is reflected in the entry *palinodia*, but not yet in *recantare*.

To Resile

From Latin *resilire*, literally "to leap back." In law, it denotes "to withdraw" from an undertaking. While it is not met in this sense prior to the end of the third century, *non constat* that it had no place earlier in popular usage. But the classical jurists prefer more sober terms like *discedere*. *Resilire* is too emotional for them: where it expresses the point of view of the party who acts— "I leap back"—it shows great eagerness to leave, and where it expresses the point of view of the party who is being left— "you leap back"—it shows disapproval of the act as arbitrary or mean.

The former nuance comes out in a passage from Pseudo-Asconius, a fifth-century work. Some manipulators had promised Verres that, for a substantial payment he would make them, they would bribe the court into acquitting him. When the selection of the judges, however, produced a result quite hopeless for them, "the whole business displeased them and they withdrew from the arrangement entered into," *displicuit totum negotium redemptoribus et resiluerunt a condicione ac placito*:[13] they scrambled out. Disapproval is contained in a complaint, brought before the Emperors in AD 293, about a woman who, having consented to a compromise and even accepted what she was to receive by its terms, "now

---

13. Pseudo-Asconius on Cicero, *Verr.* 1.6.16. Whether the commentary gives the right explanation of Cicero's speech is not here relevant. Cf. below, "To Renounce."

has withdrawn from the agreement," *nunc de conventione resiluisse*[14]: she went back on her word.

This is not to deny that, once the verb had entered legal writing, it could be applied neutrally, just like *discedere*. Ulpian discusses sale with *in diem addictio*: the seller up to a certain date may accept a better offer. An interpolated clause puts the case where the parties specially agree that, on the seller receiving a better offer, even "the buyer be allowed to withdraw," *erat nominatim actum ut liceret resilire emptori meliore condicione allata*.[15] Here *resilire* has no distinctive flavour. Interestingly, Beseler, who first noticed the post-classical provenance of the text, adduced the occurrence of "the rare word *resilire*" in support of his contention.[16]

The word never became frequent in the area of law. Du Cange quotes *a conventione resilire* from a letter of King John, of AD 1212. In the sixteenth century the liking for ancient speech led to *resilir* and "to resile" being employed for "to withdraw" in French and English. But French before long gave up this usage and even in English, though it does persist, it is not very common.[17] Neither "resilient" nor "resilience" has been drawn into the legal orbit.

To Retract

Retractare signifies, *inter alia*, "to go over something again" and "to revoke something." In antiquity, the former meaning is frequent, the latter one is confined to legal contexts and rare even there. Significantly, the former meaning alone develops an agent noun: *retractatio* is met in the sense of "reconsideration," "revision"—Augustine's *Retractationes* may be recalled— never in that of "revocation." By contrast, English "to retract," starting in

---

14. Code 2.4.17, Diocletian and Maximian. When I say the complaint was lodged in 293, I may be overestimating the efficiency of the chancellery: all we know is that it was answered in that year.

15. Digest 18.2.9, Ulpian XXVIII *ad Sabinum*.

16. Beseler, *Beitr.* 1 (1910): 86–87.

17. *The Concise Oxford Dictionary* does not list it at all. Professor Peter Stein of Cambridge in a letter expresses the view that "to resile" still carries a hint of moral disapproval.

the sixteenth century with reference to legal matters, to this day denotes "to revoke" only; and "retractation" denotes "revocation," except that, in direct imitation of Augustine, it may figure in the title of a work wherein the author re-examines a previous publication.

The details of the Latin usage are quite complicated. Not surprisingly, both the chancellery and the jurists employ *retractare* where a party "goes over something again," in particular, "resumes a process that was concluded." When we come to the meaning "to revoke," however, a division emerges. The classics, while speaking of *retractare* where the Emperor "invalidates" a transaction, seem to avoid it where a party "calls off" one. It is probably too ponderous for this case. The chancellery is less reticent and applies it here too, and so do post-classical jurists.

Heumann-Seckel[18] and the *Vocabularium Jurisprudentiae Romanae*[19] cite a fair number of instances from the Digest and the Code of *retractare* in the sense of "to resume a process." They also present a group of texts in which it denotes "to contest the result of a process with a view to resumption" (Heumann-Seckel: *anfechten, bestreiten*; Vocabularium: *reprehendere, in controversiam vocare*)—a slight extension in meaning. Two first-century decisions by a proconsul of Sardinia[20] and Domitian[21] may be added. In both, the sense lies between "to resume" and "to contest with a view to resumption."

The meaning "to invalidate" occurs in a reply by Trajan to Pliny,[22] laying down that though the Emperor had recently interdicted donations by a municipality to a citizen, donations made long ago *retractari atque in inritum vindicari non oportet*. A person "calls off" a contract in a constitution by Alexander Severus,[23] of the first third of the third century, quoted by Heumann-Seckel. Also quoted in this Dictionary is a constitution by Valerian and Gallienus,[24] AD 254. Here, however, it is the

---

18. H. G. Heumann, *Handlexikon zu den Quellen des römischen Rechts*, 9th ed., ed. E. Seckel (1907), 517.

19. *VJR* vol. 5 (1939), 199.

20. 71a.8 in Bruns, *Font.*, 241.

21. 82.17 in Bruns, *Font.*, 255.

22. Pliny the Younger, *Ep.* 10.11.

23. Code 7.26.4.

24. Code 2.50.6.

provincial governor who "invalidates" a sale. A third constitution quoted,
by Philip,[25] AD 249, shows in striking fashion that even the chancellery
is less prone in the third century than in the sixth to describe the "calling
off" of a transaction by a party as a *retractare*. In the Code, a patron *non
retractavit* a gift to his freedman. The constitution, however, is transmitted
also in the *Fragmenta Vaticana*,[26] and their reading, *non revocavit*, is surely
the genuine one.

The *Vocabularium* enters four texts under "to revoke." The first is also
given by Heumann-Seckel: Digest 3.3.39.7 = *Fragmenta Vaticana* 340b,[27]
from Ulpian.[28] But the entry is wrong: *retractare* here means "to resume a
process." We are told that if a tutor is charged with being "suspect" in his
absence, he who takes up his defence must give security that the tutor
will ratify his dealings since, otherwise, on his return, *velit retractare quod
actum est*. This is the *satisdatio rem ratam haberi*, the principal purpose
of which is "that there should not be renewed litigation about the same
matter."[29] Moreover, if a single "calling off" were envisaged, one would
expect *retractet*, "since otherwise the returned tutor might call off what
has been transacted," rather than *velit retractare*, "might wish to do so";
whereas "might wish to resume, re-litigate, what has been transacted" is
perfectly plausible.

Ulpian, incidentally, declares that the tutor's representative must
give security "also" that the tutor will ratify; that is to say, he must give
security not only *iudicatum solvi*, that the tutor will satisfy an adverse
judgment, but also *rem ratam haberi*. At first sight this speaks strongly
against the prevalent view[30] that a "suspect" tutor, if found guilty, is merely
removed but not fined. However, it is very possible that the word *etiam* is
interpolated with a view to assimilating the *accusatio suspecti tutoris* to the
actio rationibus distrahendis. Alas, this portion of the decision is preserved
in the Digest only, but illegible in the *Fragmenta Vaticana*.

25. Code 8.55.1.3.
26. *Fr. Vat.* 272.
27. Misprinted in the *VJR* as 122.
28. Ulpian IX *ad edictum*.
29. Gaius 4.98, concerning representation of plaintiff.
30. See M. Kaser, *Das römische Privatrecht*, pt. 1, 2nd ed. (1971), 363.

Next, for Digest 46.8.12.3, again from Ulpian[31]: the *Vocabularium* is guilty of the same misclassification. This time a plaintiff is represented in litigation, and defendant has received security that he will ratify. Ulpian informs us that the security can be enforced not only if the plaintiff sues afresh but also if he disregards his representative's dealings by deducting from something he owes defendant what he thinks defendant owes him. "For," he adds, "the security can be enforced by whatever mode he resumes the same transaction that has been transacted by his representative." A simple "calling off" would be expressed by "he calls off the transaction," not "the same transaction"; *eundem actum* points to a "going over something again"— "he resumes the same matter."

In Digest 24.1.7.6, Ulpian once more,[32] the reference is to the "invalidating" of a transaction by the Emperor: good, classical idiom. A wife buys from her husband land pledged to her for her dowry. A rescript by Septimius Severus and Caracalla declares the sale void if it disguises a gift. At the same time, the rescript makes it clear, Ulpian explains, that a genuine sale *non retractari*.

This leaves Digest 31.89.7, from Scaevola.[33] Here, indeed, the verb does signify a "calling off" by a party, but it is not the jurist who uses it thus. A woman sells land inherited under her husband's testament. A codicil which, in accordance with his directions, is opened after her death leaves the estate to third persons by way of *fideicommissum*. "The buyer asks whether the sale can be revoked, *retractari*, by the fideicommissaries." No need to go into the decision. The enquiry itself has been attacked by Beseler[34] as a post-classical concoction. If he is right, obviously, Scaevola is not responsible. This, however, remains true even if—as I believe— he is wrong. We know[35] that, in Scaevola's works, the question is apt to be left in the crude form in which it reached him. This is perhaps more noticeable in his *digesta* than his *responsa*, from which latter the text under discussion comes; but it is definitely the case in the *response* too. We have, then, before us a lay usage not to be attributed to the classics.

31. Digest 46.8.12.3, Ulpian LXXX *ad edictum*.
32. Digest 24.1.7.6, Ulpian XXXI *ad Sabinum*.
33. Digest 31.89.7, Scaevola IV *responsorum*.
34. Beseler, *ZRG* 50 (1930): 69.
35. See R. Samter, *ZRG* 27 (1906): 151ff.

To Renounce

"To renounce" ultimately—through French *renoncer*—derives from Latin *renuntiare*, which has two basically different meanings. The element of *nuntium*, "message," is common to both. But one proceeds from *re* in the sense of "back": "to bring back word," then, more generally, "to bring word," and finally "to declare." The present note is chiefly concerned with the other, proceeding from *re* in the sense of, "against": "to send word rescinding, calling off, refusing" and then also "to rescind, call off, refuse in person."

The second meaning appears later in the sources than the first. True, the dictionaries[36] spot it once in Plautus, but this is an illusion. A parasite would like to get a free meal with a young gentleman. As the latter pretends to be invited out himself by a friend, the former urges him to change his plans: *Iuben domi coenam coqui atque ad illum renuntiari,* "Order dinner to be cooked at home and word to be brought to that one"—scil. that you cannot come.[37] There is no justification for translating "Order the appointment to be called off to that one." The verb recurs in Plautus a dozen more times, invariably denoting "to bring (back) word."[38] Now and then it is used absolutely, just as here, without an object stating the contents of the message; for example, *nunc domum renuntio,* "now I bring back word home"—scil. that her father is unavailable.[39] It is so used in an order, *abi et renuntia,* "go away and bring word"—scil. that the lady declines to come.[40] The very expression *ad illum renuntiare* is met in a speech where it cannot possibly signify "to rescind": an unsuccessful agent is off to inform his principal of his failure, *ad illum renuntiabo qui mihi tris nummos dedit,* "I shall bring word to that one who gave me the three bob."[41]

36. See Lewis and Short, *A Latin Dictionary* (1969), 1566.

37. Plautus, *Stichus* 599.

38. Plautus, *Aulularia* 604, 783; *Bacch.* 157, 592; *Men.* 421, 1127; *Merc.* 804; *Poen.* 764; *Pseud.* 420, 430, 451; *Trin.* 995.

39. Plautus, *Merc.* 804. Cf. *Poen.* 764.

40. Plautus, *Baach.* 592.

41. Plautus, *Trin.* 995. Cf. *Men.* 1127.

In support of their treatment of the line under discussion, the dictionaries refer to the Senecas in whose work *renuntiare* does indeed stand for "to rescind, call off, refuse," and with regard to an appointment. The elder Seneca adduces Leonidas's heroic exhortation to his troops, on the morning of the day when they must all die in battle, to prepare breakfast quickly since dinner they would take in Hades; and he cites a quip by his contemporary Sabinus Asilius—the oldest jester among the orators, he calls him—*ego illi ad prandium promisissem, ad cenam renuntiassem*, "I should have given an acceptance to him for breakfast, a refusal for dinner."[42] Again, the younger Seneca tells of an occasion when Augustus *renuntiare extemplo amicis quos in consilum rogaverat imperavit*, "ordered the appointment at once to be called off to his friends whom he had asked to a conference."[43] By the time of the Senecas, however, this meaning of the verb is common, and its appearance in a context similar to one in Plautus is no adequate ground for postulating it in the latter. As a matter of fact, one could make a better case for it in other passages—such as *abi et renuntia*, already cited. Surely, we had best put up with its absence from early extant literature. It may be added that the construction in the Senecas is not quite the same as in Plautus. It is *renuntiare* with the dative, "to send a No to somebody," instead of with *ad*, "to bring word in the direction of, addressed to, somebody." All this is not to deny that phrases of the kind found in Plautus may have contributed to the growth of the other usage.

Whenever it may have come into existence, it is well documented in the later Republic. Not surprisingly—considering the element of "message"—its original field seems to be where a break is communicated, not in person, but through a third party. The two main cases are, first, the dissolution of a personal tie, like *itiam renuntiare*, "to send word rescinding the friendship,"[44] *renuntiare* to a marriage or betrothal

---

42. Sabinus Asilius, *Suasoriae* 2.12. The noun here rendered as "jester" is *scurra*, from which our "scurrilous" is descended. Seneca takes Leonidas's utterance from an orator Dorion, adding that "he believes" (*puto*) it is also recorded by Herodotus. He is right in distrusting his memory. Herodotus's long account of Leonidas, in 7.204ff., does not contain the saying. As is well known, it is recorded by Diodorus Siculus, in 11.9.4.

43. Seneca the Younger, *Clem.* 1.9.7.

44. Tacitus, *Ann.* 2.70.

partner:[45] here you do not wish to see him or her whom you discard. Actually, where marriage or betrothal is concerned, the interposing of a messenger is so prevalent that *nuntium (re)mittere* to the partner, "to send the partner a messenger," acquires the sense of "to send the partner word rescinding the association."[46] Second, the dissolution of an international alliance, *amicitiam et societatem renuntiare*, "to send word rescinding the friendship and partnership":[47] here it is impracticable to see those whom you discard. Very likely, the former application—to which we shall come back in the section on "to repudiate"[48]—precedes the latter and for a good while determines the scope of the verb in important respects. It is hardly accidental that, to begin with, what is being shaken off is always an entire relationship, not just an isolated matter. *Renuntiata est tota condicio*, "the whole business was rescinded," we read in Cicero.[49] In the two quotations from the Senecas for the first time it is a single undertaking which is declined or revoked.

At least in connection with the contract of partnership, towards the end of the Republic, *renuntiare*, "to rescind," is a step of such consequence and so much reflected on that the action noun *renuntiatio* is born.[50] It may soon have spread to the "recission" of a marriage or betrothal; but, except that is occurs in an archaic-sounding notice by Gaius about this step,[51] there is no proof.

The dictionaries, while assigning too early a date to the verb in this sense, assign too late a date to its noun: they label it as silver Latin, because it makes its debut in the Digest jurists.[52] But one of them, Paul, offers us a literal extract from Alfenus Varus, consul in 39 BC, who may actually be in turn reproducing the exact words of his master Servius Sulpicius Rufus, consul in 51 BC *Quod Servius apud Alfenum ita notat:*

---

45. Digest 24.2.2.3, Gaius XI *ad edictum provinciale.*
46. Plautus, *Truculentus* 848 (the messenger is sent by the fiancée's father to the fiancé's); Cicero, *de or.* 1.40.183; *Top.* 4.19.
47. Livy 36.3.8.
48. See below, pp. 217–18.
49. Cicero, *Verr.* 1.6.16. Cf. above, "To Resile."
50. On the significance of the coming into being of an action noun, see above, chapter 2, "The Action Noun."
51. Digest 24.2.2.2, XL *ad edictum provinciale.*
52. See Lewis and Short, *A Latin Dictionary* (1969), 1565.

esse in potestate domini, cum procuratori eius renuntiatum est, an velit ratam habere renuntiationem, "This matter Servius, as reported by Alfenus, puts thus: it is up to the principal, when the partnership has been called off to his procurator, whether he wants to ratify the call off."[53] If my partner, that is, instead of declaring the partnership at an end to me, declares it at an end to my procurator, I have the option, on being informed, of treating it as terminated either from that declaration or from now.[54] Evidently, this is deep probing into the technicalities of *renuntiare*. It is quite conceivable that Servius or Alfenus is the coiner of the noun.

The preceding paragraph,[55] incidentally, after a general observation that a partner may *renuntiare*, "rescind," a partnership through others, inquires whether and how far a partnership may be "rescinded" by the procurator of a partner. Beseler[56] draws attention to the enormous difference between the case where a partner himself sends the other partner a messenger to terminate the contract and that where the procurator of a partner, acting independently, tells the other partner that the contract is terminated. The admissibility of the former procedure, Beseler holds, can never have been in doubt. This is correct. In fact, partnership is one of those bonds where the person dissolving it will hate a meeting; more often than not recourse will be had to a messenger; and it is significant that the pre-classical jurists are exercised by the problem—and only by the problem—of a rather far-going indirectness, the intervention of a procurator. In one point Beseler overshoots the mark: the general observation at the opening of the paragraph ought not to be excised. The unsatisfactory transition from it to the rest by means of *et ideo* is due to crude abbreviation on the part of the compilers.

Already in Quintilian *renuntiare* may signify "to forgo something one likes." He who cannot improvise *civilibus officiis renuntiabit*, "should forgo the oratorical profession."[57] Pliny speaks of *inertiae renuntiare paulisper, deliciis differre paulisper*, "forsaking idleness for a while, postponing

53. Digest 17.2.65.8, Paul XXXII *ad edictum*. His presentation of the passage from Alfenus by means of an accusative and infinitive shows it to be a literal quotation.
54. See Watson, *The Law of Obligations in the Later Roman Republic* (1965), 133–34.
55. Digest 17.2.65.7
56. Beseler, ZRG 45 (1925): 466.
57. Quintilian, *Inst.* 10.7.1.

pleasures for a while."[58] Shortly before succeeding to the Principate, Suetonius writes,[59] Galba had nearly *vitae renuntiaret*, "relinquished (taken) his life." Tertullian counsels his wife, should he die before her, *nuptiis renunties*, "to forgo marriage."[60] This nuance gains strength in the Middle Ages. As a result, French *renoncer* and English "to renounce"—and even more the nouns *renonciation* and "renunciation"—very frequently imply regret, self-abnegation. Sometimes they do so even when this is not obvious at first sight. When being baptised, you are (or were) expected *abrenuntiare satanae, operibus eius, pompis eius*, "to renounce Satan, his works, his pomps"—better, "to renounce utterly": the Church prefixes an emphatic *ab* to the verb. The central idea is certainly "to reject as abhorrent." Nevertheless, even here there is a tinge of "to give up however attractive," and the third member of the triad is revealing: the pomps are reminiscent of the kingdoms of the world and their glory by which the devil may tempt the saints.[61] Similarly, when Marlowe's Faustus, longing for heaven, says "I shall renounce this magic and repent,"[62] he is aware what marvels the magic promises.

To Repudiate

Repudiare,[63] precursor of "to repudiate," belongs to *repudium*, which already the Roman lexicographers derive from *pudeo, pudor*, "to make or be ashamed," "shame."[64] They are right for once,[65] and even if they were not, the fact would remain that those employing the word believed in the connection. *Repudium* signifies "repulsion and/or revulsion on account of

---

58. Pliny the Younger, *Panegyricus* 59.2.

59. Suetonius, *Galba* 11.

60. Tertullian, *Ad Uxorem* 1.1.

61. Cf. "renouncest thou Satan" in Wykyn de Worde, ed., *Ordinary of Christian Men* (1506), listed in the *New English Dictionary*, vol. 8, ed. J. A. H. Murray (1910), 449.

62. Marlowe, *Doctor Faustus* 2.2.11.

63. See Daube, "Studies in honour of Matthew Black," *Neotestamentica et Semitica*, ed. E. E. Ellis and M. Wilcox (1968): 236ff.; and in *Orita* 8 (1969): 33.

64. Festus 281.

65. See A. Ernout and P. J. A. Meillet, *Dictionnaire éymologique de la langue latine*, part 2, 4th ed. (1959), 571.

shame." Festus quotes Verrius Flaccus (died 4 BC) as holding that it is so called *quot fit ob rem pudendam*, "since it takes place because of a shameful thing."

The noun occurs in one comedy by Plautus—three times[66]—and in one by Terence—twice.[67] In both a fiancé is backing out of the betrothal. The adjective *repudiosus*, too, is met once in Plautus.[68] A daughter objects to a scoundrelly scheme of her father's: when the day comes he wishes to give her in marriage, *faciat repudiosa nuptias*, "it may make the match repudiable." No doubt her main fear is that everyone will decline even to enter into a betrothal. True, the expression as such is wide enough to include the action of somebody unaware of her father's doings getting engaged or married to her, and then severing the tie on being informed. But in the context this is at most a secondary consideration. Accius uses *repudium* of a father's casting out of his daughter: Io reports that she is *repudio eiecta*, "thrown out by *repudium*."[69] (*Eicere* signifies the "throwing out" of a daughter-in-law in Terence.)[70] Lucilius represents a father whose daughter has been sent a *repudium* as shutting himself up at home.[71] Though the dictionaries define her as *sponsa*,[72] there is really no saying whether it is her betrothal or her marriage that has collapsed. There might be reason for a father to be dejected in either case.[73] Later on, in Valerius

66. Plautus, *Aulularia* 783f, 799.

67. Terence, *Phorm.* 677, 928.

68. Plautus, *Persa* 384.

69. Festus 281. Listed among *Unassigned Fragments* (27), but marked "from Io?," in E. H. Warmington, *Remains of Old Latin*, vol. 2 (Loeb Classical Library, 1936), 572–73.

70. Terence, *Phorm.* 437, 627, 673, 725.

71. Lucilius 29.3.931ff.; see E. H. Warmington, *Remains of Old Latin*, vol. 3 (1938), 300–1.

72. See Lewis and Short, *A Latin Dictionary* (1969), 1573. Warmington, while translating *repudium* by "bill of divorce," in a note speaks of "the prospective son-in-law." F. Munzer, in Pauly-Wissowa's *RE*, vol. 22, pt. 1 (1953), 901, assumes a marriage.

73. As we know little about the context, the situation is altogether uncertain. In fact, the person isolating himself may not be a father at all; it may be a fiancé or husband who found himself forced to send a *repudium* to his lady, somebody else's daughter. If that somebody else figured in the preceding lines which are lost, a reference to her relationship, i.e. her description as his daughter, would be nothing out of the ordinary. The possibility is considered neither by Warmington nor by Münzer.

Maximus,[74] Tacitus,[75] Suetonius,[76] the jurists,[77] *repudium* often refers to the termination of a marriage by one of the spouses (or his *paterfamilias*),[78] be it husband or wife; though, as termination by agreement is the rule, *divortium* becomes the commonest term for "divorce."[79] In a single text of the end of the fifth century,[80] a *repudium* results from agreement; and even here, it is still in the end a declaration by one only of the two parties.

Evidently, the noun always envisaged one-sided rejection; and it is probable that its original range was, if not confined to, at least inclusive of a husband's dismissal of his wife. Extension in course of time from marriage to betrothal is readily intelligible; extension the other way round, with *divortium* coming to the fore, would be harder to explain. It is suggestive, moreover, that Roman authors discussing the earliest marriage laws occasionally use *repudium* as if they had it before them in the ancient sources.[81] That the two cases from Plautus and Terence are betrothal is no serious objection. First, two cases are little to go on. Second, *repudium* by a husband was rare. Third, it was perhaps a matter unfit for comedy. (It does not come up even in Terence's Hecyra. At the start of the marriage, when the husband wants to return to bachelorhood, he hopes his wife will *abire*, "leave."[82] Once she has gone back to her parents, the question is whether or not he will *reducere* her, "bring her back as wife.")[83] Finally, the quotation from Accius does concern an established bond—between father and daughter—comparable to marriage rather than to betrothal.

By the Empire, the term *repudium* is rather innocuous—largely, it may be supposed, as a corollary of wives resorting to this expedient no less freely than husbands. Initially, however, barring exceptional circumstances, the word implies an ugly blemish in the recipient or the

74. Valerius Maximus 2.1.4.

75. Tacitus, *Ann.* 3.22.

76. Suetonius, *Tib.* 11.4, *Calig.* 36.2.

77. Gaius 1.137a; Digest 24.2.2.1, Gaius XI *ad edictum provinciale*.

78. Suetonius, *Tib.* 11.4.

79. Digest 24.2.2, Gaius XI *ad edictum provinciale*; 50.16.101, Modestinus IX *differentiarum*; 50.16.191, Paul XXXV *ad edictum*.

80. Code 5.17.9, Anastasius Theodoro, AD 497.

81. Digest 48.5.44, Gaius III *ad legem duodecim tabularum*.

82. Terence, *Hecyra* 156.

83. Terence, *Hecyra* 391 and in many subsequent lines.

recipient's group. In Plautus, the fiancée is believed to be with child from a third party. (Of course there is humorous coating and everything turns out well.) In the comedy where he uses *repudiosus*, the woman's father wants her temporarily to pose as a slave and be the subject of a fake sale: this is bound to leave a *vitium*, "a taint."[84] Terence mentions no details: they would be irrelevant to the play. Nor does the small fragment from Lucilius fill in the background. Still, the *repudium* is downputting enough to make the woman's father stay indoors.[85]

Accius's Io, it will be recalled, introduces herself: "Thrown out by *repudium* from Argos, I am long since an exile." With this must be combined another line surviving from the same drama: *Topper, ut fit, patris te eicit ira.*[86] The prevalent interpretation is represented by Warmington's rendering:[87] "With might and main, for that's the way of the world, your father in his anger cast you out." But this cannot be right, for Io was a good girl and it was only at the behest of the god, very much *contre coeur*, that her father expelled her.[88] These words must be a question put to her, most likely following upon the self-introduction just cited. Io describes herself as "thrown out by *repudium* from Argos," from her paternal home. Her interlocutor asks: "Impetuously, as happens, your father's wrath threw you out?" Whereupon she is going to narrate her unusual story. The point here of interest is that, dismissed by *repudium*, she is expected to have furnished cause for fierce measures. The *dum fit*, "as happens," fits well: it is designed to make it easier for her to tell.[89] Moreover, the conclusion finds striking support in Festus, where precisely her self-introduction is adduced as evidence for the etymology according to which *repudium* is the response to "a shameful thing."

---

84. Plautus, *Persa* 388.

85. Unless the man staying indoors is he who sent it; see above, n75.

86. Festus 352.

87. Warmington, *Remains of Old Latin*, vol. 2 (1936,) 455.

88. E.g. Aeschylus, *Prometheus Bound* 661ff.

89. Certainly Warmington's translation is not satisfactory: fierce expulsion of a daughter is just not "the way of the world." Festus maintains—on the authority of Artorius (time of Augustus) —that *topper* here means "perchance." If so, it too has the purpose of indicating sympathetic interest. Warmington, *Remains of Old Latin*, vol. 2 (1936), 315, 455, thinks Festus is wrong. I am not so sure.

In discussing "to renounce" we saw that the break with a spouse or spouse-to-be is one of those steps one may prefer to accomplish *in absentia*.[90] Some combinations of *repudium* bring this out with particular clarity: *repudium renuntiare*, where a messenger "brings word announcing the *repudium*"[91] or where by means of a messenger "you send word announcing the *repudium*,"[92] similarly *repudium (re)mittere*, "to send a *repudium*," viz., by means of a messenger.[93] Other nouns for "divorce" are never used in this fashion. *Repudium* comes from the territory of shame—a very special obstacle to immediacy: you avert your face both when put to shame yourself and when coming upon somebody else's shame.

Shame has its base in sexual commerce; and as marriage and betrothal have much to do with the latter, it is hardly surprising that a term denoting one-sided rejection should be so emphatic on shame. Yet this is far from a matter of course. There is no equivalent in Greek, for example. Curiously, the Book of Deuteronomy breathes a comparable spirit. While *repudium* "takes place because of a shaming thing" and a woman is "thrown out by *repudium* from her home," for Deuteronomy, in a case of divorce, "he found a shaming thing (the nakedness of a thing) in her and sends her out of his house."[94] Again, by the Talmudic era, transmission of the bill of divorce by messenger is a common practice.[95] Primeval Rome and Deuteronomy have in common an extraordinary austerity in respect of female morality, both substance and appearance. I have noted elsewhere[96] that "Lucrece would be as unthinkable in ancient Athens as Lysistrata in ancient Rome." According to Deuteronomy, a bride not coming to her groom as a virgin is to be put to death,[97] and the rape of a girl betrothed to somebody else is likened to murder.[98]

90. See above, pp. 211–12.
91. Plautus, *Aulularia* 783.
92. Terence, *Phorm.* 677.
93. Plautus, *Aulularia* 799; Terence, *Phorm.* 928; Lucilius 29.3.931ff.; Suetonius, *Tib.* 11.4; *Calig.* 36.2; Digest 24.2.4, Ulpian XXVI *ad Sabinum*, 24.3.38; Marcellus *singulari responsorum*.
94. Deut. 24:1.
95. *Mishnah Gittin* 1:1ff.
96. Daube, *Civil Disobedience in Antiquity* (1972) 24.
97. Deut. 22:21.
98. Deut. 22:26.

We now come to *repudiare*. A verb deriving from a noun is apt to extend beyond its parent: you may house a friend in a tent or man a faculty with women. The phenomenon is exemplified by *repudiare*, though in Plautus it is still fairly close to *repudium* and indeed, the contact with the latter remains an important influence throughout.

Plautus employs *repudiare* seven times, in five comedies.[99] In one, a woman promises one lover to effect *divortium et discordiam*, "divorce and discord," between herself and another lover who is keeping her *quasi uxorem*, "like a wife," and to dismiss him—no doubt in analogy to the ending of a marriage,[100] though an element of courtship smacks of betrothal. Whether the noun *repudium* could be applied to divorce effected by a wife already at this time must be left open. In another comedy a betrothal is declined, as also a *beneficium*, "a good turn," that would go with it, namely, the offer to take the girl without a dowry.[101] Further, a woman disowns a man who claims to be her little brother.[102] Again, *hospitium*, "friendship," "guest-friendship" is severed;[103] and lastly, *comites*, "companions," may be got rid of—the particular ones mentioned are care, misery, tribulation and so on.[104]

Two plays by Terence contain the verb. A fiancée's father turns off the fiancé.[105] Elsewhere in the same comedy, a considerable widening of the meaning is noticeable: a plan is given up.[106] Similarly, in another play, an austere way of life.[107]

Whereas *repudium* in this literature is invariably a reaction to "a shameful thing," *repudiare* has plainly begun being less circumscribed: its object may be care and misery, a plan or excessive austerity. Mostly, however, it still occurs within the original boundaries. The spurning of the "little brother" is caused by his deceitfulness, his running after a rich

---

99. Plautus, *Cist.* 451f; *Merc.* 871; *Rud.* 883; *Trin.* 455, 637; *Truculentus* 706.

100. Plautus, *Truculentus* 392–93, 420, 706.

101. Plautus, *Trin.* 455, 637.

102. Plautus, *Cist.* 451–52.

103. Plautus, *Rud.* 883.

104. Plautus, *Mer.* 870–71.

105. Terence, *An.* 249.

106. Terence, *An.* 733.

107. Terence, *Adelphoe* 858.

girl and making sport of his poor, honest sweetheart;[108] the annulment of guest-friendship by a pimp's misdeeds, more precisely, by his being called to account for them;[109] and the fiancé's rebuff in Terence by his affair with an alien he treats *pro uxore*, "as if a wife."[110]

The *repudiare* of a match in Plautus illustrates the multifaceted nature of shame. The girl's brother, who has run through the family property, opposes the betrothal, not because of any disgrace on the suitor's side, but because his side would be disgraced by giving her away without dowry. There is much discussion about what, in the circumstances, is the right kind of *pudeo, pudicus,* "shame," to resist or to accept,[111] with a rich vocabulary from this domain—*officium,* "duty,"[112] *rumor,* "reputation,"[113] *flagitum,* "scandal."[114] (The coupling of *repudiosus* and *vitium* will be remembered.)[115] Some phrases are strikingly reminiscent of Deuteronomy: *noli avorsari neque te occultassis mihi,* "will you not turn away, please, and do not hide yourself from me" in the comedy,[116] "you shall not hide yourself" in the Biblical injunctions.[117] Yet we cannot say that *repudiare* as such here signifies "to refuse a good in order to avoid shame." For it is not the brother himself who describes himself as "refusing"; it is others who urge him not "to refuse," not to disdain the offer as if it were emanating from an objectionable party.

In later writings, *repudiare* is in common use for one-sided rejection of a marriage[118] or betrothal[119] partner; and while the latter —or his or

---

108. Plautus, *Cist.* 479f, 492ff., 501.

109. Plautus, *Rud.* 868ff.

110. Terence, *Andria* 144ff., 249.

111. Plautus, *Trin.* 661, 697.

112. *Trin.* 697.

113. *Trin.* 640.

114. *Trin.* 661

115. See above, pp. 216–17.

116. *Trin.* 627.

117. Deut. 22:1, 3, 4.

118. Suetonius, *Caesar* 74.2; *Tib.* 36.1; *Gram. et rhet.* 3; Quintilian, *Inst.* 4.2.98, 7.8.2, 8.5.31; Digest 23.2.12 pr., Ulpian XXVI *ad Sabinum,* 24.2.4; Ulpian XXVI *ad Sabinum* 24.3.38; Marcellus *singulari responsorum,* 40.4.29; Scaevola XXIII *digestorum.*

119. Suetonius, *Claud.* 26.1; Digest 23.2.11, Julian LXII *digestorum.* Both marriage and betrothal are envisaged in Digest 24.2.2.3, Gaius XI *ad edictum provincial,* and 50.16.191, Paul XXXV *ad edictum.*

her circle—is often deemed evil, that is far from an inevitable feature. You may *repudiare*, for instance, in order to contract a more advantageous union.[120] Actually, making allowance for the newsworthiness of misconduct, one suspects that it played a considerably smaller part as the motive of *renuntiare* in reality than it does in the sources.

The *lex Acilia* of 122 BC deserves mention. A victim of extortion by a provincial governor, when the authorities select a Roman to plead his case, may *repudiare* him if he is *moribus suspectus*, "a person of suspect practices."[121] The relationship to a representative—a *patronus*, "patron," as he is called—is not too remote from a family tie or a guest friendship. It may be declined if the nominee's history suggests that he may not be above making deals with the other side. Plainly an imputation of "a shameful thing."

The classical jurists speak of the *repudiare* of an inheritance.[122] Originally this would happen where the estate was insolvent, hence carrying *ignominia*, "ignominy."[123] However, while in this respect quite within the old territory of the verb, this usage no longer contemplates the elimination of a personal bond. It is surely because of this difference that, when a noun for the case is wanted, *repudium* is felt to be inappropriate and preference given to an action noun formed from *repudiare: repudiatio*.[124] (Though in one medieval document at least we do find *repudium*) of a right given up in favour of the Church.)[125] Before long, both the verb and the noun cover the rejection of an inheritance on grounds other than insolvency and, indeed, the rejection of a legacy or the like.[126] Canon law *repudiatio* of a benefice is clearly an offshoot of the civil law.

Outside law, by the age of Cicero, *repudiare* and *repudiatio* are frequent even where there is no imputation of "a shameful thing." Still, nearly always (not quite always)[127] the tone is one of emotional

---

120. Suetonius, *Caesar* 21; *Tib.* 36.2.

121. Lex Acilia II.

122. Digest 1.19.2, Paul V *sententiarum*.

123. Gaius 2.154.

124. Digest 24.1.5.13, Ulpian XXXII *ad Sabinum*.

125. Du Gange, *Glossarium ad Scriptores Mediae et Infimae Latinitatis*, vol. 5, ed. nova (1739), 1280.

126. Digest 12.1.8, Pomponius VI *ex Plautio*.

127. Quintilian, *Inst.* 3.6.33.

condemnation and dissociation.[128] The dictionaries rightly supplement the renderings "to reject," "to refuse," "a rejection," "a refusal," by "to scorn," "to disdain," "a disdaining."[129]

English "to repudiate," as also French *répudier*, faithfully reflects the Latin model. A slight extension in scope occurs in the second half of the eighteenth century: the verb and its noun may now be used of the denial of a charge as absolutely unfounded, if not outrageous.[130] Another development, from the first half of that century, is more innovating: "to repudiate" in the sense of "arbitrarily to cast off an obligation." The disgrace has shifted from the person or thing disowned to the disowner. To go by Craigie[131] (and disregarding an adumbration in Cicero),[132] the starting-point seems to be a man's ruthless abandonment of his family: "If a man repudiates the charge of his wife or children, villain is a word not villainous enough for him," exclaims C. Lofft, 1837.[133] The verb is still within its traditional setting, only it is not wife and children who are thrown off but their charge, the duties owed to them. However, the new meaning fully blossoms a few years later, in connection with the "repudiation" of debts by American states, rousing the moral indignation of writers like Sydney Smith.[134] The employment of *répudier* in this field appears to be due to Anglo-American inspiration.

128. Cicero, *Phil.* 3.10.26.

129. Lewis and Short, *A Latin Dictionary* (1969), 1573.

130. See W. A. Craigie, *New English (Oxford) Dictionary*, vol. 8, pt. 1 (1910), 493.

131. Craigie, *New English (Oxford) Dictionary*, vol. 8, pt. 1 (1910), 493.

132. Cicero, *Pro Murena* 4.9.

133. As quoted by Craigie, *New English (Oxford) Dictionary*, vol. 8, pt. 1 (1910), 493. I have been unable to procure the work for inspection.

134. See Letters on American Debts in *The Works of the Reverend Sydney Smith*, , vol. 3, 3rd ed. (1845) 441ff.: Petition to the House of Congress of 1843, 441, 443, Letter II of 1843 to the *Morning Chronicle*, 451–52.

Part V

GREEK AND ROMAN REFLECTIONS ON IMPOSSIBLE LAWS[*]

Ancient jurisprudence, like modern, displays much interest in unjust, immoral, unreasonable laws, but very little in impossible ones. Yet the sources contain a certain amount of material about the latter, and it may be worthwhile to present some of it.

My selection is highly subjective; I am choosing topics to which I can make some contribution within the compass of one paper. Hence I shall leave on one side the great question which has occupied Roman lawyers for the past forty years: whether, whereas the Greeks put their trust in legislation, in the Rome of the Republic and constitutional monarchy law was essentially identified with custom, which legislation was not at liberty to overthrow. Roman statutes often end with a clause to the effect that there is no intention to abolish established law, *ius*, that ought not to be abolished. For Mommsen, the legislature was sovereign, so this clause was a voluntary self-limitation.[1] For Rotondi and Arangio-Ruiz, the legislature might only either define custom or order peripheral matters, so the clause was a necessary reservation, one which would operate even without it.[2] For Mommsen, Cicero's contention that no statute could

---

[*]Chapters 9–12 are a revised version of an address given at the 9th annual meeting of the Board of Editors of the *Natural Law Forum*.

1. Mommsen, *Röm. Staatsr.* vol. 3, pt. 1 (1887), 42–43.

2. Rotondi, "Problemi di Diritto Publico Romano," *Scritti Giuridici*, ed. by Arangio-Ruiz (1922): 370ff. [*Rivista Italiana per le Scienze Giuridiche* 44 (1920): 147ff.]. The article appeared posthumously. Arangio-Ruiz, "La Règle de Droit et la Loi dans L'Antiquité Classique," *L'Egypte Contemporaine* 29 (1938): 30ff., reprinted in *Rariora* (1946): 252ff.

deprive a citizen of his freedom[3] was an advocate's exploitation of that clause; for Rotondi and Arangio-Ruiz it was absolutely correct, indeed, freedom was only one of innumerable things no statute could touch. While Mommsen was perhaps too radical in one direction, the opposite view has its own difficulties. It is, for example, hard to reconcile with the system of *legis actio* as it prevailed at some stage at least during the Republic, when any claim to be tried had first to be pleaded before a magistrate in words exactly following those of a statute. There are, of course, scholars holding positions intermediate between the extremes.

I propose to begin with some desultory remarks, chiefly designed to convey an impression of the manifold guises the problem of impossible laws may assume. The cases offered are not, however, devoid of intrinsic interest. The exchange between Antisthenes and his fellow citizens whose legs he pulled is to my knowledge the earliest extant discussion of the problem anywhere.

Next I shall examine the assertion made by a number of Roman jurists that the civil law has no power over the rights of blood relations. No practical consequences were drawn from this doctrine; it is an illustration of a rather rare phenomenon in classical law, philosophical embellishment. Blood relationship—as opposed to the agnatic relationship between those who are in the same *patria potestas* or would be if the common ancestor were still alive—did not become important in private law till the late Republic. The regulations having regard to it were inevitably laxer than those having regard to agnatic relationship. Moreover, in Greek speculation, taken over by the Romans, the ties of blood were prominent among the sources of obligations no human lawgiver might invalidate: Antigone cannot leave "her mother's son" unburied;[4] it is her case which Aristotle in his *Rhetorica* quotes first to illustrate what is naturally just though prohibited;[5] and Cicero defines piety, which is a sector of the law

---

3. Cicero, *Caecin.* 33.95ff.; *Dom.* 29.77ff.
4. Sophocles, *Antigone* 466–67.
5. Aristotle, *Rh.* 1.13.2.

of nature, as the duty owed to one's country, one's parents, and one's other relations by blood.[6] When we consider, in addition, that even at Rome, in religion, *fas*, and in personal life, blood relationship had always been of the greatest moment, the pronouncements in question will not appear too surprising.

I shall go on to the denial by a school of Roman jurists of a lawgiver's power to extend to new situations a concept like theft, homicide, usufruct. In this case, the debate no doubt did involve practical considerations, at least in respect of the earlier instances; it is possible that in course of time the academic-linguistic side took over. What is remarkable is how the jurists—both those who object to the transfer and those who, up to a point, accept it—treat these terms of theirs in their traditional application as in accordance with nature, like, say, silence, noise, a house, a horse. To widen them is to misrepresent reality (thus those who decline the extension), unless the widened term is looked on as a different, additional one (thus those who admit the extension).

Finally I shall introduce a variety of impossibility which has so far received scant attention: laws intended to change the past. I shall say something about the so-called *damnatio memoriae*, which might go as far as to make a hated ruler not to have ruled. Above all, I shall investigate the rectification of servile birth. Even today, in societies less keen on the self-made man than in America, humble antecedents are apt to be covered up. At Rome, there were several ways in which a freedman might conceal his origin. From the formalistic-legal point of view, from the early Empire onwards, there was less need for it since, as far as public, political life was concerned, the Emperor could grant him most of the privileges of a freeborn citizen. But that was still not good enough, and from the second half of the second century the Emperor could make him freeborn. In a statute enacted by Justin, the uncle of Justinian, this idea of the conferment of free birth combines with the religious idea of the

---

6. Cicero, *Inv. rhet.* 2.22.66, 53.161.

restoration of sinners to form the basis for a grant by which the Emperor may rehabilitate penitent actresses and cleanse them of their tainted past. By this statute Justinian was enabled to marry Theodora.[7]

7. Recently Lon L. Fuller, in his book *The Morality of Law* (1964), 70–79, has devoted a valuable chapter to "Laws Requiring the Impossible." On the whole, however, the area he has in mind is not the same as that considered in this article. For instance, he deals with strict civil and criminal liability, which may (though, surely, it need not) be understood as implying a command of the impossible. Moreover, he seems to include relative impossibility. If my material lends itself to a different approach, this does not mean that his treatment is not perfectly appropriate to the problems with which he is concerned.

9

Varia

Antinomy

Perhaps at the outset attention should be drawn to the fact that a considerable sector of the art and rules of interpretation of statutes is designed to get rid of "logical" impossibility, the existence of which jurists are unwilling to admit. Suppose there are two laws, one which forbids a man convicted of extortion to speak in the assembly and another which orders an augur to designate in the assembly the successor to a deceased colleague; now an augur convicted of extortion makes a nomination in the assembly—a case recorded in *Rhetorica ad Herennium*.[1] Somehow the two *leges contrariae* must be reconciled so as to allow a decision about the case. As a rule, the premise that such a conflict is not real, can be only apparent, is tacitly assumed—but not always. Quintilian, for example, formulates it in so many words: "It is obvious to all that one statute can never contradict another as to the law as such since, if the law as such were different, the one would cancel the other."[2]

One can see that in a well-working legal system this consequence—that one would cancel the other—would be most awkward. We ought to be clear, however, that it would not be intrinsically untenable. With regard to two contradictory testamentary dispositions, the Roman ruling

---

1. Cicero, *Rhet. Her.* 1.11.20.
2. Quintilian, *Inst.* 7.7.2.

was indeed that neither of them was valid.[3] Strangely, most philosophers believe that there cannot be several quite inconsistent moral duties binding at the same time. If they were right, there would be no genuine moral drama; a little more analysis and everything will be in order. True life is less simple.

At any rate, it is partly due to the role of interpretation that we hear so little about impossible laws (partly—there are other reasons too): defects of the kind indicated, logical discrepancies and the like, are construed away.

As for laws requiring the practically impossible, they are far rarer than, say, contracts of this description; nor do they easily lead to litigation. (Among things practically impossible the Romans reckoned the touching of the sky with one's finger,[4] as did whoever coined the phrase "to cry for the moon": *tempora mutantur*.) They do play a certain part in fairy tales and nightmares, and, indeed, in theology. But I shall omit the entire complex referred to by the apostle Peter as "the yoke which neither our fathers nor we were able to bear,"[5] except to say that the long and rich jurisprudential history behind it is virtually unexplored. That the impossible order of a judge is void, and that a judgment which by the nature of things, *rerum natura*, cannot be obeyed is so lacking in force that there is no point in an appeal, is noted by the jurists.[6]

An Athenian Wit

Now for a few cases outside the more familiar legal literature.

Antisthenes, an older contemporary of Plato, recommended to the Athenians to vote that asses were horses. To the objection that that was absurd he retorted: "Yet there are generals in your city who have no experience but are merely elected."[7]

It is clearly the agreed basis between the parties that there can be no legislation for the absolutely impossible: asses are horses. At this juncture

3. Digest 50.17.188 pr., *Celsus XVII digestorum*.
4. Institutes 3.19.11.
5. Acts 15:10.
6. Digest 49.8.3, *Paul XVI responsorum*.
7. Diogenes Laertius, *Lives and Opinions of Eminent Philosophers* 6.8.

it is immaterial for us whether the accent lies on the flaw in perception, i.e., the error in declaring something to be something that it is not, or—what is more probable from the context—on the practical impossibility of turning one natural species, a useless one, into another which is of use.[8] I leave aside (since it is not ventilated by the text) the case where such a statute might make sense, namely, if it decrees that something, hitherto falling under such-and-such rules, equals something else, falling under other rules. We shall have to deal with this case below in connection with extensions of *furtum manifestum* and usufruct.[9] One is reminded, of course, of Parliament, which can do anything except make a man into a woman, yet in a sense can do even this.

Antisthenes's conclusion, however, is reached by a sleight-of-hand. He was a precursor of the Stoics and—as this anecdote illustrates—shared features with the Sophists. He steps from the impossible to the unreasonable, to the conferment of a status and function on someone unworthy. The trick is cleverly obscured by focusing on the common element, i.e., the contrast between the inferior, stupid, untrained, and the superior, valiant, disciplined. This contrast is the same whether we think of asses and horses, or of people who have never learnt the art of soldiering and proper militaries; and the emphasis on it is designed to make us overlook the difference—that while it is impossible to turn asses into horses, it is merely foolish to appoint an inadequate leader. Any two natural species would not have done for the joke. It would not have done to recommend to vote that lions were tigers or that asses were mules: as lions and tigers are both splendid and as asses and mules are both despised, these proposals would have lacked that *tertium comparationis* with the election of the generals (to wit, the contrast between the inferior and the superior) which gave the analogy its convincing look.

8. Horse and ass were apparently a favorite illustration of the efficient and the inefficient. In Plato, *Phdr.* 260B, the accent lies on the ignorance as to which is which, leading to harmful consequences. The ass can be relied on to deflate solemnity. In Digest 15.1.40 at the beginning, Marcian *V regularum*, we are told that a *peculium* "is born, declines, dies" and that, therefore, Papirius Fronto "elegantly remarked that it resembled a man." Stein points out ("Elegance in Law" *LQR* 77 [1961]: 249) that Accursius in his Gloss shows scant respect for such elegance: he notes *eadem ratione et asino*, "by the same reasoning it is also like an ass."

9. See below, pp. 256ff.

It is noteworthy that the term used in the objection to Antisthenes's proposal is *alogon*, "absurd." It is a good choice: it is general enough to cover the whole field, the unreasonable as well as the impossible.[10] Which again facilitates the translation from the latter to the former.

Caligula's Horse and Nero's Weddings

Caligula, when he consecrated himself priest in his own service, made his favorite horse a fellow priest,[11] and, had his reign not taken a premature end, he would have made him consul as well.[12] (In the recent play *The Horse*, by the Hungarian author Julius Hay, he is enabled to execute his design, with amusing results.) This horse should figure prominently in any history of legal personality: he was given a furnished house and slaves, for the entertainment of guests invited to the races in his name. Suetonius writes that "besides a marble stall and an ivory manger, and besides purple blankets and a collar of jewels, Caligula gave him also a house, his own slaves and furniture." The structure of the sentence indicates a clear distinction between gifts which, however extravagant, imply no serious assimilation to a free man's status, and house, slaves and furniture which do.[13]

The elevation of a horse to the priesthood or consulate no doubt goes further than the appointment of bad generals. To the ordinary onlooker at least it seems to trample on the offices in question, to empty them of any content. Nevertheless it is possible in that the law, sacred or secular, can lay down what an office is to mean and who is able to hold it.

The Roman historians from whom we get our information are equally outraged by the gifts to the horse and its promotion to or destination for

---

10. See Daube, *Le raisonnement par l'absurde chez les jurisconsultes romains*, lecture delivered at the Institut de Droit Romain, Paris, 1958 (mimeographed). In the passage from the *Phdr.* quoted above, the exposition of an orator who does not know what is a horse and what an ass is called *geloion*, "ridiculous"—practically synonymous with alogon, "absurd."

11. Dio, *Roman History* 59.28.6.

12. Suetonius, *Calig.* 55.3; Dio 59.14.7.

13. Suetonius, *Calig.* 55.3. Dio 59.14.7 does not mention this particular wildness, but here Caligula invites the horse to dinner and drinks his health.

office. For them, Caligula constantly overstepped the bounds of decent or even sane conduct; he posed as Jupiter, Neptune and so forth.[14] It is chiefly Caligula whom the German word *Caesarenwahnsinn* calls to mind; it was coined by Gustav Freytag[15] and achieved wide currency through Wiedemeister, who wrote as a medical. To judge fairly, however, we must remember the wider background of deification of rulers, such old stories as Xerxes having the sea lashed for insubordination,[16] ideas which, long prevalent in the East, were now rapidly gaining ground in the West. After all, the Jews were the only nation not to acknowledge Caligula as god. ("Are you the god-haters," he greeted Philo and his fellow ambassadors,[17] "who do not believe me to be a god, though I am acknowledged as such by all the other nations, and you refuse me the name?") From that—supernatural—angle, much that otherwise appears insensate is less so, and even the turning of one natural species into another would not be quite impossible. It is hardly accidental that the horse's career started with a religious honor; the consulate would have come second.

The Emperor sensed that the jurists, an unimaginative lot, did not like his doings. He threatened that he would abolish their art and at any rate make sure no opinion contrary to his wishes could be given.[18]

Nero took Pythagoras to "husband" and Sporus to "wife"[19]—transactions on about the same level as the conferment of priesthood or consulate on a horse. Our historical sources are enraged, it is all wicked, monstrous. Of course the sober ones among the Romans saw precisely how the traditionally accepted essence of matrimony was thereby infringed: a bon mot went round that it would have been a good thing if Nero's father had contracted such a marriage—a sterile one. But again, there is more to

14. Seneca, Dio, Philo, Josephus, and probably also Statius regard him as lunatic; Tacitus and Suetonius use slightly weaker language, though Suetonius speaks of *insania* (55.1) in describing Caligula's excessive devotion to his actor friends.

15. G. Freytag, *Die Verlorene Handschrift*. Freytag refers to Tacitus's chapters on Tiberius and Claudius.

16. For Caligula's emulation of Xerxes, see Suetonius, *Calig.* 19.3; Dio 59.17.7ff., 59.25.3.

17. Philo, *Legatio ad Gaium* 44.353; Cf. Philo 45.367, and Josephus, *AJ* 18.8.258, 19.5.284.

18. Suetonius, *Calig.* 34.2. Hitler's *Table Talk*, by the way, evinces an obsessive hatred of lawyers.

19. Tacitus, *Ann.* 15.37; Suetonius, *Nero* 28–29; Dio 68.28.3, 62.13.1, 63.22.4.

it. Admittedly, despite dowry, ceremonies, etc., these marriages were not meant quite seriously, were not looked on as of full legal validity not even in the sense of a noncivil marriage; a *matrimonium non iustum*. But neither were they simply mad pranks. Various religions, especially sects based in the East, provided models: nature could be overcome. We are told that, in uniting as "wife" with Pythagoras, Nero behaved like a deflowered maiden, cried and so forth. Sporus looked like the deceased Poppaea Sabina (whose death Nero had caused by a kick);[20] was perhaps regarded as a kind of Sabina rediviva.[21] At any rate Nero had him castrated "and even tried to transfigure his nature into that of a woman."[22] In Greece people prayed for progeny from this union.

Martial, after Nero, satirizes a ceremonious "marriage" between two perverts.[23] The torches, the veil, the wedding songs, the dowry—nothing was omitted. He adds: "Is this not enough for you, Romans? Or are you now waiting for an accouchement?" Back of this verse there is not only the old bon mot about Nero, but also the more serious expectations enthusiasts had entertained.

The Undeposable Augur

Before going on to the jurists, I would mention one of Plutarch's Roman Questions:[24] why is an augur absolutely undeposable—even should he be exiled as a criminal? One answer supplied is that "augur" denotes not the office but the skill. To depose an augur would therefore be like voting that a musician is not a musician, a physician not a physician.

There is no need to dwell on the unsatisfactoriness of this solution, which would clearly create quite a few augurs over and above those properly appointed: anyone with the requisite knowledge would be an

20. Tacitus, *Ann.* 16.6; Suetonius, *Nero* 35.3; Dio 62.27.4.

21. Compare Dio 63.9.5: women's masks in plays were sometimes given the features of Sabina "in order that, though dead, she might still take part in the spectacle." On the other hand, he kept a courtesan resembling his mother Agrippina while the latter was yet alive. Suetonius, *Nero* 28.2; Dio 62.11.4.

22. Suetonius, *Nero* 28.1: "*etiam in muliebrem naturam transfigurare conatus.*"

23. Martial, *Epigrammata* 12.42.

24. Plutarch, *Quaest. Rom.* 99.287E.

augur. What is, however, neatly brought out is the distinction deliberately blurred, we saw, by Antisthenes: the factual belonging to a species (ass, horse, musician, expert in augury) is not subject to a decree; the belonging to a rank (general, priest—if we mean just the rank of priest, not the skill) is.

10

Interference with Natural Rights

Pomponius on the Claims of Cognates to an Inheritance

Pomponius, in his discussion of *bonorum possessio*, the praetorian scheme of succession, explains that where *capitis deminutio minima*—such as emancipation from *patria potestas*, the head of the family's power—prevents a claim *unde legitimi*, based on civil, statutory law, there may still remain a claim *unde cognati*, based on blood relationship: "the rights of blood," he adds, "can through no civil law be destroyed."[1] The statement is one of many concerned with the effect, or lack of effect, of positive or civil law on natural law or facts.[2]

The statement is not correct. If the civil law so wishes, it can destroy the rights of blood; and, in fact, in some cases it does so. The claim *unde cognati* does not, for example, survive *capitis deminutio maxima*, loss of liberty, or even media, loss of citizenship, say, through exile or deportation.

---

1. Digest 50.17.8, *IV ad Sabinum*: "*iura sanguinis nullo iure civili dirimi possunt*" For the original context, see Lenel, *Pal.*, 2 (1889), 93.

2. Voigt's extensive inquiry into the history of the problem is still indispensable: *Das Jus Naturale*, 4 vols. (1856–75), especially vol. 1 (1856), 303ff. See also Ernst Levy's great lecture, "Natural Law in Roman Thought," *Studia et Documenta Historiae et Iuris 1–10*, vol. 15 (1949): 1–10.

True, the law cannot turn a relation into a nonrelation, an ass into a horse. But, *pace* Pomponius, it can deprive a relation of all a relation's rights. Even *capitis deminutio maxima* does not turn a relation into a nonrelation, though before the law the former is now like the latter—his rights are gone.

It might perhaps be argued that *capitis deminutio maxima* and *media* are closer to natural law, of which Pomponius would not deny that it can destroy the rights of blood. But this is a lame excuse. Moreover, there are other cases which should have given him pause. An incestuous begetter of offspring does not count as father, the offspring not as his child; and, remember, it is incest for a man to "marry" his adoptive daughter—indeed, it makes no difference if the adoptive tie is dissolved.[3] The offspring of such a union, being a bastard, has no claim *unde cognati* to his begetter's estate. So here the civil law prevents the rights of blood from even coming into existence. Again, prior to the *lex Minicia*, the child of a Roman mother and an alien father was a Roman; a child born from such a marriage after that statute was an alien—entirely outside the praetorian scheme which was confined to citizens, unable to invoke either *unde legitimi* or *unde cognati*.[4]

One might try an entirely different defense of the jurist. The remark in question is preserved in title 50.17 of the Digest, *De diversis regulis iuris antiqui*. We know that many texts in it have been slightly adjusted by Justinian with a view to obtaining a general *regula*.[5] One might ask, therefore, whether the inexactitude is not due to Justinian, Pomponius having expressed himself more circumspectly. But this is most unlikely in view of the fact that, as we shall see,[6] his contemporary Gaius repeatedly commits a similar blunder, at least once in his *Institutes*, untouched by Justinian, and that it is indeed Justinian who on this occasion tries to put it right.[7]

3. Gaius 1.59,64; Institutes 1.10.1, 12; Digest 23.2.55 pr., *Gaius XI ad edictum provinciale.*
4. Gaius 1.78; *Ulp. Reg.* 5.8.
5. See Daube, "Zur Palingenesia einiger Klassikerfragmente," ZRG 76 (1959): 198ff.
6. See below, p. 240.
7. Gaius 1.158; Institutes 1.15.3, 1.16.6. See especially 17–18.

It is easy to guess what Pomponius is driving at. The actual presence of cognation, blood relationship, cannot be abolished by any law; no law can turn a relation into a nonrelation.[8] Further, though the rights flowing from cognation, the rights of blood, can be abolished, that does not in fact happen as a result of *capitis deminutio minima*, a mere civil law change of family status. The distinctively Roman, civil law relationship of agnation, the relationship between those who are in the same *patria potestas*, or would be if the common *paterfamilias* were still alive, is indeed dissolved by such a change; it is of its very essence that it should be. At one time, private law took little notice of cognation. Now, however, that the praetor does recognize it as a source of rights, natural rights as opposed to the old civil law ones, he is only consistent in not admitting grounds of extinction peculiarly connected with the old civil law relationships. That would vitiate the main purpose of his innovation: Something like this is the—considerable—grain of truth in Pomponius's remark.

It would be a mistake, incidentally, to think that, by Pomponius's time, *capitis deminutio minima* has become a technicality with negligible practical consequences. It has not. A son emancipated, for instance, can own property of his own; the seriousness of which consequence is underlined by the praetor's request, on according him a claim *unde liberi* together with a son still in *potestas*, to make *collatio bonorum*, to bring in his possessions. The reason *capitis deminutio minima* is discounted when it comes to *unde cognati* is not that it is unimportant in itself, but that, however important, it is the kind of transaction which, where cognation is the decisive tie, it is appropriate to discount, and which, unlike, for example, deportation, one can afford to discount.

Little damage was done by a statement like that here reviewed. The classical jurists on the whole refrained from enunciating philosophical maxims. The few we do find tend to be commonplaces, repeated again and again. Their function is to justify (after a fashion) an existing state of law. Beyond that, they are merely decorative; no real inferences were drawn.

---

8. In reality, even cognation by the time of Pomponius was no longer as simply factual as that: it covered adoptive relatives so long as the agnatic tie lasted. Digest 38.8.3, *Julian XXVII digestorum*; 38.8.1.4, *Ulpian XLVI ad edictum*. I disregard this complication.

Justinian's Institutes on the Claims of Children to an Inheritance

Institutes 3.1.11, according to Ferrini,[9] comes from the *Res Cottidianae* rightly or wrongly attributed to Gaius.[10] We learn that true children emancipated, while the emancipation costs them their civil law claim to their father's estate, are given a claim *unde liberi* by the praetor; adoptive children emancipated are not only without a civil law claim to their adoptive father's estate but also get no praetorian claim *unde liberi*. The text goes on: *et recte*, "and rightly." Why? Because "a civil law reason cannot destroy natural rights, and true children or grandchildren cannot cease to be children or grandchildren by ceasing to be *sui heredes*."[11] By contrast, "adoptive children, as they obtain the right and name of a child by the civil law reason of adoption, so they lose them by another civil law reason, emancipation."[12]

This is the same mix-up as in Pomponius, except that the natural tie in question is not cognation in general, but the more specific one between father and child. Moreover, as in Pomponius, it occurs in the context of the effect of *capitis deminutio minima* on *bonorum possessio*.

The author of the passage is right in saying that a true child does not lose this quality by ceasing to be a *suus heres*. But he is slipping when he says that a true child's natural rights—the claim *unde liberi*—cannot be destroyed by a civil law transaction. It is indeed astonishing he should be so enamored of his theory as not to realize its brittleness. There is the glaring fact that an adoptive child, while in his adoptive father's *potestas*, has no claim *unde liberi* to his natural father's goods.[13] Moreover, though a child emancipated by his adoptive father regains *unde liberi* in

9. Ferrini, "Sulle fonti delle Istituzioni di Giustiniano," ed. by Albertario, *Opere* 2 (1929): 379. (This reference is the same as *Bull. Ist. Dir. Rom.* 13 [1900]: 166.)

10. Jolowicz, for example, inclines to regard the attribution as wrong or, shall we say, exaggerated (*Historical Introduction to Roman Law*, 2nd ed. [1952], 398). Honoré argues that it is right (*Gaius: A Biography* [1962], 113ff.). I am not convinced by the latter.

11. *Naturalia enim iura civilis ratio peremere non potest nec, quia desinunt sui heredes esse, desinere possunt filii filiaeve nepotes neptesve esse.*

12. *Ius nomenque filii filiaeve, quod per adoptionem consecuti sunt, alia civili ratione, id est emancipatione, perdunt.*

13. *Ulp. Reg.* 28.8.

his old family, or as Paul puts it, regains the *ius naturale liberorum*, "the natural right of children,"[14] in the very paragraph preceding that under discussion, in Institutes 3.1.10—equally, according to Ferrini, from the *Res Cottidianae*—an exception even to this right is noted. For a sound reason of expediency, even a child emancipated by his adoptive father and thus no longer under his *potestas*, if the emancipation takes place after the natural father's death, is refused a claim *unde liberi* to the latter's estate. The reason is that it should not be within the adoptive father's discretion, on the natural father's death, to place or not to place a *liber* ahead of the *legitimi*, the agnates. Plainly, if it were, he could make some unscrupulous deals.[15] Yet this rule is followed by the statement that the natural rights of *liberi* are unabolishable by the civil law.

It may be added that the remark at the end of the quotation, about adoptive children, is also far too simple: emancipation of an adoptive child, it is affirmed, deprives him of *unde liberi* in the adoptive family because what is gained by a civil law transaction is lost by a civil law transaction. There is no inevitability about this; but there were good grounds for attaching *unde liberi* in such a case to the original family. I shall not, however, pursue this matter.

Let me call attention to the interesting phrase *ius nomenque*, "right and name," where *nomen* has the connotation of something artificial, superimposed, "mere name," by contrast with the genuine, natural: adoptive children are children "by mere title of law." We shall come

----

14. Digest 38.6.4, *Paul II ad Sabinum*. For the probable scope of Paul's statements, see the following footnote.

15. In Institutes 3.1.10 as it stands, the exclusion from *unde liberi* in the old family is confined to *adrogatio*, more precisely, to a child first emancipated by his true father, then giving himself in adoption—*adrogatio*—and finally emancipated by his adoptive father. In the *Res Cottidianae*, the exclusion cannot have been so confined. It must have covered also a child given in adoption (in the narrow sense, not *adrogatio*) by his true father and then emancipated by his adoptive one. For Justinian, as a result of his great reform of adoption (in the narrow sense), Institutes 1.11.2, Code 8.47.10 of AD 530, this case no longer falls within the area of the rule at all: adoption (in the narrow sense) now leaves the rights of succession in the old family quite unaffected. Hence the curious restriction of the rule to *adrogatio*. Doubtless Digest 38.6.4, *Paul II ad Sabinum*, too, has been brought into harmony with his legislation; in the classical version, the portion *sed si naturales . . .*, now restricted to *adrogatio*, was certainly wider. My comments on Institutes 3.1.11 do not, however, depend on the exact scope of 3.1.10.

across two more instances of this use of *nomen,* Gaius 3.21 and Institutes 1.15.3.[16] To be exact, Gaius 3.21 speaks of *nomen agnationis,* "the name of agnation." The combination with *ius* occurs only in Justinian. Between *ius nomenque* in 3.1.11, descriptive of an adoptive child's position, and *iuris nomen* in 1.15.3, descriptive of agnation (*nam adgnatio iuris est nomen*), there seems to be little difference; the meaning is "a mere name, title, conferred by the law." Institutes 3.1.11, as mentioned above, probably comes from the *Res Cottidianae,* Institutes 1.15.3 in the main reproduces Gaius 1.158, but the relevant clause is an addition, be it by Justinian, be it by a pre-Justinianian reviser of Gaius.[17] In any event, as far as the extant textual evidence goes, the combination of *nomen* and *ius* in this area is later than Gaius's *Institutes.*[18]

One reservation is called for. After observing that the praetor discriminates between true and adoptive children, *Institutes* 3.1.11 continues: *et recte,* "and rightly." The opposite of what is done *recte,* I feel, is wrong, incorrect, improper rather than impossible. Accordingly, this kind of approval seems to imply that the praetor could have treated the two classes of children alike though, had he done so, he would have made a mistake; still, it would have been valid if objectionable law. It is, then, only when the *et recte* is being expanded, substantiated by a slogan, that confusion sets in. That the confusion did no harm, since no attempt was made to lift it from the sphere of theory, I have already pointed out in discussing Pomponius.

16. See below, pp. 241, 245.

17. Ferrini, *Opere,* 2:344 (*Bull. Ist. Dir. Rom.* 13:135) takes the latter view: it is a gloss that got into Gaius 1.158 prior to Justinian.

18. Theophilus, incidentally, simplifies *ius nomenque* in Gaius 3.1.11 by omitting *ius;* he translates to *onoma.* In Gaius 1.15.3 he translates *nomimon onoma,* agnation is "a legal name." Strangely, Ferrini in his Latin version of Theophilus, *Institutionum Graeca Paraphrasis Theophilo Antecessori Vulgo Tributa,* pt. 1 (1884), 70, retains a gross vulgarization introduced by previous modern editors, namely, the insertion of *civilis.* He renders *iuris enim civilis nomen adgnatio est,* "for agnation is a title of the civil law." This gets rid of the not very easy concept of *iuris nomen* and, in the process, robs the clause of any interest, makes it state the excessively obvious. (As a matter of fact, in his version as it stands the word *nomen* does not appear at all; we read *iuris enim civilis adgnatio est.* I assume, however, that it has dropped out through a slip on his or the printer's part. The edition is notorious for its misprints: Zachariä von Lingenthal, "Review of *Institutionum* etc.," ZRG 5 [1884]: 276).

Gaius on Agnates and Cognates in Connection with Statutory Tutorship

In Gaius's time a boy under age (normally, under 14) who was *sui iuris*—without a *paterfamilias*—had a guardian, often one appointed in the dead *paterfamilias*'s testament; in default of such a one, the nearest agnate was his guardian. In expounding this *tutela legitima*, which goes back to the XII Tables, Gaius in his *Institutes* writes that "the right of agnation, though not that of cognation, is destroyed by *capitis deminutio*."[19] He is thinking of *capitis deminutio minima* (*media* or *maxima* would wipe out the right of cognation as well). From the destruction of agnation by this it would follow, for example, that a person otherwise the nearest agnate, if he got himself adopted by another family, would no longer become guardian or, supposing the adoption took place after he had become guardian, would cease to be guardian.[20] Gaius continues by explaining why cognation survives *capitis deminutio*: "whereas civil law rights can be extinguished by a civil law reason, natural rights cannot."[21]

Basically, this is again the same muddle, this time in the context of the effect of *capitis deminutio minima* on *tutela legitima*. The natural tie in question is cognation, as in Pomponius; in Institutes 3.1.11 it is the tie between father and child. However, we shall see that, in several respects, Gaius's presentation is worse than that of the other two texts.

Basically, then, it is the same muddle: the misconception that natural rights are indestructible by the civil law. In reality, they are destroyed by *capitis deminutio maxima* or *media* and could be destroyed whenever the legal order so decreed. (This has, of course, been seen.)[22] Gaius himself mentions the incestuous nature of a union with an adoptive daughter, with

19. Gaius 1.158.

20. *Ulp. Reg.* 11.9.

21. *Sed agnationis quidem ius capitis deminutione perimitur, cognationis vero ius eo modo non commutatur, quia civilis ratio civilia quidem iura corrumpere potest, naturalia vero non potest.* Beseler, *Beitr.* 2 (1931): 5, in a general attack on *ratio*, brackets the relevant passage from *quia*, "whereas civil law rights . . ." This is unacceptable. Compare, below, pp. 247ff. on Digest 4.5.8, *Gaius IV ad edictum provinciale*, and below, pp. 267ff. on Digest 7.5.2.1, *Gaius VII ad edictum provinciale*.

22. See, e.g., Voigt, *Das Jus Naturale*, vol. 1 (1856), 306n33; Poste, *Gai Institutiones*, 4th ed. (1904), 92–93.

the result that any offspring would be a bastard[23] not tied to his begetter even by cognation. As for the provision of the *lex Minicia* making the child of a Roman mother and alien father an alien, Gaius himself points out[24] that this overturned the *ius gentium*, which he regards as resting on *naturalis ratio*;[25] and a little further on he observes more generally that the principle of the *ius gentium* that a child follows the mother is subject to legislative modification. The example he cites is interesting: a senatusconsult—*Claudianum*— had decreed that if a free woman has the owner's consent to cohabit with his slave, she herself would remain free but the offspring would be slaves; Hadrian found this "inelegant"—though by no means impossible—and restored the *ius gentium*, a child would share the mother's status.[26] I agree with Levy against the prevalent opinion, that in classical times *ius gentium* and *ius naturale* were not synonymous: "The one stated the fact of universal usage, the other its motivation. Moreover, while *ius gentium* was a hard and fast category indispensable to the technique of the jurists, *naturalis ratio* never obtained an organic status in their reasoning."[27] It is partly because of this vagueness of the latter notion that a misconception like that presented could come about.

The misconception recurs in two passages in Gaius's chapter on succession, though it is here less fully formulated. Commenting on the law of the XII Tables he observes that, under that code, an agnate having undergone *capitis deminutio*—again, the reference is to *minima*—is not admitted to the succession, "since the name of agnation is destroyed by *capitis deminutio*."[28] The contrast with cognation is not expressly drawn, but it clearly underlies the description of agnation as a *nomen*, "name." As in Institutes 3.1.11 just discussed, where we hear of the *ius nomenque* of an adoptive child, so in this passage "name" means "mere name," "mere civil law title," as opposed to the real, natural thing, in this case cognation.[29] The implication, then, is that the position of a cognate could not be affected by *capitis deminutio*.

23. Gaius 1.59, 64.
24. Gaius 1.78.
25. Gaius 1.1, 189.
26. Hadrian 1.83f.; see Stein, "Elegance in Law" *LQR* 77 [1961]: 248n15.
27. Levy, "Natural Law in Roman Thought," *Studia et Documenta Historiae et Iuris* 1–10, vol. 15 (1949): 11n33.
28. Gaius 3.21, *quia nomen agnationis capitis deminutione perimitur*.
29. Compare also Institutes 1.15.3, to be considered presently.

Further on, dealing with the praetorian improvements, Gaius does contrast agnation and cognation expressly. The praetor reserves a place in his scheme for cognates (though they still rank below agnates). Agnates having undergone *capitis deminutio* may still have a chance in this class since, Gaius explains, "though they have lost their statutory right, assuredly they retain the rights of cognation."[30] He does not say merely that they retain the rights of cognation. They do so *certe*, "assuredly," "obviously." Once more, what is implied is that these are rights which cannot be touched by a civil law transaction.

To return to his remark on *tutela legitima*, the muddle is less tolerable than in Pomponius and Institutes 3.1.11 in two respects. First, prima facie, from his presentation it looks as if the rights flowing from cognation survived even *capitis deminutio maxima* and *media*. He declares these rights to be unaffected by *capitis deminutio*—he does not specify, he does not put *minima*. Ordinarily, to be sure, it might be left to the reader, even a student reader, to notice that *minima* alone is intended. But in the present case, this is very slipshod, considering that, in the very next paragraph, he defines *capitis deminutio* as a change of civic condition, adding that it can be *maxima*, *media*, or *minima*.[31]

Secondly, the remark, correct or incorrect, is rather out of place. In the case of succession, the subject of Pomponius and Institutes 3.1.11, a person having dropped out of agnation, *unde legitimi*, may sometimes nevertheless have a claim based on cognation, *unde cognati*, or more narrowly, on his quality as child, *unde liberi*. But there is no *tutela* of cognates. Accordingly, whereas it is useful to point out the contrast between agnation and cognation, and stress the possible retention of the latter when the former has gone, in a discussion of succession—as also, perhaps, in one of *capitis deminutio* in general or of *capitis deminutio minima*[32]—it is not very relevant here. Certainly, where, in the absence of both a testamentary guardian and a legitimate one, an appointment is made by the magistrate, he will often in fact appoint a cognate. This may

---

30. Gaius 3.27, *Licet enim capitis deminutione ius legitimum perdiderint, certe cognationis iura retinent.*

31. Gaius 1.159.

32. But we do not really find it even in Digest 4.5.7 pr., *Paul XI ad edictum*, and 4.5.8, *Gaius IV ad edictum provinciale*: see *infra*, 19ff.

safely be assumed—from general considerations, from the ever-increasing part played by cognation, from the obligation of cognates (at least some of them) if necessary to request an appointment, from their role in *nominatio potioris* which came in soon after Gaius. But all this in no way brings in cognates as a technical class. The financial suitability of a cognate, for instance, would be more important than his nearness in degree. Moreover, friends of the family, too, would come into consideration.

What makes the remark particularly inapposite is the fact that, by the second century AD, it is no pleasure to get the appointment. Indeed, the trouble and risks are enormous. A legitimate guardian, an agnate, is perhaps still relatively free from duties. (Namely, if we reject as spurious the texts assimilating him to the guardian appointed by the magistrate. The matter is controversial.) For a guardian appointed by the magistrate—a cognate, a friend of the family—the office is definitely a burden. In a sketch of guardianship, therefore, to speak of "a right of cognation"— "though the right of agnation is destroyed by *capitis deminutio*, the right of cognation is not because a civil law transaction cannot destroy natural law rights"—is *schief*, thoughtless.

Below I shall quote a text from the Digest deriving from a section of Gaius's commentary on the provincial edict which deals with *capitis deminutio minima*.[33] Here he again proclaims the doctrine of the resistance of natural rights to civil law transactions, and though the doctrine is wrong, at least it is not misplaced.[34] In the *Institutes* Gaius, first-rate

33. Digest 4.5.8, *Gaius IV ad edictum provinciale*; for the original context, see Lenel, *Pal.*, 1 (1889), 197.

34. It might perhaps be argued that the paragraph from the *Institutes* here analyzed should be read, not together with what precedes it, as part of the discussion of *tutela legitima*, but together with what immediately follows, that is to say, as opening the excursus on *capitis deminutio* which Gaius inserts in the chapter on guardianship. In an account of *capitis deminutio*, as already observed, the contrast between agnation and cognation does make sense.

Unfortunately this is not tenable. For one thing, the paragraph in *Ulp. Reg.* corresponding to that under review unmistakably belongs to *tutela legitima*. It reads: *legitima tutela capitis deminutione amittitur*, "*tutela legitima* is lost by *capitis deminutio*." *Ulp. Reg.*11.9. We need not go into the precise relationship between *Ulp. Reg.* and Gaius's *Institutes*. Unquestionably the former work (which prevalent opinion assigns to the first half of the fourth century AD) uses either the latter or a precursor of the latter or a revised edition of the latter. The way it understands the paragraph in [*continues onto next page*]

teacher, second-rate jurist, enlivens his résumé by a commonplace maxim though it does not fit. Perhaps in the older work which he follows,[35] to be guardian still appeared as an advantage rather than a bother—which would make his talk of *ius cognationis* more pardonable. After all, right to the last we can spot traces of the original character of guardianship, if only in vocabulary.[36] Or he may have had at the back of his mind a passage like that from Sabinus which is adduced by Gellius: "Our forefathers held that a man's obligations were in this order—first to his ward, then to his guest, then to his client, next to his blood relation, finally to his relation by marriage."[37]

[*note 34 continued from previous page*] question is of considerable weight. (It is, of course, simpler and more direct; nothing is said about agnation or cognation, nothing about civil law transactions and natural rights. We are offered a straightforward statement of the effect of *capitis deminutio* on *tutela legitima*. The qualification *minima* is missing, as in the Institutes.) Equally, in the Institutes of Justinian, principally relying on Gaius's exposition, the paragraph forms the close of the title *De legitima adgnatorum tutela* (1.15.3) while the excursus *De capitis minutione* occupies title 1.16. (I shall presently say something about the modifications 1.15.3 shows compared with Gaius 1.158.) For another thing, if we treated the paragraph here inspected as opening the excursus on *capitis deminutio*, the omission of *minima* would be far more serious. In the opening sentence of an *ex professo* account, Gaius could not expect the reservation to be supplied by the reader. If this paragraph opened the law regarding *capitis deminutio*, he would really be representing the rights based on cognation as untouched even by *capitis deminutio media* or *maxima*. Of such nonsense he cannot possibly be guilty.

35. Compare below, pp. 263–64.

36. The very notion of *amittere tutelam*, "losing the guardianship," which occurs in *Ulp. Reg.* above, p. 234n34, is an anachronism in the era of the composition of that book. *Ulp. Reg.* 11.9 concerns *tutela legitima*; even this is a burden by the fourth century. In 11.7 *amittere* is used in connection with *tutela testamentaria*. Three more texts are to be added: Gaius 1.182, which if it does not exclusively contemplate *tutela testamentaria* at least includes it. Digest 4.5.7 pr., *Paul XI ad edictum*, where the object of *amittere* is all classes of guardianship (but the verb is strangely used, signifying "to effect loss," as in 4.5.6, *Ulpian LI ad Sabinum*, which, in the Digest, comes immediately before). Digest 26.4.2, *Ulpian XXXVII ad Sabinum*, which concerns *tutela legitima*, not yet too bad in Sabinus's time.

37. 5.13.5, quoting Sabinus III iuris civilis: *in officiis apud maiores ita observandum est, primum tutelae, deinde hospiti, deinde clienti, tum cognato, postea adfini.*

I ought to add that, should the Veronese palimpsest have the correct reading, *quaedam* instead of *quidem*, Gaius would be more complicated: "some civil law rights can be extinguished by a civil law reason." Some only—so there are even civil law rights defying the civil law. Kniep maintains (*Gai Institutionum Commentarius Primus* 67 [1911]) that Gaius means just this. Unfortunately he does not say what particular rights might be

Justinian's Institutes on Agnates and Cognates in Connection with Statutory Tutorship

Institutes 1.15.3 more or less copies Gaius 1.158. I put the deviations in brackets.[38] *Sed agnationis quidem ius [omnibus modis] capitis deminutione [plerumque] perimitur. [nam adgnatio iuris est nomen.] cognationis vero ius non [omnibus modis] commutatur, quia civilis ratio civilia quidem iura corrumpere potest, naturalia vero non [utique].*

Four points are noteworthy. First, Justinian inserts an explanation of the vulnerability of agnation by *capitis deminutio*: agnation is "a name of law," "a mere title of law." It will be remembered that he makes use of the notion in Institutes 3.1.11, probably drawing on the *Res Cottidianae*, and that he would also have found it in Gaius 3.21. Ferrini thinks that the explanation is a gloss that got into Gaius 1.158 prior to Justinian: quite possible.[39]

Secondly, whereas according to Gaius 1.158 agnation is always destroyed by *capitis deminutio minima*, Justinian puts *plerumque*, "generally." This is necessitated by postclassical and Justinianian reforms.[40]

Thirdly, he improves Gaius's presentation by making it quite clear that even cognation does not survive *capitis deminutio maxima* or *media*. Whereas Gaius 1.158 says that "agnation, though not cognation, is destroyed by *capitis deminutio*" (leaving it to the reader to supply *minima*), Justinian says that "agnation, though not cognation, is destroyed in general by all modes of *capitis deminutio*": by all modes, that is to say, even by *minima*. Moreover, as in Gaius (and no doubt in the *Res Cottidianae*), there follows an excursus on *capitis deminutio* (Institutes 1.16), and here

---

in point. Still, an interpretation on this basis is just possible: Gaius might, for example, be alluding to the argument he advances in 3.194—that a statute cannot turn a nonmanifest thief into a manifest one (see below, p. 257n10). It would be queer, however, to look upon this as a case of indestructibility of "civil law rights." Moreover, "some" makes too many inviolate. Again, it is not like Gaius to bring in a major qualification in such an offhandish, distracting fashion. Finally, the sentence, if taken in this way, would be rather inelegant. I incline to accept the orthodox emendation *quidem*. It is *quidem* which we find in Institutes 1.15.3, which text now falls to be examined.

38. As far as *quidem* is concerned, see my comments in the preceding footnote.

39. See above, p. 239n17.

40. See, e.g., Institutes 3.5 pr.

a special paragraph (1.16.6) is devoted to the distinction between the
effect on the right of cognation, of *capitis deminutio minima* and the other
kinds of *capitis deminutio*. The paragraph begins by expressly restricting
the survival of cognation to *minima*; it goes on to note and illustrate its
extinction by *maxima* and ends by noting its extinction by *media*.[41]

Fourthly (and most importantly for us), Justinian does realize that
the slogan of the indestructibility of natural rights exaggerates. Instead
of proclaiming, with Gaius, that a civil law transaction cannot annihilate
them, he says that it cannot annihilate them *utique*, "simply," "without ado,"
"totally"—I shall not attempt to decide between the various nuances.

The special paragraph contrasting *minima* with the other kinds
(1.16.6) shows, incidentally, a curious wording in its first portion: "As
regards the statement above, that cognation survives *capitis deminutio*, this
applies to *minima* only." The curious thing is that, in Justinian's exposition,
"the statement above" (1.15.3) is no longer so careless as its source, Gaius
1.158. It already, by means of a twofold insertion of *omnibus modis*, "by
all modes," as well as the reservation *utique*, "simply," corrects the slipshod
original (which took the restriction to *minima* for granted). It is not true
that it says that cognation survives *capitis deminutio*, period. So why does
1.16.6 represent it as saying that? This paragraph, according to Ferrini,
comes from the *Res Cottidianae*,[42] and herein may lie the explanation. In
the *Res Cottidianae*, we may suppose, Gaius 1.158 was still left unaltered;
there were not yet, as in Institutes 1.15.3, the qualifications *omnibus modis*
and *utique*. At that stage, "the statement above" was still carelessly wide,
and what is 1.16.6 in Justinian was added to put it right. The rectifications
in 1.15.3 are attributable to Justinian himself, desirous to have the law
outlined in an accurate manner from the outset; only he did not trouble
to adjust the first portion of 1.16.6.[43]

41. *Quod autem dictum est manere cognationis ius et post capitis deminutionem,
hoc ita est, si minima capitis deminutio interveniat: manet enim cognatio, nam si maxima
capitis deminutio incurrat, ius quoque cognationis perit, ut puta servitute alicuius cognati, et
ne quidem, si manumissus fuerit, recipit cognationem. sed et si in insulam deportatus quis sit,
cognatio solvitur.*

42. Ferrini *Opere*, 2:344 [*Bull. Ist. Dir. Rom.* 13:135].

43. Support for my suggestion is furnished by the two awkward successive ablatives
omnibus modis capitis deminutione, "by all modes by *capitis deminutio*," in Institutes 1.15.3.
That is not the style of the *Res Cottidianae*; it is the kind of thing resulting from an
interpolation in the course of codification.

No reason to overrate Justinian's analytical powers. The terms *cognatio,* "blood relationship," and *ius cognationis,* "the right of blood relationship," are still employed indiscriminately. There is still no precise separation between the factual and legal position.[44] After all, in Institutes 3.1.11, we have seen, the commonplace about natural rights occurs (is taken over, it would appear, from the *Res Cottidianae*) without the qualifying *utique.* Its addition in Institutes 1.15.3 is surely due to the existence of 1.16.6, dwelling on the destruction of cognation by *capitis deminutio maxima* or *media,* and reflected in the insertion of *omnibus modis* in 1.15.3. With the legal result of *capitis deminutio maxima* and *media* highlighted in such a degree, it is not surprising that, on this occasion, the defectiveness of the commonplace obtrudes itself, can no longer be overlooked.

Gaius on Natural Obligations

Digest 4.5.8, Gaius IV *ad edictum provincial,* lays down that "those obligations the fulfillment of which is considered to be of a natural kind obviously do not end by *capitis deminutio,* since a civil law reason cannot destroy natural rights." It follows, we are told, that the action for restoration of a dowry, being equitable, conceived in *bonum et aequum,* survives *capitis deminutio.*[45]

The following brief fragment, 4.5.9, Paul XI *ad edictum,* syntactically part of 4.5.8, adds "so that when the time comes the emancipated woman may sue," *ut quandoque emancipata agat.*

---

44. I also in this paper am lax in my usage and, for the sake of brevity, sometimes speak of "cognation" where I mean the rights. But I can afford it because I know, or trust, my readers will make the requisite adjustments.

45. *Eas obligationes, quae naturalem praestationem habere intelleguntur, palam est capitis deminutione non perire, quia civilis ratio naturalia iura corrumpere non potest; itaque de dote actio, quia in bonum et aequum concepta est, nihilo minus durat etiam post capitis deminutionem.* Beseler, *Beitr.* 5:17, branding *ratio* as postclassical, brackets the relevant bit from *quia* to *potest,* "since a civil law reason cannot destroy natural law rights." This is unwarranted; Cf. above, p. 240, on Gaius 1.158, and below, p. 267, on Digest 7.5.2.1, *Gaius VII ad edictum provinciale.* In "Romanistiche Studien," *Tijdschr. Rechts.* 8 (1928): 321, he reconstructs the text in too imaginative a fashion.

The jurists have in mind *capitis deminutio minima* only. The omission of the adjective is no problem: the edict they are commenting on[46] applied only to this type.[47] Hence the restriction is taken for granted.

The obligation referred to in the first part of 4.5.8 may be *naturales obligationes* in a technical sense; this is indeed the prevalent view. On this basis, however, one would expect the topic to be *capitis deminutio minima* of the debtor, whereas the example of *actio de dote* envisages *capitis deminutio minima* of the creditor, the woman. Still, the technical sense of *naturalis obligatio* is so different in different periods (and maybe with different writers of the same period) that we should not be too surprised. On the other hand, there is the possibility that the very elaborate phrase *obligationes quae naturalem praestationem habere intelleguntur* is not synonymous with *naturales obligationes*; and that it means obligations to be performed to a person defined by his natural position, irrespective of agnatic or even cognatic relationship. That would clearly include an obligation to be performed to a wife irrespective of a *capitis deminutio* she may have undergone. I shall presently adduce Digest 4.5.7pr. where, in an interpolated section, *naturaliter designari* does denote "to be defined by one's natural relationship"—though, to be sure, that text speaks of cognates, not of husband and wife.

At any rate, the resistance to *capitis deminutio minima* of obligations with a *naturalis praestatio* is explained by means of the slogan we know from Gaius 1.158 (and Institutes 1.15.3), except that it is shortened: we are spared the positive part, that a civil law transaction can extinguish civil law rights, and are given only the really significant negative one, "it cannot extinguish natural rights." I need not repeat the objections to this doctrine.

It has been alleged that these words are interpolated by the compilers.[48] This is difficult to accept; it would be too much of a coincidence for a bit from one work of Gaius, the *Institutes*, to be stuck into an extract from another, his commentary on the provincial edict. Surely he resorted to the commonplace in the latter as well as the former;

---

46. For the original context see Lenel, *Pal.* I (1889), 197, 986.

47. See Digest 4.5.2 pr., *Ulpian XII ad edictum*. As for the wording of the Edict, see Lenel, *Das edictum perpetuum*, 3rd ed. (1927), 117.

48. E.g., by Burdese, *La Nozione Classica di "Naturalis Obligatio"* (1955), 113–14.

and quite likely it is because the compilers found it there that they used this piece from Gaius instead of contenting themselves with Paul, who supplies 4.5.7 and 4.5.9. The latter is so precisely on the topic of 4.5.8 as to be introducible as, syntactically, a subsidiary clause of this fragment. It does look as if the compilers had had a special reason for preferring 4.5.8 to what was in Paul—that reason being the slogan.

Less immediately unconvincing is the proposition that what now surrounds this slogan in 4.5.8 is spurious. In the classical version, there may have been no talk of dowry. (If there was, the action must have been called *rei uxoriae*. Justinian commonly prefers *de dote*.) Indeed, there may have been no talk of "natural performance." Siber, for instance, holds that the slogan was attached to a distinction between *ius agnationis* and *ius cognationis*, just as in Gaius 1.158.[49] (It is futile to speculate whether, if he is right, Gaius here associated the slogan with *bonorum possessio* only or also, stupidly, with *tutela*.) To Siber's own arguments should be added this, that in classical writings the concept of the indestructibility of natural rights may well have been confined to succession, tutorship, and the like. It sounds rather pompous when applied to restoration of dowry, at least for classical law, where this is primarily a commercial affair; in Justinian's eyes it is indeed far more. It is demonstrable that Gaius did not think of extending the slogan to partnership. This is described by him as belonging to the *ius gentium* and therefore a universal phenomenon by natural reason;[50] yet it is dissolved if a partner incurs *capitis deminutio minima* since, he says, "by civil law reason *capitis deminutio* is equated to death."[51] However, there is no need for me to come to a decision about the original context of 4.5.8. I shall leave this question open, as also countless others arising out of this puzzling text.

Let me just note four points, though even these are not relevant to my main thesis. First, 4.5.9 may well be concerned with emancipation of

49. Siber, "Naturalis Obligatio," *Gedenkschrift für Mitteis* (1925): 16. This work of Siber's is so well argued that on occasion initial rejection has been followed by conversion: contrast Albertario's review in *Studi di Diritto Romano* 3 (1936): 55ff. [*Archivio Giuridico* 102 (1929): 230ff.] with his article "*La critica del fr. 8 D. De capite minutis IV 5, 4*," *Studia et Documenta Historiae et Juris* (1938): 529ff.

50. Gaius 3.153f: *iuris gentium est, itaque inter omnes homines naturali ratione consistit*.

51. *Quia civili ratione capitis deminutio morti coaequatur*.

a wife by her *paterfamilias* while she is married. The result would be that, should it come to divorce, she herself would sue for the dowry, instead of the *paterfamilias* with her merely in a supporting role (*adiuncta filiae persona*). My translation proceeds from this case. Other cases, however, are conceivable; for example, emancipation between divorce and *litis contestatio*—if we proceed from this situation, it would be better to translate "so that henceforth (in future) the emancipated woman may sue."[52]

Secondly, if the ending of 4.5.8 contemplates such situations, the formulation is curious. The action, we learn, *durat*, "remains," "goes on," after *capitis deminutio*. What happens is that as a result of *capitis deminutio*, the woman, up to now merely entitled to support or frustrate the action of her *paterfamilias* (being *adiuncta* to him), is entitled to bring it alone, and indeed, she alone is entitled to bring it.

Thirdly, Digest 4.5.7pr., Paul XI *ad edictum*—same provenance as 4.5.9, *capitis deminutio minima*—in its first half states that, except for *tutela legitima*, guardianship is not affected by *capitis deminutio minima*; and that *tutela legitima*, deriving from the XII Tables, is affected on the same ground as the agnatic succession of that statute, *unde legitimi* in the praetor's edict. (The present text is somewhat doctored. I am summarizing what Paul seems to have said.) The muddleheaded principle of the indestructibility of natural rights does not figure: no doubt that is why the compilers, 4.5.8, had to get it from Gaius. Nor do we find any allusion to *ius cognationis* in connection with guardianship, Gaius's particular

---

52. Digest 24.3.22.5, *Ulpian XXXIII ad edictum*. The decision that the *paterfamilias* in this case cannot bring the action is certainly correct. But the text as it stands pairs it off with the decision that he cannot bring the action if the daughter, having at first consented to it, changes her mind before *litis contestatio*: both decisions are represented as following from the rule that it is at the moment of *litis contestatio* that her consent is required. As a matter of fact, only the decision concerning her change of mind follows from this rule. We have the choice between two solutions. Either Ulpian discussed emancipation separately from change of mind, and the compilers, in order to abbreviate, threw the two cases together, inserting *vel etiam si emancipata sit* into the paragraph about change of mind. Or *secundum haec*, describing the two decisions as both of them consequences of the rule, should be excised: Ulpian would have made a fresh start with *si filia*. Beseler, *Beitr*. 3 (1913): 154ff. condemns *secundum hoc* or *haec* in general. Whether right or wrong in this, he goes too far, 159, when he simply dismisses everything in Digest 24.3.22.5 from *secundum haec* as "postclassical illustration."

blunder. Paul's comparison of the two cases of *tutela legitima* and *unde legitimi* is perfectly sound; it may well have been a traditional way, among the great classics, of presenting the matter in a survey of *capitis deminutio minima*.

The second half, *ex novis* and so on, is due to the compilers.[53] We are informed that new legislation frames the destination of both succession and guardianship in such a manner that "the persons are defined by their natural position," *ut personae naturaliter designentur*. As illustration the compilers mention the senatusconsults (*Tertullianum* and *Orfitianum*) establishing succession between mother and child. In respect of guardianship, they are probably thinking of laws like Code 5.30.4, by Anastasius, AD 498, and 6.58.15.4, by Justinian himself, AD 534. The latter ordains: "but those persons whom on the strength of the right of blood relationship we have transferred to the legitimate successions, we also subject to the burden of guardianship over one another."[54] It might perhaps be argued that already Paul had in his discussion something about natural position or rights as opposed to civil law, which provided the stimulus for *ex novis* and so on. But there is no evidence to support this, and the remark of the compilers is, for them, so *naheliegend*, so easy to hit on, they needed no help.

Fourthly, what is the relation of the doctrine in Pomponius (Digest 50.17.8) on the one hand and Gaius's *Institutes* (1.158, 3.21, 27, also Institutes 1.15.3) and the *Res Cottidianae* (represented in Institutes 3.1.11) on the other? Gaius may be indebted to Pomponius: this is perhaps still the current thinking.[55] According to Honoré, the borrowing is more likely the other way round.[56] It is also, I suppose, arguable that they independently drew on a common source or floating material. That this is the relation between Gaius and Gellius I shall suggest below with regard to a theory concerning the discovery of stolen goods in the course of a ceremonious search.[57] It would lead too far afield to go into the problem

---

53. Wissenbach, *Emblemata Triboniani* (1736), 21.

54. *Quas autem personas ex iure cognationis in legitimas successiones transveximus, eas et tutelae gravamina vicissim supponimus.*

55. E.g., Krüger, *Geschichte der Quellen und Literatur der Römischen Rechts*, 2nd ed. (1912), 201.

56. Honoré, *Gaius: A Biography* [1962], 57ff.

57. See below, pp. 255–56.

at length. Insofar as a passage from Paul quoted above[58] can be regarded as alluding to the doctrine, the most plausible assumption is that he got it from Pomponius, whom he used a great deal.

Justinian's Institutes on Natural Laws

Institutes 1.2.11 reads: "But natural laws, which are observed in all nations everywhere, being established by some divine providence, remain always firm and immutable; whereas those which each State establishes for itself are apt to be often changed, either by the tacit consensus of the people or by another statute subsequently passed."[59]

I shall not linger on this pronouncement which, in its present context at all events, is so general that what it aims at and within what limits cannot be determined. Nor, as Ferrini points out,[60] is it possible to specify its provenance. It may be the work of Justinian (this is the prevalent view);[61] it may be taken from a classical manual; it may be partly the former and partly the latter.

Curiously, Theophilus omits the mention of natural laws. He says: "But the laws of nations are administered in all nations, found from divine providence, whence they are firm and immutable ..." What significance, if any, is to be attributed to this deviation I am unable to determine. Perhaps he was put off by the discrepancy between this use of the plural *naturalia iura* in the sense of "natural laws" and its normal use in the sense of "natural rights" it means: "natural rights" in all the three remaining places in Justinian's Institutes.[62]

---

58. Digest 38.6.4, *II ad Sabinum*; see above, pp. 250–51.

59. *Sed naturalia quidem iura, quae apud omnes gentes peraeque servantur, divina quadam providentia constituta semper firma atque immutabilia permanent; ea vero, quae ipsa sibi quaeque civitas constituit, saepe mutari solent vel tacito consensu populi vel alia postea lege lata.*

60. Ferrini, *Opere* 2:334 [*Bull. Ist. Dir. Rom.* 13:126].

61. Maschi, *La Concezione Naturalistica del Diritto e Degli Istituti Giuridici Romani* (1937,) 221ff..

62. Institutes 1.15.3 and 3.1.11, which I have discussed, as well as 1.11.12. Ferrini in his Latin rendering of Theophilus adheres too closely to the Latin text of Institutes 1.2.11 (Institutionum etc. at 17). He puts *constituta*, "established" by providence. But

There have been relatively few studies in depth of Justinian's ideas on law. The proclamation by which he published the Digest in 533 is preserved in Greek and Latin; only the latter states that while the divine is most perfect, there is nothing of eternal duration in human law.[63] The Latin is generally more devotional than the Greek.[64]

---

heurethenta means "found," "discovered," possibly "devised," "invented"—not "established." He also retains *peraeque,* "everywhere," and *quadam,* "some" ("by some divine providence") though Theophilus drops both.

63. *Constitutio Dedoken* 18; *Constitutio Tanta* 18; Code 1.17.2.18.

64. See Ebrard, "Das zeitliche Rangverhältnis der Konstitutionen De confirmatione Digestorum 'Tanta' und 'Dedoken,'" *ZRG* 40 (1919): 135.

An assertion by Gaius as to the immutability of *naturalis ratio* in Digest 7.5.2.1, *VII ad edictum provinciale,* I shall consider below, 266ff., in connection with a different series of texts.

11

Interference with Facts
and Concepts

Paul on Possession

Natural rights are one thing, facts another: the latter, we may agree, the
law is powerless to overturn. But what is a fact? In the area of this inquiry,
impossible laws, the question poses itself in several ways.

One of them is illustrated by a text on possession, Digest 41.2.1.4,
Paul LIV *ad edictum*. A husband yields possession of an object (probably
land, in Paul) to his wife, with intent to make her a present: most
authorities, we learn, hold that she does now possess, *quoniam res facti
infirmari iure civili non potest*, "since a point of fact cannot be invalidated
by the civil law."

I shall not inquire whether Paul is primarily thinking of interdict
possession[1] or usucapion possession (in the sense that, if the gift were
confirmed by the husband's death, the period she had held the object
would count for her). His point is that the *ius civile*, more especially the
rule excluding gifts between spouses, cannot alter facts, and the wife's
possession is a fact. Needless to say, he is not implying that the *ius naturale*
or *gentium* could do what the *ius civile* cannot. It so happens that the
difficulty of the case is created by the *ius civile*, hence the reference to it.

---

1. So, e.g., Kaser, *Eigentum und Besitz im älteren Römischen Recht*, 2nd ed. (1956),
356ff. with strong arguments.

Indeed, for the Romans, the *ius naturale* is so essentially in line with the real world that the statement that it cannot interfere with a fact would be superfluous, even queer.

What about the minority who, we are given to understand, do not regard the wife as in possession? They would hardly claim that the law, or the civil law, can alter facts; rather that possession is not a mere fact or that, though it is, the wife's holding does not amount to it.

Hagerstrom declares the reason *quoniam . . .* interpolated.[2] Every classical jurist, he says, knew that the *ius civile* did determine whether or not a man possessed in the legal sense: a slave, for example, who withheld an object from his master did not possess. This argument, however, though not devoid of force, is not fully conclusive. The classics often support a decision by a finesounding principle which does not fit without qualification. In the field of possession in particular, inexactitudes of this kind abound.

Some passages which proclaim the unalterability of facts are concerned, not with the law as such, but with private transactions. When Celsus says that "that which is ruled out by the nature of things, *rerum natura*, can be established by no *lex*," the context—both in his original work and in the Digest—leaves no doubt that the reference is to a testamentary disposition requesting the impossible.[3] Another paragraph from the same book of Celsus's work, which in the Digest directly precedes this one, was quoted above: contradictory dispositions in a will are void. Labeo and Javolenus adopt a decision by Ofilius rejecting a legacy of "a hundred pecks of wheat each of which is to weigh a hundred pounds," since such wheat does not exist, is not *in rerum natura*.[4] Africanus discusses a legacy of "the ten I have in my chest" when in reality there are only five. A claim for more than five, he explains, would not be in accordance with reason, *ratio*, since as to the missing five the legacy may be said to refer to something not in existence, not in *rerum natura*. Pomponius and Gaius note that you may bequeath an object which, though not yet in *rerum natura*,[5] is expected to

2. Hagerstrom, *Der Römische Obligationsbegriff* 1:197f., 206.

3. Digest 50.17.188.1, *XVII digestorum*. Voigt, *Das Jus Naturale*, vol. 1 (1856), 306, seems to think of a statute. So perhaps does already Basilica 2.8.188, translating *lex* by *nomos*, and certainly the Gloss: no law will uphold a promise of something impossible.

4. Digest 33.6.7, *Javolenus II ex posterioribus Labeonis.*

5. Digest 30.108.10, *Africanus V quaestionum.*

come into existence—fruits, for example, or the offspring of a slave.[6] It is to this complex that Celsus's utterance belongs.[7]

But let us go on to an entirely different variety of the problem of what is a fact.

Gaius on Manifest Theft Extended

According to Gaius, whereas the XII Tables imposed a twofold penalty on ordinary theft, they laid down that a manifest thief, a thief caught *in flagranti*, was to be delivered over into the hands of his victim. Further, if a man's house was searched for a stolen object in the presence of witnesses and the object was found, he had to pay a threefold penalty. And again, if a search of this kind was resisted, a more ceremonious search was to be resorted to; and should the object turn up now, the theft, the XII Tables prescribed, would be a manifest one—*iubet id lex furtum manifestum esse*, "the statute decrees this to be manifest theft."[8]

Elsewhere I have tried to show that this account is trustworthy and that attempts to disprove it, though common in Romanistic literature, are misconceived.[9] Many authorities, for instance, maintain that the XII Tables spoke of one search only, the ceremonious one. This is wrong, I think. I would emphasize, however, that the argument I am about to develop is not fundamentally affected, will stand, in the main, even if modern corrections of Gaius may be deemed plausible. For this reason I shall not make constant reference to slight qualifications of my thesis which acceptance of these conjectures would entail.

---

6. Digest 30.24 pr., *Pomponius V ad Sabinum*; Gaius 2.203; Institutes 2.20.7; G. Ep. 2.5.3.

7. Not surprisingly, the idea recurs in other branches of the law. Compare, e.g., Digest 50.17.31, *Ulpian XLII ad Sabinum*, from a section on pacts and stipulations in sale. Also from sale comes Digest 18.4.1, *Pomponius IX ad Sabinum*, where sale of the inheritance of a living or nonexistent person is declared a nullity because the object is not in *rerum natura*. On a judge's order or a judgment for the impossible, Digest 49.8.3, *Paul XVI responsorum*, see above, pp. 227–28.

8. Gaius 3.183ff. See Levy, "Natural Law in Roman Thought," *Studia et Documenta Historiae et Iuris 1–10*, vol. 15 (1949), 9ff.

9. Daube, *Studies in Biblical Law* (1947), 259ff.

To begin with, then, let me quote Gaius's comment on the code's regulation: "Because of the fact that the statute decrees the theft in that case (the ceremonious search) to be manifest, there are some who write that theft becomes manifest either by statute or by nature: by statute the very theft we are discussing (where the object is found by the ceremonious search), by nature that which we expounded above (where the thief is caught *in flagranti*). But the better view is that only theft manifest by nature is to be regarded as manifest. For a statute cannot bring it about that he who is not a manifest thief should be a manifest one—no more than that he who is not a thief should be a thief, and that he who is not an adulterer or homicide should be an adulterer or homicide. That indeed a statute can bring about—that a man should be liable to a penalty as if he had committed theft or adultery or homicide even though he has committed none of these."[10]

The XII Tables, it will have been realized, meted out the same harsh treatment to a thief caught in *flagranti* and to him with whom, after he had opposed a simple search with witnesses, the object was finally discovered in the procedure *lance et licio*, "with loincloth and platter."[11] However, they dealt with the latter case in a somewhat indirect way. Instead of directly stating the punishment, instead of saying that a man convicted by this procedure should be delivered (as was a manifest thief) into the power of plaintiff, they achieved this effect by simply subsuming the case under the basic category, by simply declaring it to be manifest theft. Doubtless,

---

10. Gaius 3.194: *Propter hoc tamen quod lex ex ea causa manifestum furtum esse iubet, sunt qui scribunt furtum manifestum fieri aut lege aut natura: lege id ipsum de quo loquimur, natura illud de quo superius exposuimus. Sed verius est natura tantum manifestum furtum intellegi. Neque enim lex facere potest ut qui manifestus fur non sit manifestus sit, non magis quam qui omnino fur non sit fur sit, et qui adulter aut homicida non sit adulter vel homicida sit. At illud sane lex facere potest ut proinde aliquis poena teneatur atque si furtum vel adulterium vel homicidium admisisset, quamvis nihil eorum admiserit.* The Veronese manuscript reads *sunt qui scribunt furtum manifestum aut lege aut natura.* At a pinch this could be left unemended. Of the insertions suggested I prefer Kniep's insertion of *fieri* after *manifestum* (*Gai Institutionum Commentarius Tertius* [1917], 56), to the more popular *intellegi* after *lege*; and I do not do so only because the Veronese MS has *furtum mf* which, he ingeniously observes, might stand for *furtum manifestum fieri*, not simply for *furtum manifestum.* Anyhow he should not be represented as inserting the *fieri* after *lege*—a slip committed by David, *Gai Institutiones* (Editio Minor, 1964), 113.

11. Thus Gaius 3.193, but other understandings of the phrase are defensible.

the phrasing was *furtum manifestum esto*, "it shall be manifest theft," just as in other early instances of indirect regulation: a statute ascribed to Numa enjoined that if a man killed another with malice aforethought, *parricidas esto*, "he shall be a murderer" or "it shall be murder."[12] In a sense, another provision from the section on theft in the XII Tables themselves is comparable: if you kill a thief who comes by night, *iure caesus esto*, "he shall be lawfully slain."[13]

I shall not go into these parallels but concentrate on the paragraph pronouncing it to be manifest theft if the object comes to light in the course of the ceremonious search. At that time, the resistance from the outset and all that followed from it made the latter case a desperate matter of life and death, quite close to the former. It was quite close also in this, that, in the circumstances, there could not be a shadow of doubt as to the accused's guilt. The code, therefore, in decreeing *furtum manifestum esto*, did no violence to the facts, gave *furtum manifestum* only a slightly extended meaning. Gradually, however, the search "with loincloth and platter" became obsolete. It had vanished, say, by the middle of the Republic, and we must not assume subsequent generations to be familiar with its original setting and significance. Actually, Gellius, a contemporary of Gaius, mentions the remark of a lawyer friend of his, that only if he had studied the laws of the Fauns and Aborigines—the mythical forerunners of the Romans—could he be expected to understand institutions of that sort.[14] No wonder, therefore, that the jurists interested in the XII Tables found the formulation *furtum manifestum esto*, "it (the case where the object is found as a result of the ceremonious search) shall be manifest theft," puzzling. The problem what to make of it evidently antedates Gaius, who introduces one solution by "there are some who write."

Some hold, he says, that the statute adds to manifest theft *natura*—where a thief is caught *in flagranti*—a manifest theft *lege*—where an object is discovered by the ceremonious search. The starting point is that there is a given, "natural" manifest theft, namely, what appears as such to the ordinary man and in everyday language. The law, however, can create another: in law, an ass might be a horse. Whether, for the advocates of this

12. Festus (Paulus) 221.
13. XII Tables VIII, 12.
14. Gellius 16.10.7f.

doctrine, the species created by statute has to show a minimum of prima facie affinity with the genuine one, it is difficult to decide. Probably not. After all, it is precisely because, to them, the discovery by ceremonious search which the XII Tables subsume under manifest theft looks distinctly nonmanifest that they felt the need for an explanation, arriving at the doctrine in question. Moreover, we shall see presently that the same school of thought seems to have postulated a usufruct *lege* which had little to do with "natural" usufruct.

Gaius disagrees: there is only manifest theft *natura*, since the law has no power to turn a nonmanifest thief into a manifest one or, for that matter, a nonthief into a thief, a nonadulterer into an adulterer, a nonhomicide into a homicide. The law can only make a man punishable as if he had committed theft, adultery or homicide though in fact he has not. Note a minor carelessness: at the end Gaius forgets about the very case he is analyzing, he forgets to mention, what should be the climax of his series of things the law can do, that the law can impose a penalty as if there had been *furtum manifestum* though in fact there has been only *furtum nec manifestum*.

The starting point, as for the other doctrine, is a given, "natural" manifest theft. Indeed, this is the only species: where the present doctrine parts company with the other is in that the possibility of adding a species by statute is denied. The statute is, of course, upheld, but reinterpreted as expressing a fiction, shorthand way. It does not, as one might be led to think at first sight, make the case where an object is found by ceremonious search into manifest theft. It merely lays down that the case—which remains different—should be treated as if it were the same. Even in law, an ass cannot be a horse: we can only transfer to it the rules relating to a horse as if it were one, too.

If we look for analogies to these two doctrines in the modern debate about legal personality it is, curiously, the one mentioned first, the one Gaius rejects, which comes nearest the Fiction theory, with its assumption of a "natural" personality and one created by the law, a "legal" one. True, the Fiction theory tends to see in the legal creation something of lesser standing. This element is foreign to the Roman doctrine which puts manifest theft *natura* and manifest theft *lege* on the same level; of course, the subject of personality calls forth very special emotions. The doctrine mentioned second, the one adopted by Gaius, is highly reminiscent of what goes by the name of Symbolist, Bracket, or Collectivist theory. According to the Symbolist theory, legal personality is nothing but a device to express in an expeditious, brief fashion complicated relations between natural persons, the only ones existing. There is no personality *lege*, created by the law: the law considers only the natural person; though, for the sake of efficient, compact description of intricate arrangements, it may speak as if there were another. It is interesting that fiction thus plays a part in the Symbolist theory.[15] Certainly the nuance is not quite the same as in the Fiction theory. In a sense, indeed, there is more of a fiction: while the Fictionists do admit a legal personality though, compared with the natural person, it is fictitious, the Symbolists deny any such thing; it is merely convenient sometimes to talk as if, say, a corporation were a person. The doctrine Gaius favors is strikingly similar. The only manifest theft, theft, adultery or homicide is that *natura*. There is no manifest theft, theft, adultery or homicide *lege*. When the law decrees of something else that it shall be any of these things, all that is meant is that the consequences shall be as if one of them—the "natural" crime—had been committed.

Which of the two doctrines is the older? I would suspect that it is that discarded by Gaius: there are two kinds of manifest theft, one *natura* and one *lege*. This doctrine keeps more loyally to the wording—and spirit— of the provision which, after all, does speak of manifest theft *tout court*, "it shall be manifest theft." The doctrine which Gaius prefers—the law cannot make its own kind of manifest theft; it only treats a different case as if it were manifest theft—is considerably more daring, independent. Even this, not surprisingly, contains no trace of the modern, historical view here taken as to the origin of the difficulty felt about the statute, that it declared the case in question manifest theft because, at that time, it virtually was whereas later it lost that character.

The doctrine approved by Gaius, however, is no more his product than that he rejects. It plainly underlies the exposition of the matter in Gellius: "Those thefts which were detected by loincloth and platter the

15. The very term *Fiktion* is used by Ihering in outlining his theory in *Geist des Römischen Rechts*, 7th and 8th ed. (1924), 202n99. Other words used are "technical instrument," *technisches Intrument*, (vol. 2, pt. 2, 6th and 7th ed. [1923], 366–67; "device," *Kunstgriff*; "artifices," *Kunstprodukte*; "mechanisms," *Mechanismen* (vol. 3, 6th and 7th ed. [1924], 224f.; and "appearance," *Schein*, in the main discussion, (3:356ff). I failed to take account of this in *Studies in Biblical Law*, 296, 301, where I represent Gaius as a Fictionist.

decemvirs punished as if they were manifest."[16] It may be taken that neither did Gellius use Gaius nor Gaius Gellius, but I cannot here enlarge on the point. Nor can I go into the question whether they drew on the same source or different ones. Gellius often relied on information by word of mouth. It is clear that, around the middle of the second century AD, this was the fashionable doctrine. My hunch is that its author is Labeo; it would fit in with his role in the classification of various modes of theft to which I shall come in a moment.[17]

Gaius on Theft, Adultery and Homicide Extended

It is worthwhile to look at the parallels Gaius adduces: a statute can turn a nonmanifest thief into a manifest one no more than (1) one who is not a thief at all into a thief, (2) a nonadulterer into an adulterer or (3) a nonkiller into a killer. None of the three are chosen at random. In all three cases a problem much like that created by "it shall be manifest theft" did in fact exist.

One

The first parallel is the impossibility of decreeing a nonthief to be a thief. This refers back to a point Gaius discusses only a paragraph before, in the opening part of his section on theft.[18]

In the XII Tables we find theft accompanied by four distinguishing attributes: there is manifest theft, where the thief is caught *in flagranti*; nonmanifest theft, the ordinary case; theft taken hold of, *conceptum*, where a man's house is searched in the presence of witnesses and the object turns up; and theft inflicted, *oblatum*, where the man in whose house the object turns up was saddled with it by somebody else—the latter is liable to

---

16. Gellius 11.18.3: *ea quoque furta quae per lancem liciumque concepta essent proinde ac si manifesta forent vindicaverunt.*

17. See below, pp. 261–62.

18. Gaius 3.183, 186–87.

him. Servius, a late Republican jurist, in systematizing the law of theft, faithfully took the code as his guide. As Gaius tells us, he divided theft precisely into these four classes: manifest, nonmanifest, taken hold of, and inflicted. Sabinus accepted this classification, but Labeo demurred. He denied that taken hold of and inflicted were classes of theft on the same level as manifest and nonmanifest, his principal reason doubtless being that you could fall under these headings without being guilty of *dolus*: the man in whose house the object turns up might be innocent, and so might be the man who brought it to him, in which case one could not call them thieves. There were, Labeo argued, only the two classes, manifest theft and nonmanifest theft, whereas taken hold of and inflicted were merely actions connected with theft. (It might make a practical difference: for example, on the basis of Labeo's classification, with taken hold of and inflicted excluded from theft proper, an innocent person convicted under these heads would presumably not incur the infaming consequences imposed by the edict on one convicted of theft.) Gaius, though a Sabinian, openly sides with Labeo ("the better view");[19] and, in his description of taken hold of and inflicted, emphasizes both that in these cases the person held accountable need not be a thief (he is liable *quamvis fur non sit*) and that it is a question of the law providing two special actions on top of theft in the full sense (*nam propria actio constituta est* with regard to taken hold of, *nam propria constituta est actio* with regard to inflicted).[20]

It is quite possible that Servius and Sabinus spoke of theft taken hold of and theft inflicted as theft *lege*, in contrast to theft *natura*. Whether they did so or not, the position taken up by Labeo and approved by Gaius is that the law cannot make a nonthief into a thief, though definitely it may sanction an action against anyone who is somehow tied up with theft. It is Labeo's role in this controversy which makes me wonder whether he is not also responsible for the progressive line concerning "it shall be manifest theft."[21] Anyhow, this is the background of the first parallel, *non magis quam qui omnino fur non sit fur sit.*

19. Gaius 3.183 at the end.

20. Gaius 3.186f. That this emphasis is intentional, designed to justify Labeo's theory, follows from the little clause Gaius adds to his acceptance of that theory, 3.183: it is the better view, he says, "as will appear below"—namely, from the exposition of taken hold of and inflicted in 3.186f.

21. See above, p. 261.

I fear I must add a footnote not very flattering to Gaius. By his time, at least the action *furti oblati*, "on the ground of theft inflicted"—though probably not yet *furti concepti*, "on the ground of theft taken hold of"—lay only if there was *dolus*; in fact, it lay only if defendant had quite deliberately got rid of the object to plaintiff in order that the latter should be incriminated rather than he himself. This means that, by now, only a thief could be convicted by this action, for whether or not he was the man who had first stolen the object, this knowing, treacherous palming off clearly involved *contrectatio*, that peculiar "illicit, nasty handling" which was the essence of the delict in classical law. Gaius, therefore, should not have taken over Labeo's view without modification. He certainly should not have said that this action was available irrespective of whether the accused was a thief.

This is of course only one of many instances in the *Institutes* where one has the impression that the author is in the main writing out a more ancient work, with an occasional reference to newer developments.[22] In the present case, however, the impression becomes almost a certainty. The statement that the person held accountable under theft inflicted need not be a thief, true only in an earlier period, is made in the very same paragraph where the conflicting requirement of *dolus*, of more recent origin, is enunciated: "Theft inflicted is said to occur where the stolen object has been inflicted on you by somebody and has been taken hold of on your premises, at any rate if it was given you with the intention that it should be taken hold of on your premises rather than on those of the giver."[23] This is really explicable only if we assume that the basic text is

22. See e.g., Daube, "Book Review of *History of Roman Legal Science* by F. Schulz," *JRS* 38 (1948): 114–15.

23. Gaius 3.187: *Oblatum furtum dicitur cum res furtiva tibi ab aliquo oblata sit eaque apud te concepta sit, utique si ea mente data tibi fuerit ut apud te potius quam apud eum dederit conciperetur.* I follow De Zulueta, *The Institutes of Gaius*, 1 (1946), 215, in translating *utique si* by "at any rate if." The meaning is "though only if." In two more passages of the Institutes a rule is directly followed by this phrase, 2.76 and 2.78. They deal with the cases where you are in possession of my land and build on it, plant in it or sow it (2.76) and where you are in possession of a panel belonging to me and paint on it (2.78). If I bring an action for recovery of my land or my panel but refuse to pay your expenses, you can defeat me by an *exceptio*—*utique si*, "at any rate if," "though only if," you were a *[continues onto next page]*

simply copied from an older source, copied, indeed, in an astonishingly mechanical way: the old—"even if he is not a thief"—remains untouched next to the new—"provided it was given you with intent." Of late a few scholars have become anxious lest Gaius may have been judged too harshly by the moderns;[24] and one all-out attempt in particular has been made to raise him from the status of a second-rater commonly assigned to him.[25] But no ingenuity of argument can bring it about *ut qui classicus non sit classicus sit*. Let me note that long before Justinian, *dolus* was required in the case of theft taken hold of, *conceptum*, as well as theft inflicted, *oblatum*; and both were absorbed by ordinary, nonmanifest theft.[26]

Two

The second parallel is that a statute cannot change a nonadulterer into an adulterer. This, I guess, also comes from the older source. Under the *lex Julia de adulteriis* of 18 BC, quite a few cases not strictly adultery were dealt with *pro adulterio*, "as adultery" or "as if adultery," the guilty person was sentenced *quasi adulter*, "as adulterer" or "as if an adulterer," "under the heading of an adulterer." For example, a man knowingly marries a woman convicted of adultery; a husband fails to divorce his wife caught *in flagranti*; a spouse makes a profit from the other spouse's adultery.[27] I have given alternative renderings, "as" and "as if," because the Latin *pro* and *quasi* are both ambiguous. The idea may be either that these crimes are punishable "as adultery," the criminal "as an adulterer," i.e., they are adultery, he is an

---

[note 23 *continued from previous page*] possessor in good faith. *Utique cum* has the same force. It occurs once, in 3.96, where Gaius remarks that, except for the oath binding a freedman to render his patron certain services, we meet no oath which grounds an obligation—*utique cum quaeritur de iure Romanorum*, "though only so long as our study is the Roman law": he goes on to point out that in some foreign laws it is different.

24. De Zulueta, *The Institutes of Gaius*, 2:7ff., does his best for him, which is too good.

25. Honoré, *Gaius: A Biography* (1962).

26. Institutes 4.1.4.

27. Digest 4.4.37.1, *Tryphoninus III disputationum, pro adulterio*; Digest 48.5.9 pr., *Marcian II de adulteriis*; 48.5.34.2, *Marcian I de publicis iudiciis, quasi adulter and quasi adultera*.

adulterer, if you like adultery *lege* and adulterer *lege*; or that these crimes are punishable "as if adultery," the criminal "as if an adulterer," i.e., they are not adultery, he is not an adulterer, it is merely that we are to proceed as if we had to do with adultery and an adulterer.

Whether the statute itself spoke of *pro adulterio* and *quasi adulter* or whether these expressions are due to its early interpreters may be left open. (Very likely some such phrase did figure; it may, of course, have been *pro adultero*.) What matters is that the cases in question evidently presented the same jurisprudential difficulty as the subsumption by the XII Tables of a situation not "naturally" manifest theft under this offense. By contrast with the latter, antiquated provision, those of the *lex Julia* were of acute importance. We know, indeed, that this entire legislation evoked enormous interest among lawyers and was much analyzed. There is every reason to believe that the debate was in full swing in Labeo's lifetime. Here, then, is the setting of the second parallel, the refusal to recognize any but "natural" adultery.

Three

The third parallel—a nonkiller is not a killer—may well be Gaius's contribution. Surely it alludes to Hadrian's rescript which—perhaps more or less by way of reaffirmation—subjected attempted murder to the same penalties as the completed crime. The person guilty of attempt, the texts say, is to be sentenced *pro homicida* or *ut homicida*; either phrase is ambiguous and may mean equally "as killer" or "as if a killer." The rescript seems to have said *pro homicida*. Ulpian writes: "The words of the rescript—On the one hand he who has killed a man is normally acquitted, namely, if he did so without intent to kill, on the other hand he who has not killed but has tried to kill is sentenced *pro homicida.*" [28]

---

28. Coll. 1.6.2, Ulpian VII *de officio proconsulis sub titulo sicariis et veneficis*. In 1.6.4, which is comment on the rescript, we find *ut homicida*. *Pro homicida* also in Marcian's report of the rescript, Digest 48.8.1.3, *XIV institutionum*. *Ut homicida* again in Coll.1.7.1 [equals *Pauli Sententiae* 5.23.3], where the rescript is paraphrased but not expressly mentioned.

Gaius on Usufruct Extended

The doctrine favored by Gaius in his *Institutes* recurs in his commentary on the provincial edict, quite possibly the earlier of the two works.[29] He is discussing a senatusconsult of the end of the Republic or the early Empire—under Augustus or Tiberius—enabling a testator to leave what we call a quasi-usufruct, a right over perishable, consumable goods such as money, wine, oil: the legatee obtained ownership and by means of a *cautio* gave security for return, at the expiry of the quasi-usufruct, of things of the same quality and quantity. This *cautio* was a modification of that traditional in ordinary usufruct, over a nonperishable object, by which return of that object was guaranteed.

From what Gaius says it is obvious that the senate used the indirect method of regulating the matter that we found in the case of "it shall be manifest theft," bringing the case to be dealt with under an established category. It did not just set out the detailed rules to apply to such a legacy (though some detailed rules, e.g., as to *cautio*, did figure in the senatusconsult). Nor did it term the right as we do, a quasi-usufruct. What it ordained was that the right resulting from the legacy was, or should be, a good usufruct.

That some such language was employed is confirmed by other texts. "The senate decreed," Ulpian tells us, "that a usufruct can be left over every kind of thing that is agreed to be in any person's patrimony."[30] Similarly, in Institutes 2.4.2 we hear that "the senate decreed that also over those (perishable) things a usufruct could be created."[31] The latter text is particularly strong evidence since, as we shall see,[32] the author would much rather have it different, would much prefer the senate to have expressed itself more cautiously.

29. Digest 7.5.2.1., *VII ad edictum provinciale.* My footnote on this text in *Studies in Biblical Law*, 313, is very superficial.

30. Digest 7.5.1, *Ulpian XVIII ad Sabinum*; essentially the translation of Monro, *The Digest of Justinian* vol. 2 (1909), 44. For an alternative interpretation see below, p. 267n36. The Latin is *Senatus censuit, ut omnium rerum, quas in cuiusque patrimonio esse constaret usus fructus legari possit.*

31. *Senatus censuit posse etiam earum rerum usum fructum constitui.*

32. See below, p. 272.

This is how Digest 7.5.2.1 runs: "By this senatusconsult it is not brought about that there is a usufruct over money properly—for natural reason could not be overturned by the authority of the senate—but with the introduction of a remedy it begins to be treated as if a usufruct."[33]

One can sympathize with the bogglers at the senatusconsult, the new case having very little to do with the old, at least as far as its legal-technical structure is concerned. The affinity is chiefly in the socioeconomic function. As is well known, the senate was faced by bequests of a usufruct *bonorum* or *omnium bonorum*, over a man's goods or entire goods, which would ordinarily include perishables as well as a house, slaves, or the like. In Cicero's *Pro Caecina*, delivered in 69 BC, a man makes his son heir, leaving his wife a usufruct over all his property for life to be exercised jointly with the son.[34] Presumably, as the senatusconsult was not yet in existence, this was valid only in respect of the nonperishable objects in the estate. In the *Topica*, written in 44 BC, we find the following illustration of an argument "from the contrary": "A woman whose husband has bequeathed her a usufruct over his goods and has left full wine and oil cellars must not believe that these fall under her right. For use, not consumption, has been bequeathed (*usus enim, non abusus, legatus est*)—these are contrary to one another."[35] This passage surely reflects an interesting point in the development culminating in the senatusconsult—namely, that point when pressure for allowing a usufruct over an entire estate to cover the perishables in it was mounting, but still resisted. In the end the senate did validate such gifts,[36] and soon, if not at once, you could create a usufruct

---

33. *Quo senatus consulto non id effectum est ut pecuniae usus fructus proprie esset—nec enim naturalis ratio auctoritate senatus commutari potuit—sed remedio introducto coepit quasi usus fructus haberi.* In *Romanistische Studien*, 324, Beseler changed *naturalis ratio* into *ratio iuris*; later, in *Beitr.* 5:22, he crossed out the entire clause *nec enim—potuit*, "for natural reason could not be overturned by the authority of the senate." None of this is plausible: Cf. above, p. 240, on Gaius 1.158, and p. 247, on Digest 4.5.8, *Gaius IV ad edictum provinciale*. A valuable discussion of Digest 7.5.2.1 as well as Institutes 2.4.2 is supplied by Grosso, "Sul Quasi Usufrutto," *Bull. Ist. Dir. Rom.* 43 (1935): 248ff.

34. Cicero, *Caecin.* 4.11.

35. Cicero, *Top.* 3.17: *Non debet mulier cui vir bonorum suorum usum fructum legavit, cellis vinariis et oleariis plenis relictis, putare id ad se pertinere; usus enim, non abusus, legatus est—ea sunt inter se contraria.*

36. As the original decree contemplated legacy of the usufruct over a whole inheritance, it is conceivable that in Digest 7.5.1, quoted above, [*continues onto next page*]

over perishables separately, i.e., even apart from a usufruct over your entire assets. In juristic writings, incidentally, the noun *abusus* occurs only in three postclassical insertions in Ulpian in the Digest,[37] and one place in the postclassical *Ulpiani Regulae*;[38] in all four passages, indeed, as in Cicero's *Topica*, it denotes "consumption" in connection with usufruct. The classics clearly avoided the term because of its double meaning; it might signify "abuse."[39]

However, what was the true effect of giving the legatee ownership and imposing an obligation to return an equal amount? It was something very like an interest-free loan,[40] most rules and considerations of regular usufruct being utterly inapplicable. No wonder the senate's calling this a usufruct provoked jurisprudential comment. It should be recalled that regular usufruct itself was not all that old, so the literal meaning of the term would be close to the surface in any case. But apart from this, to describe the new institution as usufruct, especially once there could be a separate right over, say, 10,000 sesterces or 50 barrels of Falernian, not just as part of a usufruct over an entire inheritance, was an astounding

---

[note 36 continued from previous page] there is preserved a reference to just this case. If so, we might translate: "The senate decreed that a usufruct can be left over all things of which it is established that they are in a person's estate," i.e., a usufruct *omnium bonorum* includes the perishables too.

37. Digest 7.5.5.1f., *XVIII ad Sabinum*; 7.8.12.1, *XVII ad Sabinum*; 12.2.11.2, *XXII ad edictum*; see Kübler, "Exegetische und kritische Bemerkungen zu einigen Digestenstellen," *ZRG* 59 (1939): 569–70. The context in 7.8.12.1 is slightly different from that in the other texts, but even here it is right to excise *abusus*. A man who has a *usus* over land may take wood for daily purposes, apples and so on, water, *non usque ad compendium sed ad usum, scilicet non usque ad abusum*, "not to the extent of profit but of use, that is to say, not to the extent of consumption": the *scilicet* clause is an appendix both very inelegant and not really accurate. On 12.2.11.2 I shall say more below, pp. 275–76.

38. Why all occurrences are associated with Ulpian is a puzzle.

39. Kübler, "Exegetische und kritische Bemerkungen," *ZRG* 59 (1939): 569–70, denies that *abusus* in Cicero has anything to do with "consumption"; it simply means "abuse." But, for one thing, it is difficult to believe that there should be this discrepancy between Cicero and all legal texts on exactly the same subject, and for another, no better setting for Cicero's illustration can be imagined than a stage on the way to recognition of usufruct over consumable goods. What may be admitted is that the opponents of the recognition made play with the pejorative potential of the word: that is why the classics dropped it, why it is confined to preclassical and postclassical vocabulary.

40. Buckland, *Text-Book* (1963), 271.

extension of the term. With some exaggeration one might imagine a senatusconsult validating consensual conveyance by declaring it a good *societas omnium bonorum*[41]—with, indeed, quite different rules from *societas*. It is significant how much trouble the senate's method gives to a modern scholar like Levy, in a chapter where he is concerned to show that the classics did not mix up usufruct and ownership: "Regardless of the wording of the statute or a bequest, his [the beneficiary's] right *in re* was not *ususfructus* but *proprietas*."[42]

If we ask why, despite all this, the senate did assign the case in question to usufruct, the answer must make reference not only to the social and economic closeness but also to the machinery for final settlement at the expiry of the term of enjoyment. I have already mentioned that in ordinary usufruct, over a nonperishable object, at the beginning of the term, the usufructuary by means of a *cautio* guaranteed return of the object at the end. This *cautio* was a characteristic and much analyzed element in usufruct.[43] When the senate decided the time had come to recognize usufruct over perishables, it prescribed a modified *cautio* for this case—guaranteeing return of things of the same quantity and quality. The texts leave no doubt that this common machinery, the *cautio*, greatly contributed to the classification of the new case as usufruct.[44]

From the first moment there must have been controversy as to the construction of the new institution. One party must have construed it as usufruct *lege*, which in this case might be the more satisfactory solution. It is relatively easy to think of a category *lege*, of usufruct *lege*, as greatly differing from the basic category, from ordinary, "natural" usufruct. After all, legal personality greatly differs from a human person. The line taken by Gaius—in reliance on earlier authority—is less appropriate to this case than to those inspected above. The arrangement in question, he holds, is

41. Where the partners become co-owners at the moment of the contract: Digest 17.2.1.1, *Paul XXXII ad edictum*; 17.2.2, *Gaius X ad edictum provinciale*.

42. Levy, *West Roman Vulgar Law* (1951), 35. The reference to "statute" is explained by the fact that Levy—no doubt rightly—regards the senatusconsult as supplementing a statute of Augustus.

43. See the sections *Ut usus fructus nomine caveatur* and *Usufructuarius quemadmodum caveat* in Lenel, *Das edictum perpetuum*, 3rd ed. (1927), 368–69, 538–39.

44. Digest 7.5.2, *Gaius VII ad edictum provinciale*; 7.5.4, *Paul I ad Neratium*; Institutes 2.4.2.

considered as if a usufruct. But this is not really true. Except for the fact that it is upheld (but so are sale, *traditio*, marriage, and countless other dealings) and a very few specific features such as limitation to the lifetime of the beneficiary and, indeed, the *cautio*, the law accords it radically dissimilar treatment.

Gaius says that to make the new case usufruct would be contrary to *naturalis ratio*, "natural reason"; that is indeed why the lawgiver cannot do it. In the remarks on manifest theft and the like, we came across no reference to *naturalis ratio*. This may be accidental, but I do not think so. What is and what is not manifest theft, who is and who is not a thief, an adulterer, a homicide—these appeared to be straight questions concerning the external world, and a lawgiver transferring the word would simply fly in the face of facts. What is and what is not a usufruct, I suspect, was felt to be a somewhat more complicated question, having regard not just to externals but to a legal category. For the classics, a sound legal category, like a fact, had its intrinsic, unshakable characteristics,[45] and you could not arbitrarily transfer its name to a situation not showing these. Nevertheless, the blunder would be just a little less obvious than the misdescription of one fact by the name of another. It would be a blunder as to the order of things rather than the things themselves—a violation of *naturalis ratio*.

Let me add that the thrust of the statement is rather different also from that in the texts considered earlier, which insist on the unabolishability of *naturalia iura*, "natural rights." With the exception of Institutes 1.2.11, those texts are all concerned with rights grounded in family ties. Their object is less the preservation of clarity about the various legal categories than the assertion of the unlosability of certain positions in the family; they are more ethical. Neither could Digest 7.5.2.1 be reformulated with the help of the term *iura naturalia* nor those texts with the help of *naturalis ratio*: the direction of thought would be radically falsified.

The final portion of 7.5.2.1, *sed remedio introducto coepit quasi usus fructus haberi*, has been attacked by Segrè.[46] He proceeds from the

45. See Levy, "Natural Law in Roman Thought," *Studia et Documenta Historiae et Iuris 1–10*, vol. 15 (1949): 8ff. He does not, however, make my distinction. Compare also Maschi, *La Concezione Naturalistica del Diritto e degli Istituti Giuridici Romani* (1937), 258. But see also below, p. 278, and p. 285n91a, on "manifest theft."

46. Segrè, "Sul Deposito Irregolare in Diritto Romano," *Bull. Ist. Dir. Rom.* 19 (1907): 197.

orthodox interpretation to which, I must now confess, my translation does not conform. The current interpretation is that Gaius is here working with the notion of a quasi-usufruct: "But with the introduction of a remedy the arrangement came to be held a quasi-usufruct."[47] Segré feels, not unreasonably, that this notion was not yet reached in classical law. Moreover, he argues, the clause is illogical; as a logical conclusion Gaius should have stated, not that as a result of the remedy a quasi-usufruct came about, but that in this way effects analogous to usufruct were achieved.

However, this is precisely what Gaius does state.[48] Only we must not, in rendering the passage, let ourselves be misled by Institutes 2.4.2, where quas-usufruct does figure, or very nearly.[49] The proper rendering is: "But with the introduction of a remedy, the arrangement begins to be considered as if a usufruct"—exactly what Segré wants Gaius to say. The notion of a quasi-usufruct is not yet there. The doctrine corresponds to the Gaian attitude in all the cases already presented. It is carried a step or two further in Institutes 2.4.2 which, we shall see, comes from the *Res Cottidianae*. It would be rash in the extreme to dispute the authenticity of the *sed* clause.

Segré has found a large following.[50] But even those who oppose him do so on the wrong basis, trying to prove that the concept quasi-usufruct could be classical. Bonfante cites a letter by the younger Pliny[51] where

47. In this sense Monro, The Digest of Justinian, vol. 2 (1909), 44: "there came to be something analogous to usufruct."

48. As pointed out above, pp. 267–68, it is not even strictly true that the effects—the legal-technical ones—were analogous to usufruct. But within the framework of Gaius's doctrine, it is indeed the logical upshot.

49. A fortiori we must not be influenced by Digest 43.18.1.6, *Ulpian LXX ad edictum*. The meaning of *et quasi usum fructum sive usum quendam eius* is quite obscure and in any case the text is spurious. See Beseler, *Beitr.* 1 (1910): 106; Perozzi, *Istituzioni di Diritto Romano*, vol. 1, 2nd ed. (1928), 789; Kaser, *Das Römische Privatrecht*, vol. 1 (1955), 380.

50. E.g., Grosso, "Sul Quasi Usufrutto," *Bull. Ist. Dir. Rom.* 43 (1935), 248ff.; Perozzi, *Istituzioni di diritto romano* vol. 1, 2nd ed. (1928), 789; Albertario, "Il possesso dell'usufrutto, dell'uso, della habitatatio," *Studi di Diritto Romano* 2 (1941), 328 (he is far too indiscriminate in his treatment of *quasi*).

51. Bonfante, "Corso di Diritto Romano," *Diritto Reale* 3 (1933), 86. It is presumably on the strength of his argument that the concept quasi-usufruct is accepted as classical in works like Jörs-Kunkel-Wenger, *Römisches Recht*, 3rd ed. (1949), 146; Kaser, *Das Römische Privatrecht* 1 (1955), 380.

Pliny, enlarging on his affection for his slaves, writes: "I allow my slaves so to speak to make testaments and observe these as if they were legal," *permitto servis quoque quasi testamenta facere eaque ut legitima custodio.*[52] Surely, Pliny is not speaking of quasi-testaments; he is not allowing his slaves to make a particular kind of testament; the *quasi* qualifies the whole phrase *testamenta facere*; he is allowing them, in a sense, to make wills. Even, however, if Pliny did here jokingly introduce a quasi-testament, it would have little bearing on the senatusconsult we are discussing. I am not denying that the formation of a term such as quasi-usufruct would have been possible. The classics just did not form it. There are more cases of a late quasi-something being read back into earlier layers in which all that is claimed is that a set of facts is treated as if it were that something. But I forbear from going on with this.[53]

Beseler attributes *remedio introducto* to the compilers.[54] I am reluctant to assent even to this modest excision, for three reasons. First, why ever should they have inserted the idea? Secondly, we shall find words to the same effect, *per cautionem,* "by means of a *cautio*," in Institutes 4.2.4 going back to the Res Cottidianae. Thirdly, it will be remembered that Gaius follows Labeo in holding that *furtum conceptum* and *furtum oblatum*, theft taken hold of and theft inflicted, are not types of theft; they are called *furta* simply because they are actions made available in connection with this delict. The idea behind *remedio introducto* is much the same: this new institution is not usufruct; the senate calls it that because a remedy is provided—the *cautio*—connected with usufruct, indeed, typical of it, a remedy on the strength of which the case is looked on, dealt with, as if it were usufruct. That the term *remedium* is rare in classical sources should not put us off. We have before us a semiphilosophical disquisition and,

---

52. Pliny the Younger, *Ep.* 8.16.1. For what this meant in actual fact see Biondi, *Successione Testamentaria e Donazioni*, 2nd ed. (1955), 84. He does not deal with the problem here under notice. Translators mostly get the nuance wrong; e.g., Guillemin, *Pline le Jeune, Lettres*, vol. 3, 2nd ed. (Collection des Universités de France, 1959), 74: *à faire de quasi-testaments.*

53. Quasi-delict, Stein has pointed out, appears first in Basilica 60.4.1: *hosanei hamartema*; see "The Nature of quasi-delictal Obligations in Roman Law," *Revue Internationale des Droits de l'Antiquité* 5 (1958): 563.

54. Beseler, *Beitr.* 2 (1911): 121. For further intrusions alleged by him see *Beitr.* 5: 22.

besides, *remedium* is the appropriate word. *Actio*, used in the explanation of *furtum conceptum* and *oblatum*, would have been far too narrow: the effectiveness of the new arrangement was ensured by taking over from usufruct—with adjustments—a special machinery, the main component of which was the *cautio*.

Justinian's Institutes on Usufruct Extended

We come to Institutes 2.4.2, which Ferrini regards as descending from the *Res Cottidianae*.[55] Usufruct, we learn, is possible over everything except perishable, consumable goods. "For these are susceptible of usufruct neither by natural nor by civil law reason." The same (the text goes on) applies to money. "However, for the sake of expediency, the senate decreed that also over those things a usufruct could be created, so, however, that the heir be given an adequate security." After some details as to machinery, the paragraph concludes: "hence the senate has not called into existence a usufruct over those things, for it could not do that, but by means of a *cautio* it has established a quasi-usufruct."[56]

I suppose that, though gramatically the phrase "neither by natural nor by civil law reason" coordinates, puts on the same level, the two sources of law, what is meant is that, as perishables do not admit of usufruct by virtue of natural reason, neither will they admit of it in the strength of the civil law: the latter cannot go against the former.[57] This is, of course, consistent with the principle enunciated in several passages from Gaius or dependent on him. Why, in the present case, there is mention of *naturalis ratio* I have just tried to explain in connection with Digest 7.5.2.1.[58] In fact Institutes 2.4.2. makes it even clearer that it is a question of the sound order of things: the structure of usufruct, we are informed, is intrinsically averse to the inclusion of perishables.

---

55. Ferrini, *Opere* 2:334 [*Bull. Ist. Dir. Rom.* 13:126].

56. *Nam eae neque naturali ratione neque civili recipiunt usum fructum . . . Sed utilitatis causa senatus censuit posse etiam earum rerum usum fructum constitui, ut tamen . . . heredi utiliter caveatur . . . Ergo senatus non fecit quidem earum rerum usum fructum, nec enim poterat, sed per cautionem quasi usum fructum constituit.*

57. Compare Digest 3.5.38, *Gaius III de verborum obligationibus.*

58. *VII ad edictum provinciale;* see above, pp. 269–70.

The senate's awkwardly formulated regulation—awkward from the point of view of its commentators at least—was enacted *utilitatis causa*, "for the sake of expediency," that is to say, in order to assist urgent, decent needs and to prevent unfair results. This excuses some irregularity. Even so, the decree did not make the arrangement a usufruct, not even *lege*: the senate could not turn a nonusufruct into a usufruct. What it did was to introduce machinery from usufruct, a *remedium* in the language of Digest 7.5.2.1: "so, however, that the heir be given an adequate security," "by means of a *cautio*." Just so, for the advocates of this line of argument, theft taken hold of and theft inflicted were species *actionis furto cohaerentes* rather than *genera furtorum*.

In one respect the author of the text goes considerably beyond Digest 7.5.2.1 where the arrangement "is considered as if a usufruct": in Institutes 2.4.2 the senate, by upholding it, "has established a quasi-usufruct." Read on its own, the clause *quasi usum fructum constituit* could mean "it has, so to speak, established a usufruct"; but after the preceding *ergo non fecit usum fructum*, "hence it has not called into existence a usufruct," this meaning is out of the question, and a translation like "it has established a quasi-usufruct" is unavoidable. Theophilus at any rate in his Greek paraphrase takes it this way: "By the device of the *cautio* the senate contrived an imitation of usufruct."[59]

A few more points in his paraphrase may be noted. He replaces the brief motivation in the Latin original "for the sake of expediency" by "since, then, it is said that there is no room for usufruct over those things." On the other hand, for the proviso "so, however, that the heir be given adequate security" he substitutes the short phrase "by a certain device":[60] "a senatusconsult was enacted laying down that also over those things by a certain device a usufruct was to exist." In the course of explaining details, he stresses far more than the original the radical independence of the new case. The legatee receives ownership "contrary to the nature of usufruct,

---

59. *Dia tes methodou tes cautionos mimesin epenoesen usufructu.* Ferrini, *Institutionum Graeca*, 126, completely disregards the mention of *methodos*, "device," "stratagem," as he also removes the nuance of purposeful planning or scheming from the verb *epinoeo*. He translates: *per cautionem vero quasi usumfructum introduxit.*

60. *Dia methodou tinos.* Ferrini's *quadam ratione*, *Institutionum Graeca*, pt. 1 (1884), 70, is not pregnant enough.

for usufruct is over another man's property; but as there exists no usufruct according to the laws over these things, fittingly the principles of usufruct are transgressed in their respect."[61]

If, as is most likely, the classics did not arrive at the concept of a quasi-usufruct, Institutes 2.4.2 furnishes an argument for the postclassical origin of the *Res Cottidianae*. Segré, regarding the concept as postclassical, draws the inference that Institutes 2.4.2 comes not, as Ferrini asserts, from the *Res Cottidianae* but from Digest 7.5.2.1. The inference is wrong. For one thing, as we have seen, Digest 7.5.2.1 does not contain the notion quasi-usufruct: this is only read back into it from Institutes 2.4.2. For another, the vocabulary is about as unlike as it could be—*sed remedio introducto coepit quasi usus fructus haberi* over against *sed per cautionem usum fructum constituit*—a fact Segré notices but is unable to account for. The point is that, in his day, the possibility of the *Res Cottidianae* being postclassical did not yet occur, hence, he was practically driven to his mistaken conclusion.

We might, indeed, consider the possibility that Justinian altered the text of the *Res Cottidianae* in the points here of relevance. A possibility, to be sure, but an exceedingly remote one. Or again, it might even be argued that quasi-usufruct was invented by Gaius between his commentary on the provincial edict and his (genuine) *Res Cottidianae*. I am not the Jew Apella.

Paul and Ulpian on Usufruct Extended

In both the provinces of theft and usufruct, Labeo's doctrine prevailed: the law cannot turn facts which do not constitute such and such an offense or transaction into that offense or transaction, it cannot add a "legal" class to the "natural" one. Gaius, Gellius, Justinian, Theophilus—they all follow this doctrine. For usufruct, Paul and, perhaps, Ulpian may be included in the list of witnesses.

---

61. Very similar to Levy, quoted *West Roman Vulgar Law* (1951), 35. *Para ten physin tou usufructu, ho gar usufructos kata allotrias despoteias estin; all' epeide ou synesteke epi touton kata nomous ho usufructos, eikotos kai hoi kanones epi auton parabainontai tou usufructu.*

Usufruct was lost by nonuse, for one year in the case of movables, for two years in that of land. (Justinian extended these times.) But this mode of extinction did not apply to quasi-usufruct[62]—obviously, it would have made no sense, the quasi-usufructuary becoming owner of the objects, the wine, oil, money. Paul puts the matter thus: "Also if a usufruct over money is bequeathed it does not end by nonuse for a year, because it is not usufruct and the ownership of the money is with the usufructuary, not with the heir."[63] The particle *quoque* connects up with the preceding remark to the effect that, in contradistinction to usufruct (ordinary usufruct) already in existence, the action by which you may claim to have it created is not lost by nonuse. This leads on to quasi-usufruct not lost by nonuse. "It is not usufruct," Paul declares: this is in accordance with what we found in Gaius. Like Theophilus, Paul names the usufructuary's ownership of the objects as the fundamental deviation; for Theophilus, we have seen, quasi-usufruct is "contrary to the nature of usufruct, for usufruct is over another man's property."

In the course of discussing the oath which, given certain conditions, settles a right, Ulpian observes: "But if he swears that he has, or that there is owing to him, a usufruct over things over which because of consumption a usufruct cannot be created, I opine that the effectiveness of the oath should be accepted and therefore I believe that even then he should be considered to have correctly sworn and he can on the strength of the oath claim the usufruct on offering the security."[64]

---

62. Institutes 2.4; *Fr. Vat.* 46, to be discussed presently, Digest 7.5.9, *Paul I ad Neratium*; 7.5.10 pr. [equals 7.9.7.1], *Ulpian LXXIX ad edictum*. In fact, nearly all modes of extinction of usufruct proper were inapplicable.

63. *Fr. Vat.* 46, *Paul I Manualium*: *Pecuniae quoque usus fructus legatus per annum non utendo non perit, quia nec usus fructus est et pecuniae dominium fructuarii, non heredis, est.* The words *non perit* are supplied by *Huschke Iurisprudentiae Anteiustinianae quae Supersunt*, 3rd ed. (1874), 691, and certainly give the right sense. I do not see some of the difficulties Grosso, "Sul Quasi Usufrutto," *Bull. Ist. Dir. Rom.* 43 (1935): 264, has with the text.

64. Digest 12.2.11.2, *Ulpian XXII ad edictum*: *Sed si rerum in quibus usus fructus propter abusum constitui non potest iuraverit usum fructum se habere vel sibi deberi, effectum iurisiurandi sequendum arbitror ideoque tunc quoque videri eum recte iurasse puto et ex eo iureiurando posse petere usum fructum cautione oblata.* See Grosso, *Bull. Ist. Dir. Rom.* 43 (1935): 266, with whose results I am not in full agreement; my principal argument is not much affected.

To begin by taking the text as it stands, the question is whether to recognize an oath in which a quasi-usufruct is described as a usufruct. The very question implies a firm insistence on the view that it is not usufruct, be it *natura* or be it *lege*. The decision, it is true, prefers a sane and fair result to rigorous logic and, with some hesitation (*arbitror, puto,* "I opine," "I believe") the oath is upheld.

Beseler reconstructs the decision as follows: "I opine that the oath has no effect."[65] If he is right, Ulpian carried the exclusion of quasi-usufruct from usufruct to extremes—perhaps not impossible where it is a question of interpretation of an oath.

I agree with Beseler that the text is doctored,[66] but I should seek to restore it along different lines. The clue seems to me to lie in the switch from the first person in the first half of the paragraph, not here quoted, *item si iuravero,* "if I swear," to the third person in the second half, the half we are concerned with, *sed si iuraverit,* "but if he swears." Beseler puts it right by inserting *quis* into the latter case, *sed si quis iuraverit,* "but if somebody swears." This, I think, is too simple. I think that, in the original Ulpian, between the first half and the second there was a discussion which the compilers found inconvenient and dropped. The first half deals with extinction of usufruct proper. The bit dropped may have continued this theme. And even the second half, here under notice, may originally have had to do with it, pointing out—as does *Fragmenta Vaticana* 46— differences in the case of quasi-usufruct.

If so, there is no knowing the exact question Ulpian had in mind; but it was most probably not the description of a quasi-usufruct as a usufruct.[67] That this is the problem now would be the doing of the compilers.

---

65. *Et (atque) ideo, et (atque) idcirco, ideoque, idcircoque,* Beseler, ZRG 45 (1925): 462: *nullum esse effectum iurisiurandi arbitror.*

66. That *propter abusum* is not classical was noted above. Beseler cuts it out. It may, however, be an abbreviation of something like *quia usu consumuntur,* "because they are consumed by use."

67. Compare, below, p. 281, for Ulpian's attitude to a comparable problem from "infamy."

Gaius on Adoptive Relations and Ulpian on Conventional Infamy

An Excursus on In-laws

An argument from silence is apt to be precarious. Still, from our sources it does look as if the Roman jurists had embarked on an *ex professo* inquiry into an extension of a category only in connection with these two cases: the manifest theft if an object is found by ceremonious search "with loincloth and platter," and the usufruct over perishables. It is only here, it appears, that they set forth, gave explicit shape to, their theories—the category *lege* on the one hand, the explanation by means of "as if" or *quasi* on the other. Why should that be so? There would have been many other opportunities, the whole, vast field of interpretation, for example. The very term "manifest theft," as Gaius himself points out,[67a] was far from unambiguous, construed in a narrow sense by some jurists (the thief must be caught in the act, on the spot), less rigorously by others (he must be caught before having carried the object to safety).

The answer is that, in these two cases, there was legislation—known legislation—declaring a set of facts to be what prima facie it was not: "it shall be manifest theft," "it is a good usufruct." These provisions had to be made sense of and thus, in a time greatly interested in definition and classification, the discussion of principle was sparked off. In the course of it, or rather in the course of discussing "with loincloth and platter," three other cases were drawn in: theft as such, adultery, and homicide. Theft as such, because of the long-standing allied problem which had cropped up in endeavors to work out various types of theft, with theft taken hold of and theft inflicted becoming increasingly difficult to fit in; and adultery and homicide, because as to both there was also extending legislation—though these extensions were more carefully worded, with the aid of *pro*, *quasi*, *ut*.

Needless to say, if the *ex professo* ventilation of the problem is confined to a very few contexts, adumbrations and echoes abound

---

67A. Gaius 3.184. Mr. Colin Turpin, of Clare College, Cambridge, has kindly drawn my attention to this remarkable fact. Cf. above, p. 270n45, and below, p. 285n91a.

throughout the system. Above I quoted Institutes 3.1.11 on adoption,[68] and it is instructive to pay attention to the way adoptive relationships are described there and elsewhere. A few sketchy remarks must here suffice. In his *Institutes* Gaius, who rejects manifest theft *lege* and usufruct *lege*, freely speaks of "adoptive son" or "adoptive father," *filius* or *pater adoptivus*.[69] (The use of *liberi* in this area is not determined by absolutely the same factors since, though the word mostly signifies "children," its wider, basic meaning "free persons" and then "free subjects of a *paterfamilias*" is not without some influence.) Sometimes he represents them as occupying "the place of" natural relations,[70] which chimes with his thesis in regard to extensions in other fields. But he is far from consistent, as when he says: "If a woman through adoption begins to be a sister to me."[71] In Institutes 3.1.11, from the *Res Cottidianae*, the thesis seems to be carried to greater lengths: adoptive children have "the mere legal title of son or daughter," *ius nomenque*. The late classic Modestinus in his *Regulae* is not unsubtle, considering that in this kind of work a terse statement is called for: "Not only nature but also adoptions make sons of families."[72] He says not that adoptions make sons but that they make "sons of families." The latter is a more technical notion, more directly referring to the quality of the persons concerned as subjects of the heads of families. Whether adopted sons merely acquire the place of natural sons or become sons *lege* he does not decide.

Of *adrogatio*, the adoption of one *paterfamilias* by another, we know the formula designed for it by Q. Mucius Scaevola around 100 BC The popular assembly was asked: "Do you wish and ordain that Lucius Valerius be a son to Lucius Titius by law and statute just as if he were born of that father and his wife, and that to Titius be power of life and death

---

68. See above, pp. 237ff..

69. Gaius 1.137a, 2.136, 137, 147, 3.40, 41, 46, 49, 83, 84.

70. Gaius 1.59, *eamque mihi per adoptionem filiae loco esse coeperit,* "a woman who through adoption begins to be in the position of a daughter to me," 2.136, *adoptive filii naturalium loco sunt,* "adoptive sons are in the place of natural ones."

71. Gaius 1.61: *si qua per adoptionem soror mihi esse coeperit.*

72. Digest 1.7.1 pr., II *regularum; filiosfamilias non solum natura, verum et adoptiones faciunt.* Monro, *The Digest of Justinian* vol. 1 (1904), 31 under the influence of passages with "in place of," translates: "The position of *filiusfamilias* is acquired not only by nature but by adoption."

over Valerius as is to a father over a son?"[73] The archaic formula is not yet dominated by a definite, consciously held theory. Mucius's academic grandson Servius[74] would find here ammunition for his category *lege*— the person arrogated is *iure legeque filius*—but equally the "as if" school might derive comfort from "just as if he were born," *tam siet quam si esset.* I suppose that in both adoption in the narrow sense and arrogation, at all stages, the way the new relationship was thought of would depend a little on whether, in any given case, attention focused on the power-subjection aspect, the *filiusfamilias* as comparable to the *paterfamilias*'s ordinary property, or whether it focused on the more elementary characteristics of fatherhood, sonship, brotherhood, sisterhood and so on. In the former case, the difference between a true and an adoptive relation would be less conspicuous than in the latter; which means that the concept "father, son, brother, sister *lege* or *iure*" would present itself more readily in the former, that "in the place of a father, son, brother, sister" in the latter.

To give one more example from a remoter branch of the law. "Infamy" was not uncommonly incurred by a man who could hardly be considered a scoundrel; for instance, by a tutor whose negligence— negligence, not fraud—was found to have caused his ward some loss. The praetorian edict attached the same disabilities to condemnation in *actio tutelae* as to condemnation, say, in an action on the ground of theft and only slightly fewer than to condemnation in a capital trial; and in the *lex Julia municipalis* the three cases attract the same disabilities.[75] Ulpian comments: "Some kinds of opprobrium are dishonorable by nature, some

73. Gellius 5.19.9: *Velitis iubeatis uti L. Valerius L. Titio tam iure legeque filius siet quam si ex eo patre matreque familias eius natus esset, utique ei vitae necisque in eum potestas siet uti patri endo filio est.* A MS of the thirteenth century reads "become son" and "to Titius become power," *fiet* instead of *siet*; see Aulus Gellius, *Noctium Atticarum Libri XX*, bk. 1, ed. by Hertz (1883), 321. In the script of the period, *f* and *s* were very close. Nevertheless it is probable that the copyist did find *siet* a difficult thought: at this moment the sonship is not yet created. But *siet* is, of course, correct. The falling together of assertion and creation of a right is known, for instance, from mancipation; and at any rate, *siet*, occurring as it does in a question to the assembly, may well look forward to a legislative *esto.*

74. Mucius taught Aquilius Gallus and Lucilius Balbus, who in turn taught Servius.

75. Greenidge, *Infamia* (1894), 121ff.; Mommsen, *Röm. Strafr.* (1899), 805–6, 993–94.; Watson, "Some Cases of Distortion by the Past in Classical Roman Law," *Tijdschr. Rechts* 31 (1963), 76ff.

by the civil law and so to speak by the usage of the State; for example theft or adultery is dishonorable by nature, whereas to be condemned in the *actio tutelae*, that is not an opprobrium by nature but by the usage of the State. For that which can befall even a worthy man is not an opprobrium by nature."[76]

A jurist opposed to manifest theft *lege* or usufruct *lege* ought perhaps not to have recognized the dishonorable or opprobrium *more civitatis*; the logical view would have been that condemnation because of negligence is treated as if it fell under those attributes. Apart from the fact, however, that the jurists were not always logical, I argued above, in discussing quasi-usufruct, that we do not really know where Ulpian stood in that controversy.[77] To judge by the present fragment, he did not in fact follow the main trend. But to attain anything approaching certainty, a much more thorough investigation would be needed.

The fragment comes from Ulpian's chapter on *iniuriae*, attacks on the person, and Lenel seems to think that it was concerned to explain precisely what aspersions constituted actionable slander: you would be liable if you spoke of a man as found guilty of theft or adultery, dishonorable by nature, but not if you spoke of him as found guilty in an *actio tutelae*, an opprobrium only by usage of the State.[78] This is a perfectly possible context, but I incline to assume a different one. Ulpian may well have been exercised by the fact which has very understandably exercised modern authorities such as Mommsen and Watson[79]—that condemnation in the *actio iniuriarum* involved infamy though, in many cases, this would appear quite unjustifiable. It was this criticism he answered by the distinction between "natural" disgrace and "conventional" disgrace, and the *actio tutelae* came in as a further illustration: here, too, to understand the law one had to resort to this distinction.

---

76. Digest 50.16.42, *LVII ad edictum: Probra quaedam natura turpia sunt, quaedam civiliter et quasi more civitatis, ut puta furtum, adulterium natura turpe est, enimvero tutelae damnari hoc non natura probrum est sed more civitatis. Nec enim natura probrum est quod potest etiam in hominem idoneum incidere.*

77. See above, p. 277.

78. Lenel, *Pal.* 2:777; *Das edictum perpetuum*, 397, adducing Digest 47.10.15.13, from the same book by Ulpian.

79. See Mommsen, *Röm. Stafr.* (1899), 805f., 993f.; Watson, "Some Cases of Distortion by the Past in Classical Roman Law," *Tijdschr. Rechts.* 31 (1963), 76ff.

Beseler considered Lenel's suggestion implausible and labelled the fragment as spurious.[80] Why it should be necessary to deny Ulpian's authorship if the context suggested by Lenel does not convince I fail to see. I am conjecturing a different context; yet Lenel may be right, or neither of us—no reason here for condemning the fragment. Kaser tries to reinforce Beseler's excision by the strangest argument.[81] It contains the following steps. (1) *Mos civitatis* "can here signify only the feelings, views, judgment of the Roman people," *kann hier nur die römische Volksanschauung bedeuten.* (2) The main distinction in the field of infamy, however, is between cases where infamy results automatically from certain conduct (from working as a gladiator, for example—so-called "immediate" infamy) and cases where it results only from judicial conviction (the three cases in the present text all fall under this "mediate" infamy, you become infamous not when you steal, commit adultery, or are remiss in your job as tutor, but only by being convicted of theft, of adultery, or in an *actio tutelae*); and with this main distinction the one made in the present text between "natural" infamy and infamy in accordance with the *römische Volksanschauung* has no detectable connection. (3) The connection is not rendered any clearer by the final clause, *nec enim*, etc., "for that which can befall," etc., which is in any case naive. To these arguments one may reply: (1) There is nothing to justify the interpretation of *mos civitatis* as *die römische Volksanschauung.* It has its usual sense, "usage, established tradition, custom, of the State." This is contrasted with *natura* just as *lex* is in the discussion of "loincloth and platter." (2) Ulpian is plainly not concerned with the distinction between "immediate" and "mediate" infamy (a distinction which, though most useful, was worked out by Savigny).[82] All his three illustrations are cases of "mediate" infamy; there is no vestige of another. So no objection can be based on the fact that a connection with that distinction is not detectable. (3) Nor can we expect the final clause to elucidate this connection, which is not there. As for the naivete of this clause, that criticism has some weight so long as we translate *idoneus* by "suitable," "fit for the job." Then it would indeed be a little naive to say that what can befall a man suitable

80. Beseler, *Beitr.* 5:75. The words *civiliter et quasi*, already questioned by Albertario, are probably an intrusion.

81. Kaser, "Mores maiorum und Gewohnheitsrecht," *ZRG* 59 (1939): 93.

82. Greenidge, *Infamia* (1894), 38–39.

for the office of tutor cannot be disgraceful by nature. But *idoneus* shades off into "worthy," "honest,"[83] and though in the legal sources this nuance is rare, a discussion of infamy is the place for it.

May I be permitted an excursus on father-in-law, brother-in-law and so on? At first sight we seem to have before us a father *lege* or *iure*, a brother *lege* or *iure*, that is to say, a father or brother the law has added to the genuine one. The *New English Dictionary* does take this line. It explains that "in-law" means "in canon law." The contrast is with father or brother in blood, by nature. The terms with "in-law" imply that, as regards intermarriage, these persons fall under the same prohibitions as a true father, brother, and so on; they are, for this purpose, a father, brother, and so on created by the law.[84]

I am highly skeptical about what would be an amazingly early—thirteenth century—appearance in common English parlance of so sophisticated a concept. What increases my doubts is the idea that these relations should have received their designations from the forbidden degrees—especially as in some important cases a designation so based would make nonsense. My wife's brother is my brother-in-law:[85] because he is forbidden to me like my true brother? Again, stepfather and stepmother, who would best suit the category of a father and mother created by law, are not called father-in-law or mother-in-law before the sixteenth century, and the designation never quite stuck to them.[86] Last but not least, the earliest instance—about 1250—of the use of "in-law" is wife-in-law, signifying a lawfully married woman. It antedates the other uses by at least half a century. It might perhaps be argued that this is an accident of transmission. The fact remains that wife-in-law is very ancient, and that the explanation of the *New English Dictionary* does not

---

83. E.g., Cicero, *Off.* 2.62; Quintilian, *Inst.* 2.15.31; *Declamations* 376 at the beginning.

84. This account is given under "brother-in-law" (first in alphabetical order), *New English Dictionary* 1, ed. by Murray (1888), 1133. For the remaining in-laws, and also under the heading of "in-law," vol. 5, ed. by Murray (1901), 306, we are referred back to this basic entry.

85. Brother-in-law is among the early in-laws: AD 1300. See *New English Dictionary*, s.v. "brother-in-law."

86. *New English Dictionary*, vol. 4, ed. by Bradley (1901), 99; vol. 6, pt. 2, ed. by Bradley (1908) 694.

fit at all. A wife-in-law, a lawfully married woman, is not a wife added by the law to a wife in blood or by nature. She is the one wife.[87]

The correct solution seems to be this. The term wife-in-law does in fact stand at the beginning. The noun wife at that time might denote any woman married or unmarried—as *Weib* still does in German. Therefore, where her status as legitimate spouse was to be stressed, she was described as wife-in-law, i.e., wife (woman) taken in the law of wedlock. Father-in-law, brother-in-law, and so on were formed by way of extension, the attribute "in-law" referring to the area of wedlock: father-in-law, brother-in-law meant father, brother, in the area of wedlock, father, brother, of the woman who is my lawful spouse—not father, brother, added by the law to father, brother, by nature. Gradually the noun wife became narrowed down to married woman, and wife-in-law dropped out. It was from then onwards that father-in-law and so on could be and sometimes were in joke or earnest represented as father by virtue of law as opposed to the natural.

In Monstrelet's *Chronicles*, written in the fifteenth century, there occurs the expression *père en la loi de marriage*: Jean Petit in his defense of John the Fearless in 1408 mentions that the latter was made the Dauphin's father in the law of marriage.[88] This fully chimes with my view that father-in-law originally means not a father *lege* or *iure* but a father in the area of wedlock, the lawfully wedded spouse's father. In the recently published *Oxford Dictionary of English Etymology*[89] the English "in-law" is said to be coined "after AN. [Anglo-Norman] *en ley*, OF. [Old French] *en loi (de mariage)*." I have not been able to trace any evidence for *en ley*, and the only evidence for *en loi* known to me is the passage from Monstrelet just adverted to.[90] Admittedly, even should there be in fact no further evidence,

---

87. Actually, we might see indirect attestation of wife-in-law as early as about 1230, in Haili Meidenhad, *Early English Text Society*, vol. 18, ed. Cockayne (1866), 21. Women weak enough to marry are here called such as "are in the law of wedlock." At least this passage provides additional justification for questioning the derivation of "in-law" from the forbidden degrees.

88. Monstrelet, *Chronicles*, bk 1, ch. 39 towards the beginning.

89. *Oxford Dictionary of English Etymology*, ed. Onions, Friedrichsen and Burchfield (1966), 476.

90. It is cited by Godefroy, *Dictionnaire de l'ancienne Langue Franchise*, vol. 5 (1888), 17, and, from there, by the *New English Dictionary*, vol. 6. In the latter entry, the phrase is

the possibility of a Norman-French provenance of "in-law" cannot be ruled out; it makes no difference to my main point. But it could also be that it is the English, well attested from the thirteenth century, which comes first and is responsible for the French. Jean Petit, incidentally, was a native of Normandy. Let me add that, if my explanation is correct, the English (or Norman-French) development is basically much closer to the German than has so far been assumed: *Schwiegervater, Schwiegersohn* mean father, son in the area of *Schwägerschaft*, of affinity through wedlock.

Extension by Interpreters and Moralists

The Praetor

It would be interesting to see whether, and how far, the Roman jurists deemed their reflections on statutory extension of a category applicable to extension of a category by way of interpretation. Interpretation can at times assume a near-legislative stance—*Wer ein Arier ist, bestimme ich,* said Göring[91]—in which event the problem might become quite similar. However, this is too big a field for this discussion.[91a]

A fortiori the field of morality, though inviting comparison, is too big. In general, in the sphere of morality, with no trial in prospect, considerable freedom is taken with the wrongs known to the law: they are apt to be more expansively conceived. *La propriété, c'est le vol,* says Proudhon, "property is theft," *Eigentum ist Raub.* It is noteworthy, however, that in the moral writings of the Romans, there is relatively little of this. Probably the most familiar ancient illustrations are from Rabbinic and New Testament literature. Here, the moralist will frequently oppose his wider notion to the lawyer's narrower one. Take these extensions of adultery and murder: "Thou shalt not commit adultery (Exodus 20:14,

---

attributed to the sixteenth century, presumably because Godefroy refers to a 1516 edition of Monstrelet. But it is already in the fifteenth-century copies and may actually go back to Jean Petit's address.

91. Following in the footsteps of Karl Lueger; see Keller, *The City Behind the Charm* (book review), *Sunday Times* of June 12, 1966, 28.

91A. See above, p. 278n67a for a reference to the various interpretations of "manifest theft."

Deuteronomy 5:17)—not even with the eye, not even in the heart";[92] "The eye of the adulterer waiteth for the twilight (Job 24:15)—lest you should think that only he who commits adultery with his body is called an adulterer by Scripture: he also who commits adultery with his eye is called an adulterer by Scripture";[93] "Whoever looks at (or, thinks about) a woman with desire is as if he had cohabited with her";[94] "Ye have heard thou shalt not commit adultery, but I say unto you that whosoever looketh on a woman to lust after her hath committed adultery with her already in his heart";[95] "He who puts his fellow to shame in public is like a shedder of blood";[96] "He who hates his fellow belongs to the shedders of blood";[97] "Ye have heard thou shalt not kill and whosoever shall kill shall be in danger of the judgment, but I say unto you that whosoever is angry with his brother without cause shall be in danger of the judgment."[98] Anyone guilty of the essential, wicked element of the crime is included. It may well be significant, however, that in none of these quotations do we meet a simple pronouncement "He who desires another man's wife is an adulterer," "He who hates his fellow is a murderer." There are little reservations: "is called such and such," "is as if," "has done so and so in his heart," "is like," "belongs to those who." Enough—I just wanted to remind readers of this province.

Yet another inquiry I skip. I might at this juncture compare the praetor's inability (in classical law) to change the civil law directly: "the praetor cannot make heirs," says Gaius, "though when he gives persons possession of the estate, they are established in the position of heirs."[99] But let me pass on to a very different theme.

92. *Mekhilta de-Rabbi Shimeon* 111.

93. *Leviticus Rabbah* 23, Resh Laqish.

94. Kalla 1.

95. Matt. 5:27f. On the half-interpretative, half-autonomous form of this saying, as well as 5:21f., to be quoted presently, See Daube, *The New Testament and Rabbinic Judaism* (1956), 55ff.

96. *Babylonian Baba Metzia* 58b.

97. *Derekh Erets Rabbah* 10, R. Eliezer ben Hyrcanus.

98. Matt. 5:21f.

99. Gaius 3.32.

12

Interference with the Past

Nineteen-Eighty-Four

The desire to reshape the past occurs in all spheres of life; I mean actually to reshape it—not merely to feign it different or to set it to rights now and for the future, but to interfere with yesterday, to make things that did not happen to have happened and vice versa. Rationally we know that what is done cannot be undone,[1] *quod factum est infectum fieri non potest, ce qui est fait ne peut être défait, man kann das Geschehene nicht ungeschehen machen.* But the very existence of this proverb in many languages testifies to the strength and ubiquity of the impossible hope: Lady Macbeth desperately wished it were otherwise.[2]

The Rabbis discourage a prayer such as that a sound of lamentation you hear from afar may not be over one dear to you, or that the child your wife is expecting may be male. The prayer is "vain": the victim over whom they lament is already in being, as is the sex of the child conceived, and even God cannot or will not undo or remake the past.[3]

---

1. But see Davy, "Time May Go Back in Faustian Universe" (reporting an article by Stannard in *Nature*), *Observer* of August 14, 1966, p. 1.

2. William Shakespeare, *Macbeth* 5.1.75.

3. *Mishnah Berakoth* 9:3; the Hebrew for "vain" is *shav'*. Opinions diverging in varying degrees are recorded in *Palestinian Berakoth* 14a, *Genesis Rabba* 72 on Gen. 30:21; none of them, however, reckons with a retroactive intervention on the part of God. This is not the place to raise the question whether, on a rigorously mechanistic-causal view of nature, one could ever pray for anything but a miracle.

This (apparent) restriction on God is an old theological conundrum.[4]
Yet people do pray in this way, "Let it not have happened," "Let me be
the prize-winner" (on going up to the notice board). It is precisely in the
religious world that time is often felt to be conquerable. Renewal of the
pristine creation, rebirth in conversion, are examples. "Behold, I create
new heavens and a new earth, and the former shall not be remembered,"
says the prophet.[5] "Though your sins be as scarlet, they shall be white as
snow"[6]—the promise here is of more than a writing off, they will never
have been; "I will allure her into the wilderness and she shall sing there
as in the days of her youth"[7]—this means a new beginning, with all that
ever clouded the marriage annihilated; and the prayer "renew our days
as of old"[8] longs for just this miracle. (Our "to wipe the slate clean" tends
in the same direction.) A convert to Judaism becomes a newborn child
in so real a sense that his previous bloodrelations are no longer related
to him: this affects the law of inheritance and he may also, for instance,
enter into what would otherwise be an incestuous marriage.[9] The Greeks
made a person returning from abroad after being reputed dead undergo
a rebirth, a custom modern treatises on Greek law assign to the section
about fictions.[10] Plutarch, who mentions the rite, would presumably have
agreed,[11] but one may wonder whether it was not once looked on as, let
us say, three-quarters real.

4. E.g., Abraham Tucker (Edward Search), *Light of Nature*, vol. 2, pt. 1 (1768), 196–
97, in a chapter on Omnipotence discusses "absolute impossibilities which appear such
even to Omnipotence itself, such as ... annihilating time and space, undoing past events or
producing contrary ones." His explanation is that "those things imply contradictions, and
contradictions are generally held to be no objects of power as their possibility would infer
a defect rather than an enlargement of power."

5. Isa. 65:17, taken up in Rev. 21:1.

6. Isa. 1:18.

7. Hos. 2:14f.

8. Lam. 5:21.

9. E.g., *Babylonian Yebamoth* 22a, 97bf., *Palestinian Yebamoth* 12a. For certain
modifications laid down in order that he should not think Judaism was lax in questions of
incest, see Daube, *The New Testament and Rabbinic Judaism*, 113. From the middle of the
third century the principle began to be undermined: this is behind the view R. Johanan
opposes to that of Resh Laqish, *Babylonian Yebamoth* 62a.

10. J. Walter Jones, *Law and Legal Theory of the Greeks* (1956), 306.

11. Plutarch, *Quaest. Rom.* 5:264Eff.; compare *Vit., Luc.* 18.1.

In history, we call an aetiological myth one that is invented *ex post facto* in explanation and, frequently, in support of an existing situation. To some extent the story of Jacob's struggle with the angel is of this type— explaining why the Israelites abstain from certain portions of an animal.[12] Often such myths support a right. We may think of the various biblical tales showing why, though of the twins Esau and Jacob the former was the firstborn, the latter's descendants must be superior to his: an oracle before they were born, an extraordinary occurrence at birth, Esau's sale of his birthright, Jacob's success in obtaining their father's blessing.[13] Genealogies furnish prominent instances of aetiology. "To return to our wethers," says Rabelais, "I say, that by the sovereign gift of heaven, the antiquity and genealogy of Gargantua hath been reserved for our use more full and perfect than any other except that of the Messias, whereof I mean not to speak; for it belongs not to my purpose, and the devils, that is to say, the false accusers and dissembled gospellers, will therein oppose me."[14]

Exactly what was the attitude—or better, were the attitudes, or still better, were and are the attitudes—of aetiologists to the past? It would be naive to think that the phenomenon is confined to antiquity. And what the Ministry of Truth will do in 1984, we know: "Who controls the past, controls the future, who controls the present, controls the past. Oceania was at war with Eurasia, therefore Oceania had always been at war with Eurasia. As short a time ago as February, the Ministry of Plenty had issued a promise that there would be no reduction of the chocolate ration during 1984; the chocolate ration was to be reduced; all that was needed was to substitute for the original promise a warning that it would probably be necessary to reduce the ration at some time in April." This will be "reality-control," when previous descriptions and predictions will not be "altered" but "rectified."[15]

Insofar as interpretation or reinterpretation of laws purports to conform to their true meaning, the problem is closely related. As early as under the *legis actio*, the Roman experts were prepared to let a man whose

12. Gen. 32:32.
13. Gen. 25:23; 25:26; 25:33; 27:1ff.
14. Rabelais, *Gargantua*, bk. 1, ch. 1, transl. Urquhart.
15. George Orwell, *Nineteen-Eighty-Four* (1949), 37ff.

vines, *vites*, had been cut down cash in a fine the XII Tables imposed on the cutting down of trees, *arbores*.[16] There is no study on interpretation that does not revel in the presentation of judgments attributing incredible meanings to the authoritative text. The Talmud has a scene where Moses visits R. Aqiba's academy (he died under Hadrian) and cannot follow the discussion; he is satisfied, however, when assured that their decisions do go back to his revelation at Sinai.[17] Irrebuttable evidence, irreversible judgments—in particular, annulments of acts gone through or ratifications of collusive litigation—may all produce remodellings of the heretofore; as when Catherine of Aragon "was divorced and the late marriage made of none effect."[18]

In the commoner legal disputes, the urge to intervene in the past normally aims at a negative—to undo what did happen rather than to put up what did not: people quarrel or go to law when they are dissatisfied with the course things have taken. (I am not pronouncing on how far the distinction is one of substance and not merely of aspect.) An expression like *restitutio in integrum*, "restoration to the untouched position," is significant: the praetor might grant it where a person's rights had been adversely affected by some event.[19] Similarly, if a Roman returned from captivity, he recovered *pristina iura*, "his pristine rights."[20] A man suspected of trying to get out of a bargain by denying it is rebuked: "You hope to be able by dissimulation to render this unmade," *speras potesse dissimulando infectum hoc reddere*.[21] The parties to a sale might from the start agree that if the price is not paid by a certain date, the object should be *inempta*, "unbought."[22] From the international field, there is the peace treaty concluded in 321 BC by the generals of the Roman army with the Samnites who held them blocked in the narrow Caudine pass. When the army was safely back at Rome, the senate repudiated the treaty as

16. Gaius 4.11. In the case recorded by Gaius plaintiff lost because he rested his claim on a statute speaking of *vites*—there was no such statute.

17. *Babylonian Menahoth* 29b. On some aspects of the question, see Daube, "Texts and Interpretation in Roman and Jewish Law," *Jewish Journal of Sociology* 3 (1961): 3ff.

18. Shakespeare, *Henry VIII* 4.1.

19. See Buckland, *Text-Book*, 3rd ed., ed. Stein (1963), 719.

20. By the special regulation of *postliminium*: Gaius 1.129.

21. Plautus, *Mostell.* 1017.

22. *Lex commissoria*, Digest 18.3.

unauthorized. The Samnites pleaded that such repudiation was fair only if Rome "restored those legions into the defile where they were surrounded": "let everything be as if it had not happened"—*restituat legiones, omnia pro infecto sint.*[23] There were indeed some Romans who took this view: the treaty could not be shaken off "unless all was restored to the Samnites just as it had been at Caudium," *nisi omnia Samnitis qualia apud Caudium fuissent restituerentur.*[24] Naturally, expediency prevailed over scruples.

In none of these cases, however, does the law step outside the boundaries of the rational. Though the desire may be for direct alteration of the past, fulfilment is a different matter. The limitations of the latter are clearly realized. One method by which effect was given to a *restitutio in integrum* was an *actio rescissoria*, advising the judge to deliver his verdict as if the damaging event had not occurred—an open admission of it.[25] A returned prisoner did not, for example, automatically recover possession and marriage, at least not in classical law, when these were regarded as primarily factual relations; Justinian, to whom marriage meant more, introduced some reforms.[26] An object which had become "unbought" might still have to be retransferred into the vendor's ownership.[27]

"And His Place Shall Know Him No More."

Especially in the political domain, the irrational may triumph. Let us look at what we might call *abolitio memoriae*, "abolition of a person's memory." (The ancient sources contain only the verbal form *abolere memoriam*, "to abolish a memory"; the step to the category "abolition of a memory" is not

---

23. Livy 9.11.3f.
24. Livy 9.8.14.
25. Buckland, *Text-Book*, 3rd ed., ed. Stein (1963), 723.
26. *Text-Book*, 67.
27. *Text-Book*, 497. Where the contract fell to the ground under a *lex commissoria*, the Sabinians gave *actio empti* or *venditi* to settle matters, the Proculians only an *actio in factum*. This controversy, however, does not represent a rational attitude to the past on the part of the Sabinians versus an irrational one on that of the Proculians. The latter simply argue that according to the agreed, retroactive, resolutive condition no sale has come about, whereas the former give contractual actions as soon as the orbit of sale is entered. See Daube, "Certainty of Price," *Studies in the Roman Law of Sale* (1959): 32–33.

yet taken.)[28] We may begin with a modern episode. In 1933, the Oxford Union passed a resolution "in no circumstances to fight for King and country." Randolph Churchill, disgusted, moved, not another resolution to revoke this one, but a private business measure—to expunge the offending resolution from the records. Evidently, he tried to cause it not to have happened. Before his proposal could be debated (when it finally was, it was defeated), wilder men sharing his feelings tore the page from the minute book and burnt it at the Martyrs' Memorial.[29]

At Rome, the elimination of a ruler might be followed by a rescission of his decrees and the overthrow of his statutes. (There is ample discussion in modern literature of *rescissio actorum*,[30] but, again, the sources contain only the verbal *rescindere acta*.) So far so good: these are actions to reject and improve upon the past, not to influence it directly. The cutting out of the hated man's name from inscriptions goes further; and in some cases he was removed even from the *fasti*, the official calendar showing, for example, the years when he had occupied the consulate. He had never been, or at least never been in those positions of honor. The first case for which this extreme measure is evidenced is that of Marc Antony in 30 BC It is interesting that Hirschfeld, writing in the second half of the nineteenth century, found it difficult to accept that a sober chronological State register could be treated thus, getting a hole torn into it.[31]

28. It is curious that Vittinghoff, while aware that *damnatio memoriae* is modern— the sources speaking only of *damnare memoriam*—does not seem to notice that the same is true of *abolitio memoriae*. There is much to be said, however, for his contention that *damnare memoriam* refers not to the condemnation, abolition, of a person's memory but to the posthumous sentencing of a person guilty of *perduellio*: *Der Staatsfeind in der Römischen Kaiserzeit* (1936), 12–13, 47, 64ff.

29. Hollis, *The Oxford Union* (1965), 187. I asked some experts in Union affairs what would have happened if the page had not been illegally torn out and Churchill's proposal had been approved. They think that probably the page would have been not torn out, but crossed out with two huge strokes, though a tearing out would not be inconceivable.

30. E.g., Vittinghoff, *Der Staatsfeind in der Römischen Kaiserzeit* (1936), 91ff.

31. Hirschfeld, "Die Kapitolinischen Fasten," *Hermes* 9 (1875), 93: *Die Kapitolinischen Consularfasten sind keine Ehrendenkmäler, sondern ein historisches Dokument: wollte man eine vollständige Eponymenliste herstellen, so mussten auch diejenigen Männer, die geächtet waren, darin eine Stelle finden.* On 93 he does consider the conceivability (*denkbar*) of omission. Compare Mommsen's reply in the same volume, *Die Capitolinischen Magistraturtafeln*, 273ff.

Already Cicero in 56 BC, in his speech *Pro Sestio*, said of the consuls of two years before: "those consuls, if they are to be called consuls who there is nobody but thinks should be torn out not only from human memory but also from the *fasti*."[32] Translators are apt to tone it down, rendering, for example, "whose names" instead of "who" ought to be torn out.[33] Mommsen remarks that this remained a *frommer Wunsch*, a "pious wish."[34] This is true but it is not all. Three things may be deduced. First, as early as then, a quarter of a century before the suppression of Marc Antony, the possibility of such a procedure was at least in people's minds, whether or not it was in that epoch ever carried into practice.[35] Secondly, it was clearly realized that expunction from the *fasti* went beyond expunction from memory: "torn out not only from memory but also from the *fasti*."[36] Indeed, this way of putting it suggests that the more radical idea was rather novel at the time. Thirdly, the Orwellian effect of such reality control did not escape Cicero. On erasure, these men would never have held their rank: "if they are to be called consuls who should be torn out from the *fasti*." One is strongly reminded of the rewriting in 1984 of a piece in praise of Comrade Withers after he has become an "unperson."[37] Mommsen, incidentally, did perceive that men might want to make an impact on the past. In discussing the rescission of decrees, which can rarely be carried out in full, he observes: "It is simply impossible to make what has happened unhappened; and if political passion refuses to recognize this, the practical conduct of affairs will bring it back to it with absolute inevitability."[38] (I do not know whether anybody has

32. Cicero, *Pro Sestio* 14.33: *eidemque consules, si appellandi sunt consules quos nemo est quin non modo ex memoria sed etiam ex fastis evellendos putet.*

33. Gardner, *Cicero, Pro sestio* and *in Vatinium* (Loeb Classical Library, 1958), 77.

34. Mommsen, *Röm. Staatsr.*, vol. 3, pt. 2, (1888), 1191.

35. Vittinghoff, *Der Staatsfeind in der Römischen Kaiserzeit* (1936), 24, suspects that it was; I incline to think it was not.

36. Even at an earlier point in the speech, 7.17, Cicero pretends to hesitation to call them consuls, this time because of their treasonable activities—which are, of course, the reason they ought to vanish from the *fasti*.

37. Orwell, *Nineteen-Eighty-Four* (1949). I have seen a painting of a congress with a head which had once been there taken off: that man was not at the congress.

38. Mommsen, *Röm. Saatsr.*, vol. 2, pt. 2, 3rd ed. (1887), 1132: *Geschehenes ungeschehen zu machen ist eben nicht möglich; und wenn die politische Leidenschaft dies nicht gelten lassen will, führt die praktische Handhabung der Geschäfte sie mit zwingender Notwendigkeit darauf zurück.*

made a study of how much and which portions of Hitler's, Mussolini's, Stalin's new order survived the author's disgrace. I daresay the—very substantial—remnants might be divided into three kinds: such as it is practically impossible to get rid of—Mommsen's case; such as one has to concede are worth preserving; and such as, though unworthy, there is not the will to get rid of.)

It would be instructive to investigate Cicero's handlings of unpleasant occurrences in general. For instance, he regrets that a good man's downfall cannot be dismissed from memory;[39] he is sure—in the lifetime of Marc Antony—that even if the senate revoked all decrees and judgments against him, the memory of his crimes would live on;[40] he proposes to a friend that certain misunderstandings be wiped out from all their memory and lives;[41] and he declares that the sad time when he was on hostile terms with Caesar, though he cannot erase it from *rerum natura*, the realm of reality, yet he will erase it from his *animus*, heart.[42] Doubtless he knew that one can only approximate an enemy's retrospective degradation or annihilation, not achieve it. His language in regard to expunction from the *fasti* is all the more remarkable.

I am convinced that Hellenistic-Oriental influences are responsible for the removal of names from inscriptions and *fasti*. In the East this kind of thing went on from very early times.[43] The book, or book of remembrance, in which, according to the Old Testament, God inscribes those acceptable and from which he blots out those unacceptable may well be conceived in analogy to customs at earthly courts.[44] (Commentators seem to think of this book as quite in *vacuo*. Moreover they fail to appreciate its full significance; to be blotted out, for example, means no more—they

39. Cicero, *Planc.* 70.

40. Cicero, *Phil.* 12.5.12f.

41. Cicero, *Fam.* 5.8.3.

42. Cicero, *De provinciis consularibus* 18.43. The relation between forgiving and forgetting is as intricate as important. Two propositions for debate: women forgive but don't forget; old men forget but don't forgive.

43. Examples are cited by Vittinghoff, *Der Staatsfeind in der Römischen Kaiserzeit* (1936), 18–19. He leaves the question of influence open: 25. How far these Oriental excisions were designed to interfere with the past I shall not here examine.

44. Exod. 32:32f., Isa. 4:3; Mal. 3:16; Ps. 69:28; Dan. 12:1.

assume—than to be prevented from reaching the normal span of life.)[45] The destruction of a person's or group's memory is common:"I will utterly put out the remembrance of Amalek from under heaven."[46] (A modern specimen of a wish for the abolition of a person's memory—the wisher's own—is met in C.P. Snow's *The Light and The Dark*: "'I hate myself,' said Roy.'I've brought unhappiness to everyone I've known. It would have been better if I'd never lived. I should be wiped out so that everyone could forget me.'")[47] The Oriental inspiration of the actions following Marc Antony's death is confirmed by the fact that even the names of other members of his clan were erased, a collective annihilation unique in Roman history but familiar in the East.[48] Considering that his association with an Egyptian woman was a major cause of the resentment against him, it is ironical that here for the first time at Rome (or at least pretty much the first time) the authorities resorted to punitive steps ultimately, it looks, deriving from Egypt. Augustus had the excisions from the *fasti* restored, and indeed both he and Tiberius made it clear that there should be no meddling with the *fasti*.[49] Maybe their motive was not only clemency or a conciliatory purpose or consideration for the practical use of the *fasti*, but also disapprobation of irrational foreign ideas.

Recognition of Freeborn Citizen Wrongfully Kept Down

In the Republic you could free a slave, but there was no one who could make him freeborn. To be sure, already in that period, there was room for circumventing the limitation. It happened that a person, though in truth free, was mistakenly treated as a slave, a *bona fide serviens*; say, he was kidnapped and sold. The comedies of Plautus are full of men and, above all,

45. E.g., Coert Rylaardsdam, *The Book of Exodus*, in *The Interpreter's Bible* 1 (1952), 1: 1069–70; Noth, *Exodus*, trans. by Bowden (1962), 251.

46. Exod. 17:1.

47. Snow, *The Light and the Dark* (Penguin). (III The Last Attempt, 243, Self-Hatred, 28).

48. See Mommsen, *Hermes* 9:276; Vittinghoff *Der Staatsfeind in der Römischen Kaiserzeit* (1936), 21ff.

49. Vittinghoff, *Der Staatsfeind in der Römischen Kaiserzeit* (1936).

women in this condition. In such a case there might be litigation, when the judge would decide that the person was free and indeed freeborn; and let us note that even if the person was already "manumitted" by his supposed master, he might want a verdict recognizing his status—he was not a freedman, with all the disabilities that that implied, he was freeborn.[50] So far so good. But suppose now that it was a question of a person in reality a slave or a freedman, yet the judge was misled or even deliberately found in favor of his freebornship. We know of collusive procedure in this field in later times;[51] it is quite conceivable that it took place from very early. Here, evidently, so long as the fraud remained undetected, a person not freeborn would nevertheless achieve that rank.

However, the analysis of the situation would be perfectly rational, with no denial of the past: the jurists saw the facts in much the same light as they are seen today. The late classic Ulpian remarks in this or a similar context that "a matter judged is accepted as the truth," *res iudicata pro veritate accipitur*. He does not say that it is the truth; it counts as such for purposes of the law.[52]

The Empire brought changes, though they were extremely gradual. From the outset, the "golden rings," symbol of knighthood, might be bestowed on a freedman, who thereby acquired in public life the rights of a freeborn citizen.[53] It is important to realize, however, that he was not on this account looked on as literally freeborn: *ut ingenuus habetur*, "he is treated as freeborn,"[54] *ingenuus intellegitur*, "he is considered as freeborn," that is to say, for certain purposes[55]—that is all. Actually, in private life his position remained legally inferior: his former master retained all privileges

50. Compare Institutes 1.41; Theophilus 1.4.1; Code 7.14.4, *Diocletian and Maximian*, AD 293.

51. See Mayer-Maly, "Collusio im Zivilprozess," ZRG 71 (1954): 264ff.; see Daube, "Zur Palingenesie einiger Klassikerfragmente," ZRG 76 (1959): 254–55.

52. Digest 1.5.25, 50.17.207, *I ad legem Juliam et Papiam*. Compare his sober observation on a judgment concerning paternity in Digest 25.3.1.16, 3 pr., *XXXIV ad edictum*.

53. Mommsen, *Röm. Saatsr.* vol. 2, pt. 2, 3rd ed. (1887), 892ff., 517ff.; Duff, *Freedmen in the Early Roman Empire* (1928) 86ff., 214ff. On the whole I follow Duff, but on several points I differ from him as well as from Mommsen.

54. Digest 40.10.5, *Paul IX ad legem Juliam et Papiam*.

55. Digest 40.10.6, *Ulpian I ad legem juliam et Papiam*, with reference to a rescript by Hadrian.

of a patron, and above all some hold on the inheritance. (I am disregarding voluntary arrangements by which a patron could give up his claims.) *Vivit quasi ingenuus, moritur quasi libertus,* "he lives as one freeborn, he dies as a freedman."[56] Until the reign of Commodus[57] it is still true to say that it was not possible to turn one not freeborn into one freeborn with such effect that *ingenuus fit,* "he becomes freeborn."[58]

Let us look at some relevant incidents. Augustus admitted only freeborn guests to formal dinners—with the exception, Suetonius tells us, of Menas, a Greek, who had once been a freedman admiral of Sextus Pompey's, but had gone over to Augustus. Even he, Suetonius adds, was invited only after a judgment that he was freeborn.[59] *Asserere in ingenuitatem,* "to assert into freebornship," is technical of the appropriate trial,[60] and it is quite wrong to treat this term as implying an imperial grant.[61] Maybe the evidence was not scrutinized too carefully. But we

56. Digest 38.2.3, *Ulpian XI ad edictum.* Mommsen thinks that this was not always so. But his evidence is weak. He refers to Pliny the Younger, *Ep.* 8.6.4, where the senate is reported as voting that Pallas, a freedman of Claudius, should be not only entreated but compelled to wear "the golden rings." Mommsen argues that Pallas refused "the rings" in order to keep Claudius as patron—ergo he would have lost him had he accepted them. The text, however, contains no hint at this specific motivation; Pallas is depicted as of a general fake humility—he also refused money voted to him by the senate. In fact, whereas in the end he did accept "the rings," he never took the money (Epistles 7.29.1, 8.6.1, 8ff.). Mommsen is probably influenced by Tacitus, *Ann.* 12.53.3, where the senate thanks Pallas for consenting to remain among the *ministri,* "servants," of Claudius. The splendid thing Pallas does, however, is to continue in the public offices (*usui publico,* "for the welfare of the State") reserved for freedmen. The matter of a patron's private rights is certainly not in the senators' minds. Not to mention the fact that this passage is quite unconnected with Pallas's refusal of "the rings": it contemplates a judicial recognition of freebornship he might have gained—see *infra,* 60. Admittedly, if it were recognized that he had never been a slave, only believed to be one, he would have no patron; but this has nothing to do with "the rings."

57. Or possibly the close of that of Marcus Aurelius: see below, p. 305n100, on Digest 40.11.3, *Scaevola VI responsorum.*

58. See below, p. 310n112, on Digest 40.11.2, *Marcian I institutionum.*

59. Suetonius, *Aug.* 74.

60. Compare below, pp. 300–1, on Suetonius, *Vesp.* 3; also Suetonius, *Tib.* 2.2, referring to the wicked decemvir who attempted "to assert a freeborn virgin into slavery," *virginem ingenuam in servitutem asserere.*

61. This is done by Duff, *Freedmen in the Early Roman Empire* (1928), 87.

must not rule out the chance[62] that he was really freeborn and had been carried off and sold by gangsters or pirates. The risk of such capture is a recurrent theme in the historians of the early Empire;[63] and the fact that stories of this sort figure prominently in the fraudulent claims to freebornship retailed in the sources[64] is additional proof that the thing did occur—otherwise it would have been no use as a story. In his treatise *On Grammarians* Suetonius has a chapter on Gnipho, whom Cicero is said to have respected: he was born, we learn, in Gaul of free parents, *ingenuus natus*, but cast out, *expositus*, though his foster father set him free, a *nutritore manumissus*.[65]

Dio's comment on the elevation of Menas is different: Augustus gave him "the golden rings," thus lifting him above the condition of a freedman.[66] That Menas received "the rings" is not unlikely. But in confining himself to the mention of this distinction Dio is influenced by the less rigorous notions prevalent in his era. For Augustus, that would not have been enough; if it had been, there would be no point in the notice that he entertained only freeborn guests—he could simply have conferred "the rings" on anyone he fancied. Suetonius, who on this occasion names his source, Valerius Messala Corvinus, a contemporary of the events in question, is clearly right: the decisive factor in Menas's inclusion among the freeborn was the finding of the judge, honest or dishonest, that he was in fact entitled to it.

Appian, though simplifying somewhat, furnishes corroboration: Augustus "declared Menodorus (Menas) free (freeborn) from being a freedman."[67] This basically coincides with Suetonius: in accordance with the Emperor's wishes it was established that Menas was freeborn. White's rendering, Augustus "made" him freeborn, may be good English but is not exact.[68] To "make" a freedman freeborn was not—not yet—feasible.

---

62. As is done by Mommsen, Röm. Staatsr. vol. 2, pt. 2 (1887), 893; vol. 3, pt. 1, 519.

63. E.g., Suetonius, *Aug.* 32; *Tib.* 8.

64. See Mayer-Maly, "Collusio im Zivilprozess," ZRG 71 (1954), 254f.

65. Suetonius, *Gramm. et rhet.* 7. This may again be invention; even as such it would indicate the range of what might occur.

66. Dio 48.45.7ff.

67. Appian, *Bella civilia* 5.80. Appian, like Suetonius, used the work of Valerius Messala Corvinus: see Hanslik, *RE* vol. 8 (1955), 156.

68. Appian's *Roman History* 4 (Loeb. Classical Library, 1961), 513.

The Greek is *apephenen*, "declared," in the sense of "had him declared," or "found," freeborn.

Nero had a hand in two dubious promotions to freebornship. A favorite actor of his, who had been a slave of his aunt Domitia and had bought his freedom from her, with the help of the Emperor's influence succeeded in recovering the money on the ground that he had been a *bona fide serviens*, a free person erroneously kept as a slave.[69] Whether, as is generally assumed,[70] there were two trials, the first to get his status recognized and the second to recover the money, or whether, as is also thinkable, there was only one, about the money, which implicitly settled the question of status as well, is immaterial here. In either case it was the verdict of a court which, with whatever degree of partiality, established his free birth. A conferment of "the rings" would not have served. It did not make a freedman freeborn; it left the former master's position intact, and Domitia could have kept her money.

Then there was Acte, whom Nero for a time thought of marrying, in full *matrimonium iustum*. According to Suetonius she was just an Asian freedwoman, but Nero bribed high dignitaries to swear that she was *regio genere orta*, "offspring of a royal house."[71] That is to say, she or, say, her mother had been abducted and illegally reduced to a servile condition. This account, then, with the oath of witnesses purchased, clearly makes Nero procure a judicial pronouncement concerning her status. Claudius's freedman Pallas, in the view of the flattering senate, could also have obtained a judgment establishing his free birth: he too was (gave himself out as) of old royal descent. Only he was so selfless as to prefer to remain an imperial freedman and perform the functions appropriate to this rank.[72]

Dio says that *esechthe* into the house of Attalus.[73] This is capable of various interpretations. It may mean that "she was assigned" to that royal house, in the sense in which Suetonius represents Nero as foisting her on it, by means of a fraudulent trial. Some authorities, however, translate "she

69. Tacitus, *Ann.* 13.19, 27; Digest 12.4.3.5, *Ulpian XXVI ad edictum.*

70. Tacitus, *Ann.* 13.27 favors this alternative. See, e.g., Boyé, "Pro Petronia Iusta," *Mélanges Lévy-Bruhl* 32 (1959).

71. Suetonius, *Nero* 28.1.

72. Tacitus, *Ann.* 12.53.3; see above, p. 297n56.

73. Dio 61.7.1.

was adopted."[74] That would have been a different method, not a judgment confirming her noble provenance, but a covering up of her servile birth by incorporating her in a great family. It is possible that Nero considered or even resorted to both devices, adoption as well as a trial concerning her status.[75] At all events, neither Suetonius nor Dio is speaking of a grant of freebornship.

Of Vespasian's wife Suetonius tells us[76] that, prior to her marriage, she was found freeborn and a Roman citizen by a court. As for her citizenship, she was a native of Ferentum, hence a Latin by birth. Her father, however, was elected to some municipal office, which apparently in the court's view entitled him and his descendents to Roman citizenship.[77] To be sure, from Suetonius's language it may be gathered that the particular office he occupied was not normally sufficient to ground Roman citizenship. A municipal quaestor would be high enough,[78] but her father, Suetonius says, "was nothing more than a quaestor's clerk." Whether the court let it go at that or whether it assumed (rightly or wrongly) that he had risen higher it is impossible to decide.

Now we come to the part of the verdict recognizing her as freeborn. Why had this fact to be confirmed? Maybe the form of a trial to establish citizenship routinewise included the question of *ingenuitas*; or maybe Vespasian wished it confirmed from general caution. But I could also think of a more specific reason. The lady had been another man's *delicata*. Such a position was often held by a slave or freedwoman. It may, therefore,

74. E.g., Cary, *Dio's Roman History* 8 (Loeb Classical Library, 1961), 41.

75. Far be it from me to enter into the problems arising if we think of adoption. The first question is whether there was a suitable Attalid around to adopt her; Ronald Syme assures me that there was. But then, as it was presumably a case of arrogation, could a woman be arrogated? Could a freedman (freedwoman) be arrogated with all the legal effects Nero desired? I shall not say a word—except this, that the violent statement of Sabinus transmitted by Gellius 5.19.12 may have been directed against precisely this scheme of Nero's: "But this is neither permitted nor ever to be permitted, that persons of the condition of freedmen should invade the rights of the freeborn." If this is an anti-Neronian utterance, it was hardly made under Nero. We know that Sabinus lived to comment on the senatusconsult *Neronianum* of 64 BC Nero died in 68. Sabinus could still have lived.

76. Suetonius, *Vesp.* 3.

77. See, e.g., Gaius 1.96.

78. E.g., Strabo 4.1.12.186f.

have been advisable to prevent any untoward suspicions. It is noteworthy that it was her father who performed the requisite *asserere*, "asserting," in the trial:[79] that would show that there was nothing to hide. The relevant deduction is that the story contains no vestige of a grant of freebornship: a person actually freeborn has the fact established by a judgment.[80]

A letter of the younger Pliny to Trajan has been seriously misconstrued.[81] Pliny was administering Bithynia as Trajan's legate, though ordinarily this province would have been under a proconsul; and in view of a certain senatusconsult he was doubtful whether, not being a proconsul, he had the right to sit *de agnoscendis liberis restituendisque natalibus*, "in cases concerning children to be acknowledged and birth to be restored." This means litigation about paternity and freebornship— litigation, that is, as to whether or not, in certain circumstances, a man has to acknowledge a child as his,[82] or as to whether or not a man, hitherto considered a slave or a freedman, may have his free birth established. Literally, it is "birth" without "free," or even more literally, "native conditions": *natales*. The point is that only free birth is birth, a slave has no birth, no native conditions—a bit as, in English, only a gentleman has a *gens*, a family.[83] The addition of *mei, tui, sui* to *natales*, incidentally, is not uncommon:[84] it is a question of the birth, the native conditions, of the individual concerned, "my," "your," "his" birth.[85]

---

79. See above, p. 295n60.

80. Very misleading, therefore, is the account of Stein, "Flavia Domitilla," *RE*, 6 (1909) 2731, who writes that Roman citizenship was *zuerkannt*, "assigned," to her after her trial. Not to mention his description of the trial as a *Freiheitsprozess*, as if it had been a question of her freedom. Schmidlin, *Das Rekuperatorenverfahren* (1963), 90–91, like Stein, expresses himself as if the procedure had been one by which she became a citizen (*Bürgerrechtsverleihung, sie sollte römische Vollbürgerin werden*). At least, however, he clearly represents her as of free Latin birth. Fortunately, the error has no bearing on the main propositions of his book.

81. Pliny the Younger, *Ep.* 10.72; Trajan's reply in 10.73.

82. See title 25.3 of the Digest.

83. Martial 10.27.4 tells the freedman Diodorus that, notwithstanding his sumptuous birthday celebration, *nemo tamen natum te putat*, "nobody believes you born"; see Duff, *Freedmen in the Early Roman Empire* (1928), 68 and 86–87.

84. E.g., *de natalibus suis restituendis* in Trajan's reply, Pliny 10.73, *natales tui* in Code 4.19.10, *Diocletian and Maximian*, AD 293.

85. See, however, below, p. 310, on Digest 40.11.2, *Marcian I institutionum*.

The current interpretation is that Pliny is thinking of a grant of freebornship to persons of servile birth.[86] This is an anachronism; as already indicated, it was not before Commodus, some seventy-five years after Trajan, that a man of servile birth might be directly, openly turned into one of free birth. And it was in consequence of this innovation that *natales suos restituere*, "to restore an individual's free birth," came to denote "to confer free birth on one not freeborn." I shall of course say more about this.

That Pliny has in mind, not a grant of freebornship, but a judicial pronouncement on a man's status at birth is obvious. First, there is the pairing off of this procedure with that concerning paternity—surely not a grant of paternity (in most cases the man does not want to be the father) but a lawsuit to end in a finding.[87] In fact there is a definite link between the two procedures: the result of that concerning paternity is likely to bear on a later one concerning status. Secondly, Pliny asks whether he might *cognoscere*, in these matters: "find," not "make grants."[88] Thirdly, when, considerably later, the grant of freebornship to persons of servile birth became customary, it always remained the prerogative of the Emperor; it was never within a proconsul's competence. Yet Pliny reports to Trajan that people press him to deal with these cases *secundum exempla proconsulum*, "according to the practice of proconsuls."

The picture resulting from the interpretation here combated is indeed astonishing—proconsuls regularly receiving requests from slaves or freedmen to endow them with freebornship and making or declining the grant. One asks oneself what makes modern commentators thus fasten on the secondary sense of *natales suos restituere*. I suppose one factor is that the original, literal sense in which Pliny still employs the expression is not mentioned by Mommsen.[89] The initial error has produced some major consequential ones; as when Hardy explains that "the phrase was based

86. E.g., Melmoth, *Pliny, Letters* 2 (Loeb Classical Library, 1963), 372.

87. The term *agnoscere*, incidentally, "to acknowledge," conspicuous in connection with paternity, is also applied to the "acknowledgment" of an apparent freedman's true, free origin: Digest 40.14.3 pr., *Pomponius V senatus consultorum* (for the understanding of which passage it is useful to consult Code 7.14.1, *Alexander*, between AD 222 and 235).

88. The term recurs in Trajan's reply, 10.73.

89. Mommsen, *Röm. Saatsr.* vol. 2, pt. 2 (1887), 894. In fact he does not quote the letter at all—nor does Duff. For another factor making for confusion, see below, p. 313.

on the theory that the original condition of men was one of freedom."[90] This is to turn things upside down. At its inception, the phrase was quite pedestrian, referring to the trial by which a freeborn man whose status was denied him regained—or more precisely, had reconfirmed— what was his by virtue of his origin. From Commodus, it signified more and more, though even then never exclusively,[91] the Emperor's grant of freebornship to a man not freeborn. It was this usage which, we shall see, at the end of the classical era, was brought into relation with, supported by, the doctrine of universal freedom in the golden age. To place the doctrine at the beginning is to credit the rulers of the first and second centuries AD with a magnanimous visionary policy of which they were plainly innocent.[92]

Creation of a Freeborn Citizen by the Emperor

Under Marcus Aurelius there was a crisis. Difficulties of proof in trials about freebornship were felt to be so awkward that the Emperor ordered registration of freeborn children in both Rome and the provinces.[93] In the meantime, no doubt, benevolent as he was, he often as a judge pronounced in favor of free birth where the evidence was less than conclusive. It is from the reign of his successor Commodus onwards[94] that we come across in the texts a grant of freebornship by the Emperor to persons avowedly born in slavery.[95]

The term *natales suos restituere* henceforth signifies two things. On the one hand, it continues in its original meaning, "to restore a person's

90. Quoted by Melmoth, *Pliny, Letters* 2 (Loeb Classical Library, 1963), 372.

91. See, e.g., below, p. 304, on Digest 40.11.1, *Ulpian II responsorum.*

92. Leist, "Das römische Patronatsrecht," pt. 2, in *Glück, Ausführliche Erläuterung der Pandecten,* Serie der Bücher 37/8 pt. 5 (1879) 311–12, comes nearer the correct evolution of the meanings of the phrase.

93. Julius Capitolinus, SHA, *Marcus Antoninus* 9.7ff.

94. Conceivably from the end of that of Marcus Aurelius himself: see below, p. 305n100.

95. How this innovation is connected with the change in the "right of the golden rings," which (if Mommsen is right, *Rom. Staatsr.* vol. 2, pt. 2 [1887], 893–94) from Commodus no longer implied a knighthood, I shall not here investigate; see, however, Novellae 89.1 pr..

free birth, free native conditions," on the other, it now can mean "to confer free birth, free native conditions, on a person of servile birth." If the latter meaning is the more frequent in our sources, that may be simply because it raises more problems, is of greater interest to legal writers, not necessarily because it predominated in actual life. At any rate, the former sense is met, and indeed, the lawyers are fully alive to the difference between the two functions. Naturally, once there was the grant in addition to the judicial finding, the latter, whenever proceeding from the Emperor, must assume some of the former's coloring. Even so, Ulpian transmits the decision that if a person is "restored to his free birth" by the Emperor on the strength of a false affirmation of free birth, the act is vitiated.[96] This is plainly a "restoring" in the sense of judicial or quasi-judicial establishment of the status to which, if he is telling the truth, the man is entitled.[97] By contrast, the new *natales suos restituere* by way of a grant is designed precisely for a man whose servile birth is admitted.[98]

96. Digest 40.11.1, *Ulpian II responsorum*. Instead of "to restore an individual's free birth," *natales suos restituere*, it is not unusual to say "to restore an individual to his free birth," *natalibus suis restituere*; e.g., Digest 40.11.3, *Scaevola VI responsorum*, with reference to a grant of freebornship. The passive designation "restored to free birth" recurs in Code 6.8.2, *Diocletian and Maximian*, AD 294, also concerned with a grant. The nominal phrase *natalium restitutio*, "restoration of free birth," does not seem to be in use before Justinian: see below, p. 314.

97. In *Cod. Theod.* 15.14.4, Constantine, AD 326, the senate is to judge about the reinstatement of such as contend that they were arbitrarily degraded by Constantine's rival Licinius and wish *natalibus suis restitui*, "to be restored to their native conditions." In *Cod. Theod.* 5.8.1, Constantine, AD 314, *natalibus suis restituere* signifies the factual, extrajudicial restoring of a person to his position of a freeborn citizen of which he was wrongfully deprived under Constantine's rival Maxentius.

98. *Natales redere*, "to return free birth," is synonymous with *natales restituere*. The passive designation *natalibus redditus*, "returned to free birth," implies a grant of freebornship in Digest 39.2.3.1, *Ulpian XII ad edictum*. In a much later text, Code 8.50.13, *Diocletian and Maximian*, AD 294, *natales pristinos reddere*, "to return the pristine free birth," means the recognition of a true free birth. So does *ingenuitati suae reddere*, "to return somebody to his freebornship," in Code 7.14.4, *Diocletian and Maximian*, AD 293. In the *Interpretatio ad Cod. Theod.* 5.8.1 (see the preceding footnote) *ingenuitati reddere* signifies the extrajudicial handing back of a man to his freeborn position. In *Novella Maioriani* 7.5, AD 458, *natalibus suis reddere* signifies the extrajudicial handing back of a decurion's (municipal councillor's) daughter to the oppressive native dignity.

How was this grant construed? How was this correction of a man's origin by means of imperial privilege viewed? Inevitably a large element of fiction, of "as if," of conscious treatment of x as y, always remained. But in quite a few texts we can discern also something of an assumption that, supernaturally, the man was indeed changed. In some cases of legal personality, however different the historical background, we might come across parallels, but I shall not enlarge on them. One ought to remember, however, the enormous claims of certain Emperors, Commodus among them, who thought of Rome as his foundation, *colonia Commodiana*.[99]

The earliest comment we have is from Scaevola.[100] He is relatively cautious. Consulted as to whether a man whom the Emperor "has restored to his free birth" enjoys *ingenuitatis ius*, "the right of freebornship," he lays down that the recipient of this *beneficium*, "privilege," *ad omnem ingenuitatis statum restitui eum*, "is indeed restored to the complete status of freebornship." The consultation itself shows that *natales restituere* by way of a privilege, *beneficium*, is a novelty at this moment, with effects not yet universally familiar. Scaevola's construction is just within the boundaries of the rational: "the complete status of freebornship" need imply no more than treatment by the law of a person not freeborn as one freeborn, full concession to an outsider of the legal position normally reserved.for a group. Where Scaevola exaggerates is in maintaining that the extent of the grantee's rights is so obvious that the questioner need not have asked at all: "But[101] this point neither suffers nor has ever suffered any doubt, that it is established that he is restored to the complete status of freebornship." Such overemphasis is common precisely where serious doubts did or do exist but cannot be admitted; that is to say, it is not enough to refute them

---

99. Aelius Lampridius, SHA, *Commodus Antonius* 8.6ff., Dio 72.15.2; compare Pharaoh's boast "Mine is the Nile and I have made it," Ezek. 29:3, 9.

100. Digest 40.11.3, *VI responsorum*. If Scaevola was no longer alive or active under Commodus, this opinion must go back to the previous reign; I prefer a date under Commodus, but there is no evidence. *Respondit: quaeris an ingenuitatis iure utatur is quem sanctissimus et nobilissimus imperator natalibus suis restituit. sed ea res nec dubitationem habet nec umquam habuit, quin exploratum sit ad omnem ingenuitatis statum restitui eum qui isto beneficio principis utatur.* "He replied: You ask whether he whom the most sacred and noble Emperor has restored to his native conditions enjoys the right of freebornship. But this point neither suffers nor has ever suffered any doubt, that it is established that he who enjoys that imperial privilege is restored to the complete status of freebornship."

101. This "but" itself characterizes the question as unnecessary.

or declare them groundless, their very existence must be denied. Gaius uses the same method when he asserts: "nor has it ever been doubted that a decree of the Emperor has the force of a statute."[102] In Stalin's last years, it was not doubted, nor had there ever been any doubt, that he was the man by whom Lenin wanted to be succeeded. The Preamble to the *Constitution of Ghana*, 1960, says: "We the People of Ghana . . . in exercise of our undoubted right to appoint for ourselves the means whereby we shall be governed . . ."

Schulz declares 40.11.3 "a text assuredly postclassical both in form and substance": it does not show Scaevola's usual division into facts, question and reply, it is theoretical instead of dealing with a specific practical case, and question and reply are both unintelligible.[103] I admit that the original is shortened, probably in order to achieve what Schulz calls "theory," generalization. With this reservation, the *responsum* fits the state of law in Scaevola's later years better than any other period. As for unintelligibility, I hope I have removed that.

According to Ulpian, a freedman who receives "the golden rings" still owes reverence to his patron though he may occupy *omnia ingenuitatis munia*, "all public offices of freebornship"; but if he is "restored to free birth, free native conditions," the duty is gone since *princeps ingenuum facit*, "the Emperor makes a freeborn man."[104] That this opinion has regard, not to the judicial recognition of a true *ingenuus*, but to the privilege discussed by Scaevola, the grant of *ingenuitas* to one not in truth freeborn, is certain: the whole problem can arise only in the latter case. (The same consideration applies to the further texts I am going to inspect.) Ulpian, however, goes beyond Scaevola's "complete status of freebornship": the beneficiary now becomes freeborn.

102. Gaius 1.5: *nec umquam dubitatum est quin id (constitutio principis) legis vicem optineat.* I wish Honoré were right in suggesting *(Gaius: A Biography* [1962] 118ff.) that Gaius is here ironical.

103. Schulz, "Überlieferungsgeschichte der Responsa des Cervidius Scaevola," *Symbolae Friburgenses in Honorem Ottonis Lenel* (1933), 159–60, 169. Levy seems to concur: "Libertas und Civitas," *ZRG* 78 (1961): 170.

104. Digest 2.4.10.3, *Ulpian V ad edictum* (compare 6.4.3, Justinian, AD 529). *Sed si ius anulorum accepit, puto eum reverentiam patrono exhibere debere quamvis omnia ingenuitatis munia habet. Aliud si natalibus sit restitutus: nam princeps ingenuum facit.* "But if he receives the right of the rings, I believe he must display reverence to his patron though he has all the offices of freebornship. It is different if he is restored to free birth, for the Emperor makes a freeborn citizen."

A freak formulation? The further development shows that it is not that. Towards the end of the third century AD the Emperors Diocletian and Maximian distinguish: whereas "the golden rings" confer on the grantees *libertinitatis quoad vivunt imaginem, non statum ingenuitatis,*"while they live, the appearance of freedmanship, not the status of freebornship" (i.e., when they die their patrons have claims to the estate),[105] *natalibus antiquis restituti liberti ingenui constituuntur,* "those freedmen who are restored to past free birth are created freeborn citizens."[106] The "status of freebornship" here means that the person has been made freeborn.

A much-favored emendation of a statement by Modestinus now turns out to be unwarranted. Modestinus, a pupil of Ulpian's, writes as follows: "A freedman who is restored to free birth is considered as if, being made freeborn, he had not in the meantime suffered the blemish of slavery."[107] He accepts the notion that the person is made freeborn, and he concludes that the degrading life in slavery is regarded as not having occurred. Fullest consistency would perhaps have required the denial of any *medium tempus,* "meantime," between birth and now. In strictness, that is, since the person is made freeborn, there is no "as if" at all, the blemish should not only be regarded as not having been, it just has not been. I have already remarked, however, that in a construction like that before us, which refashions the past, traces of fiction inevitably remain. For Modestinus, the man is made freeborn—no fiction here; though, with a slight degree of incongruity, he does represent as a fiction the absence from the man's life of any blemish of slavery.

---

105. Compare Digest 38.2.3, *Ulpian XLI ad edictum,* quoted above, p. 297: "He lives as one freeborn, he dies as a freedman."

106. Code 6.8.2, AD 294. *Aureorum usus anulorum beneficia principali tributus libertinitatis quoad vivunt imaginem non statum ingenuitatis praestat, natalibus autem antiquis restituti liberti ingenui nostro beneficio constituuntur.* "The enjoyment of the golden rings assigned by imperial privilege confers while they (the beneficiaries) live the appearance of freedmanship, not the status of freebornship; those freedmen, however, who are restored to past free birth are created freeborn citizens by our privilege." There is much to be said for the emendation by Cujas of *libertinitatis* into *libertinis:*"the enjoyment of the golden rings confers on freedmen while they live the appearance, not the status, of freebornship." This would conform to *Fr. Vat.* 266, *Papinian XI questionum,* and Code 9.21.1 pr., Diocletian and Maximian, AD 300, with reference to the lex Visellia. My thesis is not affected.

107. Digest 40.11.5.1, *VII regularum. Libertinus qui natalibus restitutus est perinde habetur atque si ingenuus factus medio tempore maculam servitutis non sustinuisset.*

Haloander, the great sixteenth-century editor of the *Corpus Juris*, did not appreciate the force of "being made freeborn"; no doubt he also boggled at the lack of logic, the vagueness of *medium tempus*. His emendation of *ingenuus factus* into *ingenuus natus* is recommended by modern editors, Kriegel and Mommsen. We ought to read, then: "A freedman who is restored to free birth is considered as if, being born free, he had not in the meantime suffered the blemish of slavery." One reason modern authorities like the emendation is presumably that they find it easier, on this basis, to make Modestinus adhere to the fictitious character of the free birth: the grantee (they interpret) "is considered as if he were born free and had not in the meantime suffered the blemish of slavery."[108] But rational as this is, it is not what Modestinus says nor what, considering the other texts, we should impute to him.[109]

In the Eastern half of the Empire, it seems, the consequence was drawn that even a child born to a grantee prior to the grant retrospectively

108. Haloander's idea seems to have been somewhat different. He certainly kept out the supernatural creation of a freeborn man, but he did so by a more complicated route, namely, by assuming that the text concerns a person in truth freeborn, in truth *ingenuus natus*. (This was a widespread understanding—misunderstanding—of the text, still shared by Leist, "Das romische Patronatsrecht," pt. 2, *Gluck, Ausfuhrliche Erlauterung der Pandecten* [1879], 311, and, who knows, perhaps leading a shadowy life even today.) More precisely, the freedman in question had really been born free, had then fallen into real slavery (say, he was a foreign prisoner of war at Rome or a Roman criminal condemned into the mines), had then been manumitted by his master (not "manumitted" from a supposed slavery but really manumitted) and was now receiving the privilege of free birth. This man "is considered as if, being (in fact) born free, he had not in the meantime (when subsequently enslaved) suffered the blemish of slavery." The grant thus does not make a man not freeborn into one freeborn, it simply produces the fiction that a freeborn man continued free throughout his life. It must be conceded that this interpretation relieves the *medium tempus* of all difficulty. But there are decisive objections; the grant of *natales restituere* nowhere else has regard to a person really freeborn. It is incredible that, if this text were an exception, we should be left to read the whole, immense story into it. I would also point out that, if a grant of *natales restituere* to persons really freeborn and then enslaved had been known, it would have had to be quoted in Code 5.4.23.1, Justinian AD 520–23, as the closest approximation to the measure proposed in this law; but we find only the usual grant to those of servile provenance. See below, pp. 318ff.

109. On the fiction "as if he were born free" in Digest 40.11.2, *Marcian I institutionum*, and Code 5.4.23.1, just adverted to (see the preceding footnote), I shall say something presently.

gained the higher status. A constitution by Diocletian and Maximian rejects this view.[110]

A highly significant piece of evidence from outside the juristic discussion is here to be adduced: the tomb inscriptions of freedmen elevated to freebornship. As pointed out by Mommsen,[111] these inscriptions suppress the deceased's quality as a freedman. More than that. In the enumeration of the successive public offices held by the deceased they suppress those indicative of that quality, those normally bestowed on freedmen. This history writing à la 1984 seems to have been resorted to even in the case of freedmen who merely received "the golden rings" (though, as Mommsen notes, there is no concealment of the servile origin of the tutor of the Emperor Verus.) Anyhow, there is here striking confirmation that those references by lawyers to what is not far from a supernatural creation of a citizen of free birth must be taken seriously. On the inscriptions in question, the "meantime," the life of blemish, has simply never been.

Creation of a Freeborn Citizen and the Natural Law of the Beginning

Towards the end of the classical era, the development led to a brilliant theory, sponsored by Marcian, a slightly older contemporary of Modestinus. It aims at rationalization yet introduces a miraculous note of its own. "At times," he explains, "even persons born as slaves are made freeborn *ex post facto* through intervention of the law, as when a freedman has been restored to his native conditions by the Emperor. For he is

---

110. Code 6.55.6, AD 294: the probability of an Eastern addressee emerges from Mommsen, "Zeitfolge der Verordnungen Diocletians und seiner Mitregenten," *Abhandlungen der Kgl. Akademie der Wissenschaften zu Berlin,* (1860) 419ff. [*Gesammelte Schriften,* 2 (*Juristische Schriften*) (1905), 265ff.]. *Ex libera conceptus et servo velut spurius habetur nec ut decuronis filius, quamvis pater eius naturalis manumissus et natalibus suis restitutus hunc fuit adeptus honorem, defendi potest.* "A child conceived by a free woman with a slave is treated as spurious and it cannot be pleaded that he is a decurion's son, even though his natural father, manumitted and restored to his native conditions, has attained this honor."

111. Mommsen, *Röm. Staatsr.* 3:518–19.

restored to those native conditions which in the beginning all men were, not to those in which he himself is born, since he was born a slave. For such a one is treated with regard to the entire law as if he had been born free, and his patron can lay no claim to his estate. Therefore in general the Emperors do not readily restore anyone to native conditions without his patron's consent."[112]

Marcian starts by adopting the by then prevalent concept: the grant makes the freedman freeborn, his freebornship is *ex post facto* effected by the law. But then he goes on to give the matter a new twist. It is not the grantee's own native conditions which are restored to him, but the native conditions of the golden age, before slavery had made its appearance.

This doctrine has considerable advantages. We have seen that, linguistically, the term *natales restituere*, "to restore native conditions, birth, free birth," goes back to the trial by which a man in truth freeborn but somehow kept out of his rights recovers them. In the latter half of the second century AD there was introduced the bestowal of freebornship on persons admittedly not in truth freeborn. The term "to restore native conditions" was extended to this case, which, manifestly, it does not fit. There is here no restoration; there is creation, a grant. Marcian's theory does away with this awkwardness. According to him, there is indeed restoration—namely, of the ideal, primeval state of things, the position the person would have held but for the degeneration of mankind. Where he or other exponents of this doctrine still speak of a restoring of *natales sui*, "his native conditions, his free birth," instead of simply *natales*, "native conditions, free birth," we should paraphrase not "his individual free birth," but "the free birth ideally his as a member of the pure human race."[113]

A further, substantive merit of the doctrine is that it removes the need to deny the facts. The servile birth of the individual concerned can be conceded, and Marcian stresses the point: "since he was born a slave." It can be conceded seeing that what is granted is not a free birth of his own

112. Digest 40.11.2, *I institutionem. Interdum et servi nati ex post facto iuris interventu ingenui fiunt, ut ecce si libertines a principe natalibus suis restitutus fuerit. illis enim utique natalibus restituitur in quibus initio omnes homines fuerunt, non in quibus ipse nascitur cum servus natus esset. hic enim quantum ad totum ius pertinent perinde habetur atque si ingenuus natus esset, nec patronus eius potest ad succesionem venire. ideoque imperatores non facile solent quemquam natalibus restituere nisi consentiente patrono.*

113. Cf. above, pp. 301–2.

but the abstract free birth which once belonged to all men. He is freeborn in the sense of being elevated above the unnatural division of mankind. As for his servile origin in this divided society, that, in consequence of his elevation, ceases to count. But, as just remarked, it is not suppressed. Marcian at this point definitely assumes a fiction: the person, he says, "is treated as if he were born free."

While these are advances in the direction of a rational definition, the supernatural element is far from eliminated. This privileged placing of the beneficiary into the order of an uncorrupted world is also a conquest of time, though perhaps less crude than endowment with a new, personal free birth. He is still, as already observed, actually turned into a freeborn citizen: "persons born as slaves are made freeborn." Only he is made freeborn not so as to be born free in this life, but so as to participate in the universal free nativity of the golden age. As for this, life, the law, in pursuance of his restitution to the pristine, ideal world, feigns him to be of free birth. That restitution is real; the Emperor even in this doctrine has power *ex post facto* to elevate the man's past.

The original, free state of all under natural law is repeatedly affirmed by the later classics.[114] A passage in Justinian's Institutes is reminiscent of Marcian's wording: "For by natural law, at the beginning, all men were born free."[115] According to Voigt and Kalb,[116] it is indeed taken from Marcian, while Ferrini doubtfully suggests Florentinus as its source.[117] I incline to the former alternative: Marcian was an institutional writer whose new ideas greatly appealed to Justinian.[118]

There is, however, a possibility which, remote though it is, should not be passed over—that the linking of the grant with the golden age transmitted under the name of Marcian is an interpolation, maybe by the

114. Digest 1.1.4, *Ulpian I institutionum*, 1.5.4.1, *Florentinus IX institutionum*, 12.6.64, *Tryphoninus VII disputationum*, 50.17.32, *Ulpian XLIII ad Sabinum*; see Levy, "Natural Law in Roman Thought" *Studia et Documenta Historiae et Iuris* 1–10, (1949), 12ff.

115. Institutes 1.2.2, *iure enim naturali ab initio omnes homines liberi nascebantur*.

116. Voigt, *Das Jus Naturale*, vol. 1 (1856), 332, 566ff.; Kalb quoted by Ferrini: see the following footnote.

117. Ferrini, *Opere* 2:331f. [*Bull. Ist. Dir. Rom.* 13:123–24].

118. Buckland, "Marcian," *Studi Riccobono* (1936), 1:277ff. This is not to maintain that the whole of Institutes 1.2.2 rests on Marcian.

compilers themselves. Albertario and Beseler thought so."[119] I believe it most unlikely. Still, the theory propounded by the fragment would lose none of its interest.

Creation of a Freeborn Citizen and Legitimation by Rescript

What is certain is that Justinian was greatly attracted by this theory. In AD 538 he introduced a fresh mode of legitimation, to wit, by imperial rescript; and he expressly represented this innovation as modeled on the creation of a freeborn citizen: "For just as there is a mode invented by those before us which leads freedmen to freebornship, first cleansing them by another act and giving them the right of the golden rings, then restoring them to nature itself which at the beginning did not distinguish slave and free but made the offspring of man free, so we too intend the same for the matter in hand."[120] He goes on to say that originally there was no division into legitimate and bastard children; there wre only legitimate ones. Wars produced slavery; excessive desire, bastardy. The passions involved in both are the same; hence the remedy should be the same: what his predecessors thought out to deal with slavery, a grant from the Emperor, he is now extending to bastardy.

    That the grant of freebornship is here conceived in supernatural terms is evident, if only from the reference to purification. According to

119. Albertario, "Concetto Classico e Definizioni Postclassiche del Ius Naturale," *Studi di Diritto Romano* 5 (1937): 288 [equals *Rendiconti del Reale Istituto Lombardo di Scienze e Lettere* 57 (1924): 178]; Beseler, "Unklassische Wörter," *ZRG* 56 (1936): 66. The offending word which the latter is presenting in this section of his article is *ecce*. He reconstructs the text as follows: [—] *si libertinus a principe natalibus suis restitutus fuerit* [—], *perinde habetur atque si ingenuus natus esset nec patronus eius <heres fieri bonorumve eius possessionem accipere> potest* [—]. "If a free man has been restored to his conditions by the Emperor, he is treated as if he had been born free, and his patron cannot become his heir or take his goods by way of *bonorum possessio*."

120. Novellae 74.1: *hosper gar este tis tois pro hemon exeuremenos tropos hos tous apeleutherous eis eugeneian agei, prokathairon men autous heterai tini praxei kai didous autois to ton chryson daktylion dikaion, hysteron de eis auten epanagon ten physin ten doulon te kai eleutheron ex arches me diakrinasan all' eleutheron ten anthropou poiesamenen gonen, houto de kai hemeis touton de ton tropon epinooumen toi pragmati.*

Justinian, prior to the grant, the candidate is cleansed by means of the "golden rings," cleansed, that is, from the blemish of his servile origin. Justinian speaks of this procedure as coming down to him from his predecessors, and we have no reason to doubt his word on this point.[121] The grant reestablishes man's natural birthright, and that is also the object of the new grant of legitimation. The idiom of the model grant of freebornship is transferred to the grant of legitimation, the latter like the former being a *natales restituere*: the father of bastards, Justinian ordains, shall be allowed to invoke the Emperor and thus "to restore his children to nature."[122]

A year later, in a consolidating statute regarding bastards, the tenet of the primeval, universal freedom and legitimacy appears twice, first towards the beginning, in a somewhat general survey,[123] then again in the chapter setting forth the method of legitimation by rescript. Here Justinian almost word for word repeats the explanation given on the earlier occasion—that this method is analogous to the grant of freebornship; that once, under the exclusive reign of natural law, all men were born free and legitimate, slavery and bastardy being the result of war and concupiscence; and that the same passions call for the same remedy, his predecessors having found it for slavery and he applying it to bastardy.[124] What does not recur is the reference to purification by means of "the golden rings" preceding the grant of freebornship. No wonder seeing that this preliminary measure has no correspondence in the legitimation by imperial rescript introduced by Justinian.

121. It may be as early as Commodus. As mentioned above, p. 303n95, from Commodus onwards the "golden rings" no longer implied a knighthood (Mommsen). This puzzling development might be explicable by the fact that a main function of this privilege was now to be the preliminary step to *natales restituere*. The double procedure is presupposed in Novellae 18.11, of AD 536, where a man who has children from a slave woman manumits mother and children and then petitions on their behalf "both the right of the golden rings and restoration of native conditions." The law uses *palingenesia* for "restoration of free birth": see below, pp. 314–15.

122. Novellae 74.7, 2 pr. The fullest version is in 2 pr.: *tous nothous autou paidas apokatastasai tei physei kai tei anothen eugeneiai to kai gnesioteti*, "to restore his bastard children to nature and to pristine ingenuitas and legitimacy." *Eugeneia, ingenuitas*, here signifies, not freebornship, but as, e.g., in Code 11.68.4, *Valentinian, Valens and Gratian*, AD 367 (?), the status of a free Roman in a family governed by the civil law.

123. Novellae 89.1 pr.

124. Novellae 89.9 pr.

Also in 539, Justinian decisively enlarged the circle of those obtaining freebornship. He enacted that henceforth, on manumission, a slave would automatically have "the right of the golden rings and of restoration to free birth," no special grant being needed.[125] To be sure, he safeguarded to some extent the patron's position: in particular, reverence and gratitude were still to be shown him. Essentially, though, any freedman was now freeborn, a further approximation to the ideal state of the world. In the Preface to the statute Justinian proclaims that, as all goods given him by God are perfect, so he holds that the freedom given to a slave should be made pure, incorrupt, and perfect. Already ten years before, in 529, he had decreed that if a patron renounced his hold over a freedman, the latter was to be more or less in the position of one having obtained "restoration of free birth."[126]

Two terminological features underline Justinian's particular interest in the conferment of freebornship. First, it is he who, to the traditional *natales restituere*, "to restore free birth," adds the nominal phrase *natalium restitutio*, "restoration of free birth"; it is found in the statute of 529 about a patron's renunciation of his privileges.[127] This coinage reflects increased systematic thinking about the institution, also a feeling of respect for it. Modern writers without exception use the nominal phrase even when concerned with earlier centuries. I have little doubt that this antedating of the weighty-sounding designation has contributed to the antedating of the imperial grant.[128] If Pliny asked Trajan about *natalium restitutio*,[129] the temptation to think of the discretionary elevation of a man of no origin is far greater than if he asked (as he did) more modestly whether he might sit *de natalibus restituendis*.

Secondly, in Justinian's Greek legislation, both on legitimation and on manumission, several times "restoration of free birth, native conditions"

---

125. Novellae 78.

126. Code 6.4.3.3: the patron lost his right to the succession though he did remain entitled to reverence—which, at that time, i.e., prior to Novellae 78, was not due after "restoration to free birth" proper. On what the reform introduced in Code 6.4.3 did to the legislation on price in the contract of sale, see Daube, "Generalisations in Digest 18.1," *Studi Arangio-Ruiz* 1 (1952), 192ff.; and "Zur Palingenesie," *ZRG* 76 (1959): 177ff.

127. Code 6.3.4.1, 2.

128. Cf. above, pp. 295ff., especially 302.

129. See above, p. 304n96.

is represented by *dikaion paliggenesias*, literally, "the right of *palingenesia*, regeneration, rebirth."[130] I have already quoted instances of the belief, not uncommon in antiquity, that a man might undergo a second, supernatural birth.[131] Admittedly, as a glance at the dictionaries will show, the word *palingenesia* is not confined to this event. It has many shades of meaning, from distinctly theological ones to such as are hardly weighted that way— it can signify any major fresh start. (Cicero, incidently, in an otherwise Latin letter, uses it of his own "renaissance," his reinstallment after exile.)[132] However, in view of what we have just noticed and, indeed, of what we shall yet notice concerning Justinian's attitude to bestowal of freebornship, it is safe to say that his introduction of this term is not a casual matter. It indeed joins with the concept of attainment of a personal

130. Novellae 18.11 of AD 536, 78 rubric, 1, 3, 5, of AD 539. This does not entail the extrusion of "to restore to nature": 78.5.

131. See above, p. 288. At this juncture I may add that rebirth plays a remarkably small part in adoption, except for adoption by God. Professor Thomas L. Shaffer of Notre Dame Law School kindly draws my attention to the law of Indiana. He writes:

Today, in reading the Indiana statutes on adoption, I noted a provision dealing with the issuance of new birth certificates in cases where the adoption petitioner asks for a change in the child's name. One section of the most recent amendment to that statute may interest you; this is part of Sec. 2, Acts of 1957, General Assembly of Indiana, ch. 47, which is codified in *Indiana Statutes Annotated* Sec. 3–125: "When a new certificate of birth is established following adoption, it shall replace the original registration of birth, which shall be filed with the evidence of adoption, and withheld from inspection except by order of a court of competent jurisdiction. The new certificate shall show the actual place and date of birth, except the court may, if requested in the petition duly filed, decree the birthplace of the child as the place of residence of the adopting mother at the time of such child's birth, or at the time of the filing of the petition, provided such child was born within the continental limits of the United States and is less than six years of age at the time of said petition." This provision replaced ch. 146, Acts of 1941, Sec. 11, which provided on this point: "At any time after such recording of said certificate of adoption a certificate of birth shall be issued, upon request, bearing the new name of the child as shown in the certificate of adoption, the names of the foster parents of said child, . . . and there shall be no difference or distinction by way of color, size, or general substance of birth registration cards or birth certificates, whether the child be legitimate or illegitimate, adopted or of natural parentage." The old statute provided that the original birth registration remain a public record, but seems clearly to have contemplated also a sort of new birth by court decree; the new statute contemplates a new birthplace by court decree; it is not clear to me whether the adopted status of the child appears on the record under the new statute.

132. Cicero, *Att.* 6.6.4.

free birth rather than that of participation in the abstract free birth of the ideal law of nature.[133] There is no reason why Justinan should narrowly adhere to one construction of *natales restituere*: after all, he admits both into the Digest.

Before going on to the source of his fascination with bestowal of freebornship, it is useful to dispose of an episode from Plutarch's *Lucullus*, which, at first sight, might look like alluding to the contrast between freedmanship and the primeval pure freedom of all men but, in fact, does nothing of the sort.[134] When Lucullus in 71 BC captured Amisus, the grammarian Tyrannio (the Elder) was among the prisoners. Murena, then serving as legate, asked to have him as his prize and, having got him, manumitted him. Lucullus considered this procedure mean: such a scholar, he held, ought not to have been enslaved and manumitted since "the gift of seeming freedom was a taking away of the original one."[135]

The proper interpretation of the passage is as follows. It would have been open to Murena not to treat Tyrannio as a slave at all. Lucullus, Plutarch informs us, of a nobler disposition than his legate, simply allowed such citizens of Amisus as wished to live on there to do so, and to many Greeks among them he even gave clothes and money. He could have made slaves of all of them, and freedmen tied to him by subsequently releasing them, but he refrained.[136] Murena ought to have treated Tyrannio in the same way, simply leaving him free. Instead of which he made him his slave, so that, on manumission, he became his patron. Tyrannio was now free indeed, but this "seeming," factitious freedom was not his "original," genuine, unencumbered one; it was merely freedmanship. Manifestly, this has nothing to do with the doctrine of equality in the golden age. The contrast is between Tyrannio's *natales*, his freedom from birth, and the status Murena's meanness substituted for it, a status "seeming," "considered"

---

133. Significantly, in Novellae 18 and 78, with the more personal *palingenesia*, we find no lengthy description of primeval equality.

134. Plutarch, *Vit., Luc.* 19.7.

135. *Aphairesis gar en tes hyparchouses he tes dokouses eleutherias dosis.*

136. Plutarch, *Vit., Luc.* 19.6. A commander had a good deal of discretion in these matters. A story commemorating Scipio's (Scipio Africanus Major) generous behavior after the capture of New Carthage in 209 BC is told in Livy 26.50, Gellius 7.8.3ff. and Polybius 10.19. For details of the law, see Vogel, "Zur rechtlichen Behandlung der römischen Kriegsgewinne," *ZRG* 66 (1948): 398–99.

to be freedom by virtue of a legal transaction, a manufactured, lesser freedom, freedmanship.

Creation of a Freeborn Citizen and Rehabilitation of an Actress by Rescript

In a way, a strange way, *natales restituere* reaches its climax some six years before Justinian's accession to the throne, in *Codex Justinian* 5.4.23, enacted between 520 and 523, at Justinian's instance by his uncle Justin, then sole Emperor, in order to enable Justinian to marry Theodora, a penitent actress. (Justinian was then getting on to forty.) In this law the principle of *natales restituere* is carried outside its original province in a far bolder manner than in the later *Novel*, considered above, where it is transferred to legitimation. It is here extended from problems of descent to the moral sphere and the status of man as determined by his chosen way of life. While the influence of Marcian's construction is strong, the thought of recovery of the individual's own unspoilt past is also unmistakably present. The whole law is very theological and has received too little attention on the part of historians of Christian doctrine: it would surely throw light, for instance, on some controversial questions regarding sixth-century ideas on penitence. I must confine myself to points of direct interest.[136a]

Prior to this law, a citizen of senatorial rank was not allowed to marry an actress.[137] Theodora had been one, and once an actress always an actress.[138] Justin (the hand is the uncle's, but the voice is the nephew's) in

136A. For further details see now my Pope John Lecture, delivered in Spring, 1967, at the Columbus School of Law of the Catholic University of America at Washington, D.C. and published in *Catholic University of America Law Review* 16 (1967): 380.

137. *Cod. Theod.* 4.6.3 [= Code 5.27.7] *Constantine*, AD 336; Novella Marciani 4.3 [= Code 5.7.2] *Valentinian and Marcian*, 454.

138. E.g., Digest 23.2.44, *Paul I ad legem Juliam et Papiam*: a member of a senatorial family may not marry, the statute prescribes, "one who herself or whose father or mother practices or has practiced stagecraft," *quae ipsa cuiusve pater materve artem ludicram facit fecerit*. This permanency of the label, however, while applying wherever social status is in question, is not absolute. I shall not go into this complicated business, except to give an illustration relating to prostitutes. To them, too, the label once acquired stuck for good (e.g., Digest 22.5.3.5, *Callistratus IV de cognitionibus*, 23.2.43.4, *[continues onto next page]*

an introductory paragraph explains that these women should not be left
without hope, an inducement to give up their objectionable profession. In
this way, the Emperor can imitate the clemency of God, always willing to
accept the penitent sinner and "lead him back to a better state," *ad meliorem
statum reducere*. If the Emperor fails to act thus, he himself will not be
worthy of divine forgiveness.[139] So far the motivation concentrates on
forgiveness and, with it, on the forgiven person's reinstatement (*reducere*)
in his former, guiltless condition.

In the next paragraph Justin brings in, drags in, the rules of *natales
restituere*. A far-fetched comparison indeed. It would be wrong, he argues,
if a freedman could be helped but not a penitent actress—quite forgetting
that the former is innocent whereas the latter is guilty: "As it is unjust that
slaves to whom freedom has been given can by imperial relief be restored
to their native conditions and, after receiving such an imperial grant,
live as if they had never served as slaves but had been born free, whereas
women who, though they have concerned themselves with stage plays,
yet later, spurning this evil condition, have turned to better intention and
escaped from their dishonorable profession, have no hope of an imperial

---

[*note 138 continued from previous page*] *Ulpian I ad legem Juliam et Papiam*; compare *Tabula
Heracleensis* 122–23), but again only in matters having to do with social status, not, say, for
the purpose of the tax on the profession. When Caligula wished to tax even ex-prostitutes,
a special clause had to be appended to the statute, a clause which Suetonius condemns
(*Calig.* 40). As often, there is a serious problem at the bottom of a vulgar joke. Elderly
lady: "Mr. Smith, you should talk to your wife, she has called me a —." Mr. Smith: "No use
talking to her, that's her way. I've been out of the army for thirty years and she still calls
me Colonel."

139. The Emperor holds that one should by no means *eis spem melioris condicionis
adimere, ut ad eam respicientes improvidam et minus honestam electionem facilius derelinquant;
nam ita credimus dei benevolentiam et circa genus humanum nimiam clementiam quantum
nostrae naturae possibile est imitari, qui cottidianis hominum peccatis semper ignoscere
dignatur et paenitentiam suscipere nostram et ad meliorem statum reducere; quod si circa nostro
subiectos imperio nos etiam facere differamus, nulla venia digni esse videbimur,* "deprive them
of hope for a better condition, in order that, looking to it, they may more readily give up
their ill-considered and dishonorable choice; for thus we believe that we are imitating
God's benevolence and his measureless clemency towards mankind as far as is possible to
our nature, seeing that he ever deigns to pardon the daily sins of men and to receive our
penitence and lead us back to a better state; which if we fail to do too to those subject to
our power, we shall appear worthy of no pardon."

grant which would lead them back to that state in which, had there been no sinning, they could have remained."[140]

Here we have before us a blend of theories concerning a rise in status. On the one hand, as far as a freedman's promotion is concerned, Marcian's teaching is adopted, just as it is, we saw above, in several later statutes of Justinian: the personal free birth of a freedman "restored to his native conditions" is a fiction; he is looked on, the text says, "as if he had been born free." On the other hand, the grant envisaged for a penitent actress will mean her actual reinstallment in her previous, sinless position (*ad illum statum reducere in quo commorari potuerint*), in analogy to what happens when God forgives. There is less of a discrepancy than might appear at first sight. Marcian's fiction, it will be recalled, flows from an effect of the grant which is regarded as real—the turning of the grantee into a man freeborn under the ideal dispensation valid for all. In the case of forgiveness, restoration of the sinner to his own, personal state prior to the sin and restoration of the sinner to the state of innocence in the golden age more or less coincide; the former is tantamount to the latter.

The Emperor goes on to proclaim that henceforth penitent actresses may apply for an imperial ordinance granting full marriage rights. Upon such a privilege, the husbands "may be confident that the marriage will be as valid as if they had taken them to wives with no earlier dishonorable life."[141] How far this implies a fiction, how far the past is thought of as just nonexistent, is difficult to say: the particle *quasi*, here translated by "as if," is so ambiguous.

It is the immediate continuation which takes up from the opening argument the association with *natales restituere*, or rather the synonymous *natales reddere*.[142] "For, all blemish being utterly wiped out, and these

---

140. *Cum iniustum sit servos quidem libertate donatos posse per divinam indulgentiam natalibus suis restitui postque huiusmodi principale beneficium ita degere quasi numquam deservissent sed ingenui nati essent, mulieres autem quae scaenicis quidem sese ludis immiscuerunt, postea vero spreta mala condicione ad meliorem migravere sententiam et inhonestam professionem effugerunt, nullam spem principales habere beneficii quod eas ad illum statum reduceret in quo, si nihil peccatum esset, commorari potuerint.*

141. *Ita validum huiusmodi permanere matrimonium confidentibus quasi nulla praecedente inhonesta vita uxores eas duxerint.*

142. See above, p. 304n98.

women being, so to speak, handed back to their native conditions, we wish that neither shall a dishonorable designation henceforth attach to them nor shall they be any different from those who have committed no such sin."[143]

The comparison with *natales restituere* is here pushed to its limit. In the motivation, we have seen, Justinian claims that it would be an injustice to offer a route to the heights to freedmen and none to penitent actresses. Here, a penitent actress rehabilitated is said to be, in a sense (*quasi*, "so to speak"), like a freedman who has been granted freebornship; she is, in a sense, "returned to her native conditions." From the context it is probable that, at this point, the lawgiver is harking back to that doctrine which assumes that a freedman granted freebornship is actually born free, is (in the words of Modestinus) "as if, being made freeborn, he had not in the meantime suffered the blemish of slavery."[144] Just so, a penitent actress accepted by the Emperor is actually recreated, recovers the untainted life that was hers at birth. It will be noted that, in her case, the notion *restituere* (or *reddere*) *natales*, "to restore (hand back) the native conditions," fits whether we think of her as reinstated in the primeval, universal sinlessness of mankind or in her own, personal sinlessness before she became an actress. In the case of a freedman, where it is a question not of a moral lapse but of descent, the phrase fully suits only reinstatement in the abstract, primeval undividedness of rank; there is no personal free birth to reinstate him in. As pointed out above,[145] this may indeed have been among the considerations which led to the understanding (by Marcian) of the grant of freebornship as the man's restoration to the original, ideal world.

A rehabilitated actress may no longer be called an actress, a *scaenica*: this predicate is meant, of course, by the "dishonorable designation" from which the statute releases her. Indeed, there shall be no difference between her and any respectable woman. The formulation is not absolutely clear, but apparently the label is removed only for the future; it could still be said that she was once a *scaenica*. Complete annulment of the past is simply

---

143. *Nam omni macula penitus direpta et quasi suis natalibus huiusmodi mulieribus redditis, neque vocabulum inhonestum eis inhaerere de cetero volumus neque differentiam aliquam eas habere cum his quae nihil simile peccaverunt.*

144. See above, p. 307n107, on Digest 40.11.5.1, *Modestinus VII regularum.*

145. See above, pp. 312–13.

not attainable. Maybe she is thought of as having sinned in a different life.

In one respect, however, the language is as unambiguous as can be: "all blemish is utterly wiped out." The best MSS have *direpta*, "torn up." Mommsen suggests *dirempta*, "eliminated." *Direpta* is certainly unusual, and the fact that an important MS (Casinas 49) has *direptam* also speaks in his favor. Yet a very forceful, striking expression may have been deliberately chosen. I have translated neutrally with "wiped out."[146] In a parallel clause further on in the law the verb is *abolire*, "to abolish." There is no doubt as to the sense: as a result of the imperial ordinance, the woman is absolutely pure.

As already remarked, it is a strange undertaking to present the case as an extension of the principle underlying the conferment of freebornship. But we can now see the point. That institution was the nearest model of an imperial grant with a direct effect on a person's past, the nearest legal model that would render plausible the—prima facie extraordinary—denial of any blemish in a rehabilitated actress. (The term *macula* for "blemish" is well chosen: it is traditionally associated with the servile status as well as misdeeds reflecting on a person's character. It occurs in the passage just cited—"as if he had not suffered the blemish of slavery.")[147] Justinian, through his uncle, is here at work for his great love. She must be flawless—hence this tour de force.

I have the impression that some scholars believe that Justin, in the clause mentioning *natales*, is according freebornship to rehabilitated actresses who are freedwomen. Earlier legislation prohibited marriage between a man of senatorial rank and a freedwoman. In the opinion of these scholars, Justin here legalizes such a union where the freedwoman is a penitent actress whose blemish has been removed.[148] But this is an

---

146. It would be interesting to find out what is the history behind the interchangeability of *dirimere* and *diripere* assumed in a late medieval glossary on a work by Balderic of Bourgueil: see Du Cange, *Glossarium Mediae et Infimae Latinitatis* 3 (1883–7), 126.

147. Compare also, e.g., Code 7.16.9, Diocletian and Maximian, AD 293. In *Cod. Theod.* 4.6.3 [= Code 5.27.1 pr.] Constantine, AD 336, a senator who enters a forbidden marriage is declared subject to the *macula infamiae*, "the blemish of infamy."

148. Vasiliev, *Justin the First* (1950), 393: "the latter (penitent actresses) shall be regarded as free women"; Kaser, *Das Römische Privatrecht* 2 (1959), 113: "marriage with former actresses, freeborn or manumitted."

error. The law contemplates only freeborn women; Theodora's free birth was never in doubt. The extension to freedwomen came only some twelve years later, under Justinian.[149] Let me reiterate: what the clause mentioning *natales* does is to liken the reinstatement of penitent (freeborn) actresses to the bestowal of freebornship on persons of servile origin: a reinstated actress, like a freedman made freeborn, is—up to a point—a new creature, her degradation a bad dream.

Bury is skeptical about Procopius's statement that the law was needed for Justinian's marriage; he points out that, as is reported by Procopius himself, Theodora had been made a patrician some time before and a patrician, Bury argues, even if she had once been on the stage, was marriageable by a senator.[150] Assunta Nagl says that Bury gives no reason for his doubts.[151] But surely, this elevation to the patriciate is a reason, though, as we shall soon see, a bad one. Miss Nagl's comment is all the stranger as she does accept Bury's—erroneous—view that from the moment Theodora became a patrician, her profession was no longer an obstacle in the way of a marriage with Justinian. Vasiliev is remarkably confused.[152] He adopts Bury's position: having become a patrician prior to this law, Theodora no longer needed it; she was already fit for a senatorial marriage. As proof that, as a patrician, she could marry a senator, he cites *Codex Justinian* 5.4.23.4, which indeed provides that an actress receiving a high dignity is equal to one who, penitent, is granted an imperial rescript; but the provision is part of the very law we are discussing, the law enacted by Justin. There is nothing to suggest that it applied at an earlier date, when Theodora was first honored.

Here lies the fallacy of Bury's argument. What he and those dependent on him fail to appreciate is that, when Theodora became a patrician, though the dignity was no doubt recognized as eliminating the blemish of servile provenance (which she, however, did not bear), it did not yet eliminate a blemish like that of the stage; at least there was no definite ruling to that effect—the question, I guess, had never become

149. Code 1.4.33.2, AD 533. It would lead too far afield to discuss this interesting statute.

150. Bury, *History of the Later Roman Empire* 2 (1923), 29, referring to B. Panchenko, *O Tainoi Istorii Prokopiia* (1897), 74. The reference is to Procopius, *Anecdota* 9.30.

151. Pauly-Wissowa, *RE*, vol. 5, 2nd ser. (1934),1778, s.v. "Theodora."

152. Vasiliev, *Justin the First* (1950), 100ff., 389, 392ff.

acute. It is the very law here under review which, in a special paragraph, lays down that women receiving a dignity from the Emperor are to be equal to those who obtain a rescript. Indeed, the conferment of such a dignity is to remove also any blemish other than a theatrical career (say, the recipient had kept a tavern) normally an impediment to a senatorial marriage.[153] (The radical nature of the suppression of any other blemish is brought out by the term used, *penitus abolere*, just as in the case of the blemish of the stage.)[154] Legislation, then, was needed.

Two questions arise. First, why did Justin—or Justinian—bother about penitent actresses, instead of simply legislating that a woman promoted to the patriciate is cleared of her past? That would have done for the immediate purpose of the proposed union. The answer is that the lawgiver was inspired by genuine religious and moral fervor. Theodora's rise from the depths was not to be covered up; on the contrary, others were to be encouraged to emulate her. The legislation was *ad hoc* in the sense that Justinian's match was the occasion for it. But it was genuinely desired that the example should be followed. This is not mere speculation: the subsequent legislative policy of Justinian bears out what I am saying.

The second question flows from the answer to the first. Why, once it was decided to make available this wide access to senatorial marriage, a request to the Emperor acknowledged by a rescript, did Justin nevertheless add the paragraph providing elevation to high dignity—the patriciate, for instance—with the same effect? Surely, this was, above all, a gallant gesture to Theodora. She was to be spared the procedure of having to apply for a favor and obtaining no more than what she asked for. Her patriciate had been given her, the Emperor indicates, as a free manifestation of his

153. *Similes vero tale merentibus ab imperatore beneficium mulieribus illas etiam esse volumus quae dignitatem aliquam, etsi non serenissimo principi supplicaverunt, ultronea tamen donatione, ante matrimonium meruerint, ex qua dignitate aliam etiam omnem maculam per quam certis hominibus legitime coniungi mulieres prohibentur aboleri penitus oportet.* "To the women being rewarded by the Emperor with this privilege [the rescript to help them from their past as actresses] we wish to equate those who, though they did not supplicate to the Most Serene Emperor, have been rewarded with some dignity by an unsolicited gift before marriage; by which gift it is meet that also any other blemish on account of which women are prohibited from being united with certain men, be utterly abolished."

154. I do not know why Vasiliev, *Justin the First* (1950), 394 represents the statute as using *stigma* at this point instead of *macula*. No MS has *stigma*. Not that it matters much.

goodwill; at least this is what I think he is conveying when he speaks of women "who, without supplicating to the Most Serene Emperor, have nevertheless been rewarded with some dignity by a spontaneous gift." By adding this paragraph which declares recipients of an imperial honor suitable partners for senators, Justin succeeded in combining his general religious-moral aim with personal considerateness. It should be observed that this provision concerning women dignitaries is distinctly subsidiary to that concerning women petitioners. It is the latter whose fitness for senatorial unions is established in the principal part of the statute; and it is the former who, in a relatively short paragraph, are equated to them. It is not the latter who are equated to the former.

It is just conceivable, however, that there is a little more to this subsidiary rule. Elevation to a dignity wipes out, we have just found, not only the blemish of the stage but also any other blemish obstructing a noble marriage. The rescript cures only the blemish of the theater; elevation to a dignity can do more. It is just conceivable that the lawgiver, while unwilling to make blemishes other than the theater generally venial, and therefore keeping them out of the rescript, did deem it wise to ensure that Theodora at least should be eligible for a noble marriage even should the stage not have been her only sin. In the concluding chapter I shall have occasion to say something about reports depicting her as a prostitute. Justin would never admit such a charge; at the same time it may have been considered wise to have a clause which would legalize the marriage whatever view one took.

We have seen that a rehabilitated actress is no longer an actress, is in fact no different from a woman who never lapsed. It is only logical that the law should enjoin that "daughters of such women, if they are born after the cleansing of their mother's former life, are not considered daughters of actresses."[155] Among marriages forbidden to senators had been also that with an actress's daughter. From now a daughter born after the mother's rehabilitation is automatically excluded from the ban.

The provision is admirably placed at such a point in the statute as to make it quite clear that it covers rehabilitation by means of a dignity like the patriciate as well as rehabilitation by means of a rescript. The expression

---

155. *Filiae huiuscemodi mulierum, si quidem post expurgationem prioris vitae matris suae natae sint, non videantur scaenicarum esse filiae.*

by which rehabilitation is referred to is also very general, covering both methods: "cleansing of the former life." Very likely this paragraph was put in with a view to any female offspring that might ensue from Theodora's marriage with Justinian. We know that they hoped for children, though in vain.[156] The term *expurgatio*, incidentally, "cleansing," occurs nowhere else in the Roman legal sources—but it will be remembered that we found Justinian speaking in Greek of a *prokathairein*, a "purifying beforehand," of freedmen through "the golden rings."[157]

Daughters born before rehabilitation, the law adds, need an imperial rescript, which will be granted them if the mother is either rehabilitated or dead, and which will give them marriage capacity "as if they were not the daughters of an actress mother."[158] So with regard to them, a fiction will result.[159] The only daughter, it follows, who remains debarred from a first class marriage is one whose mother is alive and unredeemed. The lawgiver knew what he was doing: in this case, the husband would acquire undesirable connections. Theodora's illegitimate daughter from her earlier life, if a noble marriage were intended, would need and be entitled to a rescript. That this daughter was the fruit of her mother's premarital affair with Justinian is claimed by Bury,[160] but seems incredible to me. The argument from silence alone is overwhelming: there is no testimony lending the slightest support to his conjecture. The question does not affect my conclusions.

The Rehabilitation of Theodora

Eros and Agape

I should like to append some further comments on this statute though they are not required by my subject. The unwarranted dismissal of Procopius's

156. Nagl, Pauly-Wissowa, *RE*, vol. 5, 2nd ser. (1934),1782.

157. Novellae 74.1, see above, p. 312.

158. *Quasi non sint scaenicae matris filiae.*

159. Rigorous insistence on retroactivity of rehabilitation might—though it need not—lead to the conclusion that even in this case the mother is in fact no actress; compare above, p. 308, as to a rejected view about retroactivity of the grant of freebornness.

160. Bury, *History of the Later Roman Empire* 2 (1923), 27.

notice that the statute was designed to enable Justinian to marry Theodora leads to a good deal of more basic misrepresentation. For Vasiliev, "the law was merely one step in the progress of the emancipation of women, which goes back to the fourth and fifth centuries and was in accordance with Christian sentiments."[161] This is an exaggeration. Certainly the law marks a stage in a more or less steady advance. But that such advance was not its immediate central purpose comes out in many ways. Why were no other female sinners considered worthy of a chance? Why no female sufferers with far better claims and far more comparable to slaves or freedmen? Daughters of women keeping taverns, for example, were included only in a *Novel* of AD 542.[162]

Ex-prostitutes were perhaps never under Justinian entitled to rehabilitation (except if promoted to high dignity, a contingency which, after Theodora, would hardly ever again be of more than academic interest). In the Digest they are still definitely interdicted to the senatorial class,[163] and it is extremely doubtful whether, as seems universally held,[164] the interdiction was lifted by *Novel* 117 of the year 542.[165] Procopius both in his official and secret writings tells us about the seclusion offshore of ex-prostitutes in Justinian's reign.[166]

Beyond question Theodora had led a dissolute life; if we distrust Procopius's secret history, the fact is confirmed by John of Ephesus, a Monophysite who cannot enjoy transmitting anything unfavorable to a benefactress of his party. In law, it would make all the difference whether she had been a prostitute or only come near being one. I believe that she was free with her favors and not averse to earning money that way, but that she was not technically a prostitute.[167] At any rate, the long, principal portion of *Codex Justinian* 5.4.23 is evidently meant to convey the impression

161. Vasiliev, *Justine the First* (1950), 395.

162. Novellae 117.6.

163. Digest 23.2.43.4, *Ulpian I ad legem Juliam et Papiam.*

164. Buckland, *Text-Book* (1963), 115; Kaser, *Das Römische Privatrecht* 1:113 (1955).

165. Novellae 117.6 allows the women defined as "abject" in *Cod. Theod.* 4.6.3 [= Code 7.27.1 pr] *Constantine*, AD 336; Novella Marciani 4.3 [= Code 5.5.7.2], *Valentinian and Maximian*, 454. But these are freedwomen, tavern keepers, the daughters of tavern keepers and the like—not prostitutes.

166. The difference between the official account in Procopius, *Ktismata* 1.9.1ff. and the secret one in Procopius, *Anecdota* 17.5f. is priceless.

167. For a legal definition see Digest 23.2.43ff. pr., *Ulpian I ad legem Juliam et Papiam.*

that she was guilty of acting only, and the comparative lightness of this lapse is cleverly insinuated by the phraseology.[168] Moreover, the continued harshness of the legal order in respect of prostitutes may be partly owing to the determination to avoid confusion: Theodora had never been that low. Doubtless in practice this distinction between actress and prostitute was sometimes blurred, especially between a variety or circus actress and a prostitute slightly better than "infantry."[169] But the law differentiates most definitely, and the principal part of Justin's statute is emphatically—overemphatically—about actresses only. I argued above that, conceivably, in the clause concerning the rehabilitation of a patrician, the removal of all blemishes indiscriminately—not only of that caused by acting—may be intended inconspicuously to legalize Theodora's marriage even should she be deemed guilty of worse than acting. Procopius, who surely knew *Codex Justinian* 5.4.23 well and understood its religious-moral component, is very nasty in stating that this law made possible the marriage between men of senatorial rank and prostitutes;[170] though, if my suspicion about that paragraph concerning women dignitaries is justified, it is not surprising he was alive to that aspect and made the most of it.

Whether or not Biondi subscribes to Bury's suggestion that Justinian did not need the law for his marriage is not clear; at all events, he gives no hint at the possibility of any selfish motive. In his book on Justinian as a Catholic ruler, he confines himself to the affirmation that, contrary

168. *Indigna honore conversatio,* "company incompatible with honor"; *improvida et minus honesta electio,* "ill-considered and dishonorable (less honorable) choice"; *scaenicis sese ludis immiscere,* "to involve oneself with the stage"; *mala condicio,* "evil condition"; *inhonesta professio,* "dishonorable profession"; *mala et inhonesta conversatio,* "evil and dishonorable company"; *inhonesta vita,* "dishonorable life"—none of these expressions are very harsh, especially when we consider what scathing language the laws can use. The women are said to be impelled by *sexus imbecillitas,* "the weakness of their sex." The term recurs only in Digest 16.1.2.2, *Ulpian XXIX ad edictum,* in connection with a senatusconsult forbidding women to undertake liability for others. Justin may well be intending to evoke the idea that women become actresses under pressure from selfish men. Compare, e.g., Code 1.4.33, Justinian, AD 534, or also, with regard to prostitutes, Procopius, *Ktismata* 1.9.2f. Digest 16.1.2.2 is often held interpolated (e.g., Beseler, *Beitr.* 2 (1911): 106; *Beitr.* (1913): 106. Vogt, *Studien zum Senatusconsultum Velleianum* (1952), 8, without good reason, I think, but it does not matter.

169. *Peze* in Greek: Procopius, *Anecdota* 9.11; see translation by Dewing, *Procopius* 6 (Loeb Classical Library, 1954), 105.

170. Procopius, *Anecdota* 9.51.

to Procopius's malicious report, the law is "a veritable hymn to the redemption of women and the benevolence of God, whom the lawgiver seeks to imitate";[171] and again, in his *magnum opus* on the Christian law of Rome, though he quotes the statute more than half a dozen times, he never once makes mention of its *ad hoc* object—it is just an example of Christian pity for the sinner and facilitation of repentance.[172]

He cites the words, "We hold that their lapses should be remedied by a suitable means, and we ought not to deprive them of the hope for a better condition, in order that, looking forward to this, they may more readily give up their ill-considered and shameful choice,"[173] and he adds, "Who does not see in these phrases the distant echo of the gospel episode of the adulterous woman (John 8:3–11)?"[174] Aristotle in his *Rhetorica* counsels that, unless the answer desired to your rhetorical question is 100% obvious, you should at once state it yourself.[175] Biondi disregards this advice, to his cost. I do not see it, or at least I find there is room for doubt: the passage from John deals with an adulteress caught *in flagranti*, and furthermore, there is no significant verbal affinity whatever between it (i.e., its Latin versions) and Justin's law. (The words *mulier* and *peccare* are common to both, but they are too unspecific to be relevant. For the rest, the dominant notions in John are *accusare* and *condemnare*, "to accuse" and "to condemn,"[176] and these are absent from the statute.) Biondi continues: "Towards those women the lawgiver feels not contempt but humane understanding calculated to bring about penitence and redemption." Ambiguous language, "those women," *quelle donne*, since, as a matter of fact, the kinds of women contemplated in the *pericope de adultera* and this law are quite different.[177]

171. Biondo Biondi, *Giustiniano primo principe e legislatore cattolico* (1936), 62–63.

172. Biondo Biondi, *Il diritto romano cristiano* 1 (1952): 138; vol. 2 (1952), 164, 166, 168; vol. 3 (1954), 86, 326, 427, 437.

173. *Cum competenti moderatione sublevandos (lapsus) esse censemus mimimeque eis spem melioris condicionis adimere, ut ad eam rem respicientes improvidam et minus honestam electionem facilius derelinquant.*

174. Biondi, *Il diritto romano cristiano* 2: 166.

175. Aristotle, *Rh.* 3.18. I am aware that Aristotle has in mind a speech to an audience that can intervene—not a piece of writing.

176. *Ubi sunt qui te accusabant? nemo te condemnavit? Nec te condemnabo.*

177. Biondi himself offers a detailed exposition of the sanctions on adultery. *Il diritto romano cristiano* 3: 473ff.

A similar rhetorical question is put a little further on. He writes that the law provides for the rehabilitation of actresses who—he quotes— "spurning their evil condition have turned to a better intent and have fled their dishonorable profession, have embraced a worthier life and have turned to decency."[178] "Who does not hear," he asks, "in these provisions the echo of the gospel warnings concerning prostitutes who convert (Matthew 21:32)?"[179] When we look up Matthew, we find that publicans and prostitutes believed the Baptist; the Pharisees, though offered more evidence, showed no repentance: *Venit enim ad vos Joannes in via justitiae, et non credidistis ei, publicani autem et meretrices crediderunt ei, vos autem videntes nec poenitentiam habuistis postea, ut crederetis ei.* I cannot hear the echo.

The law under notice is permeated by the spirit of Christianity and rich in categories deriving from the New Testament, directly or indirectly.[180] Yet overidealization ultimately enhances neither the stature of Justin or Justinian nor the value of their legislation as an *exemplum*, as a stimulus and guide—not to mention what it does to the gospel. What is most moving about the law is the peculiar fusion of self-interest and generosity. (Nero had proceeded very differently when he planned marriage with a freedwoman—and even that association is not devoid of deeply touching features.[181]) The primary impulse comes from Justinian's passionate resolve to marry Theodora; a splendid resolve, nothing wrong in it, but still a personal cause. He has, however, thought profoundly about their relation, about why they find themselves confronted by such difficulties, and about why it is right to remove them. The law makes use of what he has learnt; and while assisting him, it extends relief to many sufferers and, indeed, propagates sentiments of a kind that must inevitably lead to further progress. No point in dehumanizing this measure. Some fifteen years later, at the age of fifty-five, in the *Novel* which introduces legitimation by rescript, he avowed: "For we know, though we are lovers of chastity, that nothing is more vehement than the fury of love."[182]

178. *Spreta mala condicione ad meliorem migravere sententiam et inhonestam professionem effugerunt . . . commodiorem vitam amplexae fuerint et honestati se dederint.*

179. Biondi, *Il diritto romano cristiano* 2:168.

180. Though compare also sentiments like Seneca, *Clem.* 1.7.1f.

181. Suetonius, *Nero* 50: "His nurses Egloge and Alexandria, with his concubine Acte, deposited his remains."

182. *Ismen gar, ei kai sophrosynes esmen erastai . . . ouden einai manias erotikes sphodroteron.*

Index of Sources

www.ingramcontent.com/pod-product-compliance
Lightning Source LLC
Chambersburg PA
CBHW020406100426
42812CB00001B/220